Taxcafe.co.uk Tax Guides

# How to Save Inheritance Tax

By Carl Bayley BSc FCA

## Important Legal Notices:

Taxcafe®
TAX GUIDE – "How to Save Inheritance Tax"

**Published by:**
Taxcafe UK Limited
67 Milton Road
Kirkcaldy KY1 1TL

Email address: team@taxcafe.co.uk

Nineteenth Edition – December 2023

ISBN 978-1-911020-86-8



**Disclaimer**
Before reading or relying on the content of this Tax Guide, please read the disclaimer.

## Disclaimer

This guide is intended as general guidance only and does NOT constitute accountancy, tax, investment or other professional advice.

1. The author and Taxcafe UK Limited make no representations or warranties with respect to the accuracy or completeness of this publication and cannot accept any responsibility or liability for any loss or risk, personal or otherwise, which may arise, directly or indirectly, from reliance on information contained in this publication.

2. Please note that tax legislation, the law and practices of Government and regulatory authorities (e.g. HM Revenue & Customs) are constantly changing. We therefore recommend that for accountancy, tax, investment or other professional advice, you consult a suitably qualified accountant, tax adviser, financial adviser, or other professional adviser.

3. Please also note that your personal circumstances may vary from the general examples provided in this guide and your professional adviser will be able to provide specific advice based on your personal circumstances.

4. This guide covers UK taxation only and any references to 'tax' or 'taxation', unless the contrary is expressly stated, refer to UK taxation only. Please note that references to the 'UK' do not include the Channel Islands or the Isle of Man. Foreign tax implications are beyond the scope of this guide.

5. While, in an effort to be helpful, this tax guide may refer to general guidance on matters other than UK taxation, Taxcafe UK Limited and the author are not expert in these matters and do not accept any responsibility or liability for loss which may arise from reliance on such information contained in this guide.

6. All persons described in the examples in this guide are entirely fictional. Any similarities to actual persons, living or dead, or to fictional characters created by any other author, are entirely coincidental.

7. The views expressed in this publication are the author's own personal views and do not necessarily reflect the views of any organisation he may represent.

## About the Author

Carl Bayley is the author of a series of 'Plain English' tax guides designed specifically for the layperson and the non-specialist. His aim is to help families, landlords, and other business owners understand the taxes they face and make savings through sensible planning and by having confidence to know what they can claim. Carl's speciality is his ability to take the weird, complex world of taxation and set it out in the kind of clear, straightforward language taxpayers can understand. As he often says, "My job is to translate 'tax' into English."

Carl enjoys his role as a tax author, as he explains, "Writing these guides gives me the opportunity to use the skills and knowledge learned over more than thirty years in the tax profession for the benefit of a wider audience. The most satisfying part of my success as an author is the chance to give the average person the same standard of information as the 'big guys' at a price everyone can afford."

Carl takes the same approach when speaking on taxation, a role he undertakes with great enthusiasm, including his highly acclaimed annual 'Budget Breakfast' for the Institute of Chartered Accountants. In addition to being a recognised author and speaker, Carl has spoken on taxation on radio and television, including the BBC's 'It's Your Money' programme and BBC Radio 2's Jeremy Vine Show.

Carl began his career as a Chartered Accountant in 1983 with one of the 'Big 4' accountancy firms. After qualifying as a double prize-winner, he began specialising in taxation. He worked for several major international firms until beginning the new millennium by launching his own practice, through which he provided advice on a wide variety of taxation issues; especially property taxation, inheritance tax, and tax planning for small and medium-sized businesses, for twenty years, before deciding to focus exclusively on his favourite role as author and presenter.

Carl is a former Chairman of the Tax Faculty of the Institute of Chartered Accountants in England and Wales, and was a member of the Institute's governing Council between 2003 and 2023. He is also a former President of ICAEW Scotland and member of the ICAEW Board. He co-organised the annual Practical Tax Conference from 2002 to 2019.

Aside from his tax books, Carl is an avid creative writer and has just published his debut novel, *Trinity of Souls*. When he isn't working, he takes on the equally taxing challenges of hill walking and horse riding: his Munro tally is now 106 and, while he remains a novice rider, his progress is cantering along nicely. Carl lives in the Scottish Borders, where he enjoys spending time with his partner, Linda. He has three children and his first grandchild arrived in April 2021.

## Dedication and Thanks

At its heart, this book is, of course, about relationships. It seems appropriate, therefore, for me to dedicate it to those who represent the most important relationships in my life.

***For the Past,***
To Diana, the memory of your love warms me still. Thank you for bringing me into the light and making it all possible. To Arthur, your wise words still come back to guide me; and to my loving grandmothers, Doris and Winifred. Between you, you left me with nothing I could spend, but everything I need. Also to my beloved friends: Mac, William, Edward, Rusty, Dawson, and the grand old lady, Morgan. Thank you for all those happy miles; I still miss you all.

***For the Present,***
To the lovely lady Linda, bless you, my princess; I'm so proud of you. Thank you for bringing the sunshine back into my life, for opening my ears, and putting the song back into my heart. Also to Ollie, the world's oldest puppy: thank you for these happy miles.

***For the Future,***
To James, a true twenty-first century gentleman and one of the nicest guys I have ever met. To Robert, the 'chip off the old block', who is both cursed and blessed to have inherited a lot of my character; luckily for him, there is a lot of his mother in him too! And to Michelle, one of the most interesting people I have ever met. I am so very proud of every one of you and I can only hope I, in turn, will be able to leave each of you with everything you need. Finally, to Sebastian: welcome to the world, wee man.

**Thanks** are due to:

The Taxcafe team, past and present: for their help in making these books more successful than I could ever have dreamed; my old friend and mentor, Peter Rayney: for his inspiration and for showing me tax and humour can mix; Rebecca, Paul, and David: for taking me into the fold at the Tax Faculty and their fantastic support at our Practical Tax Conference over many years; Gregor: for the 'brain-storming' sessions and those extraordinary ideas that spring from his lateral thinking; Jane Evans: for some useful practical insights; Jonathan Woodwards and Alan Sacks: for their helpful constructive comments.

And last, but far from least, thanks to Nick for giving me the push!

**C.B., Roxburghshire, December 2023**

## Contents

# Chapter 1

# Introduction

## 1.1 A PERSONAL NOTE

I'll make no bones about it. I find the concept of taxing people for dying morally repugnant. So I have an especially strong desire to help people save Inheritance Tax.

To be honest, I have always found this a difficult subject to write about: not because of the undoubted technical complexities – as a tax author, I am well and truly accustomed to that. No, I find this particular tax difficult to write about from an emotional perspective, because it is, inevitably, largely about death. My first introduction to the topic, as a young accountancy student, came within weeks of my own mother's death and that, perhaps, may be why I have always found the subject somewhat distressing.

Nonetheless, as a professional tax writer, I have always tackled this subject to the best of my abilities and strived to give readers the quality of information and guidance they deserve, just as in all my guides. I am confident I have succeeded in this aim and I believe the guide you have here is as comprehensive and detailed as anyone could wish for.

But to help me, and I hope you too, deal with the emotional aspects of the subject, I have always tried to inject some humour into the topic. Sometimes, particularly in the last few years, I have wondered if this humour is still appropriate and whether, perhaps, I should re-write the guide to reflect a more serious tone. I have considered this approach but, in the end, I still believe in trying to put a smile on people's faces (including my own), even when tackling such an emotive issue. So, the humour, such that it is, remains. If I offend anyone, I sincerely apologise, but I hope most readers will simply smile at my efforts.

When it comes to tax, I firmly believe no-one should ever pay more than their fair share. Taxpayers have every right to undertake sensible planning measures to legitimately reduce, or delay, their tax bills; especially to protect their family.

That's what this guide is all about. And, whatever form your family takes, be it a traditional spouse and children, or be it a collection of people connected only by the fact you want to take care of them, I fervently hope this guide helps you protect it.

## 1.2 THERE ARE TWO CERTAINTIES IN LIFE

Generally speaking, I find the oldest sayings are the truest. One old saying is, 'There are two certainties in life: Death and Taxes.'

The point where these two great 'certainties' meet is Inheritance Tax, and it is through the medium of this tax the Government will aim to get its final pound of flesh from you, just as you have departed this life.

Most people spend their lifetime trying to accumulate a reasonable amount of wealth, to take care of themselves in old age and then pass on any remaining surplus to their children. Much of the Government's fiscal policy is aimed at encouraging this behaviour.

It is somewhat unfair then, that without careful planning and a great deal of pre-emptive action, many families will ultimately face a huge Inheritance Tax bill. Unchecked, this tax bill will rob your family of a significant proportion of their rightful inheritance: up to 40% of it, in fact.

Most people are absolutely appalled at this prospect, which, of course, is where Inheritance Tax planning comes in!

Inheritance Tax, as we know it today, arrived in 1986, the brainchild of Margaret Thatcher and her then Chancellor, Nigel Lawson. The tax is actually little more than a re-branding of its predecessor, Capital Transfer Tax, which, in turn, had replaced the earlier and rather more Draconian Estate Duty that, in its day, had played a major part in turning many of Britain's stately homes into amusement parks!

It is quite ironic that Inheritance Tax should have such a long lineage because it is, of course, usually one's descendants who will suffer its effects.

The principal difference between Inheritance Tax and its predecessors is the fact there is a general exemption for most lifetime transfers to other individuals. This is part of the reason behind accusations the Labour Party once made to a previous Conservative Government that they had allowed Inheritance Tax to become a voluntary tax, paid only by the unwary, ill-advised and unprepared taxpayer, while wealthier taxpayers took expensive professional advice and avoided the tax.

Certainly there was, and still is, an element of truth in this accusation. In recent years, however, it has become increasingly difficult to avoid this hated grave-robber's tax, with a host of measures introduced by Governments of all persuasions designed to block many of the popular methods used by families attempting to plan for the inevitable.

Help seemed to be at hand in 2007 when the Conservatives proposed a massive increase in the nil rate band exemption to £1m. Although this did not materialise for many years and, even then, it had been watered down beyond all recognition by a host of 'ifs', 'buts' and 'maybes', it did at least prompt the then Labour Government into making nil rate bands transferable between spouses. Suddenly, overnight, it seemed almost every married couple, civil partnership, widow, widower and surviving civil partner had effectively doubled their nil rate band.

Since then, however, things have taken a turn for the worse: as it seems all our politicians are happy to break their promises when it comes to

Inheritance Tax. Alistair Darling kicked off the era of broken promises in 2009 when he announced the planned increase in the nil rate band set for the following year would not go ahead. Worse still, he went on to announce a five year freeze in the nil rate band at its 2009 level of £325,000.

Soon afterwards, the Conservatives became the senior partner in the Coalition Government. Sadly, their promised increase in the nil rate band was swiftly shelved and Labour's freeze adopted in its place. Since then, the freeze has been extended several times, most recently by current Chancellor, Jeremy Hunt. In his November 2022 Autumn Statement, he announced a further, additional two-year freeze, bringing it to a total of nineteen years!

Incredibly, we are now stuck with the 2009 nil rate band of just £325,000 until at least 2028. Not since 1946 has it remained the same for so long.

Inflation has already severely eroded the value of the nil rate band and its real value will reduce even further between now and 2028. This will undo most, if not all, of the benefit of the transferable nil rate band regime introduced in 2007 (and those who are single or divorced never had that benefit anyway).

Make no mistake about it: the nineteen-year freeze in the nil rate band is a significant tax-raising measure. As the value of the band decreases in real terms, the Government's Inheritance Tax take is steadily increasing.

On top of the many broken promises about the nil rate band, George Osborne unleashed more misery in 2013, when he introduced a raft of new rules to restrict the deduction of liabilities. As one might expect, these blocked a number of popular planning techniques. However, what will be less apparent to most people is that the rules also lead to some astonishingly unfair results, especially when a family business is passed on to the next generation.

We will look at the impact of these rules in more detail later, but it is clear to me they severely undermine the original intention of helping small and medium-sized businesses survive their owner's death. The additional Inheritance Tax burden placed on many families will inevitably threaten many businesses' chances of survival.

In 2015, Osborne finally returned to that promise of a £1m nil rate band. And what a mess he made of it! Instead of the simple £1m nil rate band he had promised, he created an additional 'residence nil rate band'. Claiming the new relief amounted to the equivalent of a £1m nil rate band, "Promise Made, Promise Delivered!" was somewhat disingenuous, since getting the required level of exemption necessitates a complex combination of circumstances.

What Osborne did was rather like me promising to give one of my children £1,000 tomorrow, no strings attached; but, instead of doing as I said, waiting thirteen years then telling them I would give them £1,000, but only if they got married, bought a house, and provided me with grandchildren. That's what I call, "Promise Made, Promise Broken."

Despite the many changes to the Inheritance Tax regime, what remains true to this day is the fact it is the moderately wealthy members of society who suffer the greatest proportionate burden.

The problem for many people in the middle wealth bracket is they face a fundamental dilemma. On the one hand they have, on paper, sufficient wealth to leave their family with a substantial tax burden. On the other hand, they do not really have a great deal of disposable income, despite leading reasonably modest lifestyles. This means the simple expedient of just giving all their surplus wealth away is, in practical terms, simply not an option.

This all too common 'asset rich/cash poor' situation that many people find themselves in is exacerbated by increases in property values over recent decades, which have pushed more and more people into the Inheritance Tax bracket. Despite Osborne's desperately convoluted attempt at deluding us into thinking he'd fulfilled his promise, property values are still the number one cause of most people's Inheritance Tax burden.

As ever, there remain two effective ways to avoid Inheritance Tax: die poor, or plan ahead. Most of us find the first option somewhat unpalatable and also quite difficult to achieve without a remarkable sense of timing!

In the past, planning ahead was seen as the prerogative of the very wealthiest members of society, leaving the moderately wealthy to pick up the bill. However, my aim in this guide is to help put an end to this situation. If the Government is still prepared to allow Inheritance Tax to be even partly 'voluntary', albeit to a far lesser extent than previously, then why should ***anyone*** volunteer?

Early and careful planning is the key to reducing the eventual Inheritance Tax burden on your family and you don't need to be a millionaire to do it. Or to ***need*** to do it either, for that matter! Besides which, a great many people are surprised to discover when they add up all their assets they are, in fact, millionaires anyway: on paper, at least.

While some tax can still be saved through last-minute planning, a great deal more unnecessary tax can be avoided by planning for death and taxes throughout your lifetime. Read on and I will show you how.

## 1.3 GUIDE OVERVIEW

In this opening chapter, we start by taking a brief look at some background issues important to an understanding of the rest of the guide, including giving consideration to the future of Inheritance Tax and what it may mean for you and your family.

Following that, in Chapter 2, we will cover some of the basics, including how the tax is calculated and who pays it. All of this comes under the general heading of 'know your enemy', because it is important to understand what you're up against before you start to make plans to combat it.

We then move on, in Chapter 3, to look at the main exemptions available at any time, both during your lifetime and on death; as well as those only available on death.

Chapters 4 and 5 look at the area of lifetime transfers, including the additional exemptions available and how to maximise them.

The first five chapters prepare us for Chapter 6, which is devoted to Inheritance Tax planning for married couples, widows, and widowers (including civil partners). The changes introduced in 2007 fundamentally altered the Inheritance Tax planning landscape for married couples. In many cases, something that was the best advice before is now the very last thing you should do!

Married couples therefore need to consider everything contained in the rest of this guide in the context of the guidance set out in Chapter 6. The chapter also includes an analysis of the position facing widows and widowers, with guidance on crucial tax-saving action that needs to be taken by the recently bereaved.

Even those who are currently single or divorced will benefit from Chapter 6, as it includes guidance on the potential Inheritance Tax benefits of marriage.

Chapter 7 covers the important area of business property relief, perhaps the most valuable piece of equipment in our Inheritance Tax planning armoury; as well as agricultural property relief, which can also be highly beneficial.

We then move into the realm of trusts in Chapters 8 and 9 and we will see what powerful tools these vehicles can provide in the battle against Inheritance Tax.

In Chapter 10 we look at the tremendous opportunities pension savings can provide to allow your wealth to escape Inheritance Tax and be passed to your heirs, or even further down the generations, tax efficiently. However, there are also pitfalls to be wary of, and we will see that avoiding Inheritance Tax is only part of the story, as there are both other tax benefits, and other tax costs, to watch out for.

Chapter 11 builds further on this all-important broader view by reminding us there is a bigger picture than merely saving Inheritance Tax, and here we widen our sights to take in other aspects of estate preservation. This is reinforced in Chapter 12 with a look at the interaction between Inheritance Tax and Capital Gains Tax.

In Chapter 13, we look at passing on the family home. Here we will take a detailed look at some of the practical implications of the residence nil rate band, as well as some of the other planning techniques available to shelter the family home from the Government's most despised form of taxation.

Chapter 14 focuses on the powerful long-term planning strategy of family investment companies, which has the potential to save landlords and other investors millions of pounds in Inheritance Tax. After that, in Chapter 15, we look at some other more advanced planning techniques.

In Chapter 16, we cover perhaps the most drastic of all planning techniques, with a guide to emigration, as well as a look at the advantages available to those who have successfully achieved it.

Chapter 17 provides a useful whole life timetable for effective Inheritance Tax planning, which puts everything we have learned into context and also reassures us, while it's never too early to start planning, it's never too late either!

Chapter 18 covers the planning a bereaved family can still carry out even after someone has died. While this is not the ideal time for truly effective Inheritance Tax planning, it is surprising how much can still be achieved if the deceased's family acts quickly.

This extensive guide, fully updated for the drastic changes introduced over the last few years, and the latest planning ideas available today, has something of value for everyone, and provides a valuable tool in the battle against the Government's most despicable form of taxation.

## 1.4 TERMINOLOGY, ABBREVIATIONS, AND EXAMPLES

Throughout this guide, you will see me refer to 'married couples' and 'spouses', as well as 'widows' and 'widowers'. In each case, the tax treatment applies equally to married couples of all types and to civil partners.

Any references to 'married couples' should be taken to also include registered civil partnerships; any reference to the taxpayer's 'spouse' will also include their civil partner where relevant; and any reference to 'husbands' or 'wives' will include spouses of the same gender and civil partners. Similarly, any reference to 'widows' or 'widowers' includes surviving civil partners.

For the avoidance of doubt, I would, in particular, point out the spouse exemption covered in Section 3.3 and all the planning issues covered in Chapter 6 apply equally to same sex spouses and civil partners. However, it remains important to remember, unless specified to the contrary, the tax treatment being outlined applies to legally married couples and legally registered civil partners only.

Inheritance Tax, like many other UK taxes, is administered by reference to the UK tax year, i.e. the period of twelve months ending on 5th April. Thus, for example, the 2023/24 tax year is the year ending 5th April 2024. References to the 'tax year' in this guide should be construed accordingly.

Other periods are also important for Inheritance Tax purposes and a reference to 'seven years' or 'more than two years', for example, means a strict period of calendar years rather than tax years.

Trust concepts and terminology are key to an understanding of Inheritance Tax planning. As well as the various types of trust, we will encounter important concepts such as 'interest in possession' and 'life interest'. A full explanation of trust terminology will be given in Chapter 8.

Another important concept in Inheritance Tax is 'domicile'. Broadly speaking, domicile is similar to nationality and for most people it will be obvious whether or not they are UK domiciled. Nevertheless, this analogy is not entirely accurate and domicile can sometimes be a highly complex matter. We will return to a detailed examination of this concept in Chapter 16.

Long-term UK residents and certain other individuals are also deemed to be UK domiciled for tax purposes. We will look at the rules governing deemed domicile in Section 16.3. Throughout the rest of this guide, unless specifically stated to the contrary, any reference to a UK domiciled individual includes those who are deemed UK domiciled. Similarly, a non-UK domiciled individual means someone who is neither UK domiciled under general principles nor deemed UK domiciled.

In legal terms, the word 'property' has a wide application and can mean any form of asset, including cash. Sometimes though, when we talk about 'property' we mean land and buildings: legally termed 'real property'. In this guide, I will use the word in both its common meaning and its legal meaning, and leave the context to make it clear which I mean on each occasion.

Life expectancies quoted throughout this guide are as per the Office for National Statistics (ONS). Naturally, these take no account of personal circumstances.

Throughout the guide I have allowed myself a few abbreviations. Some of them, like 'UK', are in common usage. I will explain what the others mean the first time I use them and they are all set out again in Appendix D for ease of reference. Large amounts, such as £1,000,000 or more are abbreviated by use of the letter 'm'. For example, £2,500,000 will be written as '£2.5m'.

**Ignorance is Bliss**

For the sake of illustration, throughout this guide I am generally going to ignore the following, which have become too small to have any significant impact. They will, however, produce small savings in practice, where relevant:

- The Capital Gains Tax (CGT) annual exemption (£6,000 for 2023/24; £3,000 thereafter)
- The dividend allowance (£1,000 for 2023/24; £500 thereafter)

**Which Annual Exemption?**

Confusingly, from 2024/25 onwards the annual CGT exemption and annual exemption for IHT will be the same amount: £3,000. They are, however, two completely different exemptions, operating in completely different ways, for different taxes. Throughout this guide, unless expressly stated to the contrary, any mention of the annual exemption means the annual exemption for IHT, covered in Section 5.2.

**Property Taxes**
Inheritance Tax planning often involves the transfer of UK property. This will sometimes lead to tax charges arising on the transfer in the form of some variation of Stamp Duty. The type of Duty arising will depend on which part of the UK the property is located in, as follows:

| | |
|---|---|
| England: | Stamp Duty Land Tax (SDLT) |
| Scotland: | Land and Buildings Transaction Tax |
| Wales: | Land Transaction Tax |
| Northern Ireland: | Stamp Duty Land Tax (SDLT) |

The rules applying under each form of Duty are broadly similar. There are some variations in the rates, however. Details of the rates applying to all UK property are included in the Taxcafe guide *How to Save Property Tax.*

For the sake of simplicity, I will refer only to SDLT throughout the rest of this guide, but similar charges will arise on property in Scotland or Wales, except the Duty will have a different name and will be charged at different rates.

**About the Examples**
This guide is illustrated throughout by a number of examples. Unless specifically stated to the contrary, all persons described in the examples in this guide are UK resident and domiciled for tax purposes.

In preparing the examples I have assumed the UK tax regime will remain unchanged in the future except to the extent of any announcements already made at the time of publication. However, if there is one thing we can predict with any certainty, it is that change **will** occur. The reader must bear this in mind when reviewing the results of the examples.

## 1.5 WHY WORRY?

Of course, ***you*** won't actually have to pay the Inheritance Tax (IHT) on your own estate. Furthermore, for many people, everything can safely be left to their spouse free from IHT.

And if you have no other dependants or potential beneficiaries but just resent paying any unnecessary tax, you can simply leave it all to charity.

But most people ***do*** have someone they care about. Usually they have children, other family, or friends whom they want to see benefit from the assets they have built up in their lifetime and they don't want to see the Government taking 40% of it away.

Even if, in the first instance, you are leaving everything tax free to your surviving spouse, your accumulated wealth will eventually be hit by IHT if you don't plan ahead.

As we will see later in the guide, you need to take action ***now*** to safeguard your family's future prosperity. Alternatively, you may be the potential beneficiary yourself, trying to get an elderly relative to plan for the preservation of ***your*** inheritance. Either way, there is plenty to worry about!

**But Am I Wealthy Enough to Worry?**

Most people are quite surprised to discover just how much they are actually worth. How often have you heard someone say, "I'm worth more dead than alive"? Very often, especially as we get older, it's true (in pure financial terms only, of course).

This is basically because it takes an enormous amount of capital just to support one person. When that person dies, the capital that was previously tied up in supporting them is freed (after the Government gets its share!)

Hence, although you may not feel particularly wealthy, you may still find you have a large potential IHT bill. You'd be amazed just how many 'paper millionaires' there are these days. Take a look at this example:

***Example:*** *Rosemary is a divorcee with no children of her own: although she is very close to her two younger sisters and their children. She owns a fairly average sized detached house, which her ex-husband transferred to her under the terms of their divorce settlement. The house is bigger than she really needs, but she has fond memories of the many holidays her nephews and nieces spent there, so she is quite attached to it. She has been advised its current market value is £550,000.*

*Rosemary is retired and lives off her savings and an investment portfolio she managed to accumulate after her divorce. Although these produce an annual income of only £20,000, their total value is approximately £430,000.*

*Rosemary also has some jewellery, some silver, and a few antiques. Altogether, these are worth £15,000. Lastly, she has a small car, worth £5,000.*

*Nobody would call Rosemary rich by any stretch of the imagination. She's living off only £20,000 a year. But add it all up and you will find she is a millionaire. This means Rosemary's family has a potential IHT bill of £270,000!*

And you don't need to be anywhere near as 'wealthy' as Rosemary to have an IHT problem. Once your estate is worth over £325,000, you have a potential exposure to tax at 40% on the excess (subject to any transferable nil rate band: see Chapter 6; and any available residence nil rate band: see Section 3.4). £325,000! What's that these days? A house, a car, a few savings, and you're easily there!

So, yes, generally speaking, if you can afford to buy this guide, there is a strong chance you are wealthy enough to worry about IHT!

## 1.6 A GUIDE TO EFFECTIVE INHERITANCE TAX PLANNING

All tax planning needs to be undertaken carefully and in full knowledge of the circumstances of the taxpayer's individual situation. This is probably never more true than in the case of IHT, where a detailed review of the individual's situation is vital.

In this guide, I have provided a detailed examination of current IHT law on the basis of our present understanding. However, it is important to understand that further changes or restrictions could be introduced at any time and the precise meaning of some areas of law will only become apparent when tested in court: possibly many years from now.

I have highlighted some of the more popular planning techniques currently being used successfully by taxpayers wishing to protect their wealth from the scourge of IHT, or which are at least currently believed to work.

HM Revenue and Customs (HMRC) does, however, have very wide powers to enable it to closely examine any IHT planning technique and will do its utmost to overturn any planning strategy when the law permits it to. The associated operations rules and general anti-abuse rule covered in Section 11.11 are both particularly wide-ranging in this regard.

For these and many other reasons, the reader must bear in mind the general nature of this guide. Individual circumstances vary and the tax implications of an individual's actions will vary with them. It is always vital to get professional advice before undertaking any tax planning or other transactions that may have tax implications.

**The Challenge**
The great challenge with IHT planning is that much of the position will only be determined when an individual dies. Hence, since IHT law is constantly changing, no-one can be sure of having avoided this evil tax until they are safely tucked up in their grave!

For most people that will be many years from now, so there is plenty of time for the Government to move the goalposts, which means we have to keep an eye on them all the time. None of this means you shouldn't undertake IHT planning, especially given that the earlier you start, the more you are likely to save. But it does mean, in addition to taking professional advice when putting your plans into effect, you should also commission a regular professional review to determine whether your planning remains effective. Every IHT planning technique runs the risk of being undermined by changes in the law and these can happen at the stroke of a pen: especially when there is a change of Government.

In fact, it may not even be IHT you are trying to avoid. In January 2020, an all-party parliamentary group on 'inheritance and intergenerational fairness' published a report calling for some radical changes to the UK's death tax regime, including replacing IHT with a 'Death Tax' and lifetime 'Gift Tax'.

The current Government has shown no interest in these proposals, but it is possible a future Government might adopt some of them. Or it may do something completely different; or simply carry on tinkering with the current regime, as every Government for the last forty years has done.

Personally, I think taxing death, or personal gifts between family members, is completely immoral and just plain wrong. If it was up to me, IHT would be abolished tomorrow. However, I'm sorry to say that looks unlikely in the foreseeable future, regardless of what Government we are lumbered with.

We cannot predict what exactly is going to change. But I am sure something will. So, while death is certain, the tax regime you will face is not. Despite this, early and effective IHT planning is still the best way to protect your family, whatever the future may hold.

Chapter 2

# Inheritance Tax Principles

## 2.1 TRANSFERS OF VALUE

"Inheritance Tax is payable on death. Everyone knows that, don't they?"

Like so many things 'everyone knows' (like 'man will never fly' and 'an iceberg will never sink a ship'), this is **WRONG!**

Now, admittedly, it is true that by far the biggest part of the IHT the Government collects arises on the occasion of someone's death. Furthermore, most of the remainder arises due to attempts to offload some wealth before then. However, what actually triggers IHT is not death but a 'transfer of value'.

In principle, IHT is chargeable on any transfer of value made by any person at any time. Thankfully, however, there are a number of exemptions and these help ensure we don't have to pay the Government 40% every time we give the kids their pocket money.

The reasons we tend to think of IHT as applying mainly on death are three-fold:

i) On death, we are inevitably forced to transfer our entire wealth to others, thus causing, for most of us, the biggest transfer of value of our lives
ii) Most lifetime transfers to other individuals are exempt, or at least only become chargeable in the event of death within seven years
iii) The name of the tax implies (falsely) that it is only related to death

**What is a Transfer of Value?**
A transfer of value occurs whenever you dispose of something and, as a result, your total net wealth is reduced. Your total net wealth is referred to as your 'estate' and we will explore this concept further in Section 2.5.

What you are disposing of may be money or any other asset with monetary value. Furthermore, it is the reduction in your net wealth that generates the transfer of value, not necessarily the value of the asset disposed of. We will see an example of this a little later.

Any disposal of wealth by way of a 'transaction at arm's length' between unconnected persons is not treated as a transfer of value. Hence, the most basic transactions in life, such as buying the weekly groceries, will not be classed as a transfer of value, even though your total net wealth is inevitably reduced. Furthermore, when dealing at arm's length with unconnected persons, merely striking a poor bargain will not be a transfer of value.

Even a transaction with a connected person (see Appendix B) will still not give rise to any transfer of value if it is carried out in the same way as it would have been if it had been an arm's length transaction.

### The Amount of the Transfer of Value

A transfer of value occurs whenever you make a disposal that is not at arm's length and, as a result, there is a reduction in your total net wealth (your estate). The simplest type of transfer of value is therefore a straightforward gift. If you give someone £10,000 in cash, that is a transfer of value of £10,000, if you give someone a painting worth £5,000, that is a transfer of value of £5,000.

A transfer of value also occurs when sales take place between connected persons at an undervalue, or an overvalue. If you sell your son a painting for £2,000 when it is, in fact, worth £10,000, that is a transfer of value of £8,000; if you buy a car from your daughter and pay her £5,000, when the car is worth only £1,000, that is a transfer of value of £4,000.

But what is important to remember is that it is the reduction in the value of your overall estate that gives rise to the transfer of value.

***Example:*** *Bjorn has a set of six antique chairs worth £20,000. He gives his son, Benny, one of the chairs. The value of a single chair, which is not part of a complete set, is only £1,500.*

*However, the transfer of value here is not the value of Benny's single chair. No, the transfer of value is the reduction in the value of Bjorn's estate. Previously, he had a set of chairs worth £20,000. After the gift to Benny, he has five chairs worth £1,500 each, a total of £7,500. Hence, the reduction in the value of Bjorn's estate, and thus the amount of the transfer of value, is £12,500.*

## 2.2 WHO IS LIABLE FOR INHERITANCE TAX?

For UK domiciled individuals, IHT arises on the net value of their entire estate (see Section 2.5) at the time of their death, wherever situated, less:

i) The nil rate band (NRB): £325,000 for deaths occurring between 6th April 2009 and 5th April 2028
ii) Any transferable nil rate band (TNRB) available (see Section 6.2)
iii) Any other applicable exemptions & reliefs (Chapter 3)

IHT also arises on certain lifetime gifts and other transfers (Chapter 4)

### Non-Domiciled Individuals

Non-UK domiciled individuals are generally only liable for IHT on UK assets, including land and buildings situated in the UK. Certain UK assets are also exempt from IHT when held by a non-UK domiciled individual. For further details, see Section 3.7.

Again, the liability arises on death or in the event of certain lifetime transfers that we will cover later. We will take a detailed look at the concept of domicile and the planning opportunities it provides in Chapter 16.

## 2.3 WHO ACTUALLY PAYS THE TAX?

Despite my comments in Section 2.1, most IHT does arise on death and, naturally, the deceased is not around to pick up the bill. So who actually has to pay the tax?

Subject to the points below, the usual default position is the liability for IHT arising on death falls on the personal representatives, who must settle the tax out of the general assets of the deceased's estate.

Where the deceased has left a Will, their executors are their personal representatives. In the case of a person dying intestate (without a valid Will), the person applying for a grant of representation (i.e. probate), or confirmation in Scotland, will be the personal representative.

Where no personal representative has been appointed by the court within twelve months after the end of the month of death then the deceased's beneficiaries will be required to fulfil the obligations regarding payment of IHT, delivery of accounts, etc, which would normally fall on the personal representatives.

It is, however, possible for the Will to direct that a beneficiary should bear the tax on a legacy themselves. This can be useful to avoid the extra cost of 'grossing up' (see Section 2.8).

A beneficiary becoming entitled to a life interest in property under the terms of a Will must generally bear the tax arising on their legacy.

For property already held in trust, but which is included in the deceased's estate for IHT purposes (as explained in Chapter 8), the tax may fall on the trustees or on another beneficiary of that trust, depending on the exact circumstances.

### Lifetime Transfers

The primary responsibility for any IHT arising immediately on lifetime transfers falls on the transferor. It is possible, however, to stipulate that the transferee should bear any IHT arising (see Memorandum 2 in Appendix C).

Additional IHT liabilities frequently arise when the transferor dies within seven years of a lifetime transfer. These liabilities usually fall on the transferee. IHT on lifetime transfers is examined in more detail in Chapter 4.

## 2.4 HOW MUCH TAX IS PAYABLE?

On death, IHT is levied, generally at one single rate of 40%, on the entire value of your estate, less certain exemptions. The most important exemptions are the NRB, which is £325,000 for deaths occurring between 6th April 2009 and 5th April 2028, the exemption for transfers to spouses (see Section 3.3), and the residence nil rate band (RNRB) (see Section 3.4).

Personal representatives of widows or widowers may be able to claim up to double the current NRB and RNRB where the first spouse to die did not fully utilise their NRB or RNRB. We will cover this subject in detail in Chapter 6.

**Lifetime Transfers**

Where a lifetime transfer gives rise to an immediate IHT charge, the rate applying is 20%, sometimes known as the lifetime rate. Extra tax will often become payable on lifetime transfers in the event of the taxpayer's subsequent death within seven years and we will look at this in detail in Section 4.5.

Transfers made directly to spouses are usually tax free. Furthermore, the £325,000 NRB can be deducted from the total value of transfers made in the last seven years. As we shall see in Chapter 4, this is very important because it means tax-free transfers equivalent to the NRB can be made every seven years.

## 2.5 WHAT IS YOUR ESTATE?

Your 'estate' means everything you own, including land and property, shares and securities, savings accounts, cash, antiques, jewellery, paintings, your car, your furniture and anything else with any monetary value whatsoever.

Two things that can usually be excluded, however, are your pension savings and any life insurance proceeds, as these are generally held in trust on your behalf and do not fall into your estate. Nonetheless, there are some pitfalls to watch out for, so we will take a detailed look at pensions in Chapter 10, and life insurance in Section 11.8.

Many people assume other tax-advantaged products, such as Individual Savings Accounts (ISAs) are exempt from IHT because they are supposedly tax-free. Unfortunately, this is not the case and ***ALL*** assets held directly in your own name have to be included in your estate, regardless of their treatment for Income Tax or CGT purposes.

Income arising up to the date of death must also be included (e.g. unpaid state pensions, annuities, salary, accrued bank interest, etc).

Also included in the deceased's estate will be: the net value of any assets held on their behalf in certain types of trust (see Chapter 8); the value of any relevant gifts with reservation (see Section 4.8); and the value of any assets they elect to have included in their estate in order to prevent an Income Tax charge (see Section 11.12).

For the purposes of IHT, any non-exempt transfers of value made in the seven years prior to death will also effectively be brought back into the deceased's estate. Reduced IHT rates do, however, apply to transfers of value made at least three, but less than seven, years prior to death.

Any liabilities, such as your mortgage, overdrafts, bank loans, credit card bills, outstanding utility bills, etc, may generally be deducted; although restrictions may sometimes apply (see Section 2.10). You may even deduct outstanding Income Tax or CGT liabilities!

Reasonable funeral expenses may be deducted. What is reasonable depends on your standard of living. (In one extreme case, the expense of a private army providing a funeral honour guard was deemed reasonable.)

Sadly, the costs of obtaining UK probate and administering your UK estate may ***not*** be deducted; although the costs of obtaining foreign probate and realising the value of foreign assets (e.g. selling them) may be deducted up to a maximum of 5% of the value of those assets, where these are subject to UK IHT (see Section 2.2).

In summary, subject to a few adjustments, your estate is basically your total net worth, excluding pension savings (usually). All the property transferred on your death is subject to IHT in the same way, whether it transfers under the terms of your Will, by intestacy, by survivorship (for jointly held property), or by any other means.

Many people take out insurance policies to cover outstanding liabilities, such as credit card bills or bank loans, if they should pass away unexpectedly. The result of this is that these liabilities would not be deductible from the value of the estate as they were automatically settled on the taxpayer's death. It would be far better to make provision for such liabilities by other means (see Section 11.8) and thus ensure they are deducted from the value of your estate for IHT purposes. As we shall see in Section 2.10, it remains important that the liability is actually settled out of the assets of the estate.

Household personal effects are generally overvalued, resulting in unnecessary overpayments of IHT. The valuations most people have on their personal effects (jewellery, antiques, silverware, etc,) tend to be insurance valuations. However, the amount on which IHT is payable should only be the open market value of the assets and this is often considerably less.

## 2.6 THE BASIC CALCULATION ON DEATH

To illustrate the basic IHT calculation, let's take a look at a simple example:

***Example:*** *Arthur has been careful with his money all his life. At the time of his death in December 2023, his estate amounts to £3m. Arthur has been divorced for many years and his Will leaves his entire estate to his son, Tony. Hence, there are no exemptions available, other than the NRB. (We will see why the RNRB is not available in this case in Section 3.4.)*

*The first £325,000 of Arthur's estate is exempt from IHT, as it is covered by the NRB. The remaining £2.675m is charged to IHT at 40%, giving rise to a charge of £1.07m!*

The tax is of course reduced (or even eliminated) where there is an exempt beneficiary such as the deceased's surviving spouse or a charity. These exemptions are explored further in Sections 3.3 and 3.5 respectively.

The example above is about as simple (and painful) as it gets. In other cases there will be more than one beneficiary. This will not alter the total amount of IHT payable (unless any of them are an exempt beneficiary), but it may affect who ends up bearing the tax.

***Example:*** *John dies with a total estate worth £1m. He leaves his nephew, Paul, a house worth £300,000 on condition he settles any tax arising. He leaves his eldest son, George, the sum of £250,000 in cash, stating in his Will that this sum should be free of all taxes, and he leaves the remainder of his estate to his younger son, Richard.*

*There are no exemptions available apart from the NRB. (By leaving his house to his nephew, John is unable to claim the RNRB: see Section 3.4. We will also assume there is no TNRB available: see Section 6.2.) Hence, the IHT arising is £1m – £325,000 = £675,000 x 40% = £270,000.*

*This amounts to 27% of the total value of the estate, so this is the effective rate applying in this case, sometimes known as the 'estate rate'. As Paul has to settle the IHT on his bequest directly, he will pay IHT at the estate rate of 27% on the value of the house, giving him a liability of £81,000 (£300,000 x 27%).*

*As George's bequest is free of tax, John's personal representatives must pay the remaining £189,000 (£270,000 – £81,000). This means John's estate is effectively divided up as follows:*

| | |
|---|---|
| *Paul:* | *£300,000 (the value of the house)* |
| *George:* | *£250,000 (his tax-free legacy)* |
| *Richard:* | *£261,000 (£1m – £300,000 – £250,000 – £189,000)* |
| *HMRC:* | *£189,000 (with a further £81,000 payable by Paul)* |

The £261,000 received by Richard after dealing with specific legacies and paying the IHT due is often referred to as the 'residue'. In effect, as the recipient of the residue, Richard is suffering the IHT on both George's legacy and his own. In Section 2.8, we will see what happens when there is also an exempt beneficiary.

## 2.7 MAKING THE PAYMENT

IHT arising on death is normally due six months after the end of the month of death. Hence, in the case of Arthur who died in December 2023, it will be due by 30th June 2024. Personal representatives may sometimes have to pay the tax earlier, however, as the liability is triggered when they deliver their accounts for probate or confirmation purposes.

This same payment date applies to all IHT arising on death; both on the deceased's estate and gifts made within the previous seven years (Section 4.5).

The personal representatives may elect for any tax on land or buildings within the deceased's estate to be paid in ten equal yearly instalments, commencing six months after the month of death.

If the property concerned is subsequently sold, however, then the remaining unpaid IHT relating to that property becomes payable immediately.

Interest is charged on, and added to, payments made by instalments. Interest is also charged on late payments. The applicable interest rate is currently 7% (it is generally set at 2.5% over the Bank of England base rate). This is the same rate as is used for most other major taxes: clearly, the Government has no sympathy for bereaved families suffering both financial turmoil and emotional distress!

At the current interest rate, the cost of paying a 40% IHT bill by instalments is increased to a total effective rate of 52.6%. When interest arises on either instalments or other late payments of IHT, there will be no Income Tax relief for it.

The beneficiaries could perhaps borrow the money to pay their IHT bills. Sadly, however, the IHT is regarded as a personal liability and the interest on such borrowings would also generally be ineligible for Income Tax relief.

There is a potential way around this problem if the beneficiary re-mortgages their home to pay the IHT bill. If they subsequently move out of their home and adopt it as a rental property, they will be eligible for Income Tax relief on the mortgage interest against their rental income. The beneficiary could then move into one of the inherited properties and adopt it as their new home.

Alternatively, the beneficiary may be able to obtain Income Tax relief by re-mortgaging one or more rental properties up to the level of their market value at the time of introduction into the rental business.

The obvious step might therefore seem to be to re-mortgage an inherited property, use this to pay the tax and then rent that property out. The problem, however, is that the IHT may have to be paid before the beneficiary can take title to the property. The beneficiary's own home may provide the answer to this problem once more.

***Example:*** *Cheryl inherits her Aunt Sarah's house but has an IHT liability of £100,000 to settle. Cheryl therefore re-mortgages her own home and uses this money to pay the IHT. After taking title to Sarah's house, Cheryl mortgages that property and uses the funds to repay the mortgage on her own home. Cheryl then rents out Sarah's house and is able to claim her mortgage interest against the rental income.*

If an inherited property is already a rental property, interest relief will only be available on borrowings against the property up to its value when it was first rented out.

Interest relief for borrowings on residential rental property is now restricted to basic rate only for Income Tax purposes. Furthermore, while HMRC generally accepts that interest relief is due under the circumstances described above, some resistance does arise from time to time. If any problems arise over this issue, refer HMRC to Example 2 in BIM 45700 in their own manuals.

Subject to these issues, the techniques described above provide at least some relief for the cost of financing IHT bills: after all, relief at the basic rate of 20% is better than no relief at all. For a full discussion on the issues surrounding interest relief on rental property, see the Taxcafe guide *How to Save Property Tax*.

If it becomes necessary to sell one or more inherited properties in order to pay IHT, there is one crumb of comfort in the fact there is unlikely to be much CGT to pay, as we shall see in Section 12.2.

**Paying Tax on Lifetime Transfers**
Where IHT becomes payable on a lifetime transfer, it is due as follows:

i) Gifts made between 6th April and 30th September: IHT is due on 30th April in the following year.
ii) Gifts made between 1st October and 5th April: IHT is due six months after the end of the month in which the gift is made.

From a pure cashflow point of view, the best day to make a chargeable gift is 6th April. (This has other potential benefits too, as we shall see in Section 5.2; although it does need to fit in with the rest of your planning.)

**Repayments**
Where there is an overpayment of IHT, the rate of interest applying to the repayment of the excess is just 3.5%. This scandalous differential in the rates of interest on under- and overpayments effectively means the Government is making an additional profit of 3.5% (7% less 3.5%) from the many bereaved families who are forced to make estimated IHT payments in an effort to meet the Government's deadlines!

## 2.8 GROSSING UP

The amount of IHT payable on a specific asset or bequest may be affected by whether it is paid by the personal representatives. This is due to the procedure known as 'grossing up'. The rationale behind grossing up is that where the personal representatives are bearing the tax, this effectively represents an additional transfer of value.

However, grossing up can only apply to the IHT arising on death where there is also an exempt beneficiary (see Section 2.6). It is that exempt person, or body, often the surviving spouse, who will ultimately suffer the impact of the grossing up.

Hence, we are ***only*** concerned with grossing up (on death) where there is a mixture of exempt and non-exempt beneficiaries and the personal representatives are bearing the IHT on one or more bequests to a non-exempt beneficiary.

The grossing up process is rendered more complex where there are any exemptions available. This will apply in the majority of cases since the NRB is usually available for a start. However, for the sake of illustration, I will start with an example where there are no exemptions available, apart from the spouse exemption. This might occur, for example, where the deceased has made gifts in excess of the NRB within the last seven years (see Section 4.5).

***Example:*** *In 2018, Winston made a gift of £400,000 to his son, Stuart. Sadly, Winston dies in March 2024. The total value of his estate is £2.75m. He has no TNRB entitlement and the RNRB will not be available due to tapering (see Section 3.4). Hence, in summary, the only exemption available is the spouse exemption.*

*Winston leaves a property worth £160,000 to his nephew Pete on condition he settles any tax arising. He also leaves his daughter Julia the sum of £480,000 in cash, stating in his Will this sum should be free of all taxes. He leaves the remainder of his estate to his widow, Cynthia.*

*As Pete has to settle the IHT on his bequest directly, he will pay IHT at a straightforward rate of 40%, i.e. £64,000. The IHT on Julia's bequest will, however, be paid by Winston's personal representatives. This brings grossing up into play. In other words, Julia's bequest must be grossed up to account for the IHT being paid out of Winston's estate.*

*The grossing up factor is two-thirds. Hence, an additional two-thirds must be added to Julia's bequest, producing a grossed-up amount of £800,000 (£480,000 x 2/3 = £320,000 + £480,000 = £800,000). The IHT due on this bequest is £320,000 (£800,000 x 40%). As can readily be seen, this is equal to the amount of the grossing up, meaning the personal representatives can give the original sum of £480,000 to Julia free of any further tax liabilities.*

In this example, it is Cynthia who effectively ends up bearing the tax on Julia's bequest since it reduces the amount remaining to be distributed to her. Furthermore, as the tax is paid by the personal representatives, it is increased from the £192,000 it would have been if Julia had paid it, to £320,000 instead. The rate of IHT on the bequest has effectively increased from 40% to 67%. If the family are in agreement, this outcome can be avoided by using a deed of variation (Section 18.1) to alter the terms of the Will so the beneficiary bears the tax and it is thus reduced back to 40%.

The two thirds rate of grossing up shown in the above example is very much the worst case scenario. Where any exemptions are available, these are taken into account first, before applying grossing up, meaning the overall effective rate can be much reduced. To see how this applies in practice, let's return to the example with a couple of modifications.

***Example Revisited:*** *On further investigation, it turns out Winston's gift to Stuart was actually made in 2016 (this is why it is so important to document gifts properly: see Section 4.3), so Winston's NRB is available after all. A later Will is also found in which Winston states that his personal representatives should bear the tax on the property left to Pete. Hence, grossing up will now apply to both legacies.*

*The total of Pete and Julia's legacies amounts to £640,000. From this, the personal representatives can deduct Winston's NRB of £325,000, leaving the sum of £315,000 subject to grossing up. As before, the grossing up factor is two thirds, producing a total IHT liability of £210,000 (£315,000 x 2/3). Winston's estate is therefore distributed as follows:*

| | |
|---|---|
| *Pete:* | *£160,000 (the value of the property)* |
| *Julia:* | *£480,000 (her tax-free legacy)* |
| *Cynthia:* | *£1,900,000 (£2.75m – £640,000 – £210,000)* |
| *HMRC:* | *£210,000* |

*If the personal representatives wish to pay the IHT on Pete's property by instalments (Section 2.7), this element can be calculated on a simple pro rata basis: £210,000 x £160,000/£640,000 = £52,500.*

As before, it is Cynthia, the exempt beneficiary, who effectively ends up bearing the cost of the grossing up.

**More Complexity**

You may be wondering why I changed the example so the personal representatives were bearing the tax on Pete's legacy. This was done purely for the sake of illustration. Where, in addition to there being exemptions available, there is also a mixture of legacies on which the beneficiary is bearing their own tax, and legacies on which the personal representatives are bearing the tax, the grossing up calculations become extremely complex. Nonetheless, the principles remain that IHT being borne by the personal representatives must be grossed up to account for the additional transfer of value, and the exempt beneficiary ultimately suffers the consequences.

Grossing up can also apply to lifetime transfers, although a lower grossing up rate of one quarter applies. See Section 4.2 for further details.

## 2.9 COLLECTION OF TAX

As we saw in Section 2.3, liability for IHT may fall on any of: the transferor, transferee, the deceased's personal representatives, or the deceased's beneficiaries. Naturally, HMRC will, in the first instance, attempt to collect the tax from the correct party. However, if they encounter difficulty in collecting the tax, they will look to any other party to the relevant transfer of value.

Hence, in the case of IHT arising on death, if a beneficiary is required to pay their share of the tax under the terms of the deceased's Will, but is unable to do so, HMRC will collect it from the personal representatives out of the remaining assets of the estate. Furthermore, the tax may then have to be grossed up (see Section 2.8).

Conversely, a beneficiary who should have received a bequest free from IHT could end up having to bear part of the IHT arising when there are insufficient liquid funds left in the remaining estate.

Transferees should usually bear any extra tax arising when the transferor dies within seven years of making a gift (see Section 4.5) but this rule will also be overridden if HMRC finds it necessary.

***Example:*** *In July 2021, George, a single man, gave his old friend Andrew £500,000 to help him out. Sadly, things continue to go from bad to worse for Andrew and, in 2023, he is declared bankrupt.*

*In March 2024, George dies and the earlier gift to Andrew becomes chargeable to IHT. George had also made earlier chargeable transfers in excess of his NRB during the seven years prior to July 2021, so the gift to Andrew is fully exposed to IHT (see Section 4.5). As HMRC will be unable to collect the IHT due from Andrew, they will look to George's personal representatives to pay the tax out of the assets of the estate. Instead of the original £200,000 (at 40%), however, the IHT due on this gift will now be £333,333 (two-thirds: see Section 2.8).*

In short, HMRC doesn't really care who pays the tax, as long as it is collected. This is why it will often make sense to take out term insurance to cover IHT costs arising in the event of an early death and we will look at this further in Section 11.8.

## 2.10 LOANS AND OTHER LIABILITIES

A number of restrictions apply to the deduction of liabilities for IHT purposes. In this section, I will cover the general principles and look at how they apply in a few practical scenarios. As we progress through the guide, I will also look at how the restrictions affect various IHT planning techniques. Note that, for the examples in this section, I am going to assume for the sake of illustration that neither the TNRB, nor the RNRB apply.

### Liabilities on Death

Subject to the restrictions discussed below, the general rule is that all the deceased's liabilities are deducted from the general assets of their estate. In particular, except as noted below, unsecured liabilities are not usually deducted from the value of assets eligible for payment of IHT by instalments (i.e. land and property: see Section 2.7).

However, some liabilities are, in the first instance, specifically allocated as follows:

- Secured loans (e.g. mortgages) are allocated against the assets on which they are secured
- Business liabilities (see Sections 7.8 and 7.11) are allocated against the value of the relevant business
- Foreign debts are allocated against foreign property

Where the liabilities exceed the value of the relevant assets, the excess will again generally be deducted from the general assets of the estate. These allocations under general principles may be altered by the additional rules and restrictions discussed below.

**Restrictions**

Liabilities may generally only be deducted from the value of the deceased's estate where the liability is actually discharged (i.e. paid) out of the assets of the estate. The only exception to this rule arises where there is both a commercial reason for the non-payment of the liability; and the non-payment does not give rise to any tax advantage (or any such advantage that arises was not a main purpose behind the non-payment).

For there to be a valid commercial reason for the non-payment, it is necessary to show either that the liability was due to an unconnected party operating on an arms' length basis, or that an unconnected party operating on an arms' length basis would have accepted the non-payment.

As far as tax advantages arising out of the non-payment are concerned, this provision is very wide-ranging and generally covers any situation where any person enjoys any saving or deferral of any kind of tax. However, it only applies where the non-payment of the liability gives rise to a tax advantage: not simply because the liability itself creates a tax advantage.

***Example 1:*** *Leona dies and leaves her house to her daughter Alexandra. The house is subject to a mortgage. The lender allows Alexandra to take over the mortgage so that it does not need to be repaid immediately. The lender is an unconnected party operating on an arms' length basis so, although the mortgage has not been repaid out of Leona's estate, it may still be deducted for IHT purposes.*

***Example 2:*** *Gareth lends £20,000 to his father, Simon, on condition it be repaid on the later of Simon and his wife's deaths. Simon dies first. The loan is not repaid at that time. Allowing a loan to be repaid on the second of a couple's deaths is a normal commercial arrangement. Hence, although Gareth is a connected party, the non-payment of the loan at the time of Simon's death does not prevent the loan being deducted from the value of Simon's estate for IHT purposes.*

This example shows it is possible for a loan from a connected party to not be repaid immediately and still be deductible from the deceased borrower's estate: provided the non-payment is permitted on a normal commercial basis.

It is, however, vital that the loan documentation is drawn up correctly. If, for example, the loan agreement merely stated 'the lender may *permit* the loan to be repaid on the second death' then an unconnected party operating on an arms' length basis would generally call for the loan to be repaid on the first death: unless the loan were secured (on the borrower's home or other property) and subject to interest at a commercial rate. (Such interest would of course give rise to Income Tax liabilities for the lender.)

In other cases, a liability is only likely to be deductible if:

- It is a secured loan on full commercial terms and one or more of the deceased's beneficiaries takes over the liability together with the asset on which the loan is secured,
- It is an arms' length commercial arrangement, which one or more of the deceased's beneficiaries takes over (e.g. a business overdraft), or
- It is repaid out of the assets of the deceased's estate

**Paying Liabilities Out of the Estate**

There are a number of ways in which liabilities may be paid out of the assets of the estate in order to qualify for deduction for IHT purposes.

Firstly, of course, the personal representatives can simply pay the liability out of cash held by the deceased or the proceeds of sale of the deceased's assets. There is no restriction where the cash or assets are themselves exempt (e.g. foreign bank accounts held by a non-UK domiciled individual).

Alternatively, the deceased's personal representatives could take out a new loan and use it to repay the liabilities. The new loan would need to be charged against the estate's assets. It would then need to be repaid by selling some of the assets of the estate before they are passed to the beneficiaries, or taken over by one or more of the beneficiaries inheriting those assets.

A new loan used to repay the deceased's liabilities could come from any source: including the deceased's beneficiaries.

**Life Insurance & Pension Fund Death Benefits**

If a life insurance policy has been written in trust so that it falls outside the deceased's estate (see Section 11.8), it is vital the proceeds are not used directly to settle the deceased's liabilities, as these would not have been paid out of the assets of the estate and would not be deductible. The same applies to most pension fund death benefits (see Section 10.2).

Life insurance proceeds or pension fund death benefits could, however, be paid out to one of the deceased's beneficiaries who could then lend those funds to the deceased's personal representatives to enable them to pay the deceased's liabilities.

***Example 3:*** *Sharon dies leaving a house worth £800,000. She had a life insurance policy written in trust which yields £250,000 and she owed her son Jack £200,000: the total of a number of loans he made to her in her latter years.*

*If Jack's loan is not repaid, it cannot be deducted from Sharon's estate and her IHT liability will be £190,000 (£800,000 – £325,000 = £475,000 x 40% = £190,000). If the life insurance proceeds are paid directly to Jack to settle his loan then the loan will not have been settled out of the assets of Sharon's estate and her IHT liability will again be £190,000.*

*Instead, the life insurance proceeds are paid out to Sharon's sister, Kelly. Kelly then lends £200,000 to Sharon's estate. The loan is charged against Sharon's house. Sharon's personal representatives use the £200,000 borrowed from Kelly to repay Jack, meaning his loan can be deducted from Sharon's estate for IHT purposes.*

*This reduces Sharon's IHT liability to £110,000 (£800,000 – £200,000 – £325,000 = £275,000 x 40% = £110,000).*

*Sharon's house is then passed to Kelly subject to the £200,000 charge against it. Since the charge is in Kelly's name, she can then have it removed.*

In theory, a similar strategy could be used where Jack was the sole beneficiary of both Sharon's estate and the life insurance policy. It would, however, be vital to ensure Jack's original loan was repaid by way of a new loan from him to the estate and not repaid directly out of the insurance proceeds. In such a case, a good lawyer who knew their way around all the necessary documentation would be essential!

**Liabilities Incurred to Acquire Relievable Property**

Certain types of business property, agricultural property, and woodlands are eligible for relief from IHT. We will look at these types of 'relievable property' and the relevant reliefs in detail in Chapter 7.

Liabilities incurred to finance the acquisition, enhancement or maintenance of relievable property, must be taken to reduce the value attributed to that property (subject to the comments below regarding liabilities incurred before 6th April 2013).

A liability is deemed to have financed relievable property where it is used directly or indirectly for that purpose. Guidance issued by HMRC indicates they are taking a very broad view of what can be taken to have indirectly financed relievable property. An example of some of their thinking on this subject is included in Section 7.27 although, as ever, it must be emphasised that HMRC guidance is not the law and it is for the courts to decide whether such a case would actually be caught in practice.

**Liabilities Incurred Before April 2013**

Liabilities incurred before 6th April 2013 are exempt from being attributed to relievable property and may generally be deducted from the general assets of the deceased's estate (subject to the other rules described in this section and the treatment of business liabilities discussed in Section 7.11).

However, where a liability incurred before 6th April 2013 is refinanced or varied on or after that date, it will be treated as a new liability and will then be caught by the rules discussed above.

This means replacing or varying loans or other liabilities incurred before 6th April 2013 that have been used, directly or indirectly, to finance business property, agricultural property, or woodlands, in any way, could lead to significant increases in your IHT liability.

I will look at the practical implications of the restriction on liabilities incurred to acquire relievable property in more detail in Chapter 7.

**Liabilities Incurred to Acquire Excluded Property**

A similar restriction operates where liabilities are incurred to acquire 'excluded property'. This generally means foreign property and certain other assets owned by non-UK domiciled individuals, but see Section 3.7 for further details.

Liabilities incurred to finance the acquisition, enhancement or maintenance of excluded property, must be taken to reduce the value attributed to that property. In effect, this means such liabilities are non-deductible for UK IHT purposes. This restriction applies to liabilities incurred at any time: there is no exemption for liabilities incurred prior to April 2013.

Once again, any liabilities which have indirectly financed the acquisition, enhancement or maintenance of excluded property are caught by this restriction and HMRC is taking a very broad view of the scope of this provision.

***Example:*** *Astrid is single and domiciled in Germany. She owns a house in Liverpool worth £600,000. She mortgages her UK house for £400,000 and uses the money to buy some shares on the London Stock Exchange. A year later, she sells her shares, realising an overall gain, and uses the proceeds to buy a house in Germany. A short time later, Astrid dies. She is subject to UK IHT on the full value of her house in Liverpool (after deducting her NRB). Her mortgage cannot be deducted because it has been used indirectly to acquire excluded property (her German house).*

In this example, Astrid has realised an overall gain on her shares and hence the entire mortgage on her Liverpool house is deemed to have indirectly financed her German property. If she had made a loss on her shares, part of the mortgage would remain deductible from the value of her UK property.

For example, let's say Astrid sold her shares for £375,000 and used this sum to buy her German property. She would then be able to deduct £25,000 (her loss on the shares) from the value of her Liverpool property for UK IHT purposes.

**Interest-Free Loans**

HMRC's IHT manual states: "The grant of an interest free loan repayable on demand is not a transfer of value (because the value of the loan is equal to the amount of it)." [IHTM 14317]

This opens up significant IHT planning opportunities and we will see several possible applications of this principle in this guide. In some cases, however, it will be essential for the loan to be repaid out of the assets of the deceased's estate in order for the planning to work as intended. We will look at the practical implications arising as we consider the relevant planning techniques throughout the guide.

**Artificially Created Debts**

No deduction is allowed for an artificially created debt where, in effect, the debtor themselves had originally provided the assets or funds which later gave rise to the debt. For example, if a father gifted some money to his son and then borrowed it back, there would be no deduction from the father's estate for this debt.

## 2.11 QUICK SUCCESSION RELIEF

Quick succession relief provides some partial relief from IHT when a transferee dies within five years of receiving an earlier transfer on which IHT was paid, or on which IHT later becomes payable (remembering tax can arise up to seven years after the original transfer). The amount of relief is given by the formula: 'Percentage' x Original Tax x Net Transfer/Gross Transfer.

The 'Percentage' is 100% where the transferee dies no more than a year after the original transfer. It then reduces in steps of 20% the day after each anniversary of the original transfer until, after five years, the relief is no longer available.

***Example:*** *In May 2021, Ewan died leaving a legacy of £1.2m to his daughter, Kirsty; and the rest of his estate to his widow. Kirsty bore the IHT arising, which amounted to £350,000, leaving her with a net sum of £850,000. Sadly, in December 2023, Kirsty is killed in a boating accident, and leaves her estate to her friend Shane. Kirsty's executors claim quick succession relief of: 60% x £350,000 x £850,000/£1.2m = £148,750.*

*If we assume the value of Kirsty's estate is equal to the same net sum of £850,000, and the only other exemption or relief available is the NRB, the IHT payable by her executors will be £61,250 (£850,000 – £325,000 = £525,000 x 40% = £210,000 – £148,750).*

Despite the relief, the same funds that originally flowed from Ewan have still suffered a total of £411,250 (£350,000 + £61,250) in IHT, equivalent to 47% of the amount in excess of the NRB.

Quick succession relief can also apply where either the first or second transfer (or both) was a lifetime transfer made within seven years of the transferor's death. It is not to be confused with taper relief (see Section 4.5), however, as the two reliefs operate independently of each other.

## 2.12 SIMULTANEOUS DEATHS

Where two or more individuals die simultaneously, or in circumstances where it is not possible to determine who died first, for legal purposes in England and Wales, the oldest person is deemed to have died first (then the next oldest, etc).

Where the older person has left any funds or other assets to the younger person in their Will then, for IHT purposes, those funds or assets are still taxed in the same way, regardless of the younger person's death. However, they are not included in the younger person's estate for IHT purposes, and hence are not taxed again due to their death.

One of the most important consequences of this principle is that, where a married couple die simultaneously and the elder spouse leaves some or all of their estate to the younger spouse in their Will, that part of their estate escapes IHT completely. This arises because those assets are covered by the spouse exemption on the elder spouse's death and are effectively ignored on the younger spouse's death.

This beneficial result (beneficial for IHT that is) does not arise if the elder spouse dies intestate (see Section 11.7 for details of what happens then) or if the elder spouse's Will contains a clause requiring the younger spouse to survive them by a specified period before becoming absolutely entitled to the assets.

In Scotland the position is different and the deaths are treated as having occurred at the same instant for all purposes. Hence neither person is treated as surviving the other and for both legal and IHT purposes the assets pass as specified in the deceased's Wills or under the laws of intestacy, as appropriate (Section 11.7). The same generally applies in Northern Ireland, although there are exceptions.

## Chapter 3

# The Main Exemptions

### 3.1 WHAT IS AN EXEMPTION?

IHT exemptions come in many different forms. Some are based on value, others on the relationship between the transferor and the transferee, still others on the nature of the transferee alone and some even on the circumstances of the transferor's demise.

Some exemptions have a general application, others apply only to lifetime transfers, and others only to transfers on death. In Chapter 5 we will look at IHT exemptions that apply only to lifetime transfers. In this chapter we concentrate on exemptions that apply regardless of whether the gift or transfer is made during the transferor's lifetime or on death; or that apply only on death.

### 3.2 THE NIL RATE BAND (NRB)

The NRB is probably the most important exemption for the vast majority of people. As the name suggests, an IHT rate of nil is applied to the first part of your estate, which falls within this band.

The amount of NRB available depends on the date of death (or the date of transfer in the case of chargeable lifetime transfers: see Section 4.2). The current NRB applying to deaths or chargeable lifetime transfers between 6th April 2009 and 5th April 2028 is £325,000.

Any part of the NRB that was not used on the earlier death of the deceased's spouse may additionally be claimed. This means up to double the normal amount of NRB may be available on the death of a widow or widower. This has enormous implications for IHT planning for married persons and we will look at this subject in detail in Chapter 6.

Despite this, it remains important to note that each individual has their own NRB. I will come back to this point and explain its significance later.

Until 2009, the NRB was generally increased in line with inflation, based on the increase in the Retail Prices Index. However, in 2010 Labour Chancellor Alistair Darling announced a five year freeze at its 2009/10 level of £325,000. This disgraceful departure from Gordon Brown's earlier promise to increase the band to £350,000 was later compounded by another despicable 'U-turn' from George Osborne, who abandoned his party's plans to increase the NRB to £1m and extended Darling's five year freeze to twelve!

In the March 2021 Budget, just as we were within weeks of finally coming to the end of Osborne's twelve year freeze, Rishi Sunak extended the freeze by a further five years, to bring it to a total of seventeen years; and then, most recently, in the November 2022 Autumn Statement, Jeremy Hunt added yet another two years, to bring this fiscal ice age up to its current expected duration of ***nineteen years!***

We are therefore stuck with a NRB of £325,000 until ***at least*** 5th April 2028.

Inflation for the period from September 2009 to September 2021 totalled 43.3%, and the subsequent year to September 2022 saw this increase to a total of 61.5%. This means, if Gordon Brown had kept his promise in 2010, and the NRB had then kept pace with retail price inflation thereafter, it should have been around £510,000 by 2022/23 and £575,000 for 2023/24.

If we assume an annual inflation rate of, say, 5% over the next four years, by 2027/28 we would have expected the NRB to be around £700,000. That means the Government will be collecting an extra £150,000 from many bereaved families because of the freeze. In fact, as we shall see later in the guide, in some cases it will be a lot more.

**The Impact of Property Prices**

But that is just retail price inflation. The largest source of IHT, by value, comes from property (land and buildings). Hence, it is more appropriate to compare the NRB's lack of growth with house price inflation.

Even before the current nineteen year freeze began in 2009, the NRB was failing to keep pace with house price inflation, so let's go back a little further to see just how bad the situation really is.

Over the period from June 1997 to January 2023, average UK house prices increased by ***368%!*** Hence, if the NRB, which was £215,000 in 1997, had been increased, as seems most appropriate, in line with house price inflation, it should have stood at around £1,010,000 by now. Furthermore, if we assume house prices continue to grow at a relatively modest average rate of 5% per year, by 2027/28 we would have expected to see a NRB of about £1,250,000.

That will leave many homeowners facing around £370,000 in extra IHT simply because of the Government's failure to keep pace with property prices. Admittedly, this reduces to around £300,000 where the RNRB is available but, as we shall see in Section 3.4 this will not always be the case. How's that for stealth tax!

**The Future of the Nil Rate Band**

To be frank, after so many broken promises, I have long since given up believing anything we are told about the future of the NRB. However, among the many contradictory announcements made by various Chancellors was a proposal that the NRB would be increased in line with the Consumer Prices Index (CPI) once the freeze comes to an end (if ever). The CPI is the Government's preferred inflation measure, as it is generally lower than the far more realistic Retail Prices Index (RPI), which is a much more accurate reflection of what we all see in the shops.

Historically, the CPI runs at around 1% to 1.5% less than the RPI (it is currently 3.4% less!). Hence, even when the current, seemingly endless, freeze finally comes to an end, using this lower index will severely slow the rate of increase in the NRB and lead to even greater shortfalls in the long-term when compared to house price inflation. And it is the long-term that matters when we look at IHT planning!

Predicting the future is always difficult, but it is something one has to do to some degree when engaged in long-term planning. Hence, for the remainder of this guide, unless stated to the contrary, any predictions about the NRB beyond 5th April 2028 will be based on the assumption that, after that date, it is increased annually in line with the CPI, and this lower inflation measure averages 2.5% per annum. Each year's increase, as calculated under this assumption, is also rounded up to the nearest £1,000. I have also applied the same principles to forecast increases in the RNRB from 2028/29 onwards.

However, I must emphasise, this assumption, and the consequent future NRBs and RNRBs used in some of the examples in this guide, is only my 'best guess' used purely for the sake of illustration.

## 3.3 THE SPOUSE EXEMPTION

Except as noted below, transfers of property made directly to your spouse are completely exempt from IHT. This covers both lifetime transfers and transfers on death. The general exemption for transfers to a spouse opens up a wealth of planning opportunities, which we will return to in detail in Chapter 6.

**Transfers to a Non-Domiciled Spouse**
The general exemption for transfers to a spouse usually operates without limit. However, in the case of transfers from a UK domiciled individual to their non-UK domiciled spouse, the exemption is restricted.

It is possible to remove this restriction if the foreign domiciled spouse elects to 'opt in' and be treated as UK domiciled for IHT purposes. We will look at this election, its benefits and pitfalls, in more detail in Section 6.15.

In the absence of any such election covering the time at which a transfer is made from a UK domiciled individual to their non-UK domiciled spouse, only a maximum of £325,000 may be covered by the spouse exemption. This limit is equal to the amount of the NRB, but is a separate exemption.

The limit applies on a cumulative basis and, once exceeded, any further transfers, both during the transferor's lifetime and on death, will be treated just like any other transfer made to a person other than their spouse. One single limit applies for the whole of the transferor's lifetime, even if they are divorced or widowed and later marry another foreign domiciled person. Prior to April 2013, the limit was £55,000.

***Example:*** *Donna is UK domiciled but married to Sean who is US domiciled. In 2012, Donna gave Sean £60,000 and, in 2023, she gave him a further £300,000.*

*£55,000 of Donna's first gift is covered by the spouse exemption, the remaining £5,000 is not. £270,000 of Donna's second gift is covered by the spouse exemption, the remaining £30,000 is not. The exempt amount is derived by deducting the previous exempt amount (£55,000) from the new limit (£325,000).*

*In 2025, Donna divorces Sean and marries Guy who is domiciled in France. In June 2031 when the NRB is £361,000, Donna gives Guy £50,000. £36,000 of this gift is covered by the spouse exemption; the remaining £14,000 is not. The exempt amount is derived by deducting Donna's previous cumulative total of exempt transfers (under the spouse exemption) from the current limit (which is equal to the current NRB in 2031/32). [£361,000 – £55,000 – £270,000 = £36,000]*

The amounts not covered by the spouse exemption remain eligible for other exemptions in the same way as transfers to any other person. As these are lifetime transfers, many of the exemptions covered in Chapter 5 would be available. Any amounts still not covered by any exemption would be potentially exempt transfers (PETs) and would only become chargeable to IHT in the event of Donna's death within seven years (see Chapter 4).

Furthermore, it is important to note I have assumed each of the gifts in the example was a capital transfer of value. Many transfers between spouses will not be a capital transfer of value and would be exempted under one of the provisions covered in Sections 5.4 to 5.6. Where these provisions apply, there is no capital transfer of value and any payments do not need to be counted towards the spouse exemption limit.

For transfers on death in excess of the limit, the NRB is available in the usual way, meaning a UK domiciled spouse will often be able to leave up to £650,000 to a foreign domiciled spouse free from IHT where they have not previously used any of their spouse exemption.

This does depend on whether they have any other beneficiaries and on whether they have made other chargeable transfers in the previous seven years. In other words, once the spouse exemption has been exhausted, the non-domiciled spouse is in the same position as any other beneficiary (unless they 'opt-in': see Section 6.15).

We will look at IHT planning for married couples with mixed domicile in Section 6.14.

**Transfers from a Non-Domiciled Spouse**

There is no restriction on transfers in the opposite direction: from a foreign domiciled spouse to a UK domiciled spouse. Why would there be: such transfers may eventually increase the tax haul. Beware, however: these transfers may have foreign tax implications!

**Other Exceptions to the Spouse Exemption**

The general exemption for transfers between spouses is also restricted in a few other circumstances. The exemption may be lost where the transfer:

i) Only takes effect after the expiry of another third party's interest, or after the expiry of some other period of time,
ii) Is dependent on a condition that is not satisfied within twelve months, or
iii) Is made as consideration for the transfer of a reversionary interest in some other property

Despite point (i), it is nonetheless acceptable to have a condition in your Will that your spouse must survive you by a certain period before becoming absolutely entitled to an asset. Some people do this in order to ensure assets pass directly to their ultimate intended beneficiaries under these circumstances. Such a condition may, however, backfire in the event of you and your spouse dying together: as assets which could otherwise have escaped IHT will be exposed to tax (see Section 2.12 for details).

**Transfers into Trust for the Benefit of a Spouse**
The spouse exemption does not generally apply to a transfer into trust during the donor's lifetime. Transfers on death that confer an 'Immediate Post-Death Interest' (Section 8.12) on a surviving spouse are eligible for the spouse exemption.

**What is a Spouse?**
For IHT purposes, a spouse must be your legally married husband or wife or your legally registered civil partner.

A 'spouse' is not specifically defined in tax legislation but, for IHT purposes, HMRC takes the view that the exemption continues to apply to any transfer between persons who are still legally married at the time of that transfer. Unlike CGT, the IHT exemption for transfers between spouses continues to apply to separated couples right up until the granting of a decree absolute (see Section 12.6 for further details on the spouse exemption applying for CGT purposes).

Hence, transfers between spouses on separation or as part of divorce proceedings will be covered by the exemption if made before the granting of a decree absolute. See also Section 5.6 regarding another potential exemption that may apply under these circumstances.

Generally speaking, a couple who are legally married under the laws of another country will similarly be recognised as legally married for tax purposes in the UK. This will even include polygamous marriages when they are legally valid in the taxpayer's country of origin. In such cases, the spouse exemption limit discussed above must be applied to the cumulative value of transfers made to all the transferor's non-UK domiciled spouses.

The spouse exemption applies only to married couples. There is no exemption for transfers to common-law partners! If you intend leaving most of your estate to a common-law partner, try to get married before you die. Deathbed marriages have been known to save ***millions*** of pounds in IHT and it is one planning device that is almost impossible for HMRC to overturn. It worked for Ken Dodd, after all!

## 3.4 THE RESIDENCE NIL RATE BAND (RNRB)

The RNRB provides an additional exemption on qualifying residential property. It operates in addition to the 'normal' NRB but is only available on death. Where the RNRB applies, it takes priority over the NRB (i.e. it is used first). For deaths occurring between 6th April 2020 and 5th April 2028, the maximum RNRB available to a single individual is £175,000. Like the NRB, it has been frozen until 2028. (See Section 3.2 regarding forecast future RNRBs beyond 2028 used in the examples in this guide.)

### Qualifying Property

In order to qualify for the RNRB exemption, a property must have been the deceased's private residence at some point during their ownership. Generally, the property will also need to be in their estate at the time of their death (i.e. still owned by them); except that:

- Property included in their estate under the gifts with reservation rules (Section 4.8) may qualify. (It must have been gifted to one or more direct descendants, as described below.)
- The downsizing provisions allow the exemption to be claimed where a more valuable qualifying residence has been sold in the past, or where the deceased no longer has a qualifying residence at the time of death. We will look at these provisions in detail in Section 13.11.

If an individual dies still owning more than one qualifying property, their personal representatives may elect which property the exemption applies to.

Where an individual resides in job-related accommodation, a property they had acquired with the intention of adopting as their private residence may qualify for the exemption. See the Taxcafe guide *How to Save Property Tax* for further details regarding job-related accommodation.

### Closely Inherited

Subject to the exceptions noted above, the RNRB exemption only applies where the property is passed, on death, to a direct descendant of the deceased. Step children, adopted children and foster children are all accorded the same status as natural children for this purpose. A child who was the deceased's step-child at any time is included. 'Step-child' only includes children of a legally married spouse, and not children of an unmarried partner.

Generally, the property must pass directly to one or more direct descendants in order to qualify. However, the property may also qualify where it is passed to a trust for the benefit of one or more of the deceased's direct descendants. Only certain types of trust qualify for this purpose, as detailed in Section 8.6.

***Example:*** *Nicki divorced her husband many years before her death in June 2023. She leaves her estate, worth £600,000, to her daughter. Nicki's estate includes her former home, which is worth £250,000 at the time of her death. The RNRB exempts £175,000 of the value of Nicki's former home. This reduces her taxable estate to £425,000 before deduction of her main NRB of £325,000, which reduces it to £100,000. The IHT payable on Nicki's estate at 40% is thus £40,000.*

**Mortgages and Loans**

Any mortgages or other loans secured over a property generally have to be taken into account when allocating the RNRB. For example, where a property worth £250,000 is passed to the deceased's son, but the property was subject to an outstanding mortgage of £180,000 at the time of the deceased's death, the exemption will be limited to just £70,000: as this is the net equity value falling into the deceased's estate.

Exceptions may arise, however, where the outstanding mortgage or loan must be allocated to a different asset, or is not deductible from the estate at all: see Section 2.10 for further details of the relevant scenarios where this may arise.

**Tapering**

The RNRB is withdrawn from estates worth in excess of £2m. This withdrawal is at the rate of £1 for every £2 by which the estate exceeds this threshold. The threshold has been frozen at its current level until 5th April 2028.

***Example:*** *Ollie has an estate valued at £2.1m at the time of his death in January 2024. This exceeds the threshold by £100,000, so his available RNRB is reduced by £50,000, from £175,000 to £125,000.*

The withdrawal of the RNRB means it may effectively be lost if the deceased's estate exceeds £2.35m. This effective threshold may be as high as £2.7m where the deceased is a widow or widower, for the reasons explained below.

The value of the deceased's estate for the purpose of tapering is as detailed in Section 2.5, including items (i) to (iii) listed in that section. The estate is valued before deducting any reliefs: so even qualifying business property and assets the deceased is leaving to their spouse will be counted.

Transfers of value prior to death are ***not*** included for the purpose of tapering, however. We will look at the potential planning implications of this in Section 17.17.

In many cases, the tapering rules could mean there is an effective marginal rate of IHT of ***60%*** on the value of the estate falling into the bracket from £2m to £2.35m; or even up to £2.7m in the case of many widows or widowers. This potentially makes planning measures to reduce the amount of the estate within this bracket one and a half times as valuable (e.g. reducing the estate by £10,000 could save up to £6,000 in IHT).

**Unused Exemption Passing to Spouse**

Like the main NRB, any unused proportion of the RNRB passes to the deceased's spouse. This is not automatic, however: the additional transferred RNRB must subsequently be ***claimed*** by the spouse's personal representatives when that spouse also dies.

Tapering applies to the amount that may be transferred. Hence, for example, in Ollie's case above, only 71.43% (£125,000/£175,000) of his RNRB would transfer to his spouse if he did not use it himself.

The RNRB was introduced on 6th April 2017. Where a married individual died before that date, their entire RNRB is deemed unused and transfers to their widow or widower. This transfer also remains subject to tapering where the deceased spouse's estate was worth in excess of £2m.

Put simply, this means all widows and widowers whose late spouse died before 6th April 2017, with an estate worth not more than £2m, are entitled to double the normal amount of RNRB (hence, they are entitled to up to £350,000 at the rates applying until at least 5th April 2028).

For deaths after 5th April 2017, the fact the RNRB is used first, in priority to the NRB, means the amount of TNRB arising may sometimes be enhanced. We will look at some of the planning issues regarding transfers of unused NRBs and RNRBs to widows and widowers in Chapter 6. In both cases, it is important to remember it is the unused ***proportion*** that transfers, not the unused ***amount***.

See also Section 6.3 for guidance on using the RNRB on the first spouse's death where the couple's combined estate exceeds £2m.

## 3.5 GIFTS TO CHARITIES & OTHER EXEMPT BODIES

**Gifts to Charity:** Generally, gifts to charity are exempt from IHT. This covers both outright gifts and transfers to a charitable trust. A charity is defined as 'any body of persons established for charitable purposes only'. For gifts and legacies after 31st March 2024, the exemption will apply to UK-registered charities only.

For gifts and legacies before 15th March 2023, the exemption also applied to similar organisations based anywhere in the European Union, Iceland, or Norway. For charitable organisations based outside the UK to qualify, they had to meet the same criteria as would apply to an organisation wishing to register as a charity in England.

For gifts and legacies during the transitional period between 15th March 2023 and 31st March 2024, the exemption continues to apply to non-UK charities that had already been accepted as a qualifying organisation by HMRC as at 14th March 2023.

It is easy enough to ensure lifetime gifts are made to UK-registered charities only, but it is also essential for individuals to review their Wills to ensure any charitable legacies will still qualify for the exemption: especially if they are hoping to benefit from the additional relief explained in Section 3.6.

**Gifts to Housing Associations:** Transfers of value attributable to land in the UK and made to registered social landlords are exempt from IHT.
**Gifts for National Purposes:** Gifts to organisations such as the British Museum or any of the other bodies listed in section IHTM11224 of HMRC's manuals are exempt from IHT.

**Gifts to Political Parties:** Gifts to qualifying political parties are exempt from IHT. Funny that, isn't it? To qualify, the party must either have had at least two members elected to the House of Commons, or have received no fewer than 150,000 votes in total and had one member elected to the House of Commons, at the last General Election.

## 3.6 CHARITABLE LEGACIES

Charitable legacies are fully exempt from IHT: provided the charity meets the criteria examined in Section 3.5. An additional relief also applies where the deceased leaves 10% or more of their 'net estate' to charity. The net estate for this purpose is the deceased's remaining estate after deducting the NRB and other applicable IHT exemptions and reliefs.

Where the estate qualifies for the additional relief, a discount of 10% applies to the IHT rate. In other words, the IHT rate on the remaining estate is reduced from 40% to 36%.

***Example:*** *Carter, a divorced man, dies in May 2023 leaving an estate valued at £1m. He leaves £67,500 to the local dog and cat home (a registered charity) and everything else to his niece, Yvonne.*

*Deducting the NRB of £325,000 from his estate leaves Carter with a net estate chargeable to IHT of £675,000. He has given 10% of this amount to charity, so the IHT rate on Yvonne's inheritance is reduced to 36%.*

*After deducting the charitable legacy (which is exempt), and the NRB, the chargeable estate amounts to £607,500, so the IHT payable at 36% is £218,700. Yvonne will therefore inherit a net sum of £713,800 (£1m – £67,500 – £218,700).*

If Carter had not left anything to charity, the IHT bill would have been £270,000 and Yvonne would have received a net sum of £730,000. The relief does not leave the non-charitable beneficiary better off than they would have been without the charitable legacy, so it is not worth contemplating such a legacy just to save IHT. But, if you are planning to leave a sizeable amount to charity, it is certainly worth checking whether you will meet the 10% threshold.

If, in our example above, Carter had left £60,000 to charity, his chargeable estate would have amounted to £615,000 (£1m – £60,000 – £325,000), giving rise to an IHT bill, at 40%, of £246,000. Yvonne's net inheritance would then have been just £694,000 (£1m – £60,000 –£246,000). Hence, increasing the charitable legacy by £7,500 would actually leave her £19,800 better off overall!

**Planning Issues**

For many years, it was thought it was not possible for charitable legacies to be 'topped up' to the required 10% threshold by way of a deed of variation (Section 18.1). Recent changes suggest HMRC may now allow this, although, being a cautious man, I would prefer not to rely on it. There are also a number of practical difficulties with deeds of variation, so my suggestion would generally be to make the appropriate provisions in your Will. As no-one can be sure exactly how much their net estate will be, this requires a formula-based approach to ensure the correct result.

As we saw in our example, however, there is no point making charitable legacies just to save IHT: your main beneficiaries will still suffer an overall cost equal to at least 24% of the legacy, even after taking account of the relief.

But, as we also saw, where charitable legacies are already planned, there may be an overall saving for your main beneficiaries if you can top up those legacies so they reach the 10% threshold. The question is: when does a top up become worthwhile?

The answer is your main beneficiaries will generally be better off if you top up your charitable legacies to the 10% threshold when you would otherwise have left charitable legacies equal to more than 4% of your net estate.

For example, in Carter's case, he had a net estate of £675,000, so Yvonne would benefit from an increase in his charitable legacies to the 10% threshold if he had already planned to give more than £27,000 to charity anyway.

Finally, remember, as explained in Section 3.5, for deaths occurring after 31st March 2024, a legacy will only count as a charitable legacy for the purposes of this relief where the recipient organisation is a UK-registered charity.

## 3.7 EXCLUDED PROPERTY

Certain assets are excluded from charge to IHT. This exclusion is generally dependent on the residence or domicile status of the individual holding the assets, although it can also depend on the nature of the asset alone. These assets may also be exempt when held in a trust: we will look at that further in Section 9.10.

**Non-Domiciled Individuals**

Non-UK domiciled individuals are not subject to IHT on foreign assets. They are also exempt from IHT on holdings in authorised unit trusts or open-ended investment companies.

However, UK residential property held indirectly by non-UK domiciled individuals (e.g. through a company, trust, or more complex structure) remains subject to IHT. The proceeds of sale of such UK residential property is also subject to IHT for a further two years. Minor interests in UK residential property that amount to less than 5% of the individual's worldwide property interests are disregarded for the purpose of these rules.

Non-UK domiciled individuals who are domiciled in the Channel Islands or the Isle of Man are also exempt from IHT on certain types of savings certificates, premium bonds, and deposits with the National Savings Bank or a trustee savings bank.

**Foreign Currency Bank Accounts**
Foreign currency bank accounts held by a non-UK domiciled individual at the time of their death are generally exempt from IHT, even when held with a UK bank or the Post Office. For the purpose of this exemption, the deceased must also be non-UK resident at the time of death.

UK bank/Post Office accounts covered by this exemption are not technically 'excluded property' as this is a separate exemption.

**Government Securities (Gilts)**
Gilts acquired after 5th April 2013 and held by a non-UK resident individual are generally exempt from IHT.

This provides tremendous scope to make IHT savings as it is far easier and generally quicker, to achieve non-UK resident status than to become non-UK domiciled (see Chapter 16). Remarkably, UK government securities may be exempt from IHT far sooner than foreign assets. Hence, an investment in gilts may be a good strategy for anyone looking to retire abroad, or even just spend a few years away from the UK.

It is important to ensure you are beneficially entitled to the gilts at the time of death, or the exemption does not apply. HMRC are on the look-out for last-minute purchases where the buyer may not yet have obtained beneficial ownership.

Not all gilts carry the same advantages, however. In the case of FOTRA (free of tax to residents abroad) securities issued before 29th April 1996; or 3½% War Loan issued at any time; it is necessary to be both non-ordinarily resident in the UK and non-UK domiciled. For other gilts issued between 29th April 1996 and 5th April 2013, and earlier issues of gilts that did not originally have FOTRA status, it is necessary to be non-ordinarily resident in the UK. Becoming non-ordinarily resident will generally mean being non-UK resident for at least three years, although this is subject to the details of each individual case.

## 3.8 OTHER EXEMPTIONS

**National Heritage Property:** Have you ever wondered why so many stately homes are open to the public? Well, just like the bricked-up windows in Georgian houses and the roofless buildings we used to see back in the 1970s, it's all because of tax. IHT arising on transfers of national heritage property can be deferred when the owners give an undertaking to conserve and protect the property. They will also need to provide reasonable access to the public. The conditions to be satisfied to claim this exemption are somewhat complex, including, in most cases, the need for the property to be pre-eminent for its national, scientific, historic or artistic interest.

**Death on Active Service:** There is a complete exemption from IHT arising on the death of a person from wound, accident or disease contracted while on active military service. A certificate issued by the Ministry of Defence is required to support a claim. The exemption extends to emergency service personnel killed in the line of duty, or whose death is accelerated due to injuries sustained in the line of duty, and to aid workers dying under similar circumstances, or due to a disease contracted while providing aid. Serving and former police officers or service personnel who are targeted because of their status are also covered by the exemption.

**Medals and Awards:** The value of medals and certain other awards is exempt from IHT when these have never been purchased for consideration in money or money's worth. Hence, the exemption only applies to the original recipient and their subsequent heirs.

Chapter 4

# Lifetime Transfers

## 4.1 INHERITANCE TAX ON LIFETIME TRANSFERS

In Section 2.1, we established what triggers IHT is not death, but a transfer of value. Despite this, however, very few transfers made during a person's lifetime actually give rise to any immediate IHT liability. The reason for this seemingly contradictory position is the fact lifetime transfers to another individual are treated as potentially exempt transfers (PETs): free of IHT after seven years.

We will return to this concept in Section 4.3 because it remains important to realise 'potentially exempt' effectively also means 'potentially taxable' and many lifetime transfers are therefore still potentially subject to IHT.

## 4.2 CHARGEABLE LIFETIME TRANSFERS

As explained above, many lifetime transfers are potentially exempt. However, lifetime transfers of value by an individual to a company, or any trust other than a disabled trust, a bare trust, or a charitable trust, ***will*** be chargeable (i.e. taxable) lifetime transfers.

Before 2006, it was generally only transfers of value to a company or discretionary trust that represented chargeable lifetime transfers. Some readers unfamiliar with the nature of trusts may not feel this change is particularly restrictive until I tell you many insurance premiums represent a transfer of value into trust (although most are exempt for other reasons, as we will see).

Chargeable lifetime transfers may be ***immediately*** chargeable to IHT, depending on the cumulative value of such transfers made by the transferor within the last seven years. The main incidence of chargeable lifetime transfers arises on transfers into trust, which we will be covering extensively throughout the rest of the guide, particularly Chapters 8 and 9. We will look at transfers into companies, and how to avoid any immediate IHT charges on them, in Chapter 14.

The amount of the chargeable transfer is arrived at by deducting any available exemptions (Chapters 3 and 5) from the transfer of value. The amount on which IHT is actually chargeable is then the lower of the amount of the chargeable transfer, or the sum derived as follows:

| | |
|---|---|
| Other chargeable transfers within the last seven years | X |
| PLUS | |
| This chargeable transfer | X |
| LESS | |
| Nil rate band | (X) |

Only one NRB may be deducted when calculating the IHT on a chargeable lifetime transfer. The TNRB (see Section 6.2) applies only on death.

IHT on lifetime transfers is charged at half death rates, i.e. 20%. Where other chargeable transfers made in the last seven years already equal or exceed the amount of the NRB, the tax due on the current chargeable transfer is simply a straight 20%.

***Example*** *(I will ignore all exemptions and reliefs, other than the NRB): Two years ago, Elvis gifted investments worth £50,000 into a discretionary trust, giving rise to a chargeable transfer. No IHT was payable at the time, as this was well within his NRB. Elvis now gifts his former home, Graceland, worth £375,000, into a discretionary trust (for the purpose of this example, it doesn't matter whether this is the same trust), on condition the trust settles any IHT arising. The trust's IHT liability is calculated as follows:*

| | |
|---|---|
| *Previous chargeable transfers within last seven years* | *£50,000* |
| *Plus this chargeable transfer* | *£375,000* |
| *Equals cumulative chargeable transfers* | *£425,000* |
| *Less nil rate band* | *(£325,000)* |
| *Amount chargeable* | *£100,000* |
| | |
| *IHT payable at lifetime rate (20%)* | *£20,000* |

***Alternative Scenario with Grossing Up***
*If Elvis had settled the IHT himself, it would have been subject to grossing up, as follows:*

| | |
|---|---|
| *Amount chargeable, as before* | *£100,000* |
| *Grossing up factor – one quarter* | *£25,000* |
| *Grossed up amount* | *£125,000* |
| *IHT payable at lifetime rate (20%)* | *£25,000* |

In this example, Graceland was Elvis's ***former*** home. This is an important point since, as we will see later in the guide, it is more difficult to make an IHT-effective transfer of your current home.

If Elvis were married, he could have avoided any IHT on his gift of Graceland by first transferring it into joint names with his spouse before they both jointly gifted it to the discretionary trust. Each of them would have made a chargeable transfer of only £187,500. Even after taking his previous chargeable transfer into account, Elvis would then be covered by his NRB.

Elvis's spouse would also be covered by their NRB as long as they had not made other chargeable transfers within the last seven years in excess of £137,500. (Elvis's spouse must be under no obligation to make the subsequent transfer to the ultimate intended recipient.)

**Avoiding Grossing Up**
In the above example, we looked at the position where the IHT is paid by the transferee (the trust), as well as where it is paid by the transferor (Elvis himself).

More tax is generally payable where the transferor is settling the liability. This is because the transferor is deemed to be making a gift not only of the original asset transferred, but also of the tax arising. This, in turn, is because the transfer of value is calculated by reference to the reduction in value of the transferor's overall estate and the payment of the IHT arising naturally increases the amount of that reduction.

The bad news is, in the absence of any evidence to the contrary, the transferor is assumed to be liable for any IHT. Hence, if care is not exercised, you may find the value of any gifts you make turns out to be 25% more than you expected. The way to avoid this is to draw up a memorandum that stipulates the transferee is to pay any IHT arising: see Memorandum 2 in Appendix C.

## 4.3 POTENTIALLY EXEMPT TRANSFERS (PETS)

Lifetime transfers made by an individual to another individual, a bare trust, or a disabled trust, are generally PETs, which fall out of the IHT net after seven years. Transfers made ***by*** a trust are subject to different rules and we will explore these in Chapter 8.

**Exceptions**
The following transfers will not be treated as PETs:

- Transfers to your UK-Domiciled spouse (these are fully exempt, except as noted in Section 3.3)
- Transfers to your non-UK Domiciled spouse that are covered by the spouse exemption (see Section 3.3)
- Any other transfer covered by another general or lifetime exemption (see Chapters 3 and 5). This will be of no practical consequence unless the transferor dies within seven years of making the transfer
- Any transfer that does not result in an increase in the value of the transferee's estate (see further in Section 4.4)
- Transfers of value caused by alterations to share capital, loan capital, or other rights in most private companies
- A transfer of value to a disabled trust that does not consist of a transfer of property into the trust (see further in Section 4.4)

**What Do We Mean By 'Potentially Exempt'?**
Put simply, these transfers are ***potentially*** exempt because all the transferor has to do is survive seven years after making the transfer for it to become fully exempt and completely free of any IHT liability (subject to the gifts with reservation rules: see Section 4.8).

In the meantime, the transfer is treated as if it is exempt (i.e. no IHT is due) and only becomes chargeable if the transferor dies within seven years of the date the transfer was made. If the transferor is still alive at the beginning of the seventh anniversary of the transfer, full exemption is achieved.

***Example:*** *On 4th August 2016, Chuck gave £1m to his little brother, Richard. Sadly, on 10th August 2023, Chuck is electrocuted while playing his electric guitar* *in a rainstorm. The gift to Richard was a PET and, since Chuck survived the requisite seven years (just!), this sum is exempt from IHT on Chuck's death.*

If Chuck had died a week earlier, IHT would have been payable on his gift to Richard (see further in Section 4.5 below). Hence, it is essential to have the documentary evidence to prove the gift took place when it did. A memorandum along the lines shown in Appendix C should suffice for this purpose. See also Section 4.7 regarding the timing of gifts made by cheque.

## 4.4 PROBLEMS WITH PETS

One little known, but potentially important, point about PETs is there must be an increase in the value of the transferee's estate in order for the transfer to qualify. Furthermore, where the transferee is a disabled trust, there must be an actual gift of property into the trust.

**Any transfers that do not qualify as PETs as a result of failing to meet these requirements will be chargeable lifetime transfers, unless some other exemption is available to cover them.**

Examples of transfers that do not increase the transferee's estate might include:

i) A grandparent paying their grandchild's school fees. The grandchild, while receiving an indirect benefit, does not enjoy any increase in the value of their estate.
ii) Paying an insurance premium on a policy held for someone else's benefit. The value of the policy remains the same before and after payment of the premium, so there is no increase in the value of the transferee's estate.
iii) A parent paying the maintenance costs for their adult child's house. The value of the house may not necessarily be increased through routine maintenance, so neither is the child's estate.

Each of these payments might, of course, be exempt under the 'normal expenditure out of income' exemption (Section 5.5). It therefore only matters that they are not PETs when they are not already exempt under that exemption or one of the other exemptions we will examine in Chapter 5.

Nevertheless, in IHT planning, it is important to understand the status of every transfer of value. Remember that chargeable lifetime transfers must effectively be accumulated over a seven-year period and IHT charges will result if the cumulative total exceeds the NRB.

Hence, a transfer made today, which turns out to be a chargeable lifetime transfer instead of a PET, could cause additional IHT charges to arise at any time over the next seven years, even if the transferor survives throughout this period.

**Looking after your PETS**

In the first situation outlined above, the grandparent could avoid the problem by giving the necessary funds to cover the school fees to the child's parent, who would then pay the school fees themselves.

Alternatively, the parent could contract to pay the school fees, with the result that the payment by the grandparent gives rise to an increase in the value of the parent's estate, thus meaning a PET has taken place. The key point is that the grandparent should not contract directly with the school unless they can be certain the normal expenditure out of income exemption will apply.

The second situation above is perhaps the one most likely to be covered by the normal expenditure out of income exemption. In other cases, the position might be rectified by giving the money to pay the premium to the beneficiary, who then pays it themselves, although this does depend on who the policyholder is and whether the policy is held in trust. We will return to the subject of insurance premiums in Section 11.8.

The position in the third situation above is perhaps arguable. In a case like this, there is a PET to the extent the value of the child's house is increased as a result of the work paid for by the parent. The remainder of the parent's expenditure, however, represents a chargeable lifetime transfer (unless covered by another exemption).

***Example:*** *Joe's daughter, Sam, would like to have her house completely redecorated. Joe offers to get the work done at his own expense. He contracts for a decorator to do the work, which is then carried out at a cost of £20,000. Joe has therefore made a transfer of value of £20,000.*

*Before the redecoration work, Sam's house was worth £300,000. Immediately after the work, it is worth £308,000. Joe has made a PET of £8,000 (the increase in the value of Sam's house). The remaining spending of £12,000 will be a chargeable lifetime transfer (unless covered by other exemptions).*

Joe could have prevented any chargeable lifetime transfer very easily by simply giving all the money for the work to Sam and leaving her to contract for the work and pay the bill herself. Alternatively, if Sam had contracted for the work herself and was therefore liable for the decorator's bill, Joe could settle that bill and this would also be a PET as Sam's estate increases when her liability is settled. Either way, it is sensible for Sam to contract for the work!

If Joe were contractually liable for the work on Sam's house, but he gave Sam the money to pay the bill and she settled it, this could result in further PETs of £20,000 both from Joe to Sam and from Sam to Joe, as well as the transfers already described in the example above. If ***either*** of them died within seven years, this could result in additional IHT liabilities arising.

The requirements for a transfer to qualify as a PET where the transferee is a trust are even more restrictive. If Sam's house was held by a disabled trust for her benefit, the only way for Joe to fund the redecoration work as a PET would be for him to give the trust £20,000. The trustees could then contract and pay for the work.

If Joe settled the decorating bill, this would be a chargeable transfer regardless of who had contracted for the work. Settling a debt on behalf of a disabled trust will not qualify as a PET.

## 4.5 DEATH WITHIN SEVEN YEARS OF A LIFETIME TRANSFER

For CGT purposes, death is often a good tax-planning strategy. The same cannot be said of IHT.

Both chargeable lifetime transfers and PETs made in the seven-year period prior to death are effectively brought back into the deceased's estate for IHT purposes. This applies whether any IHT was payable at the time of the original transfer or not.

Subject to the tapering provisions set out below, IHT becomes payable at the death rate (40%) on transfers made within the seven years prior to the transferor's death. Any IHT paid on the original transfer may be deducted, so that just the excess arises on death.

The additional IHT liabilities arising are usually the responsibility of the transferees. In other words, the situation may be like this: "I'm very sorry to hear about your father, son, but do you remember that gift of £10,000 he gave you two years ago? Well, I'm afraid you're going to have to pay some tax on it." Now do you see why I call it an 'immoral and evil tax'?

The best way to avoid unwanted liabilities falling on transferees in the event of your death within seven years is to record your intention to bear any tax arising in a memorandum at the time of the gift (see Memorandum 3 in Appendix C). Alternatively, you can make a specific bequest in your Will in respect of the IHT falling on the transferee.

To avoid doubt, it is probably best to do both. There are two problems with both of these approaches, however. Firstly, the payment of IHT arising at the time of your death from out of your estate will itself represent another transfer of value and hence grossing up at full death rates may apply (see Section 2.8).

Secondly, the primary responsibility for any IHT arising on death remains with the transferee. If there are insufficient funds remaining in your estate to cover the tax, the transferee will still have to foot the bill. In practice, it often makes more sense for the transferee to take out term insurance on the life of the transferor in order to cover any potential IHT arising on the latter's death.

Conversely, the transferor will often be concerned to ensure any IHT arising on earlier gifts does not come out of his or her estate and thus reduce the value of the net estate passing to their primary beneficiaries.

In theory, of course, the IHT arising on transfers made in the last seven years of the transferor's life should be paid by the transferees. However, as we saw in Section 2.9, HMRC is more concerned with collecting the tax than with who gets hurt. To put matters (reasonably) beyond doubt, it is therefore wise to use a memorandum specifying the transferee's responsibility for any IHT arising (see Memorandum 2 in Appendix C). Sadly, however, even this will not help if the transferee simply does not have the ability to pay.

**Tapering**

Fortunately, there is some relief when death occurs at least three, but less than seven, years after the lifetime transfer. In these cases, the rate of IHT arising on death is tapered as follows:

| **No. of years after transfer before death occurs:** | **Proportion of 40% Death Rate payable** |
|---|---|
| Less than 3 | 100% (=IHT @ 40%) |
| At least 3, less than 4 | 80% (=IHT @ 32%) |
| At least 4, less than 5 | 60% (=IHT @ 24%) |
| At least 5, less than 6 | 40% (=IHT @ 16%) |
| At least 6, less than 7 | 20% (=IHT @ 8%) |

Thanks to the tapering provisions, IHT savings may start to arise once the transferor has survived three years. Hence, even if you don't think Great Aunt Maude stands any chance of lasting seven years, it may still be worth looking at getting her to make some gifts.

The reductions in the amount of IHT payable apply from the date of the relevant anniversary. The savings only relate to the lifetime gifts made by the deceased. Tapering has no effect on the amount of IHT payable on the estate itself. Tapering can therefore only produce a saving where the deceased has made lifetime gifts in excess of the NRB.

In the case of chargeable lifetime transfers (see Section 4.2), the tapering provisions could result in the final IHT liability on death being less than the amount already paid. Unfortunately, this simply means no further IHT is due; it does not result in any repayment.

In calculating the IHT due on each transfer made within the seven years prior to death, any chargeable transfers in the seven years before ***that*** transfer must be taken into account. For this reason, chargeable lifetime transfers made up to fourteen years previously may continue to have an impact on the IHT arising on the transferor's death.

The calculation of the tax arising on transfers made within the seven years prior to death is almost a repeat of the calculation we saw in Section 4.2 for a chargeable lifetime transfer, except that:

- The full death rate (40%) is used
- Tapering relief (as set out above) is applied
- The NRB available at the date of death is used in the calculations, rather than the NRB applying at the time of the transfer
- Any unused NRB on the earlier death of the deceased's spouse is also available (see Section 6.2 for further details)
- PETs made in the seven years prior to death must be brought into the calculation

***Example*** *(I will again ignore any exemptions and reliefs, except the NRB): Roy is a lifelong bachelor and a kind, generous, rich old man. Sadly, despite how much his nurses try to handle him with care he dies on 3rd December 2023. Roy made no chargeable transfers prior to 2013 but, in the last decade of his life, he made the following gifts:*

- *On 10th December 2013, he gave £200,000 in cash to the Wilbury Discretionary Trust*
- *On 1st December 2016, he gave £50,000 in cash to his nephew George*
- *On 13th January 2017, he gave another £145,000 in cash to the Wilbury Discretionary Trust. He paid £5,000 in IHT at that time (grossing up applied)*
- *On 8th May 2019, he gave his friend Jeff some shares in the Electric Light Company Inc. At that time, these shares were worth £50,000*
- *On 4th December 2020, he gave his friend Tom some shares in Heartbreakers.com plc, which were worth £80,000 at that time*
- *On 24th August 2021, he gave his friend Bob £100,000 in cash*

*The IHT payable by each of these transferees on Roy's death is as follows:*

***The Wilbury Discretionary Trust (First Gift):*** *Roy's first gift to the Trust in December 2013 was made more than seven years prior to his death. This gift itself will therefore not be subject to IHT on his death. However, because gifts to discretionary trusts are chargeable transfers, it will have an impact on other gifts made in the following seven years.*

***George:*** *Roy's gift to George was a PET made more than seven years prior to his death. On the seventh anniversary of that gift, 1st December 2023, it became fully exempt and hence can now be completely ignored for the purposes of calculating the IHT arising on Roy's death.*

***The Wilbury Discretionary Trust (Second Gift):*** *Due to grossing up, Roy's second gift to the Trust in January 2017 was deemed to have been £150,000. As this gift was within the last seven years of Roy's life, it is effectively pulled back into his estate for the purposes of his IHT calculation. Furthermore, in calculating the IHT now due on this gift, we must also take account of his previous gift to the Trust, as that first gift was a chargeable transfer made within the seven-year period prior to the second gift.*

*The gift to George in December 2016 can be ignored as this has become fully exempt. The cumulative total of chargeable lifetime transfers made by Roy up to the time of the second gift to the Trust was therefore £350,000. After deducting the NRB of £325,000, there remains a chargeable sum of £25,000.*

*As the gift took place more than six, but less than seven, years before Roy's death, IHT is chargeable at 20% of the death rate, i.e. 8%. Hence the IHT charge arising on Roy's death is £2,000. As this is less than the IHT already paid by Roy at the time of the gift (£5,000), no further IHT is payable.*

***Jeff:*** *Roy's gift of shares to Jeff in May 2019 was a PET. Unfortunately, as Roy has died within seven years of making that gift, it has now become a chargeable transfer. Both of the gifts to the Wilbury Discretionary Trust took place within the seven-year* *period prior to the gift to Jeff, so the cumulative value of chargeable transfers at this point is £350,000, meaning the NRB has been fully exhausted and the gift to Jeff is fully chargeable to IHT.*

*However, since the gift took place more than four, but less than five, years before Roy's death, IHT is only chargeable at 60% of the death rate, i.e. 24%. Jeff therefore has an IHT liability of £12,000 (£50,000 x 24%).*

***Tom:*** *Tom is going to be heartbroken. His gift took place just one day short of three years before Roy's death. IHT is therefore payable at the full death rate, 40%. Furthermore, the cumulative value of total chargeable transfers within the previous seven years now amounts to £400,000, made up as follows:*

| | |
|---|---|
| *First gift to Wilbury Discretionary Trust* | *£200,000* |
| *Second gift to Wilbury Discretionary Trust* | *£150,000* |
| *Gift to Jeff* | *£50,000* |
| *Total* | *£400,000* |

*Both gifts to the Wilbury Discretionary Trust are included as they both took place within the seven-year period prior to the gift to Tom. The gift to Jeff is also included, as it has now become a chargeable transfer due to Roy's death within seven years. Tom therefore has an IHT liability of £32,000 (40% x £80,000).*

***Bob:*** *This gift took place within the last three years of Roy's life, so there is no tapering of the IHT liability. The cumulative value of total chargeable transfers within the seven years prior to this gift amounts to £280,000, made up as follows:*

| | |
|---|---|
| *Second gift to Wilbury Discretionary Trust* | *£150,000* |
| *Gift to Jeff* | *£50,000* |
| *Gift to Tom* | *£80,000* |
| *Total* | *£280,000* |

*The first gift to the Wilbury Discretionary Trust is not included as it took place more than seven years before the gift to Bob. Adding Bob's own gift to the above figure gives a total of £380,000. From this, we are able to deduct the NRB of £325,000, leaving Bob with a chargeable transfer of £55,000. Bob's IHT liability is therefore £22,000 (40% x £55,000).*

The total value of chargeable transfers in the last seven years of Roy's life amounts to £380,000. His NRB is therefore already exhausted before we even begin to look at his estate.

The next point to note is that the oldest gift in our example, made almost ten years before Roy's death, had a major impact on the recipients of his later gifts, despite the fact it was made well before the critical seven-year period.

It is also interesting to note the oldest gift within the seven-year period did not give rise to any more IHT for the recipients of that gift. This will often be the case for chargeable lifetime transfers made more than five years prior to the transferor's death.

This position may be altered, however, where there are significant amounts of PETs made within seven years of the transferor's death, but prior to the chargeable transfer in question.

As we saw in the example, these two earlier gifts used up Roy's NRB, which had a major impact on some of the later transferees. This was particularly unfortunate for Tom, since a mere seven days' delay to his gift would have meant the first gift to the Wilbury Discretionary Trust would have been made more than seven years previously. Tom's gift would then have been completely covered by the NRB.

Where practical, it may make sense to leave a seven-year gap after making a large chargeable lifetime transfer before making further chargeable or PETs. Naturally, of course, delaying your gifts carries other conflicting risks, which you will need to weigh up. However, a delay of just seven days in order to bring the NRB back into play would surely make sense!

By the time of Bob's gift in 2021, part of the NRB was available once more, thus giving him a lower IHT bill on a larger gift. This ably demonstrates that, with careful planning: **the NRB is available to each of us not just once a lifetime, but once every seven years!**

While none of us knows exactly when we have seven years left to go, it is also worth bearing in mind that gifts in the last seven years of your life will be dealt with chronologically when you die.

Although kind old Roy cannot really be blamed for the final outcome in the example, things might have turned out fairer if he had made some of the smaller gifts first.

**A Final Observation**

As discussed in Section 3.2, the NRB had originally been due to increase to £350,000 in 2010 but was, instead, frozen at its 2009/10 level of £325,000. By 2023/24, the NRB should perhaps be something like £575,000 (even if only increased in line with retail price inflation), £250,000 more than it actually is. At first glance, one might think this freeze could only cost a maximum of £100,000 (£250,000 x 40%) in extra IHT on the occasion of one person's death. Think again!

In our example above, the freeze in the NRB has effectively cost Jeff £12,000, Tom £32,000, Bob £22,000, and will also cost Roy's estate an extra £78,000: a total of £144,000. In fact, the freeze in the NRB could cost some bereaved families up to £400,000 in extra tax in 2023/24; and perhaps as much as £600,000 by 2027/28.

## 4.6 RELIEF FOR REDUCTION IN VALUE

Where IHT becomes payable on the transferor's death within seven years of making a lifetime transfer of property that has subsequently reduced in value, the transferee may claim relief from IHT in respect of that reduction in value.

To claim relief, the following conditions must be satisfied:

i) The property transferred must not be tangible moveable property with a predictable useful life not exceeding fifty years (e.g. a car, or other machinery), and
ii) Either:
  a) At the time of the transferor's death the property is still held by the transferee or their spouse, or
  b) The property has been sold by the transferee or their spouse by way of a sale at arm's length to an unconnected person

When such a claim is made, the IHT on that transfer is calculated by substituting the property's market value at the relevant date for its value at the date of the transfer. Where the property is still held by the transferee or their spouse at the date of the transferor's death, the relevant date is the date of death. Where the property has been sold in an arm's length transaction with an unconnected party, the relevant date is the date of the sale.

The amount of relief given is the reduction in value of the transferred asset itself, without taking account of other assets that may have affected the amount of the transfer of value (see Sections 2.1 and 11.3).

The relief cannot be used to obtain any repayment of IHT that arose immediately on a chargeable lifetime transfer (see Section 4.2); it applies only to the tax arising on the donor's death.

The IHT on any other transfers and on the deceased's estate is unaffected. This is because the value of the transferred property is reduced only for the purposes of this relief and not for the purposes of calculating cumulative chargeable transfers in any seven-year period.

***Example:*** *At the time of Roy's death, Jeff still holds the shares in the Electric Light Company Inc. that Roy gave to him when they were worth £50,000. Unfortunately, they are now worth only £30,000. Nonetheless, Jeff is pleased to discover he can reduce his IHT bill to just £7,200 (£30,000 x 24%: see Section 4.5).*

*Tom is also very excited at the prospect of a relief claim under these provisions as his shares in Heartbreakers.com plc fell rapidly in value after Roy gave them to him and Tom eventually sold them for just £1,000.*

*According to Tom's calculations, he should therefore be able to reduce his IHT bill to just £400 (£1,000 x 40%). However, it transpires that Tom sold the Heartbreakers.com plc shares to his son. This was not an arm's length sale to an unconnected party and Tom's IHT bill remains £32,000 (see Section 4.5). Heartbroken again!*

The IHT liabilities for Roy's personal representatives and Bob are unaffected by Jeff's claim. (Nor would they be affected by Tom's claim if it had been valid.)

It does not matter whether Tom sold his shares to his son at market value. Because he and his son are connected, Tom loses his ability to claim relief for his shares' reduction in value. He therefore ends up with some shares that are virtually worthless and an IHT liability of £32,000.

A transferee holding property that was transferred to them less than seven years ago, and which has reduced in value since then, would be wise to avoid making any transfers of that property other than a sale at arm's length to an unconnected person, or a transfer to their spouse.

## 4.7 TIMING AND EVIDENCE

A gift made by cheque is deemed to be made when the cheque is cleared by the transferor's bank. This will inevitably cause a slight delay to the date the gift is deemed to take place. While the delay may be slight, it could have disastrous consequences.

If the cheque clears after the transferor's death, for example, it will no longer be regarded as a lifetime gift and will form part of the transferor's estate on death. This will mean none of the lifetime exemptions can apply, including the annual exemption and small gifts exemption.

For the sake of certainty, it may often be worth incurring the additional cost of putting the cheque through same day clearing.

Alternatively, where the transferor has access to online or telephone banking facilities, it might be more efficient for them to make their gifts by way of electronic transfer. While the point has not yet arisen in a suitable court case, it would seem logical to assume gifts made by way of electronic transfer will be treated as having been made when the funds are deducted from the transferor's account. While this will undoubtedly speed up the process, it will remain vital to prepare suitable documentation to evidence the gift. HMRC will try very hard to get assets back into the deceased's estate in order to increase the amount of IHT payable.

To prevent questions like, "How do we know this money wasn't just a loan; can you prove she didn't expect you to repay it?" or, "Yes, we know your parents gave you the house, but what about the contents; there's nothing to prove they gave them to you," it is vital gifts are evidenced. Furthermore, it is important the documentary evidence of the gifts is specific about exactly what is being gifted.

Appendix C contains some brief examples of memoranda recording gifts. In practice, it will often make sense to record further detailed information; especially details of household contents intended to be included in a gift of property.

## 4.8 GIFTS WITH RESERVATION

To give something away so that it is no longer part of your estate for IHT purposes, you need to completely deprive yourself of that asset and any enjoyment of it. Any purported gifts where you retain a beneficial interest in the gifted asset are ineffective for IHT purposes and are effectively treated as still being part of your estate.

For example, if you 'give' a painting to your son but keep it in your house then you are still enjoying that asset and it remains part of your estate for IHT purposes.

These types of transfer are known as 'gifts with reservation'. This is a particular problem when looking at the family home and we will return to this subject in Chapter 13.

Broadly speaking, a gift with reservation occurs whenever:

i) The transferee does not obtain genuine possession and enjoyment of the gifted asset,
ii) The transferor is not excluded from enjoyment of the gifted asset, or
iii) The transferor has some form of contractual right over the gifted asset

We have already seen an example of (i): the gifted painting being kept in the transferor's house. An example of (ii) would be to give a holiday cottage to your daughter, which you then use for a month each year. An example of (iii) would be to grant yourself a lease over your own property then transfer the freehold to your children.

Although you have to be excluded from the enjoyment of a gifted asset, there is a little leeway. If you give your son a painting, which he keeps in his house, there is no need to wear a blindfold every time you visit.

The strict rule is that the transferor must be 'virtually' excluded from the enjoyment of the asset. Mere incidental enjoyment of a gifted asset when making a short visit to the transferee is permitted. Hence, if you give your daughter a house and visit her for dinner once every six months, you will not have a problem. If, on the other hand, you stay at the house every second weekend, there will be a gift with reservation.

Thankfully, one group of gifts that would otherwise almost always fall foul of the gift with reservation rules are generally exempted from these provisions: gifts covered by the spouse exemption (see Section 3.3).

**Unforeseen Changes in Circumstances**

In the case of a property that a transferor has gifted to a relative, there will not be a gift with reservation if the transferor is forced to move back into that property due to an unforeseen change in circumstances whereby he or she is unable to care for themselves due to ill health, old age, or infirmity.

This, for example, may cover the situation where a person has transferred a property to their son or daughter and some years later has to move into the property so their family can care for them.

The move back into the property must be for the provision of 'reasonable care and maintenance' by the transferee who must also be a relative. You can't just move back in because you'd like to see a bit more of the grandchildren.

This change must also be unforeseen. If you are already ill when you make the gift, the gift with reservation rules will still apply.

### What's So Bad about Gifts with Reservation?

Plenty! Firstly, although the gift is ineffective when it comes to excluding the gifted asset from your estate, it is nevertheless still a transfer of value and could give rise to an IHT charge if you die within seven years, or even an immediate charge in the case of a transfer into trust (see Section 4.2).

Some relief is given to prevent a double charge, but it does not entirely eliminate the problem. Where the transferor dies within seven years of making a gift with reservation, two IHT calculations must be prepared. Firstly, IHT is calculated as if the transfer had never taken place and you still owned the gifted asset at the date of your death. A second IHT calculation must then be prepared on the basis that the transfer did take place.

The bad news is the calculation that produces the greatest amount of IHT is then used. In other words, the tax payable is the greater of the amount payable on the transfer **or** the amount payable on the asset deemed to still be in your estate on death!

Generally, where the gifted asset is increasing in value, we would expect the greater tax to arise by including the asset in the estate on death. The overall effect of this is to render the gift ineffective for IHT purposes. However, in some cases, the second calculation will produce the greater tax, meaning the transfer has actually cost your family more. We will see an example of one way this might arise in Section 13.12. In short, a gift with reservation where that reservation still applies at the time of the donor's death is at best ineffective and at worst may even increase the total IHT due.

Secondly, the gifted asset will also be included in the transferee's estate, thus giving rise to a possible double charge. Thirdly, although the gift is ineffective for IHT purposes, it will still be a disposal for CGT purposes. This means CGT liabilities may still arise on the gift. Furthermore, the transferee may not be entitled to the same reliefs as the transferor would have been if they had retained the asset. We will look further at the potential impact of this in Chapter 12.

### Reservation Reliefs

Assets treated as still being part of your estate on death under the gifts with reservation rules remain eligible for a number of important reliefs, including the RNRB (Section 3.4), business property relief (Chapter 7), and agricultural property relief (Section 7.28). We will take a closer look at the position where the RNRB applies to a gift with reservation of the family home in Section 13.12.

### What Happens If the Reservation Ends?

If the reservation ends during the transferor's lifetime, a new transfer is deemed to take place. For example, if a mother gave a house to her two sons in 2004, but continued to live in it until 2023, there would be a deemed transfer of the house in 2023. This time the transfer **is** effective for IHT purposes. It is treated as a PET, so it will not cause any immediate IHT charges, but it does give rise to a few problems.

The main problem, of course, is that the transferor will have to survive at least seven years after the reservation ends before the transferred asset is exempt from IHT. Furthermore, the value of the deemed transfer will be the asset's value at the date the reservation ends, not the date of the original transfer.

Deemed transfers on the cessation of a reservation are also ineligible for a number of reliefs, including the RNRB and annual exemption (Section 5.2).

If the transferor dies within seven years of the cessation of a reservation, the property subject to the reservation will effectively fall into the deceased's estate. Hence, the mother in our example would need to live until at least 2030 for her transfer of the house in 2004 to be exempt from IHT. If she should pass away before then, the value of the house when she moved out in 2023 will effectively be brought back into her estate. However, since there has now been an IHT-effective lifetime transfer (albeit in 2023 rather than 2004), the RNRB will not be available to exempt any of the house's value.

Where both the original transfer and the deemed transfer on cessation of the reservation take place within the seven years prior to the transferor's death, it will again be necessary to prepare two IHT calculations: one including the original transfer and one including the deemed transfer. Once again, the calculation producing the greater amount of tax will be used. The RNRB will not be available to exempt any of the transferred asset's value in either calculation under these circumstances.

## 4.9 WHY NOT JUST GIVE IT ALL AWAY?

After reading Section 4.3, you may have been thinking that avoiding IHT is simple. All you need to do is give everything away to your family and survive seven years. Well, yes, in theory, in the right circumstances, simply giving your property away during your lifetime can be an effective way to avoid IHT.

Certainly there is no problem with giving away whatever parts of your estate you can afford to. Just remember to make sure the gifts are PETs and then take good care of yourself for seven years. (Or take out some term insurance to cover the IHT risk: see Section 11.8.)

Unfortunately, however, in practice, there are a few catches. Firstly, as we have already seen, any gifts where you retain a beneficial interest are treated as still being part of your estate.

Secondly, even where a transfer appears to avoid the gifts with reservation rules, there may be an Income Tax benefit-in-kind charge applying if the transferor continues to enjoy the use of the asset. This charge may also apply to any future use by the donor of an asset purchased with gifted funds (see Section 11.12).

Thirdly, when gifting assets other than cash, you may be exposed to CGT. Most lifetime gifts are treated like a sale at current market value for CGT purposes. (Here there is no problem with the family home, as it is generally exempt from CGT under private residence relief: this issue is fully explained in the Taxcafe guide *How to Save Property Tax*.)

Lastly, in practice, you cannot simply give all your assets away because you will need something to live off for the rest of your life. This may include the need to pay care home fees at some point in the future: an issue we will discuss further in Section 11.6.

So, it's fine if you're happy to spend the rest of your days in a monastery or nunnery; or live off your last £325,000 (for at least seven years) but, in reality, very few people would be happy to follow such a drastic course of action. Hence, at this point, we need to start looking at what exemptions and reliefs are available and how you can use them to best effect.

## Chapter 5

# Lifetime Exemptions

### 5.1 ABSOLUTE EXEMPTION

There are a number of exemptions available to cover lifetime transfers. These are absolute exemptions, not dependent on whether you survive for any particular period.

Transfers covered by these exemptions would be free from IHT even if you were to pass away the very next day, or even on the way home from the lawyer's office. (Don't laugh: I know of one sad, but true, case where the taxpayer was knocked down by a bus outside the lawyer's office!)

These exemptions therefore provide very useful IHT planning tools under the right circumstances. Sadly though, the monetary values of the exemptions covered in Sections 5.2 and 5.3 have remained the same since 1981 and 1975 respectively. These values are long overdue for an increase, since retail price inflation alone should have increased them more than five-fold by now!

### 5.2 THE ANNUAL AND SMALL GIFTS EXEMPTIONS

The first £3,000 of any transfers of value, which are not otherwise exempt, that each individual makes in each tax year, are exempt from IHT. Married couples have an annual exemption of £3,000 each. If the annual exemption is not used one year, it may be carried forward and can be used in the next tax year if that following year's annual exemption is fully exhausted.

The annual exemption may not be very large, but it is important to bear it in mind when undertaking IHT planning. Making best use of the exemption is a matter of timing. The ability to carry it forward one year gives you a second chance, but the use of the annual exemption should nevertheless be reviewed at least every other year. A couple who manage to make effective use of the annual exemption in the final few years of their lives will save around £20,000 in IHT.

According to HMRC, the taxpayer's annual exemption must be applied on a strictly chronological basis. In their view, the exemption must be utilised against any PETs taking place before chargeable lifetime transfers made later in the same tax year. This could have some unfortunate consequences.

***Example:*** *Brian gives £6,000 to his brother Carl on 6th April 2023. This (according to HMRC) uses up Brian's annual exemptions for 2022/23 and 2023/24, despite being a PET.*

*On 10th April 2023, Brian gives £331,000 to the Wilson Phillips Discretionary Trust for the benefit of his many nephews and nieces. Unfortunately, this means he has made a chargeable lifetime transfer. After deducting the NRB of £325,000, the remaining £6,000 must be grossed up at the rate of one quarter, giving Brian an IHT bill of £1,500. If, instead, Brian had made his gifts in the opposite order, his annual exemptions would have been deducted from his chargeable transfer, leaving £325,000, which would be covered by his NRB, leaving no IHT to pay.*

HMRC's interpretation on this point is based entirely on a flaw in the drafting of the IHT law. What Parliament actually intended was for the annual exemption to be used first against any chargeable lifetime transfers, with any excess remaining available to cover PETs if they subsequently became chargeable on the transferor's death.

This difference in interpretation will affect not only those making large chargeable lifetime transfers in excess of the NRB, like Brian in the example above, but also the transferees calculating their own IHT bill in the event of the transferor's death within seven years. In the latter case there will be winners and losers but, in the former, only HMRC can be the winner!

In practice, I would always advocate planning your affairs on the basis of HMRC's interpretation wherever possible. Chargeable lifetime transfers should therefore be made earlier in the tax year than PETs whenever possible.

But, if you find you are already in a position where their interpretation is putting you at a disadvantage, you should argue for the law to be applied as it was quite clearly intended by Parliament: an argument frequently used by HMRC, so why shouldn't the taxpayer argue the same!

Transfers made on the same day are treated as simultaneous. Any available annual exemption is divided between the same-day transfers in proportion to their value.

**The Small Gifts Exemption**

There is also a general exemption for outright gifts of up to £250 to any one person each tax year. This exemption applies to any number of such small gifts to separate persons each year. It can only apply to straightforward gifts to other individuals and cannot apply to transfers into trust. A married couple may each use this exemption separately in their own right.

The small gifts exemption only covers gifts **up to** £250. Unlike the annual exemption, it does not cover the first part of a larger gift. Hence, a gift of £251 is not covered by this exemption at all. It should also be noted that the exemption has to cover all gifts to the same person in the whole tax year.

The small gifts exemption cannot be used in conjunction with the annual exemption. In other words, it is not possible to exempt gifts totalling £3,250 to the same person by using both exemptions together.

## 5.3 GIFTS IN CONSIDERATION OF MARRIAGE

It's an expensive business when the kids get married, but it does provide an additional opportunity for some IHT planning. Gifts made in consideration of marriage are exempt from IHT up to the following limits:

| | |
|---|---|
| • Parents: | £5,000 |
| • Grandparents, Great-Grandparents, etc: | £2,500 |
| • One party to the marriage to the other: | £2,500 |
| • Other donors: | £1,000 |

All these limits apply on an individual basis and the relationships referred to must be to one of the parties to the marriage. Hence, for example, the groom could receive £5,000 from each of his parents, £2,500 from each of his grandparents, and £1,000 from each of his aunts and uncles; while the bride could receive the same from her family.

Alternatively, the bride's family could make their gifts to the groom or the groom's family could make their gifts to the bride. And all the same applies where there are two grooms or two brides.

Additionally, within the same exemption (and within the same overriding limits set out above), gifts could be made to a trust for the benefit of:

i) One or both of the parties to the marriage
ii) Children of either or both parties to the marriage
iii) Future spouses of children of either or both parties to the marriage
iv) A future spouse of either party to the marriage
v) Children of any subsequent spouse of either party to this marriage and future spouses of those children

This all sounds terribly complicated, but it means the marriage provides an opportunity to put some money into trust for both living and unborn children of either or both parties without giving rise to a chargeable lifetime transfer.

To fall within the exemption, gifts must be made on or shortly before the marriage and must be fully effective when the marriage takes place. For example, 'I give you my property at Valotte on condition you marry my daughter.'

Where the gifts exceed the limits shown above, the excess may be covered by the annual exemption, if available. Otherwise, the excess will be treated like any other lifetime transfer, as explained in Chapter 4.

For the purpose of this exemption, a parent includes the parent of an illegitimate child, adopted child, or legally recognised step-child (see Section 3.4: the same principles apply here) and, as explained in Section 1.4, all of the above applies equally to same sex marriages and registered civil partnerships.

## 5.4 MAINTENANCE OF FAMILY

Anything you do for the maintenance of your family (as defined below) is exempted from being a transfer of value for IHT purposes. Just as well since otherwise, every time you bought the weekly groceries you would be at risk of causing an IHT liability! This covers expenditure for the maintenance of your spouse, plus any expenditure for the maintenance, education or training of:

- A child of either you or your spouse who is either under 18 or still in full-time education or training on the last 5th April prior to the time of the relevant expenditure.
- Any other child who is not in the care of a parent and is under 18 on the last 5th April prior to the time of the relevant expenditure.
- Any other child who has been in your care for a substantial period and was still in full time education or training on the last 5th April prior to the time of the relevant expenditure.

Your child for the purposes of this exemption includes a stepchild, adopted child or illegitimate child. One major absentee from this list, however, is your unmarried partner and hence, technically, any expenditure for the maintenance of a common-law co-habiting partner could be a transfer of value. Thankfully, however, such expenditure will generally be covered by the normal expenditure out of income exemption (Section 5.5), or the exemption for transfers not intended to confer a gratuitous benefit (Section 5.6): since most transfers of value in an unmarried couple are simply domestic cost-sharing arrangements.

Even so, this might still present a problem in a few cases, as a large part of a co-habiting partner's expenditure in the last seven years of their life could potentially be subject to IHT (sugar daddies and cougars beware!) Furthermore, since much of this maintenance expenditure will not increase the value of the transferee's estate, it might even be considered a chargeable lifetime transfer!

The maintenance of family exemption also extends to expenditure that represents a reasonable provision for the care or maintenance of a dependent relative. A dependent relative for this purpose is your widowed, separated or divorced mother or mother-in-law (by concession, an unmarried mother may also be included, as long as she is genuinely financially dependent on you); or any other relative of yours or your spouse's who is incapacitated by old age or infirmity, as a consequence of which they are unable to maintain themselves.

HMRC should, for example, accept that renting a property for your elderly and financially dependent relative to live in represents reasonable provision for their maintenance. They will not, however, accept buying a property for them and transferring it into their name to give them added security, as being reasonable care or maintenance.

This exemption is useful when an individual pre-deceases one of their parents, or where someone is providing care or maintenance for a disabled relative, such as a sibling or adult child.

## 5.5 NORMAL EXPENDITURE OUT OF INCOME

Lifetime transfers are exempt to the extent that:

i) They are part of the normal, habitual, or typical, expenditure of the transferor,
ii) Taking one year with another, they are made out of income (i.e. not out of capital), and
iii) The transferor is left with sufficient net income to maintain his or her usual standard of living

This is an extremely useful exemption, since there is no financial limit to the amount that can be covered if the transferor can afford it. However, it must be said that, since the expenditure has to come out of income, the exemption, while extremely useful, cannot be used to reduce the capital value of your estate exposed to IHT. In other words, it's a case of preventing things from getting any worse, rather than making them any better.

The amount of gifts or other expenditure involved does not need to be exactly the same every year, as long as it is part of a regular pattern. All of the following might potentially be covered as long as they meet the three tests set out above:

- Giving your son £10,000 every year
- Giving your daughter a sum of money every year, which you increase annually in line with retail price inflation (or use the CPI if, like the Government, you don't feel so generous)
- Paying your granddaughter's school fees
- Giving your nephew all your dividend income every year
- Buying your brother a new car every three years
- Passing all the income you receive from a trust each year over to your elderly father
- Paying a monthly life insurance premium on a policy in favour of your daughter

**Maintaining Your Usual Standard of Living**
It is generally accepted this test is met if the transferor is left with sufficient income to maintain his or her usual standard of living ***on average***. For this purpose, it is generally understood HMRC is willing to consider the position over a three-year period (for example, surplus income remaining from 2023/24 might be used to fund exempt gifts made in 2024/25 or 2025/26, provided these are normal, habitual expenditure).

It has also been suggested that HMRC does not generally question the validity of gifts out of income if they do not, in total, exceed one third of the transferor's net annual after-tax income. Nevertheless, I imagine they would still scrutinise any case where they had reason to think otherwise!

In some circumstances, the transferor might reasonably gift a greater proportion of his or her income and still maintain their usual standard of living, e.g. a very wealthy person with a very frugal lifestyle. I have, however, met the 'chicken and egg' situation where HMRC has argued the transferor's modest standard of living arose ***because*** of the expenditure in question. To avoid this argument, there will clearly need to be some surplus income remaining most years, on average.

HMRC regards income for the purposes of this exemption as net, after-tax income. Furthermore, not everything that is treated as income for Income Tax purposes will be regarded as income for the purposes of the exemption. (Yet another example of HMRC having their cake and eating it!)

There are, for example, cases where the proceeds of sale of company shares may be treated as income for Income Tax purposes. This often occurs as a result of specific statutory provisions relating to employee shares. The underlying nature of this deemed income would, however, remain capital, and hence this would not be income that could be relied upon for the purposes of the normal expenditure out of income exemption.

For a self-employed transferor, income for the purposes of the exemption would generally be based on the results shown in their business accounts. Hence, income will be arrived at after deducting items such as depreciation and business entertaining, even though these are not allowed for Income Tax purposes. As stated above, however, the full Income Tax charge will need to be deducted from the accounts income in order to arrive at the net after-tax income available for the purposes of the exemption.

Tax exempt income such as dividends and interest within an ISA, or winter fuel payments and attendance allowance, may be included as income for this purpose. However, items that form an effective income stream, but which are actually capital in nature, cannot generally be counted. This includes the annual tax-free 5% withdrawal from an investment bond; loan repayments received from family investment companies (see Chapter 14) or loan trusts (Section 9.9); payments from a discounted gift trust (Section 9.8); and other director's loan account repayments (Section 7.21).

**Habitual Gifts**

Establishing a gift as being part of your normal, habitual expenditure is a question of fact. The matter will be determined by looking at the particular facts of each individual case and considering the behaviour of the transferor over a number of years.

HMRC will usually consider expenditure to have become normal, or habitual, when it has been made three times, with the intention of continuing to make further similar payments. It is, however, possible to establish a gift has become part of your normal, habitual expenditure even if you should die after only one such gift. This is because the exemption will still apply if it can be shown it was the transferor's intention to make the gift regularly on a habitual basis.

A contractual commitment to make regular payments will usually be accepted as evidence of an intention to make the expenditure part of the transferor's normal pattern of expenditure. In the absence of such a commitment, some other documentary evidence of the transferor's intentions is advisable.

Establishing an intention to make a gift on a habitual basis will require some evidence to prove it. For example, if you intend paying your niece's school fees on a regular basis, it would be wise to write a letter to the school confirming this. If you should then unfortunately pass away soon after paying the first set of fees, the letter will confirm this payment was intended to be normal habitual expenditure and thus exempt from IHT (as long as the other requirements set out above are also met).

Another good way to establish an intention to make a gift on a habitual basis is to set up a standing order. This shows a clear intention to make a series of gifts. (See Section 17.16 for another reason standing orders are a good idea.)

To be covered by this exemption, the relevant gifts or expenditure must also be maintained on a regular basis. Hence, you must keep making your habitual gifts every year (or such other period as is your habit). Unlike the annual exemption, there is no scope for carrying this exemption forward!

**The Danger of Irrelevance**

Where the gifts concerned are made directly to another individual, this all only becomes relevant when the transferor has died within seven years since, otherwise, the gifts will be PETs in any case (see Section 4.3). Unfortunately, what this means in practice is the true status of these transfers is generally not established until after the transferor's death, leaving a great deal of uncertainty for their beneficiaries. It is vital, therefore, to maintain records of your normal expenditure out of income throughout your lifetime, to assist your executors in establishing the correct position when dealing with your estate after your death.

## 5.6 OTHER EXEMPT TRANSFERS

There is a general exemption for a transfer that is not intended to confer a gratuitous benefit on the transferee. An important example of such a transfer is one made as part of a divorce or separation agreement. Proposed changes to the CGT rules for transfers made by separated or divorcing spouses now give rise to even greater opportunities to benefit from this exemption and we will look at these in more detail in Sections 6.6 and 12.6.

Settlements between common-law partners might also be covered under this exemption, as well as simple transactions, such as friends sharing the cost of a holiday or restaurant bill.

Transfers of value made for the purposes of a trade, and thus allowable for Income Tax, are exempt from IHT. This covers paying your employees' wages, for example; including employees who are also family members, provided they genuinely earn those wages.

There is also an exemption for payments securing pension or other retirement benefits for an employee of the transferor, who is not otherwise connected with the transferor, or the widow, widower, or dependants of such an employee. Payments securing pension benefits for family members are not covered by this exemption (but could be covered by other exemptions).

Chapter 6

# IHT Planning for Married Persons

## 6.1 SCOPE OF THIS CHAPTER

In this chapter, we are going to take a detailed look at the IHT planning opportunities available as a consequence of marriage. We will cover people who are married now; widows and widowers; and those contemplating marriage in the future. There is even a little planning idea for those who are currently single in Section 6.4.

Everything that applies to married people applies equally to civil partners and everything that applies to a widow or widower applies equally to a surviving civil partner.

Unless expressly stated to the contrary, it is assumed throughout this chapter that both spouses are (or were) UK domiciled, or have (or had) elected to be treated as UK domiciled at the relevant time (see Section 6.15).

## 6.2 THE TRANSFERABLE NIL RATE BAND (TNRB) & RESIDENCE NIL RATE BAND (RNRB)

Any proportion of the NRB that is unused on a married person's death is transferable to their spouse. In simple terms, this means all widows and widowers are potentially entitled to a double NRB. Furthermore, since we all have the potential to become a widow or widower one day, this means we all have the potential to double our NRB. As we will see in Section 6.7, this has turned a great deal of IHT planning on its head!

The TNRB must be claimed by the widow or widower's personal representatives within two years of the widow or widower's death. No claim is necessary on the first spouse's death and it does not matter how long ago the first spouse died.

Furthermore, it does not matter whether the first spouse actually had any assets at the time of their death. Even if they died penniless, their widow or widower can still claim a TNRB.

It is the ***proportion*** of the NRB unused on the first death that transfers, not the amount. This means the widow or widower benefits from any increase in the NRB since their spouse's death.

In the simplest case where none of the NRB was used on the first spouse's death the widow or widower will be entitled to a double NRB. For widows or widowers dying between 6th April 2009 and 5th April 2028, this amounts to £650,000 (regardless of when the first spouse died).

Where some of the first spouse's NRB was used, the amount transferred to the survivor will be reduced.

***Example:*** *Lee died on 1st September 2002 when the NRB was £250,000. She left a legacy of £100,000 to her son Peter and her remaining estate to her husband Lenny. 60% of Lee's NRB was unused (£150,000/£250,000) and transfers to Lenny.*

*Lenny dies in January 2024 and is entitled to his own NRB plus a further 60% transferred from Lee. His total NRB is thus:*

| | |
|---|---|
| *Own NRB:* | *£325,000* |
| *NRB transferred from Lee (£325,000 x 60%):* | *£195,000* |
| *Total NRB available* | *£520,000* |

Similar principles apply to the transfer of a spouse's RNRB, although this is subject to the tapering provisions explained in Section 3.4. Further details on the amount available are included in Sections 3.4 and 13.11.

***Example Continued:*** *As Lee died in 2002, she would not have used any of her RNRB. If her estate was worth no more than £2m at the time of her death, her entire RNRB will therefore transfer to Lenny, giving him a total RNRB at the time of his death in January 2024 of £350,000: made up of his own RNRB of £175,000 and Lee's unused RNRB of £175,000.*

*Combining his RNRB of £350,000 with his enhanced NRB of £520,000 (see above) gives Lenny a total potential exemption of £870,000. He will, however, have to meet the rules outlined in Section 3.4 in order to benefit from the RNRB element of this exemption.*

## 6.3 USING THE RESIDENCE NIL RATE BAND ON FIRST DEATH

As explained in Section 3.4, tapering provisions apply to reduce the amount of RNRB available on the death of an individual with an estate worth in excess of £2m. Hence, where a married couple's ***combined*** net assets exceed £2m, it may be worth ensuring the RNRB is utilised on the first spouse's death since, otherwise, it will be reduced or eliminated through the tapering that applies on the second death.

Where a married couple's combined net assets exceed £4m, there are also potential savings to be made by keeping one spouse's estate to no more than £2m. In that way, the poorer spouse will retain their full RNRB entitlement.

To use that entitlement, it may also be necessary to leave some property qualifying for the RNRB directly to a direct descendant on the poorer spouse's death. For this reason, it would generally be preferable for the poorer spouse to be the one with the shorter life expectancy, although this may require a little negotiation among the family!

In the case of smaller combined estates worth less than £2m, there may be other reasons why it is wise to use the RNRB on the first spouse's death in preference to using any, or more, of their NRB.

As we know, both the NRB and RNRB are frozen at their current levels until at least 5th April 2028. Thereafter, we would expect both bands to increase at approximately the same rate in future years. Hence, for married persons dying after 5th April 2020, preserving either part of the TNRB or an equivalent amount of the RNRB for transfer to their widow or widower can be expected to have broadly the same value in future.

However, the RNRB has a quite restricted application whereas the TNRB is generally available against any assets in the widow or widower's estate and is not tapered away for more valuable estates. Since the TNRB is far more flexible, it will therefore generally make sense to use the RNRB on the first spouse's death in preference to the NRB, wherever possible.

As we saw in Section 3.4, the RNRB is used in priority to the NRB where both are applicable to the same legacy, but sometimes the use of the RNRB will depend on what assets are being inherited, and by whom.

***Example:*** *David dies intestate (see Section 11.7) but had always said he would like to leave either his Cornish cottage or an equivalent amount in cash to his daughter, Angie, and the remainder of his estate to his wife, Iman.*

*The family are about to enter a deed of variation to put his wishes into effect and are uncertain whether to pass the Cornish cottage, worth £140,000, to Angie, or to give her the equivalent sum in cash. The cottage is eligible for the RNRB, so if this goes directly to Angie, only 20% of David's RNRB (£35,000/£175,000) will remain unused and will transfer to Iman. Alternatively, if Angie takes £140,000 in cash, this will use up part of David's NRB, leaving only 56.9% (£185,000/£325,000) to transfer to Iman.*

*Iman dies many years later, when the NRB stands at £434,000 and the RNRB is £235,000. She leaves an estate worth £2m, which includes one property eligible for the RNRB: Starman House, worth £300,000. Neither she nor David ever owned a private residence worth more than this, so the downsizing provisions (Section 13.11) are not relevant.*

***Scenario 1: Angie took the cottage; Iman leaves her Starman House:*** *Iman has a full TNRB entitlement, plus her own RNRB and 20% transferred from David. This gives her a total exemption of £1.15m (£434,000 x 2 + £235,000 + £235,000 x 20%). Her chargeable estate is thus reduced to £850,000, giving her an IHT bill of £340,000.*
***Scenario 2: Angie took the cash; Iman leaves her Starman House:*** *Iman is entitled to her own NRB plus a further 56.9% transferred from David. She has a potential entitlement to both her own RNRB and David's. These would total £470,000. However, Starman House is only worth £300,000, so that is as much RNRB as she is able to claim. Hence, Iman's total exemption is only £980,946 (£434,000 + £434,000 x 56.9% + £300,000). Her chargeable estate is thus £1,019,054, giving her an IHT bill of £407,622.*

As we can see, if Angie had taken cash on David's death, rather than using the RNRB by taking the cottage, this would ultimately cost Iman an additional £67,622 (£407,622 – £340,000). This is effectively the cost of the RNRB's rather restrictive nature when compared with the TNRB.

That cost would be the same if Iman left Starman House to any other direct descendant (see Section 3.4), but what if she wanted to leave it to someone else?

***Scenario 3: Angie took the cottage; Iman's sister inherits Starman House:*** *Iman has a full TNRB entitlement, but cannot claim any RNRB. Her total exemption is £868,000 (£434,000 x 2), giving her a chargeable estate of £1.132m and an IHT bill of £452,800.*
***Scenario 4: Angie took the cash; Iman's sister inherits Starman House:*** *Iman is entitled to her own NRB plus a further 56.9% transferred from David. She cannot claim any RNRB. Her total exemption is just £680,946 (£434,000 + £434,000 x 56.9%), giving her a chargeable estate of £1,319,054 and an IHT bill of £527,622.*

This time, the decision to allow Angie to take cash on David's death will ultimately cost Iman an additional £74,822 (£527,622 - £452,800).

In summary, it may often make sense to 'cash in' the RNRB on the first death, including cases where the surviving spouse may have an estate worth more than £2m on their death; may not own any private residence worth at least twice the RNRB; or may not wish, or not be able, to leave their private residence to a direct descendant.

## 6.4 NIL RATE BAND TRANSFERS IN PRACTICE

Applying the TNRB system in practice is fraught with problems. The first spouse may have died many years ago with a total estate that was clearly nowhere near the amount of the NRB. No-one will have given much thought to IHT at that time since it was clearly irrelevant.

Now, many years later, we will be faced with the prospect of attempting to ascertain how much of the NRB was used at that time. The first question is 'how much was the NRB?' Here, at least, HMRC has been helpful and has published the NRBs going back to 1914. These can be found at: www.gov.uk/government/publications/rates-and-allowances-inheritance-tax-thresholds-and-interest-rates

Where the first spouse died before 1986, they will have been subject to a different tax regime but the previous equivalent of the NRB is used for the purposes of calculating the TNRB. However, there is a particularly nasty problem for widows and widowers whose spouse died before March 1975. Under Estate Duty, there was no general exemption for transfers to spouses. For deaths between 21st March 1972 and 12th March 1975 there was a limited exemption of £15,000. Prior to that, there was no spouse exemption at all.

Hence, where the first spouse died before 13th March 1975, there may be little or no TNRB available even if the first spouse's entire estate passed to their widow or widower. The families of those who have been widows or widowers for a long time could be badly affected by this.

There will of course be some straightforward cases where the first spouse did not use any of their NRB. This will include cases where the first spouse:

- Died after 12th March 1975 and left their entire estate to their widow or widower,
- Left their entire estate to their widow or widower except for a private residence that was fully exempted by the RNRB (Section 3.4),
- Left everything to charity,
- Had nothing of any financial value, or
- Died on active service (see Section 3.8)

Remember, however, the first spouse may have used some of their NRB if they:

- Made transfers of value in the last seven years of their life (Section 4.5),
- Made any gifts with reservation (Section 4.8), or
- Elected to include an asset in their estate in order to prevent an Income Tax charge (Section 11.12)

***Example:*** *When Pete died in March 2006, he left everything to his civil partner, Roger. However, Pete had also given £96,250 to his friend Keith in 2002. The gift to Keith in 2002 became chargeable on Pete's death. This was not important at the time as Pete left his entire estate to his civil partner, but it meant Pete used £96,250, or 35% (£96,250/£275,000), of his NRB. Only 65% of Pete's NRB therefore transfers to Roger, or £211,250 at current rates.*

**Practical Problems**

The impact of even small gifts and legacies made by the first spouse could be quite significant. In practice, we may therefore see extensive queries from HMRC whenever a TNRB is claimed. In other words, whenever a widow or widower dies with an estate worth more than the NRB, we can expect to face detailed enquiries regarding the first spouse's estate and any transfers they may have made in the last seven years of their life. For married couples who are both still alive, it is therefore vital to keep accurate records of all transfers that take place.

**Planning Opportunities for Single People**

It is possible we may in future see more detailed provisions designed to restrict the TNRB and perhaps, in particular, to prevent separated couples from benefitting. This would reduce the attractiveness of some potential planning. In the meantime, however, there are some interesting planning ideas for people who are currently single.

As things stand, a surviving spouse will benefit from any unused NRB on the death of a spouse at any time, even many years before their own death. Once a person has a TNRB, they can remarry and preserve the benefit of their TNRB by following the planning strategies set out in Sections 6.9 to 6.11. Hence, a potential IHT planning measure is to marry someone with a much shorter life expectancy and very few assets, wait for them to die, and benefit from a TNRB that could ultimately save your family up to £130,000. Add in an extra RNRB as well and the savings could be up to £200,000.

## 6.5 REMARRIAGE

It is, of course, not unusual for a widow or widower to remarry. Furthermore, some people (particularly widows) go on to outlive two or more spouses. Sadly, however, a widow or widower can only be entitled to a maximum of one TNRB regardless of how many spouses they bury.

***Example:*** *In 1987, Liz married Eddie. He died in 1995 leaving Liz his entire estate. She remarried in 1998, to Richard, who died in 2001 and also left her his entire estate. Although Liz has survived two husbands, neither of whom used any of their NRB, she is only entitled to one TNRB. Liz herself dies in March 2024. Her personal representatives may therefore claim a NRB of £650,000, comprising her own NRB plus one TNRB.*

A widow or widower whose spouse used part of their NRB may, however, continue to accumulate further TNRB through remarriage until such point as they have accumulated a total of one additional NRB.

***Example:*** *Kurt died in 1991 when the NRB was £140,000, leaving a legacy of £70,000 to his cousin Dave and the remainder of his estate to his wife, Courtney. Courtney is thus entitled to a TNRB of 50% from Kurt.*

*In 1998, Courtney remarried to Michael. Sadly, in August 2023, Michael died, leaving a house worth £260,000 to his sister Kylie and the rest of his estate to Courtney. Kylie's legacy used up 80% of Michael's NRB so, this time, Courtney is only entitled to a TNRB of 20%.*

*Courtney can, however, add her two TNRBs together to give her a total 70% of TNRB. If she should die before 6th April 2028, her personal representatives could therefore claim a TNRB of £227,500 (£325,000 x 70%) in addition to her own NRB of £325,000.*

*If Courtney were to remarry again and subsequently be widowed a third time, she would be entitled to claim any unused NRB on the death of her third spouse up to a maximum of 30% (a further 30% would bring her up to a total of one TNRB).*

The key point is many widows and widowers will already have the maximum amount of TNRB when they remarry. We will look at the IHT planning consequences of this in Section 6.8.

### Taking the Residence Nil Rate Band into Account

Similar principles apply to ensure a widow or widower who remarries can only ever be entitled to a maximum of one additional RNRB. Those who outlive more than one spouse will again be able to accumulate additional proportionate amounts of RNRB until they reach an additional 100%.

At first glance, one might expect someone like Courtney, in our example above, to already be entitled to a full additional RNRB, since her first husband died before the exemption became available. However, it is important to remember, if his estate was worth in excess of £2m at the time of his death, tapering would apply and the proportion of RNRB passing to Courtney would be reduced (see Section 3.4 for more details).

## 6.6 SEPARATION & DIVORCE

As we saw in Section 3.3, for the purposes of the spouse exemption, a couple continue to be regarded as married for IHT purposes throughout any period of separation and right up until the granting of a decree absolute. As far as we know, it is reasonable to assume the same definition of marriage can be used in applying the TNRB system.

In other words, even if the couple were separated at the time of the first spouse's death, it appears the surviving spouse will still be entitled to claim any unused proportion of the first spouse's NRB or RNRB. This could save their family up to £200,000 at current rates.

However, the practical difficulty facing the surviving spouse will be ascertaining how much of the first spouse's NRB and RNRB is available to claim. This will make any tax planning more difficult. In some cases, where the couple have been separated for many years, the survivor may not even know their spouse has died!

One thing they will know, if they can at least ascertain that their late spouse died before 6th April 2017 with an estate not exceeding £2m, they will definitely be entitled to a full transferrable RNRB.

### Divorce

Divorce was always a costly business! Now, there is a further cost: the loss of the TNRBs. If the IHT definition of married continues to apply as set out in Section 3.3 a separated couple will both continue to have the potential to claim any part of their estranged spouse's NRB or RNRB that is unused on the spouse's death.

If the couple divorce the TNRBs will no longer be available to either of them. Hence, for IHT purposes, it makes sense for separated couples to stay married. If your ex is not that well off when they die, you may benefit!

In many cases, it is the couple's children who will ultimately benefit from any TNRB or RNRB, which provides even more incentive to stay married. If you do decide to divorce, however, there are some useful IHT planning opportunities available at that time.

### Inheritance Tax Planning on Separation and Divorce

As we saw in Section 5.6, transfers not intended to confer a gratuitous benefit are exempt from IHT. This provides the opportunity to put property into trust as part of a formal, legal divorce or separation agreement without creating a chargeable lifetime transfer. Not only is this probably preferable from a practical perspective (e.g. the ex-spouse's interest can be terminated in the event of their re-marrying), it also means the property will not fall into the ex-spouse's estate and can later pass to the children without a 40% charge on the ex-spouse's death.

While the property can pass into the trust free from IHT under this exemption, anniversary and exit charges may still apply (see Chapter 8). Nevertheless, on balance, the technique will often be beneficial overall.

Note that exemption from IHT does not necessarily mean a transfer of property is exempt from other taxes. In particular, it is not possible to hold over capital gains arising on a transfer into a trust for the benefit of your own minor children (see Section 9.4). However, a proposed new exemption for transfers on divorce or separation currently going through Parliament will mean a transfer of the whole or a part share in the formal marital home may be exempt from CGT under these circumstances: see Section 12.6 for details.

## 6.7 INHERITANCE TAX PLANNING FOR MARRIED COUPLES

When the TNRB was introduced in 2007, it completely changed the IHT planning landscape for married couples. Before then, the first step was always to ensure the first spouse to die would use their NRB effectively. Now, in most cases, this is no longer necessary, as any unused NRB will transfer to the surviving spouse. In fact, there is a case for saying the best planning now is to ensure none of the NRB is used on the first spouse's death.

The important point to remember is the surviving spouse is able to claim whatever ***proportion*** of the NRB is unused on the first spouse's death. The ***amount*** of that claim will depend on the amount of the NRB at the time of the widow or widower's death. This means some former IHT planning techniques may sometimes have a disadvantageous effect.

***Example:*** *John and Dee were a married couple. Some years ago, they took professional advice on their IHT position. Following this advice, they amended their Wills to implement a 'Widow's Loan Scheme' (Section 6.11) when the first of them died. The effect of the scheme was to ensure the first of them to die would utilise their NRB. The survivor would then be able to deduct an amount equal to that NRB from their estate. This was good planning at the time since, as things stood, this was likely to save John and Dee's family over £100,000 in IHT.*

*John died in 2005 when the NRB was £275,000 and the Widow's Loan Scheme was put into action. A sum of £275,000 was left to a discretionary trust. Dee inherited the remainder of John's estate and, following one of the mechanisms explained in Section 6.11, was left owing a sum of £275,000 to the discretionary trust.*

*At this point everything seemed fine. Dee still had her own NRB and would also be able to deduct her debt of £275,000 from her estate. In effect, to begin with, this was the same as having a TNRB.*

*However, once the actual TNRB system was introduced in 2007, Dee was put at a disadvantage. While the NRB went on to be increased to £325,000, the value of her debt to the discretionary trust remained just £275,000. Already the obsolete planning implemented in 2005 is going to cost her family an extra £20,000 in IHT (£50,000 x 40%), but things may get even worse.*

*Dee lives on for many years, through many changes of Government and much political manoeuvring and eventually dies when the NRB is £1.5m. On her death, Dee's NRB and her debt to the discretionary trust add up to £1.775m of effective exemption (provided the debt is settled out of the assets of her estate: see Section 2.10).*

*If John had not implemented the Widow's Loan Scheme, however, his NRB would have been unused and would have transferred to Dee. On Dee's death, her personal representatives would have been able to claim a TNRB of £1.5m in addition to her own NRB, giving her estate total effective IHT exemption of £3m.*

In this example, the earlier planning has resulted in the loss of £1.225m worth of IHT exemption for Dee's family. This would cost the family up to £490,000 in extra IHT at today's rates. The reason for this is the fact the NRB increased by £1.225m during the period between John and Dee's deaths.

This gives us the general principle that a married couple's family will lose out to the extent of:

- The proportion of the NRB used on the first spouse's death TIMES
- The increase in the NRB between the first spouse's death and the second spouse's death TIMES
- The rate of IHT at the time of the second spouse's death

**What Does This Mean for IHT Planning for Married Couples?**

Using any of the NRB on the first spouse's death may potentially have a detrimental effect on the second spouse's death. The first spouse may use part of their NRB through any of the following:

- Legacies to anyone other than their spouse or one of the exempt bodies in Section 3.5
- Chargeable lifetime transfers in the last seven years of their life
- PETs in the last seven years of their life
- Gifts with reservation (Section 4.8)
- An election to include an asset in their estate in order to prevent an Income Tax charge (Section 11.12)

Any of the above now put some or all of any married person's NRB in jeopardy and may have a detrimental effect on their spouse's IHT position.

This means any transfer of value by a married person that does not enjoy immediate complete exemption carries an element of risk. This is particularly relevant to PETs, as well as chargeable lifetime transfers covered by the transferor's NRB (see Chapter 4 for further details).

Before 2007, it was fair to say such lifetime transfers could be made with an attitude of 'there's nothing to lose'. If you survived seven years, there was no problem, if you survived three, there might be some benefit and, if you died sooner, the position was probably no worse than it would have been anyway.

But now every lifetime transfer by a married person not covered by one of the absolute exemptions set out in Chapter 5 puts their spouse's TNRB at risk.

***Example:*** *In January 2018, Richard gave his son Zak a gift of £65,000. This was a PET as Richard had already used up any other available exemptions. Sadly, Richard dies in March 2024 and leaves his entire estate to his wife Barbara. The earlier gift to Zak becomes chargeable and uses up 20% of Richard's NRB. This means Barbara receives a TNRB of only 80%. Whatever the NRB may be when Barbara dies, she will lose out on 20% of it because of Richard's gift to Zak.*

At this point, it is tempting to suggest married people should avoid making any lifetime transfers not covered by an immediate exemption. This is not the case; it only means many such transfers now carry a degree of risk that they might actually make the position worse.

On the other hand, lifetime transfers by married people will often still be beneficial, such as when the transferor survives at least seven years; the transferor's spouse already has a TNRB from a previous marriage (see Section 6.5); or the assets grow in value faster than the increase in the NRB.

***Example Revisited:*** *Let us suppose the gift from Richard to Zak in our previous example comprised quoted shares worth £65,000. Let's also suppose these shares increase in value at an average compound rate of 5% per year until Barbara's death in early 2038. This means Zak's shares will be worth £172,500 at the time of Barbara's death.*

*If the shares had not been transferred to Zak, they would still have been in Barbara's estate and would thus increase her IHT liability. Instead, the gift to Zak means the shares are not in Barbara's estate, but she loses 20% of the TNRB. Hence, if the NRB for 2037/38 is less than £862,500 (£862,500 x 20% = £172,500), the family will be better off overall because of Richard's original gift to Zak.*

**It may still be worthwhile for a married person to use part of their NRB on the transfer of funds or assets that will grow in value faster than the rate at which the NRB increases.**

Following this principle in practice may be difficult, as it involves a good deal of 'crystal ball gazing'. Will a future Government increase the NRB significantly at some stage? Will the current freeze be extended for even longer? Will we be stuck with simple inflationary increases for many years after 2028? No-one can say.

For a lifetime transfer, there is the added bonus that any growth in the value of the transferred asset up to the point of the transferor's death is effectively free of any IHT cost. In our example, for instance, it was the value of the shares when they were transferred in 2018 that was used to calculate the restriction in Barbara's TNRB, not their value at the date of Richard's death (which may have been around £87,000 at our forecast growth rate).

Furthermore, the freeze in the NRB until 2028 provides the transferred asset with a significant head start. At a 5% annual growth rate, assets transferred now could be worth over 27% more before we even begin to see any increase in the NRB.

**Planning On the First Death**

At this point, it seems reasonable to say most married couples will be better off if they **do not** use any of the planning techniques previously designed to utilise the first spouse's NRB without actually passing any wealth to other beneficiaries at that time.

We saw an example of the detrimental effect such planning could have in John and Dee's case above. The planning techniques set out in Sections 6.9 to 6.11 are therefore no longer beneficial for most married couples.

The position may differ where one or both of the couple have remarried following the death of a previous spouse. We will look at planning for these couples in Section 6.8. It is mainly for the benefit of these couples that the techniques set out in Sections 6.9 to 6.11 are still included in this guide.

Those couples aside, any other married couple should now generally avoid using any scheme that simply uses up the first spouse's NRB without actually passing any assets or funds to other family members.

What is less certain is whether it is worth using the first spouse's NRB on genuine legacies to other family members. Here we must go back to the principle set out above, i.e. such legacies may be worthwhile if they consist of funds or assets that will grow faster than the rate at which the NRB increases.

In the case of a legacy, however, the proportion of TNRB lost will be based on the value of the relevant asset at the date of the first spouse's death. This means the growth rate must be greater than in the case of a lifetime transfer before the legacy is worthwhile for IHT purposes.

Remember also that the reduction in the surviving spouse's TNRB caused by a legacy to another beneficiary is permanent. A gift of the same asset from the surviving spouse to another person would instead be a PET and would be exempt if that spouse survives another seven years.

In many cases, therefore, and especially where the survivor still has a long life expectancy, it may be preferable to avoid legacies to other beneficiaries. Subject to the comments below, the family will often achieve a better overall result if the surviving spouse makes lifetime transfers instead.

**Passing on Wealth Tax Efficiently**

Of course, it's all very well me telling you not to give your children (or other beneficiaries) anything unless they are going to invest it at better rates of growth than the NRB, but what if they need money now, or you simply want to help them out?

In most cases, you will probably give them money during your lifetime and this will be a PET. As we know, this will lead to a reduction in the TNRB if the person making the PET dies within seven years.

You will therefore reduce the risk of a reduction in the TNRB if the spouse with the longer life expectancy makes the PET. This is not foolproof, but it improves your chances.

Remember, you can pass wealth to your spouse first free from any IHT risk and they can then make the PET if they choose to do so. However, you cannot make it a pre-condition of a gift to your spouse that they will pass that gift on to another person. If any such condition existed, the first gift is ignored and you will be treated as having made the gift directly to the ultimate recipient, meaning you will have made the PET.

Alternatively, you may wish to pass some wealth to someone other than your spouse when you die. As we have already discussed, a direct legacy has the drawback of causing a permanent reduction in the amount of TNRB that can ultimately be claimed against your spouse's estate.

You may therefore wish to consider passing the wealth to your spouse and leaving it in their hands to decide what to do. This would enable the surviving spouse to make appropriate gifts as PETs. If the survivor lives another seven years, these will be exempt from IHT and the full TNRB will be available against the rest of their estate.

As with a lifetime transfer, it is imperative there is no prior agreement that your spouse will pass the assets or funds to another person. You **must** leave the decision entirely in their hands. This point is crucial, and is explored in Section 6.12, where we will also see it is often wise for the surviving spouse to wait at least two years and a day after the first spouse's death before making any transfers of assets or funds inherited from their late spouse.

Another way you can help your children (or anyone else) without putting your spouse's TNRB at risk is to make loans instead of gifts. A loan does not represent a transfer of value, so there is no impact on your NRB if you should die within seven years: although, of course, the value of the loan remains in your estate.

The loan can be unsecured and interest free, but it is wise to document it. If it should later turn out that you are the surviving spouse, you can, if you wish, simply waive the debt, thus turning the loan into a gift at that stage. As long as you survive seven years after the waiver, the value of the original loan will escape IHT on your death. As with the loan itself, it is important to document the waiver.

## 6.8 THE SECOND TIME AROUND

Where one or both of a married couple have remarried following the death of an earlier spouse, the position may be different to that outlined in the previous section. This is because one or both of them may already have a TNRB entitlement.

If, however, the whole of the previous spouse's NRB was used on their death then the current married couple will be in the same position as a 'first time' couple and should go back to Section 6.7 for guidance on their IHT planning position.

This, for example, may apply to someone like Dee (see the first example in Section 6.7) and any future spouse she may have. As you may recall, Dee's late husband carried out some IHT planning which, while it made sense at the time, has now proved disadvantageous. This will be a common scenario for individuals who were widowed before October 2007 and subsequently remarry.

**Existing Transferable Nil Rate Band Entitlement**

Leaving such cases to one side, let's now focus on those who already have some entitlement to a TNRB. As explained in Section 6.5, a widow or widower cannot claim more than one additional NRB. This, in turn, means we are back in the position where some or all of the NRB of the first spouse in the current couple to die will effectively go to waste unless we undertake some appropriate planning. Let me explain this further with an example.

***Example:*** *When George died a few years ago, he left a sum equal to half the NRB to his son Ravi and the rest of his estate to his wife Patti. Patti is therefore already entitled to claim an additional 50% TNRB or £162,500 at current rates. Patti is now married to Eric (who has never married before). At the moment, Eric and Patti's Wills both leave everything to each other.*

*If Patti dies first, her NRB will go unused and will transfer to Eric. The additional half NRB that transferred from George to Patti will go to waste. If Eric dies first, his NRB will go unused and will be available to transfer to Patti. However, as Patti already has half a TNRB, she will only be able to claim half of Eric's unused NRB and the other half will go to waste. Either way, whether Eric or Patti dies first, half a NRB will go to waste!*

As we can see, where one of a couple already has an entitlement to part of a previous spouse's unused NRB, that entitlement will go to waste if the couple do not plan effectively.

Where the previous spouse's NRB was completely unused, that whole NRB may potentially go to waste. At current rates, that amounts to £130,000 worth of wasted tax relief.

Whatever amount of TNRB is already available the current couple will achieve the best result by ensuring the same proportion of NRB is used on the first of their deaths. We will look at how this is done in the next few sections.

**Double Second-Timers**

Where both of the current couple already have some entitlement to a TNRB, the amount potentially going to waste on the first death will be the sum of their existing entitlements. Preserving both existing entitlements in this case will necessitate the first spouse to die using all their existing TNRB plus all or part of their own NRB.

***Example:*** *Buddy died some years ago and used 25% of his NRB. His widow, Holly, later remarried to Waylon, who was a widower himself. Waylon's previous wife Jenny had used 60% of her NRB when she died. As things stand, Holly is entitled to a 75% TNRB and Waylon is entitled to a 40% TNRB. The couple's existing entitlements total 115% and this is how much will go to waste without effective planning.*

*Holly and Waylon therefore both draw up Wills to put a Widow's Loan Scheme into effect on their death that will utilise 115% of the value of the NRB at that time. (I am assuming each of them has enough wealth to do this.)*

*If Holly dies first, the Widow's Loan Scheme will use up all her existing TNRB entitlement, plus 40% of her own NRB, leaving a further 60% TNRB entitlement to transfer to Waylon. If Waylon dies first, the Widow's Loan Scheme will use up all his existing TNRB entitlement, plus 75% of his own NRB, leaving a further 25% TNRB entitlement to transfer to Holly. Either way, the survivor will end up with a full TNRB entitlement and none of the couple's existing entitlement will have gone to waste.*

In the case of a couple who both have an existing entitlement to a full TNRB, the amount of additional relief that can be preserved in this way will be equal to double the NRB. At current rates, this amounts to £260,000 worth of tax relief.

Before we look at how to use an existing TNRB entitlement effectively, it is worth pausing to consider whether we think it is worth the effort. Most married couples now only have a potential exposure to IHT when their combined total wealth exceeds £650,000. In some cases, where there is a suitable qualifying property and the couple intend to leave it, or its eventual sale proceeds, to their children, the potential exposure will only be on wealth in excess of £1m (due to the RNRB: see Section 3.4).

The planning we are now considering is designed to increase the point at which the couple's IHT exposure begins to an even greater level, often as much as £975,000 or even £1.3m: PLUS whatever further exemption they can achieve with the RNRB.

Whether this is worthwhile really depends on how large an estate you anticipate the second spouse having at the time of their death. I can only leave you to judge that, but I will give you an example to think about first.

***Example:*** *Aaliyah and Marsha are a married couple who have both been married before and both already have an existing entitlement to a full TNRB. When Marsha dies in December 2023, Aaliyah is advised there is no need to carry out any IHT planning since the property she has just inherited is worth £650,000 and is therefore covered by her NRB plus her existing TNRB entitlement.*

*However, between 2023 and Aaliyah's death in March 2034, property prices triple. [This is the same as the increase that occurred during the period of equal length, from June 1997 to September 2007, so this is entirely possible!]*

*When Aaliyah dies, her property is worth £1.95m, but the NRB is just £381,000 and the RNRB is £205,000 (see Sections 3.2 and 3.4 respectively). Even after claiming her two TNRBs, this leaves £778,000 (£1.95m – 2 x £381,000 – 2 x £205,000) of Aaliyah's estate exposed to IHT, costing her family £311,200.*

*Worse still, if Aaliyah has no direct descendants to pass her property to (not everyone does, Mr Osborne!), then £1.188m (£1.95m – 2 x £381,000) of her estate will be exposed to IHT, robbing her beneficiaries of £475,200 of their rightful inheritance. If only they had done some planning when Marsha died!*

Why a nephew, niece, lifelong friend, or step-child from an unmarried partnership should suffer an extra £164,000 in IHT defies all understanding!

## 6.9 USING THE TRANSFERABLE NIL RATE BAND

As explained in the previous section, many 'second time around' couples will benefit from using all or part of the first spouse's NRB plus, in some cases, their existing entitlement to a TNRB. The amount of additional relief generated in this way may be up to double the NRB, producing savings of up to £260,000 at current rates.

***Example:*** *Thomas died in March 2024, leaving his net estate worth £3m to his brother, Arthur (who is also Thomas's executor). Thomas was a widower who had survived two wives: Alice who died in 2005, without using any of her NRB, and Doris, who died in November 2023.*

*After claiming the TNRB to which Thomas was entitled, as well as Thomas's own NRB, Arthur is left to bear IHT at 40% on £2.35m (£3m – 2 x £325,000), i.e. £940,000.*

*However, within Thomas's estate there was a property worth £650,000 that he had inherited from his second wife, Doris. Doris herself had been entitled to a TNRB as a result of a previous marriage to Tony, who had died some years ago without using any of his NRB.*

*Since Doris left the property to her husband and it was exempt anyway, both her NRB and her TNRB (from Tony) were never used. What Doris should have done was leave her property to Arthur. No IHT would have been payable on her death, as her property was covered by the sum of her NRB and her TNRB entitlement.*

*But when Thomas died later, his estate would have been worth £650,000 less, i.e. £2.35m. After deducting Thomas's NRB and TNRB entitlement, Arthur would have had to pay IHT at 40% on just £1.7m. Arthur's IHT bill would thus have been £680,000, giving him a saving of £260,000. In effect, Arthur would have benefited from four NRBs instead of just two!*

The non-spousal legacy (e.g. the one from Doris to Arthur in the above example) does not need to be one specific property. It could be a whole group of assets, or simply worded as a legacy equal to the appropriate multiple of the NRB to be paid out of the general assets of the estate.

**What if You're Not That Well Off?**
The non-spousal legacy strategy is pretty simple to follow when, like Thomas and Doris above, there are plenty of assets around. The problem for some second time around married couples is they can't afford to simply give their children, or other beneficiaries, up to £650,000 when one of them dies.

The surviving spouse will need to retain sufficient assets to support them for the rest of their life including, in most cases, the family home. As we shall see, there are some planning strategies available to deal with this dilemma.

**Too Much of a Good Thing?**
When including a non-spousal legacy or any other technique designed to use all or part of your NRB, in your Will, it is usually best not to word the legacy as a specific sum.

What you may wish to do instead is draft your Will so it includes a legacy equal to the appropriate proportion of whatever the NRB happens to be at the time of your death. That way, the amount of the legacy will automatically adjust in line with the NRB (when the happy day does ***finally*** come at last that the NRB starts to increase again!)

This may have some practical drawbacks, however. If a future Government were to drastically increase the value of the NRB, this strategy could cause some practical problems for your family.

'What's the problem,' you say: after all, you can just amend your Will if that happens. Probably, yes, and if you keep the situation under review you will be able to do this. But what happens if you no longer have legal capacity (see Section 17.16) at that time? To guard against this possibility, you may also wish to place a cap on the maximum value of the legacy.

**What about the Residence Nil Rate Band?**
You will also need to factor the RNRB into your planning. It is likely that anyone with an existing TNRB entitlement will also have an entitlement to their former spouse's RNRB: although this will not always be the case, for the reasons we explored in Sections 3.4 and 6.3. Nonetheless, where one or both of the current spouses have an existing entitlement to a previous deceased spouse's unused RNRB, this may provide scope for some further savings.

***Example Revisited:*** *Let's take the same facts as before, except we will say Arthur was Thomas's son rather than his brother, and the property Doris initially left to Thomas was worth £1m and was a qualifying property for RNRB purposes. Let us also say Doris, Alice, and Tony all died with estates worth less than £2m.*

*None of this would alter Arthur's IHT bill of £940,000 if Doris had left her entire estate to Thomas. However, if Doris had left her property worth £1m to Arthur (instead of Thomas), it would have been fully exempted by her own NRB, her TNRB (from Tony), her RNRB and the RNRB transferred from Tony (£325,000 x 2 + £175,000 x 2 = £1m).*

*Thomas's estate would now be worth £2m, meaning he would be entitled to his own RNRB and the one transferred to him from his first wife, Alice. If his estate included a qualifying property worth at least £350,000, or the sale proceeds from such a property (see Sections 3.4 and 13.11), this would provide a further exemption of £350,000, leaving him exposed to IHT on just £1m (£2m – £325,000 x 2 – £350,000) and giving Arthur an IHT liability of just £400,000.*

In conclusion, a non-spousal legacy on the first death in a second time around couple could produce savings of up to £540,000!

**If Only We'd Known About This Before!**
Don't despair if you think you've left it too late. Any of the methods described in this guide that are available to utilise a TNRB or a former spouse's RNRB can be put in place through a deed of variation made within two years of the relevant spouse's death. See Section 18.1 for further details.

**Estate Equalisation**
One thing you cannot do, even with a deed of variation, is put money into the hands of the deceased!

For a second time around married couple with some existing TNRB entitlement, it is therefore important to ensure both spouses have sufficient net assets in their own right to utilise the appropriate proportion of the NRB on their death (plus the RNRB where appropriate).

## 6.10 WILL TRUSTS

One method for using an existing TNRB is to set up a discretionary trust through your Will (see Chapter 8 for an explanation of discretionary trusts).

Assets with a value equal to the appropriate proportion of the NRB (which will otherwise go to waste: see Section 6.8), are left to the trust. The surviving spouse will be one of the beneficiaries of the trust and, in practice, can retain all the benefits of ownership of the assets within the trust. This can be achieved by ensuring the trustees exercise their discretion in such a way that the surviving spouse receives the income from, and enjoyment of, the assets.

There is, however, a danger HMRC may attack this type of discretionary trust on the basis it is really a de facto interest in possession trust. This would mean the trust constituted an 'immediate post-death interest' (see Section 8.12). This, in turn, would mean the assets of the trust remain in the surviving spouse's estate for IHT purposes, thus rendering this planning void.

Nevertheless, this type of Will trust should still work where the trust is genuinely discretionary in nature. This would necessitate avoiding the usual letter of instruction to the trustees stating the surviving spouse is to receive all income from the trust. It would also be wise to ensure other beneficiaries did, indeed, receive some trust income.

This method cannot be used to utilise a transferred RNRB. It is also generally unsuitable for IHT planning with the family home, although we will see some variations that may be suitable in Chapter 13.

Some standard 'off the shelf' Will trusts will give rise to an interest in possession and are thus of no use for this type of planning. This can even apply to standard Will trusts provided by some quite reputable organisations. As usual, this just goes to show there is no substitute for taking proper professional advice.

## 6.11 THE WIDOW'S LOAN SCHEME

Another method for utilising an existing TNRB is to leave a specific legacy of a sum equal to the appropriate proportion of the NRB (see Section 6.8) to a discretionary trust in your Will and the remainder of your estate (or most of it) to your spouse. Your spouse would be a beneficiary of the trust, together with other family members (usually).

There are a number of variations to this method but, in essence, the basic principle is that all (or most) of the deceased's assets are passed to the surviving spouse who therefore ends up owing a sum equal to the appropriate proportion of the NRB to the trust.

The 'charge scheme' is one such variation and, unlike the simple Will Trust (Section 6.10), it is well suited to IHT planning with the family home. Under this scheme, the trust initially takes possession of the deceased's share of the family home and then takes a charge over it for a sum equal to the required proportion of the NRB. The deceased's share of the property is then passed to the surviving spouse subject to the charge.

When the surviving spouse subsequently dies, the amount of this charge is deductible from their estate (subject to the points below regarding payment of the debt), thus effectively providing relief for the TNRB that would otherwise have gone to waste (see Section 6.8).

Some experts suggest that where the charge scheme is being used, the surviving spouse should not be an executor of the deceased's estate. It is not absolutely clear if this would actually be a problem, but it is wise to play it safe in these matters.

The so-called 'debt scheme' is a simpler variation of the Widow's Loan Scheme, but has some technical problems that can lead to difficulties if the main bread-winner turns out to be the survivor.

Another variation that appears to avoid such technical problems is to leave the appropriate proportion of the NRB to a discretionary trust and leave the remainder of your estate to an interest in possession trust for the benefit of your spouse, rather than to your spouse directly.

As explained in Section 8.12, the interest in possession trust is entitled to the spouse exemption, but will be left owing the appropriate sum (which you need in order to utilise the existing TNRB) to the discretionary trust.

Once again, the debt due to the discretionary trust will be deductible from the surviving spouse's estate on their subsequent death (subject to the points below regarding payment of the debt).

There is a school of thought that it may be necessary for the discretionary trust to charge interest on the loan to make the Widow's Loan Scheme effective. Although some interest charged could be passed back to the surviving spouse (as a trust beneficiary), this would still lead to an Income Tax cost (see Section 8.20).

**Payment of the Debt**
In most cases, it will be essential that the debt due to the discretionary trust is actually repaid out of the assets of the surviving spouse's estate (see Section 2.10). Where an interest in possession trust is used (as described above) the debt will need to be repaid from the assets of that trust.

In many cases, this will be easy to achieve by simply selling some or all of the assets of the estate (or the interest in possession trust, as the case may be) and making a suitable cash payment to the discretionary trust. In other cases, one of the alternative techniques outlined in Section 2.10 may be used instead.

As discussed in Section 2.10, there may also be cases where the debt is structured on a sufficiently commercial basis that it can be left outstanding. This would generally require, as a bare minimum, that:

- The loan is subject to interest at a commercial rate
- The interest is actually paid to the discretionary trust (see Section 8.20 regarding the Income Tax consequences of this)
- The loan is secured
- The loan is taken over by a person or persons who do not pose a greater risk than an arms' length lender would generally be willing to accept

Whichever variation is followed, the Widow's Loan Scheme cannot be used to utilise a transferred RNRB. It is a complex scheme, so professional advice is essential. Despite its name though, it does work equally well in principle for a widower.

## 6.12 THE SPOUSE BRIDGE

A spouse with a longer life expectancy can be used as a 'bridge' to transfer assets to children or other beneficiaries.

Assets are transferred to the spouse either during lifetime or on death and this transfer is exempt from IHT (subject to the points in Section 3.3). The spouse can then transfer the assets to the children as a PET (Section 4.3) and, as long as the spouse survives for seven years after that transfer, IHT is avoided.

In theory, any spouse will do for this strategy, including an estranged spouse who the transferor has not yet divorced, or a spouse who is not a parent of the children who are ultimately supposed to benefit.

***Example:*** *Tremela divorced her ex-husband many years ago and has single-handedly managed to raise her daughter, Alisha, as well as building up a large portfolio of investment properties. Tragically, Tremela has found out she has only a short time to live and wishes to leave everything she owns to Alisha, who is now a young adult.*

*Tremela has been friends with Brian for many years and now decides to marry him. When Tremela dies a short time later, she leaves £325,000 to Alisha but leaves the rest of her estate to Brian. No IHT is due as everything is covered by either the NRB or the spouse exemption. Brian can then give Alisha all the property received from Tremela and, as long as he survives seven years, IHT will be avoided.*

To date, HMRC has not had any success in challenging the validity of a marriage, but there are still a few potential problems with this strategy. Firstly, PETs of anything other than cash may give rise to CGT liabilities. However, transfers of recently inherited assets should not usually give rise to significant CGT liabilities due to the 'uplift on death' (see Section 12.2).

Secondly, where there is an informal request asking the beneficiary under a Will to transfer inherited property to another person and the beneficiary does indeed make the transfer within two years of the deceased's death, the transfer is treated as a direct transfer from the deceased to that other person.

This particular provision can be side-stepped by either making a lifetime transfer to the spouse (but see further below) or by the spouse waiting two years and a day after the deceased's death before passing the assets to the ultimate recipient. While the latter approach may mean suffering some CGT on the capital growth in the assets' values, this cost is likely to be considerably less than the IHT at risk.

Thirdly, and perhaps more importantly, there is the question of whether the transferee spouse will behave as the transferor hopes. They cannot be forced to pass the assets to the children, or the initial transfer will be ignored.

Preliminary transfers to a spouse are a perfectly good way to avoid or reduce IHT liabilities, as long as there is no obligation on the transferee spouse to make the subsequent transfer to the ultimate recipient. If, however, the arrangement for the second transfer is already in place, the initial transfer to the spouse would be disregarded and the position would revert to that given by a single transfer direct from the transferor spouse to the ultimate recipient.

A similar method that might be used to pass assets to a minor child is set out in Section 9.7.

**Further Hazards for Lifetime Transfers to Spouses**

Where the initial transfer to the spouse is a lifetime transfer then, even with no fixed arrangements for the assets to be passed to the children, there is still some risk HMRC might invoke the associated operations rules (Section 11.11).

That initial transfer would then again be ignored, resulting in the loss of the spouse exemption. How anyone could do this in the face of such a terrible tragedy as Tremela's premature death escapes me, but that is the nature of IHT!

In the more usual case of a married couple still living together at the time of the initial transfer, this risk is greatly reduced, as HMRC does not usually attack arrangements between married couples still living together.

In the case of a separated couple, or a marriage of convenience like Tremela and Brian, the risk of such an attack is greater, but may possibly be avoided if the transferee retains the assets for a few years before passing them to the ultimate recipient.

Finally, it is important to remember a lifetime transfer to a spouse means foregoing the 'uplift on death' for CGT purposes (see Section 12.2), so it will often be inappropriate for investment property and other appreciating assets. Furthermore, separated spouses only enjoy the CGT exemption for transfers between them for a limited period: see Section 12.6 for details.

## 6.13 THE FAMILY DEBT SCHEME

A sale of an investment asset to your spouse can be used as a means to reduce the value of your estate for IHT purposes without increasing the value of theirs to the same extent.

The asset, such as an investment property, is sold to the spouse for any price up to its full market value. Although the transfer is not a gift, the sale still represents a transfer between spouses and is exempt from both IHT and CGT.

Some form of Stamp Duty will be payable in many cases, however, and the rates involved can sometimes be quite prohibitive (see the Taxcafe guide *How to Save Property Tax*). Nonetheless, SDLT can currently be avoided (until 31st March 2025) on residential property sold to a spouse for a consideration not exceeding £250,000. In the case of non-residential property, there is no SDLT due where the consideration does not exceed £150,000.

If you sell shares to your spouse, Stamp Duty will be payable on the sale consideration at the rate of 0.5%.

The sale consideration is left outstanding as a loan; or an 'IOU' if you like. The vendor spouse then gives the 'IOU' to their children or other intended beneficiaries. This is a PET, meaning the value of the 'IOU' will be exempt from IHT if the vendor spouse survives seven years. This provides the reduction in the vendor spouse's estate since they no longer hold either the original asset or the 'IOU'.

On the purchasing spouse's death, the value of the 'IOU' will be deducted from their estate: ***provided*** the sum due under the 'IOU' is actually paid out of the assets of their estate (see Section 2.10). This will cancel out some or all of the value of the transferred property.

This method is generally used for investment assets not qualifying for business property relief (see Chapter 7), including rental property. The debt does not fall foul of the artificially created debt rules (Section 2.10) since there is an actual sale of property from one spouse to the other and the debt is owed by the purchaser.

## 6.14 MARRIED COUPLES WITH MIXED DOMICILE

In Section 16.3, we will see how a non-UK domiciled person acquires deemed UK domicile when they have been resident in the UK for 15 or more years. However, they lose their deemed UK domicile once they commence a fourth consecutive tax year of non-UK residence. This opens up some interesting planning ideas for married couples with mixed domicile.

***Example:*** *Jim is UK domiciled but has significant foreign assets. His husband Farrokh is domiciled in Zanzibar but has lived in the UK for over 20 years and therefore has deemed UK domicile for tax purposes.*

*Jim can transfer all his foreign assets to Farrokh and this transfer will be fully exempt from IHT. Farrokh could then leave the UK and would automatically lose his deemed UK domicile at the beginning of his fourth tax year of non-UK residence. All of Jim's foreign assets, now held by Farrokh, would then be free from UK IHT.*

"Couldn't Jim achieve the same result by emigrating himself?" you may ask. Yes, he could, but, as we shall see in Chapter 16, it would be much harder for him to shed his UK domicile whereas, for Farrokh, it will be automatic.

This strategy is effective for IHT purposes, but may not be for CGT. While the transfer itself will be free from CGT, Jim would be subject to CGT on a future sale of the assets if Farrokh was still UK resident at the time of the transfer and Jim is UK resident at the time of the sale. One way around this might be to make the transfer after Farrokh has ceased to be UK resident but before the end of the period he continues to have deemed UK domicile.

There may also be foreign tax implications arising on the transfer, and it is vital these are taken into account.

## 6.15 THE OPT-IN ELECTION

A non-UK domiciled individual with a UK domiciled spouse may elect to 'opt-in' and be treated as UK domiciled for IHT purposes. A non-UK domiciled widow or widower who had a recently deceased UK domiciled spouse may also make an election.

Where the UK domiciled spouse is still alive, the election may be backdated by up to seven years; where the UK domiciled spouse is deceased, the election must be made within two years of their death and may be backdated by up to seven years prior to that date.

The person making the election must be non-UK domiciled under general principles but they are not barred from making it if they have deemed UK domicile (Section 16.3).

Where both spouses are deceased, the personal representatives of the non-UK domiciled spouse may make the election on their behalf (subject to the time limits described above).

**Impact of Election**

The effect of the opt-in election is that the non-UK domiciled spouse is treated as UK domiciled for IHT purposes with effect from whichever date the election is specified to apply from (subject to the limits described above).

The election is irrevocable and hence will apply for the remainder of the electing spouse's lifetime and on their death: unless they become non-UK resident for a period of four consecutive tax years, in which case the election automatically ceases to apply.

While the election generally means the non-UK domiciled spouse is treated as UK domiciled for IHT purposes, there are a few exceptions:

- Government securities and other UK assets with excluded property status (see Section 3.7), will retain that status
- The provisions of any applicable Double Tax Treaty (see Section 16.1) are unaffected
- Double tax relief will continue to be available where the person is also subject to IHT (or a similar tax) in another country

The election does not alter the non-UK domiciled spouse's status for the purposes of Income Tax or CGT.

**Advantages of Making the Election**

- Complete exemption from IHT on all transfers from the UK domiciled spouse to the non-UK domiciled spouse during lifetime (from the date on which the election becomes effective) and on death
- The ability to use an unlimited spouse exemption to transfer assets into an immediate post-death interest trust free from IHT (Section 8.12)
- The ability to obtain a full TNRB on the UK domiciled spouse's death (where the entire estate is left to the non-UK domiciled spouse)
- Other exemptions, such as the annual exemption (Section 5.2) will not be used up by lifetime transfers to the non-UK domiciled spouse after the election becomes effective
- The ability to carry out planning mechanisms available to UK domiciled spouses (e.g. the spouse bridge in Section 6.12)
- Unlimited exemption from the gifts with reservation rules (Section 4.8) on transfers between spouses after the election becomes effective

**Disadvantages of Making the Election**

- The non-UK domiciled spouse's entire worldwide estate will be subject to UK IHT (subject to the terms of any Double Tax Treaty)
- Transfers of assets, including foreign assets, by the non-UK domiciled spouse to anyone other than the UK domiciled spouse may potentially use part of the non-UK domiciled spouse's NRB and reduce the TNRB available
- The non-UK domiciled spouse would be unable to use an excluded property trust (see Section 9.10) to shelter assets they held on or after the date the election becomes effective. They could, however, set up an excluded property trust before the election becomes effective. In this case, it is vital to ensure the election is not backdated prior to the date assets are transferred into the trust.
- The pre-owned assets charge (Section 11.12) may apply to foreign assets enjoyed by the non-UK domiciled spouse (unless held within an excluded property trust before the election becomes effective)
- Lifetime transfers of foreign assets by the non-UK domiciled spouse may be chargeable lifetime transfers or may become chargeable lifetime transfers in the event of their death within seven years

It is important to consider the impact of backdating an opt-in election where the non-UK domiciled spouse has made transfers of foreign assets, or funds held abroad, to anyone other than their spouse. It may also be worth considering making such transfers before making an opt-in election, although the CGT implications should be considered where the non-UK domiciled spouse is UK resident. Foreign tax implications should always be considered too.

**In Summary**

While the decision whether to make an opt-in election is something that requires professional advice, it seems fair to say, in general terms, that an opt-in election is likely to be beneficial where the UK domiciled spouse has the majority of the couple's assets.

On the other hand, the election is likely to be disadvantageous where the non-UK domiciled spouse has substantial foreign assets, or may acquire them in the future (e.g. by way of their own inheritance).

**Planning Revisited**

It may be possible to adapt the planning set out in Section 6.14 so it works where the non-UK domiciled spouse has previously made an opt-in election.

***Example:*** *Whitney is UK domiciled but has significant foreign assets. Her husband Bobby had a domicile of origin (see Section 16.2) in Massachusetts but elected to opt-in and be treated as UK domiciled with effect from 6th April 2013. Some years later, Whitney transferred all her foreign assets to Bobby.*

*In March 2024, Bobby moves to Jamaica and ceases to be UK resident. On 6th April 2028, after four consecutive years as a non-UK resident, Bobby's opt-in election automatically ceases to apply. As a result, the foreign assets formerly held by Whitney are now exempt from UK IHT.*

See Section 6.14 regarding the potential CGT risks under this strategy, which apply equally here.

It is generally more difficult to achieve non-UK residence if you still have a UK resident spouse. Having said that, it is probably easier for Bobby to achieve non-UK residence than for Whitney to achieve non-UK domicile!

The strategy outlined in the example is appropriate for those who have made an opt-in election some time earlier: well before leaving the UK. If the election were made only a short time before the non-UK domiciled spouse left the UK, it is likely HMRC would seek to block this planning strategy.

Chapter 7

# The Tax Benefits of Business Property

## 7.1 INTRODUCTION

Where the appropriate conditions are satisfied, relief is available on the transfer of relevant business or agricultural property. The two reliefs are known, quite appropriately, as 'business property relief' and 'agricultural property relief'. For the rest of this guide, to save a little space, we will refer to them as BPR and APR respectively.

As a result of BPR and APR, it is possible to pass on many family businesses free from IHT. Care must be exercised, however, as there are a great many pitfalls awaiting the unwary. In particular, property rental businesses will very rarely qualify for relief and other businesses where the use of land or buildings by customers is one of the main elements are also at risk. We will look at this issue further in Sections 7.4 and 7.5 and some ways to potentially resolve the problem in Sections 7.6 and 7.22.

Another major problem is caused by the rules relating to deduction of liabilities (see Section 2.10). These rules create a whole extra set of problems for business owners looking to pass their business to the next generation. In some cases, these rules may effectively wipe out the benefit of the relief: we will see an example in Section 7.10.

The reliefs for business and agricultural property apply, in principle, to both lifetime transfers and transfers on death, although, as we shall see in Section 7.18, there are extra conditions to be met in the case of lifetime transfers.

In many cases, relief is given at 100%, meaning the transfer of the business or agricultural property may potentially escape IHT altogether. Where relief is given at less than 100%, the relief is given before applying other exemptions (such as the annual exemption or the NRB). Where relief is available at 50%, this effectively doubles the value of these other exemptions.

***Example:*** *Cliff has an industrial building worth £662,000 on which BPR is available at the rate of 50%. He wishes to transfer the building to the Marvin-Welch Discretionary Trust. This will be Cliff's first chargeable lifetime transfer. After BPR at 50%, the chargeable transfer is reduced to £331,000. Cliff's annual exemptions for the current and previous years are still available. Deducting these (at £3,000 each) leaves a chargeable transfer of £325,000, which is covered by Cliff's NRB.*

There is a risk IHT liabilities could arise if Cliff dies within seven years of making this transfer. We will return to the subject of BPR on lifetime transfers in Section 7.18.

Technically, no actual claim is required, as these reliefs apply automatically when the relevant conditions are met. In practice, one still has to claim the conditions have been met though.

These reliefs also apply to the anniversary and exit charges for trusts (see Chapter 8). Naturally, the trust will need to meet all the necessary conditions, including the minimum ownership period (see Section 7.16). In practice, the trust will generally need to hold business or agricultural property for at least two years before passing it to a beneficiary in order to obtain the relief.

## 7.2 JUST HOW USEFUL IS BUSINESS PROPERTY RELIEF?

BPR is available on transfers of business property that meet each of the following three conditions:

- The business concerned is a qualifying business (see Sections 7.3 to 7.6),
- The asset itself is relevant business property (see Section 7.7), and
- The asset has been owned by the transferor for the relevant minimum period (see Section 7.16)

There is no requirement for the business to be located in the UK (but see Section 7.28 regarding agricultural property).

There is absolutely no limit to the amount of BPR a taxpayer may claim where the qualifying conditions are met. The relief could potentially be used to completely exempt an estate worth **billions** of pounds from IHT!

An obvious piece of IHT planning is therefore to maximise the value of assets qualifying for BPR within your estate. We will return to this in Section 7.20.

But BPR isn't just for those with an existing business. The relief provides a useful mechanism to give IHT-exempt funds to family and friends, as we shall see in Section 7.25. There are even some types of investment that may qualify, as we shall see in Section 7.26. Furthermore, it generally takes just two years for assets to achieve exemption through BPR, which is much better than the seven-year period for PETs.

Sadly, however, it is all too easy to lose BPR by failing to meet the qualifying conditions at the appropriate time. There are some particularly nasty pitfalls to watch out for with BPR. In fact, not only is the relief very easy to lose, but this also has a tendency to happen at the point in life when IHT planning is becoming most important.

There is also the problem that some quite normal commercial structures will leave the business owner with BPR at just 50% on their most valuable asset when they could so easily have had 100%.

Furthermore, the rules on liabilities incurred to finance relievable property (see Section 7.10) mean some business owners will enjoy little or no benefit from BPR. Worst of all, refinancing an existing loan could lead to the loss of relief in some cases (see Section 7.14).

Given the importance of this relief and the ease with which it can be lost, we will now take a long, detailed look at the relevant qualifying conditions. Some of this gets quite technical but it is important for anyone wanting to benefit from what is arguably the most powerful way to save IHT.

## 7.3 QUALIFYING BUSINESSES

For this purpose, any business is a qualifying business as long as it is being carried on with a view to profit and does not consist wholly or mainly of dealing in securities, stocks or shares, or land and buildings, nor of making or holding investments (except for the holding company of a trading group).

This may not initially sound too restrictive but, as we shall see, the definition of what constitutes 'making or holding investments' can be a great deal broader than what one might normally think, especially in the case of land and buildings.

Despite this, Lloyd's underwriters generally qualify for at least some BPR and the businesses of market makers or discount houses on the Stock Exchange also generally qualify. As in many fields of taxation, special rules apply.

**What is a Business?**
Case law suggests a business exists where at least some of the following six tests apply. Namely, the activity being undertaken:

- Is a serious undertaking earnestly pursued, or a serious occupation
- Is an occupation or function actively pursued with reasonable or recognisable continuity
- Has a measure of substance as measured by the value of supplies made
- Is conducted in a regular manner on sound and recognised business principles
- Is predominantly concerned with the making of supplies to consumers
- Involves the supply of goods or services of a kind which, subject to differences in detail, are commonly made by those who seek to profit by them

Where some or all of the above tests are satisfied, the activity will constitute a business and will generally qualify for BPR unless it falls under one of the exclusions outlined above. However, even though it may be accepted a business exists, the intention to make a profit remains essential. The profit motive requirement means businesses like stud farms or the business activities of artists or authors may sometimes be ineligible for the relief.

Preparing a credible business plan would provide valuable supporting evidence that you had a reasonable expectation of making a profit from your business. A documented annual review of the plan will also be useful, as the profit expectation test must be met at the time of the eventual transfer.

However, a business plan will not help if it clearly bears no resemblance to your actual behaviour.

## 7.4 PROPERTY INVESTMENT OR LETTING BUSINESSES

Unfortunately, as so often seems to be the case in UK taxation, property investment or letting businesses are generally not accepted by HMRC as qualifying businesses for the purpose of BPR.

The HMRC view is that holding investment property and collecting rent does not constitute a business for BPR purposes (although this does not seem to stop them collecting tax on income generated by this 'non-business' activity!)

Sadly, HMRC's view is supported by the fact it was specifically stated the letting of land would not qualify for BPR during the parliamentary debates when the relevant rules were first enacted.

Doubtless, those of you with property letting businesses will think this is unfair. This is certainly what the executor of a certain Mrs Burkinyoung thought in 1995 when he made a claim for BPR on the furnished flats Mrs Burkinyoung had been letting.

Unfortunately, when the case got to court, the judge decided otherwise, holding that Mrs Burkinyoung's properties were only investments and did not constitute a 'business' for IHT purposes.

It also turns out it would not have helped the Burkinyoung family if the late Mrs Burkinyoung had instead been letting out commercial property. In another case, BPR was denied where the deceased's business consisted of letting out small industrial units. Once again, the judge held that the lettings amounted to the mere holding of investments.

**Ancillary Services**
That same judge went on to say the provision of security services, heating, or cleaning as part of the terms of the lease would still not be sufficient, in his opinion, to create a qualifying business. The judge felt these services would be merely incidental to the holding of investments, even though he acknowledged such services would constitute a qualifying business if provided independently of the letting business. Separating out ancillary services into a separate business may therefore provide landlords with scope to get BPR on at least part of their business.

In a later case, property maintenance services were added to the list of ancillary services that would be regarded as merely incidental to the holding of investments. Again, therefore, it might be helpful to separate these out into a separate business.

**Does Size Matter?**
You may think, perhaps, the reason the cases referred to above were lost could be that the letting businesses concerned were too small. Sadly, this is not the

case since, in yet another case a company letting out more than a hundred properties was still not regarded as having a qualifying business.

**Furnished Holiday Lets**

I don't know where they get these judges from, or why they persist in regarding property letting as an easy and passive way to make a living. Nevertheless, as the law stands, it appears the only type of rental properties that might occasionally attract BPR are furnished holiday lets.

The rules for BPR on furnished holiday lets are very restrictive and far from clear. They are dependent on case law rather than any statutory definition and, just because a property qualifies as a furnished holiday let for Income Tax and CGT purposes (as explained in the Taxcafe guide *How to Save Property Tax*), doesn't mean it will qualify for BPR.

Historically, the view generally taken was that furnished holiday lets might be accepted as a business for BPR purposes when the lettings were predominantly short-term (e.g. a week or fortnight) and the owner was substantially involved with the holidaymakers' activities. However, following a recent spate of cases that have gone against the taxpayer, it now seems the courts are willing to support HMRC's view that furnished holiday lets will not generally qualify for BPR, even when significant services are provided to tenants.

Nonetheless, there is room for some hope as the taxpayer was successful in one recent case: although it seems the bar has been set very high when it comes to what constitutes being substantially involved with holidaymakers' activities.

The successful case concerned the late Mrs Graham and her daughter, who provided guests at their self-catering holiday flats with the use of a solar-heated outdoor pool, extensive well-maintained gardens, a sauna, games room, laundry, barbecue area, and guest lounge with books.

All these facilities were regularly maintained. A golf buggy and bicycles could also be hired and each flat was supplied with fresh flowers, homemade food and drink, bed linen, towels, toiletries, and cleaning materials. Furthermore, guests were provided with a welcome pack and refreshments on arrival and the property owners were on hand to help take in shopping, organise birthday and other celebrations and advise on local activities.

There was no doubt this was a business (even HMRC accepted that), but the question in court was whether it was a business of 'making or holding investments' or whether this was outweighed by other components such as the services provided and the onsite facilities.

The taxpayer won in this case but, like me, you are probably shocked there was ever any doubt over the issue. You will be even more shocked to hear that, when the judge gave his decision, he stated this "was an exceptional case which does, ***just***, fall on the non-investment side of the line."

*"Just!"* It beggars belief, but there it is. The courts seem to think you need to lavish the level of personal care given by Louise Graham (the deceased's daughter) before a furnished holiday let can qualify for BPR.

**Furnished Holiday Let Summary**
There is no doubt that a very high level of involvement with holidaymakers is required before a furnished holiday let might qualify for BPR. Services provided to tenants will need to be far beyond the normal level where landlords merely provide maintenance and cleaning services. Significant additional facilities will need to be provided. In the vast majority of cases you simply have to accept the relief will not be available and plan accordingly.

In the rare cases where you are able to turn the property into something more like a holiday park (as Louise Graham did), you might succeed but it will be far from certain. (See Section 7.30 for a good way of testing the position)

**In Conclusion**
Investment property is highly unlikely to qualify for BPR. You will usually need to be using property in a qualifying trading business. A few furnished holiday lets may qualify, but this will be quite rare.

## 7.5 BUSINESSES EXPLOITING LAND (AND BUILDINGS)

A great many businesses involve the 'exploitation of land'. This is a legal term to cover any situation where the use, by customers, of land or buildings is a vital component of the business.

Before everyone panics, let me first reassure you I am not talking about businesses where the customer merely enters the land or buildings in order to be provided with goods or services. Hence, retail businesses, restaurants, cafes, health professionals, and most other trading businesses are unaffected. The problem only arises where the customer has some form of right to use the land or buildings themselves. In these cases, HMRC will often attempt to argue the business consists merely of the holding of an investment.

The best defence against this argument is to show the provision of services or sale of goods is essential to the business. The customer must want the goods or services provided rather than the use of land or buildings alone. Many taxpayers have failed in BPR claims where the services provided were merely ancillary to the use of land or buildings rather than being core to the customers' needs.

There is a key distinction between land or buildings held as an investment that will generate income in its own right, as opposed to land or buildings that are an essential component integral to some other business activity. HMRC has a tendency to regard all businesses that involve the use of land or buildings by customers as being investment businesses, but this is not always the case.

Let's take a look at how the exploitation of land argument has been interpreted in some specific types of business.

**Hotels:** Hotels do not usually fall foul of the 'making or holding investments' rule and hence generally qualify for BPR. There may, however, be problems for hostels, guest-houses or hotels with long-term residents.

**Serviced Offices:** Generally speaking, serviced offices do not qualify for BPR as the services provided are regarded as merely ancillary to the rental of the offices. In one case, the office tenants were provided with meeting rooms, receptionist, restaurant, gallery area, gym, hair salon, and social events: and yet the court ***still*** denied BPR on the basis that what the tenants really wanted was office space and the additional services supplied were merely incidental. (Note that, as explained in Section 7.4, if ancillary services were provided by a separate business then ***that*** business might qualify for BPR.)

**Property Development:** While dealing in land and buildings does not qualify for BPR, a property development business will qualify and both the business's own trading premises (and other assets) and the land and buildings held as trading stock will be covered by the relief.

**Livery Businesses:** In another case, HMRC tried to deny BPR for a livery business, arguing that, if similar accommodation and services were provided to humans rather than horses, the business would be regarded as akin to a furnished holiday let and thus merely the holding of an investment (see Section 7.4 regarding BPR for furnished holiday lets).

Luckily this rather peculiar analogy did not convince the judge: perhaps partly because it is difficult to envisage the owner of a furnished holiday let worming their guests, or checking them for lameness and bloating.

The late owner's son (also her executor) argued that a livery business was more akin to a children's nursery than a furnished holiday let, since the owner was responsible for the animals' health and wellbeing. In the end, the judge accepted the business offered significantly more than the right to occupy a parcel of land and hence BPR was allowed.

**Stately Homes:** Stately homes open to the public may be covered by BPR. In one case, a claim for BPR was upheld by the court when just 78% of the property was open to the public. Despite the fact that 22% of the property was closed to the public, the whole property qualified as it had to be viewed as a single asset and, furthermore, the entire exterior was important to the paying public's enjoyment of the property.

The implication is that any building, of which more than 50% is used for the public's enjoyment, as part of a commercial enterprise, might qualify for BPR. This would surely also extend to private museums and other similar enterprises, as long as the profit motive (see Section 7.3) is present. (All is not lost where less than 50% of the property is used for business purposes, as we shall see in Section 7.8.)

**Caravan Parks:** Caravan parks have occupied a lot of the courts' attention when it comes to BPR. To date, there have been five major cases on the subject. So far, the score is HMRC 3 - Taxpayers 2. In essence, the taxpayers lost the cases where the majority of income came from site fees or pitch fees (which are basically a form of rent) but won the cases where the majority of income came from the provision of other services or sale of caravans.

Most recently, the long and tortuous case of *George & Loochin (Stedman's Executors)* was eventually decided in favour of the deceased's executors when it reached the Court of Appeal. This case concerned a caravan park where a major proportion of the business income comprised site fees for the storage of caravans and mobile homes. However, the saving grace for this caravan park was the fact that 72% of those fees were absorbed by overheads, mainly the upkeep of common parts of the park.

Nevertheless, HMRC still argued the site fees represented income from the exploitation of land and the caravan park business was thus tantamount to the mere holding of an investment.

Thankfully, the judge in the Court of Appeal stated the holding of property as an investment was only one component of the business and did not prevent it from qualifying for BPR. He found it difficult to see why an active family business of this kind should be excluded from BPR just because a necessary component of the business was the holding of land.

This last judgement tells us a few things:

- An 'active' business should qualify for BPR
- Caravan parks are very much a borderline case, as they are partly concerned with the exploitation of land
- You get a better quality of judge in the Court of Appeal

But seriously, any business that involves some element of exploitation of land runs a risk of not qualifying for BPR.

**General Guidelines**

The key to obtaining BPR is to ensure the majority of the business income comes from the provision of services and not from the mere exploitation of land. We will look further at the question of what constitutes the majority of the business income in the next section.

**Life Interests in Land**

The cases where difficulty arises due to the exploitation of land argument involve taxpayers who actually own that land. Naturally, this means their estate is extremely valuable, which is why the BPR claim is so important.

It has been established, however, that a taxpayer who only held a life interest in land could not be held to have a business that consisted of making or holding investments. That taxpayer's business therefore qualified for BPR, which was very useful since, as we shall see in Chapter 8, there are some cases where the underlying assets in which the deceased had a life interest have to be included in their estate.

This provides a possible method for ensuring a business that could potentially fall foul of the exploitation of land problem will qualify for BPR. The drawback, however, is that BPR is only given at the rate of 50% where the transferor had a life interest in the property rather than absolute ownership (see Section 7.7).

Nevertheless, in some cases, BPR may be maximised by splitting the ownership of the business from the ownership of the underlying land and placing the land in a life interest trust. This should enable the owner to claim 100% relief on the business and 50% relief on the land when there may have been no relief at all if they had owned both the business and the underlying land outright.

***Example:*** *Tom owns a caravan park in South Wales. On his death, he leaves the park business to his wife Joan and the land on which the park is set to a life interest trust with Joan as the beneficiary. Tom's NRB is unused and therefore transfers to Joan (see Section 6.2).*

*On Joan's subsequent death in March 2024, her executors claim 100% BPR on the park business, worth £750,000, and 50% BPR on the park land, worth £1.3m. After BPR, the chargeable value of the land is reduced to £650,000 and this is covered by Joan's NRB plus the TNRB received from Tom: leaving no IHT to pay.*

*If Joan owned both the park business and park land outright, she might not have been eligible for any BPR. The IHT arising on the park would then have been at least £560,000 (£750,000 + £1.3m – £650,000 = £1.4m x 40%).*

The drawback to this technique is it may mean 50% relief on the value of the underlying land has been sacrificed if, in fact, the business would have qualified for BPR anyway. A better approach may therefore be to only put the structure described above into place via a deed of variation after a BPR claim on the first spouse's death has already failed. (See Section 7.30 for further details on how to safely test the position on the first spouse's death.)

The method described above is based on an old case that was only won in the Court of Appeal on a 2-1 majority. It is therefore possible this decision could be overturned one day!

## 7.6 WHAT DOES WHOLLY OR MAINLY MEAN IN PRACTICE?

As stated in Section 7.3, a business will not qualify for BPR if it consists wholly or mainly of dealing in securities, stocks or shares, or land and buildings, or making or holding investments. Naturally, however, it follows that while it cannot consist wholly or mainly of these activities, it can still consist partly of them.

Quite simply, 'wholly or mainly' means 'at least 50%'. "50% of what?" I hear you ask. Case law has sometimes, though not exclusively, interpreted the 50%

test as relating to net profits. To be on the safe side, however, I would suggest trying to ensure the business consists of qualifying activities to the extent these account for over 50% of each of the following:

- Turnover (i.e. sales)
- Gross profit
- Net profit
- Proprietor's time
- Employees' time
- Assets employed in the business (although, as we have seen already, land employed in the business may be regarded in a number of ways)

**Hybrid Businesses**

It is important to remember what is required for BPR purposes is that the business consists wholly or mainly of qualifying business activities. If the wholly or mainly test is met then the whole business will qualify, including those parts that are not themselves qualifying activities. This has important IHT planning implications as it means BPR may be available in respect of an investment business component that represents a minority element of a qualifying business.

***Example:*** *Ray and Dave run a property business, Kink Properties, in partnership together. Kink Properties derives around 75% of its income from property development and the remainder from property letting. While HMRC would argue that part of the business amounts to the non-qualifying activity of holding investments, the main part, property development, represents a qualifying activity. Kink Properties therefore qualifies for BPR. Furthermore, the whole business qualifies, including the investment properties.*

To get relief on the whole value of the business, it is important to ensure all the assets held by the business are actually used in the business. A completely unrelated quoted shareholding, for example, might be regarded as a non-business asset and would thus be ineligible for relief.

There is an important distinction between business assets used in a non-qualifying part of the business (like Ray and Dave's investment properties), which do attract relief, and assets that are not business assets at all (like those unrelated quoted shares), which are excluded from relief. Assets excluded from relief are known as excepted assets and we will return to this concept again in Section 7.8.

## 7.7 RELEVANT BUSINESS PROPERTY

The following types of property may qualify for BPR at 100%:

i) An interest in a qualifying unincorporated business (i.e. a sole trade or profession, or a share in a partnership)
ii) Unquoted shares in a company carrying on a qualifying business
iii) Unquoted securities (e.g. loan stock) in a company carrying on a qualifying business that, either alone, or with other unquoted shares or securities, give the transferor control of the company

Other types of property may qualify for relief at 50%:

iv) Quoted shares or securities in a company carrying on a qualifying business that, either alone, or together with other quoted shares or securities, give the transferor control of that company

v) Assets held personally by the transferor but used wholly or mainly for the purposes of a qualifying business carried on by a company under the transferor's control, or a partnership in which the transferor is a partner (or was prior to death in the case of transfers on death)

vi) Assets held in an interest in possession trust on behalf of the transferor and used wholly or mainly for the purpose of a business under the transferor's control or a business carried on by a partnership in which the transferor was a partner. (This applies only to interests in possession deemed to form part of the transferor's estate for IHT purposes: see Chapter 8)

A partnership includes a Limited Liability Partnership (LLP). Members' capital accounts in a partnership carrying on a qualifying business will qualify for BPR but members' loan accounts do not. This is a particular problem for LLPs.

'Unquoted' means not listed on a recognised stock exchange. Shares that are only traded on the Alternative Investment Market (AIM) are not 'listed' and thus qualify as unquoted for BPR purposes.

In general, any stock market recognised by the laws of the country in which it is situated will usually be regarded as a recognised stock exchange and shares traded there will therefore be treated as quoted.

The legislation refers only to whether the shares or securities themselves are quoted. HMRC's notes, however, refer to a 'quoted company'. This will seldom make any difference, but there remains the question of how to treat unquoted classes of shares or securities issued by a company that has a stock market quotation for another class of shares or securities. On a strict interpretation of the legislation, I would argue these continue to be unquoted, but it's not a point I would like to rely on.

Most shares in small or medium-sized private companies carrying on a qualifying business qualify for BPR under heading (ii), and hence the issue of control is not important for the shares themselves. However, control is essential in the case of shares, securities, or other assets falling under any of headings (iii) to (vi).

Furthermore, an important point to note about headings (iii) and (iv) is that it is only shares or securities that actually contribute to the transferor's control of the company that qualify for BPR. For example, a shareholder who controls a quoted company by means of voting ordinary shares will not be entitled to BPR on non-voting preference shares in the same company. It also follows that very few securities (loan stock, etc.) will qualify for BPR.

Control is generally taken to mean the transferor is able to control over 50% of the voting powers on all questions affecting the company as a whole. A transferor holding 50% of the voting shares plus the right to a casting vote will also have control. In deciding whether the transferor can control the requisite proportion of voting power, we can include: shares held by their spouse; shares transferred by them or their spouse to a charity, or other exempt body, after 15th April 1976 and still held by the transferee body at any time within the last five years; and shares treated as part of their estate or their spouse's estate (e.g. some types of interest in possession: see Chapter 8).

Control need only exist immediately before the relevant transfer. The availability of BPR is unaffected by whether control is lost as a result of the transfer in question: although, of course, subsequent transfers may be affected.

When planning a transfer of shares that may result in a loss of control of the company, it may therefore make sense to make other transfers first, such as smaller transfers of shares or securities falling under headings (iii) or (iv), or transfers of property used in the company's business falling under headings (v) or (vi).

A company held 50/50 by two individuals is not under the control of either individual. Hence, unless those individuals are a married couple, this means there can be no relief for any property under headings (v) or (vi). Subject to commercial requirements, it may therefore make sense to make a slight change to the company shareholdings so that one of the individuals has control and will be eligible for relief.

## 7.8 WHAT IS THE VALUE OF A BUSINESS?

The value of an unincorporated business is made up of the total value of all the assets of the business, including goodwill, less any business liabilities. The assets and liabilities of the business are all those items a purchaser would take into account in order to ascertain a value for the whole business.

Business liabilities (like trade creditors, for example) need to be deducted in arriving at the value of the business. Loans and other liabilities are not generally deducted in arriving at the value of the business but may need to be deducted from that value for the purposes of a BPR claim. We will look at the distinction between these two types of liabilities in more detail in Section 7.11.

Money owed to a transferor by their own business cannot be included as an additional asset in a BPR claim.

Non-business property on which business loans are secured cannot be included as part of the value of the business. However, loans and other liabilities incurred to purchase or finance the business may need to be deducted from the value of the business for the purposes of the BPR claim. Again, we will look at these in more detail in Section 7.11.

### Excepted Assets

The general rule is that BPR is not available on the value of an asset which has neither been used wholly or mainly for business purposes for the period of two years prior to the transfer, or the period since acquisition, if less; nor is required for the future use of the business.

In the case of property falling under heading (v) in Section 7.7, however, the rule is revised so that, in order to qualify for BPR, the asset in question must have either been used for the purpose of the business of the partnership or company throughout the two years prior to the transfer; or have replaced a similar previous asset (see Section 7.17) and the two assets taken together were used in the relevant business for a combined total period of at least two years within the five-year period prior to the transfer.

Remember, as discussed in Section 7.6, the asset only needs to be used in the business. In the case of a hybrid business qualifying under the wholly or mainly rule, the asset might be used in a non-qualifying component of the business and could still qualify for BPR.

**Buildings with Partial Business Use**

In Section 7.5, we saw that a building used at least 50% for business purposes would qualify for BPR as a result of the wholly or mainly rule. In many cases, however, a smaller proportion of a building may be used for business purposes. Examples might include a dentist, doctor or vet using part of their home for an office, waiting room and surgery; or a shopkeeper using the ground floor of their three-storey house as shop premises.

In cases like this, HMRC permits a BPR claim in respect of the business portion of the property, provided this portion is used exclusively for business purposes. This applies to claims under headings (i), (v) or (vi) in Section 7.7.

## 7.9 BUSINESS PROPERTY RELIEF FOR SHARES AND SECURITIES

In Section 7.7, we examined the conditions that need to be satisfied before shares or securities may qualify for BPR. However, just because the shares or securities do, in principle, qualify for BPR, does not necessarily mean the whole value of those shares or securities qualifies.

In order to calculate the available BPR, it will be necessary to take into account any excepted assets held by the relevant company. The definition of excepted assets for this purpose is the same as the general definition given in Section 7.8 (not the revised one for transfers under heading (v)).

***Example:*** *Tommy owns 60% of the share capital in Pinball Ltd, a trading company operating amusement arcades. The company has total assets valued at £1m, net of business liabilities. However, this includes £300,000 in cash held in a deposit account, which is surplus to the company's business requirements and not used in its trade.*

*The total value of Tommy's shares is £600,000. However, 30% of the company's value is attributable to a non-business asset (the surplus cash). Hence, Tommy's BPR must be restricted to £420,000, leaving £180,000 (or 30%) chargeable to IHT.*

In the above example, we ignored the value of goodwill. Any goodwill in the company's business would be a trading asset and would increase the proportion of the shares eligible for BPR.

***Example Revisited:*** *If Pinball Ltd had trading goodwill worth £200,000, the total value of its assets would be £1.2m. The £300,000 of surplus cash would represent just 25% of the company's assets and Tommy's BPR would be increased accordingly.*

Valuing company shares is a highly complex subject worthy of an entire book in its own right. It is necessary to take account of goodwill and all the company's liabilities. There is no distinction here between business liabilities and other liabilities such as loans. The company's tax liabilities will also need to be taken into account (this may sometimes include the potential tax arising if it were to sell its assets at current market value: although this depends on the valuation method used).

To establish what ***proportion*** of a company's value is based on excepted assets, however, we continue to follow the principles outlined in the previous section regarding the valuation of a business.

***Example Part 3:*** *Let's suppose that Pinball Ltd has a £100,000 Corporation Tax liability and also owes Roger, the company's founder, £500,000: a long-term loan he gave to the company many years ago. These liabilities reduce the value of the company (including goodwill) to £600,000, but the £300,000 of surplus cash still represents just 25% of the total value of its net business assets (£1.2m).*

*Tommy's shares are now worth just £360,000 (£600,000 x 60%), but he may still claim BPR of £270,000 (£360,000 less 25%).*

**Cash on Deposit**
Just because a company has cash on deposit does not necessarily make that cash an excepted asset. The question is whether that cash is surplus to the company's business requirements. In a case like Pinball Ltd, it will often be possible to argue at least some of the cash is required for working capital. Exactly how much will depend on the circumstances of each case.

Cash held by a company for a specific identifiable business purpose may also be included as a business asset.

***Example:*** *Johnny owns San Quentin Ltd, a company he originally formed to own and operate a nightclub, 'Ring of Fire'. In August 2023, San Quentin Ltd sells Ring of Fire for £1m. The company keeps the money on deposit because Johnny is actively looking for a new nightclub San Quentin Ltd can buy. Sadly, however, Johnny dies before the company can buy the new nightclub.*

*Johnny leaves his San Quentin Ltd shares to his son, Sue. Thankfully, full BPR is available on the shares because the cash held on deposit was earmarked for a specific business purpose.*

This example is based on a real case (but with different names: especially the boy named Sue), which the taxpayer's executors won.

In another case, however, a similar claim was denied when the executors claimed surplus funds were being held pending a suitable business opportunity. The court felt this was too vague and cash on deposit could only be counted as a business asset when it was required for a palpable business purpose. Hence, in Johnny's case, if he had decided he'd had enough of the nightclub business and was looking for another investment opportunity, BPR would have been denied.

The key to maintaining full BPR on shares in a company holding surplus cash is to have an identifiable business requirement for that cash. This should be documented in business plans, cashflow projections, directors' board minutes, etc. It is also worth noting the same surplus cash would not generally qualify for BPR when held personally. Hence, it may often make sense to retain business sale proceeds within a company when intending to reinvest them.

**Other Investments**
Other short-term investments held by the company might be eligible for inclusion as business assets if the same rationale as set out above regarding surplus cash can be established. Alternatively, as we saw in Section 7.6, the company may have a hybrid business, and the investments might therefore be business assets in their own right.

HMRC accepts the holding of investments by a company may often be part of its normal business activities, although they will still attack cases where they perceive the company is simply being used as a repository for non-business assets in order to artificially increase the amount of BPR available.

**Financing the Company**
Loans and other liabilities incurred by a shareholder in order to purchase company shares, or to finance the company in some other way, may need to be deducted from the value of the borrower's shares when claiming BPR. We will look at this issue in more detail in Section 7.12; as well as the position where a shareholder lends funds to their own company.

## 7.10 FINANCING A BUSINESS

As explained in Section 2.10, liabilities incurred by the transferor to finance the acquisition, enhancement or maintenance of qualifying business property, must be deducted from the value of that property for BPR purposes. Liabilities incurred before 6th April 2013 are exempt from this rule, but this exemption can easily be lost. We will return to this point in Section 7.14.

These rules apply equally to all forms of qualifying business property (as listed in Section 7.7). Their most frequent application will be to unincorporated businesses (sole traders and partnerships), which we'll look at in this section and the next, and company shares, which we'll look at in Section 7.12. Nonetheless, the principles explored in this section (and in Sections 7.14 and 7.15) apply equally to all forms of qualifying business property.

***Example:*** *In 2019, Amy (who is single) borrowed £600,000 by remortgaging her house and used the money to buy a trading business, 'The Wine House'. In March 2024, Amy dies. She leaves her house to her sister Adele and she leaves The Wine House to her brother, Pete. By this point, her house is worth £1m and The Wine House is worth £800,000. Amy's Will specifies both beneficiaries are to bear the tax arising on their legacies.*

*The Wine House is eligible for BPR, so it can be passed to Pete without any IHT liability. However, the deemed value of The Wine House for BPR purposes is only £200,000, as Amy's mortgage must be deducted from its actual value of £800,000.*

*Amy's executors arrange for her house to be transferred to Adele subject to the existing mortgage (this satisfies the requirement for a commercial reason for non-repayment: see Section 2.10). Adele therefore acquires a house with equity of just £400,000 (£1m – £600,000). However, she will be liable for IHT on the full £1m value of the house (less Amy's NRB) because the mortgage has been set against the value of The Wine House.*

*This gives Adele an IHT liability of £270,000 (£1m – £325,000 = £675,000 x 40% = £270,000), which amounts to 67.5% of the value of her inheritance!*

These rules create an incredibly unfair result. The IHT due on Amy's house falls on Adele, but she is denied any relief for the mortgage she has taken over. She ends up facing liabilities totalling £870,000 by inheriting a house worth only £1m. Meanwhile, Pete obtains a business worth £800,000 free from any liabilities at all!

Business owners who have borrowed to finance their business may wish to consider adjustments to legacies to prevent such unfair results. Amy could have left an additional £240,000 to Adele and specified this was to be charged against the assets of The Wine House. This would have compensated Adele for being denied relief for the mortgage on Amy's house.

In addition to the unfairness seen above, these rules could also lead to the collapse of many businesses.

***Example:*** *In 2018, Dusty borrowed £1m by mortgaging her house and invested it in her business. Over the next few years, she borrowed further sums by way of personal loans, credit cards, etc, in order to fund her business.*

*In 2023, Dusty, who has never married, dies and leaves her entire estate to her brother Tom. At this point, her house is worth £1.2m and the other debts she incurred to fund her business total £300,000.*

*Tom will be denied any relief for the mortgage over Dusty's house or the other debts she has incurred to fund her business, so he will be left with an IHT bill of £350,000 (£1.2m – £325,000 = £875,000 x 40% = £350,000). Leaving the business to one side for the moment, Tom has inherited a house worth £1.2m but faces total debts of £1.65m (the mortgage of £1m, other debts of £300,000, and IHT of £350,000).*

*Hence, even if Tom were to sell Dusty's house, he would still face liabilities of £450,000 (more after taking sale costs into account). If Tom had no significant assets of his own, this would have to be funded from Dusty's business meaning that, in all likelihood, Tom would be unable to continue trading.*

It is worth noting the amount of BPR Dusty receives is drastically reduced. If her business had been worth, say, £1.5m, she would have received BPR of just £200,000 (£1.5m less £1m mortgage less £300,000 of other liabilities).

**Business Property with Lower Value than Liabilities**
In the last example, I assumed Dusty's business had a value in excess of the liabilities she incurred to fund it (£1.3m). Where the value of the business property is less than the outstanding liabilities incurred to finance it, the excess liabilities may be deducted from the remainder of the owner's estate.

***Example Revisited:*** *Let's take the same facts as above, but assume Dusty's business is worth just £800,000 at the time of her death. The liabilities incurred to finance her business total £1.3m, but it will now only be necessary to set £800,000 of these against the value of the business. This leaves £500,000 that can be set against the remainder of her estate, reducing Tom's IHT bill to £150,000 (£1.2m – £500,000 – £325,000 = £375,000 x 40% = £150,000).*

In this revised example, Dusty receives no BPR at all: since the value of her business for this purpose is reduced to nil.

I assumed throughout both versions of the example that Dusty's liabilities are eligible to be deducted from her estate (see Section 2.10).

**Inherited or Transferred Liabilities**
Where a beneficiary takes over a liability secured on an inherited or transferred asset, the treatment of the liability in their estate, or on any lifetime transfers ***they*** make, is unaffected by the treatment applied to the transferor.

Hence, in the examples in this section, the mortgages taken over by Adele and Tom would be fully deductible from their estates if they were to die while these liabilities were still outstanding.

## 7.11 DEDUCTING LIABILITIES: UNINCORPORATED BUSINESS

As explained in Section 7.8, business liabilities must always be deducted in arriving at the value of an unincorporated business. Loans and other liabilities incurred to finance the business will only need to be deducted from the amount of BPR available when the liability was incurred after 5th April 2013 (but see Section 7.14 for further details). To see what this means in practice, let's look at a typical business.

***Example Part 1:*** *Duffy has her own business with qualifying business assets worth a total of £2m. She also has the following liabilities:*

| | |
|---|---|
| *Trade creditors* | *£200,000* |
| *Business overdraft* | *£20,000* |
| *Long-term business loan* | *£300,000* |
| *Hire purchase liability on own car* | *£10,000* |
| *Hire purchase liability on employees' cars* | *£25,000* |
| *Income Tax on business profits* | *£30,000* |
| *Mortgage on her home* | *£500,000* |
| *Loan from her brother Warwick* | *£250,000* |

*The trade creditors are a business liability and must therefore be deducted from the value of the business. In most cases, a business overdraft is an integral part of the business, meaning it would usually need to be taken into account in order to ascertain a value for the business and is therefore a business liability. There will be some cases where this does not apply, but we will assume the overdraft is a business liability in this case.*

*The long-term business loan is not classed as a business liability for BPR purposes. This is because a purchaser looking to buy the business would not usually take over the loan. The loan therefore only needs to be deducted from the value of the business if it was taken out after 5th April 2013. In this case, we will assume the loan was taken out in 2012.*

*It is questionable whether Duffy's own car is an asset of the business. While she may use it for business purposes, a purchaser looking to buy the business is unlikely to want to buy the car. Hence, as the car is not a business asset, the hire purchase liability on it does not need to be deducted from the value of the business.*

*The employees' cars are assets of the business: they will (most likely) transfer with the employees who are, in turn, an integral part of the business. Hence, the hire purchase liabilities on these cars are business liabilities and must be deducted from the value of the business.*

*Duffy's Income Tax bill is a personal liability. It does not matter that it has arisen on business profits; it will not need to be deducted from the value of her business.*

*Duffy's mortgage will only need to be deducted from the value of her business if it was taken out after 5th April 2013 and has been used in any way, directly or indirectly, to finance her business. In this case, we will assume the mortgage was taken out in 2012, has not been varied in any way since then, and has been used to finance Duffy's business.*

*Duffy borrowed the money from her brother in 2014 and used it to purchase some business assets and reduce her business overdraft. This loan will therefore need to be deducted from the value of Duffy's business for BPR purposes.*

*Duffy dies in December 2023. The following liabilities must be deducted from the value of her business for BPR purposes:*

| | |
|---|---|
| *Trade creditors* | *£200,000* |
| *Business overdraft* | *£20,000* |
| *Hire purchase liability on employees' cars* | *£25,000* |
| *Loan from Warwick* | *£250,000* |
| *Total:* | *£495,000* |

*While they were incurred to finance her business, the long-term business loan and mortgage on Duffy's home do not need to be deducted because they were taken out before 6th April 2013. The loan from Warwick will have to be deducted, however, as this liability was incurred after 5th April 2013.*

*Duffy's BPR will be reduced to £1.505m (£2m – £495,000). Her family's IHT bill will be increased by £100,000 because the loan from Warwick cannot be deducted from the general assets of her estate (£250,000 x 40% = £100,000).*

The position will get even worse if Duffy subsequently refinances either her long-term business loan or her mortgage. Let's return to the example to see the effect of this.

***Example Part 2:*** *In 2021, Duffy remortgaged her house for £800,000 and used the new loan to pay off both her old mortgage and her long-term business loan. All other facts outlined in Part 1 above remain the same at the time of her death in 2023. The liabilities to be deducted from the value of her business for BPR purposes are now as follows:*

| | |
|---|---|
| *Trade creditors* | *£200,000* |
| *Business overdraft* | *£20,000* |
| *Hire purchase liability on employees' cars* | *£25,000* |
| *Mortgage* | *£800,000* |
| *Loan from Warwick* | *£250,000* |
| *Total:* | *£1,295,000* |

*Duffy's BPR is reduced to just £705,000 (£2m – £1.295m). None of the liabilities listed above can be deducted from the general assets of her estate. Compared with the position in Part 1 above, this will cost her family a further £320,000 in IHT.*

See Section 7.14 for further details on the perils of varying a loan taken out before 6th April 2013.

## 7.12 DEDUCTION OF LIABILITIES FOR COMPANY OWNERS

As explained in Section 7.9, when calculating the value of shares that qualify for BPR, all of the issuing company's liabilities need to be taken into account. The owner of the shares will also need to deduct liabilities incurred after 5th April 2013 that they have used to directly or indirectly finance their shareholding or maintain or enhance its value.

To demonstrate these principles in practice, let's look at a similar example to the one we used in Section 7.11 but, this time, the qualifying business property is company shares.

***Example Part 1:*** *Robbie owns all the shares in a trading company, Old Swinger Ltd. We will assume the value of the company before taking account of any liabilities is £2m (in practice, valuing company shares is a more complex process than this). The company also has the following liabilities:*

| | |
|---|---|
| *Trade creditors* | *£200,000* |
| *Business overdraft* | *£20,000* |
| *Long-term business loan* | *£300,000* |
| *Hire purchase liability on Robbie's car* | *£10,000* |
| *Hire purchase liability on employees' cars* | *£25,000* |
| *Corporation Tax due* | *£30,000* |
| *Loan from Robbie's brother Mark* | *£250,000* |
| *Total:* | *£835,000* |

*All these items are company liabilities and must therefore be taken into account in establishing the value of the company and Robbie's shares. In this case, we will assume it is appropriate to simply deduct them from the value described above, leaving a net value for Robbie's shares of £1.165m (£2m – £835,000).*

*(I am assuming Robbie's car is a company asset. If it was his own private car then neither the car nor the hire purchase liability on it would be taken into account)*

*In 2012, Robbie mortgaged his house for £500,000 in order to buy his shares in Old Swinger Ltd. As this liability was incurred before 6th April 2013, it does not need to be taken into account for BPR purposes. Hence, as things stand, the value of Robbie's shares for BPR purposes remains £1.165m.*

The rules regarding deduction of liabilities will generally have less impact on company owners than other business owners, since all company liabilities have to be deducted in any case. However, company owners remain vulnerable to the perils of varying existing loans taken out outside the company before 6th April 2013 (see Section 7.14).

***Example Part 2:*** *In 2021, Robbie remortgaged his house for £800,000 and used the new loan to both pay off his old mortgage and lend £300,000 to Old Swinger Ltd to enable the company to repay its long-term business loan. All other facts, as per Part 1 above, remain the same at the time of his death in December 2023.*

*The value of Robbie's shares remains unaltered (£1.165m). The company has paid off its long-term loan but has simply replaced this liability with another: the debt due to Robbie. However, Robbie's estate now includes the £300,000 debt due from Old Swinger Ltd as an additional asset. This asset is not eligible for BPR (see below).*

*Robbie's new mortgage was taken out after 5th April 2013, so any part used, directly or indirectly, to finance the purchase of his shares, or enhance their value, must be deducted for BPR purposes and cannot be deducted from the general assets of his estate.*

*The £500,000 used to repay the original mortgage has been used indirectly to finance Robbie's shares and is thus caught by these rules. This sum must therefore be deducted from the value of Robbie's shares, reducing his BPR to £665,000 (£1.165m – £500,000).*

*The £300,000 Robbie loaned to the company did not enhance the value of his shares, which was the same before and after he made the loan. Hence this part of his new mortgage can still be deducted from the general assets of his estate. However, as the loan has become an additional chargeable asset in its own right, there is no overall IHT saving. The change in Robbie's position caused by the remortgaging is as follows:*

| | ***Before*** | ***After*** |
|---|---|---|
| ***Chargeable Assets:*** | | |
| *Shares in Old Swinger Ltd* | *£1,165,000* | *£665,000* |
| *Loan to Old Swinger Ltd* | - | *£300,000* |
| ***Less Deductions:*** | | |
| *Business property relief* | *£1,165,000* | *£665,000* |
| *Mortgage* | *£500,000* | *£300,000* |

*Before the remortgaging, there was a net £500,000 available to be deducted from the general assets of Robbie's estate, now there is nothing left. The remortgaging will therefore cost Robbie's family an additional £200,000 (£500,000 x 40%) in IHT.*

**Loans to Your Own Company**
In Part 2 of the example, we saw the impact of lending money to your own company. From the company's perspective, the borrowed funds will enhance its value but this will be matched by the liability due to you. Hence, there is no overall impact on the company's value.

You will have a new asset: the debt due to you from the company. This will need to be included in your estate. A debt due to you from your own company, often known as a director's loan account, is a separate asset in its own right and is highly unlikely to attract BPR. The treatment of director's loan accounts is examined further in Section 7.21.

In summary, lending money to your own company will not generally provide you with any additional BPR and will not immediately save any IHT. Naturally, however, there are many good reasons why you might lend money to your company and we will revisit this topic in Section 7.13.

**Rights Issues**
In Section 7.20, we will look at the potential benefits of rights issues for increasing the amount of BPR available to a company owner. In that section, it is assumed the company owner has substantial private wealth available to fund the rights issue. Funding the rights issue by way of borrowings will not work so well, however.

***Example Part 3:*** *The facts are the same as in Part 2 above except that, instead of lending £300,000 to the company, Robbie subscribes for additional shares by way of a rights issue. The value of the company has now increased to £1.465m (£1.165m + £300,000) because there is no debt due to Robbie to match the liability that has been paid off.*

*Robbie will not have acquired any additional asset: he will only have enhanced the value of his existing shareholding. As a result of this, however, the entire £800,000 of Robbie's new mortgage must now be deducted from the value of his shares for BPR purposes because it has all been used, directly or indirectly, to finance the purchase of his shares, or enhance their value. The end result is thus as follows:*

| | |
|---|---|
| ***Chargeable Assets:*** | |
| *Shares in Old Swinger Ltd* | *£665,000 (£1,465,000 – £800,000)* |
| ***Less Deductions:*** | |
| *Business property relief* | *£665,000* |
| *Mortgage* | *Nil* |

*The overall position remains the same as in Part 2 and, once again, the remortgaging will have cost Robbie's family an additional £200,000 in IHT.*

## 7.13 BORROWING TO INVEST IN YOUR BUSINESS

The examples in Sections 7.10 to 7.12 demonstrate the fact that new borrowings used to finance your business, by any means, will not give rise to any immediate IHT savings. Refinancing or varying earlier borrowings taken out before 6th April 2013 will often lead to additional IHT costs and should be avoided wherever possible.

Naturally, however, financing your business will usually have other benefits and it is hoped the value of your business will increase as a result. This may lead to some indirect IHT savings as future growth in your business's value will be sheltered by BPR whereas future growth in funds or investments held privately outside the business would be fully exposed to IHT.

In other words, the real benefit lies in making sensible commercial investments through the medium of a qualifying trading business and thus increasing your BPR as you grow your business (provided such investments do not endanger the business's trading status: see Section 7.6).

## 7.14 LIABILITIES INCURRED BEFORE APRIL 2013

As explained in Sections 2.10 and 7.10, liabilities incurred before 6th April 2013 are exempt from the rules we have been looking at over the last few sections. However, any variation in the terms of such a liability will make it a new liability for these purposes and will mean it must be deducted from the value of the relevant qualifying business property.

We have seen the disastrous consequences in several examples already, but it is vital to understand, in addition to a complete refinancing of those existing liabilities, those same consequences may arise in the event of other, less significant, variations in the terms of the liability, such as:

- Changes to the term (period) of a loan
- Changes in the security for a loan
- A change from fixed interest to variable interest, or vice versa (unless such a change is already part of the existing terms)
- Additional advances on the same loan account

The last point is not entirely certain but it is far safer to arrange for additional advances to be treated as a separate loan account. While the additional advances would still be subject to the new rules, the exempt status of the existing balance should be protected.

Simple changes in the interest rate on a loan should not cause any problems: provided such changes are within the original terms of the loan.

Where there is a change in the lender that is beyond the borrower's control (e.g. where one bank takes over another's mortgage book), I would argue strongly this does not create any new liability as it must be within the terms of the original contract (since it does not require the borrower's consent).

## 7.15 MULTIPLE TRANSFERS

Over the past few sections, we have seen how liabilities incurred after 5th April 2013 to finance qualifying business property must be deducted from the value of that property on a transfer of value. This applies to any chargeable transfer, including:

- Transfers on death
- Chargeable lifetime transfers (see Section 4.2)
- PETs becoming chargeable on the transferor's death within seven years (see Section 4.5)
- Trust anniversary and exit charges (see Sections 8.18 and 8.19)

Once a liability has been taken into account on one chargeable transfer, it cannot be taken into account again on another transfer made by the same transferor (except where the earlier 'transfer' was a trust anniversary charge). Remember, however, that a PET only becomes a chargeable transfer if the transferor dies within seven years.

***Example:*** *In 2014, Woody mortgaged his house for £1m and used the money to purchase shares in a trading company, Movenelo Ltd. In 2023, Woody gives his shares in Movenelo Ltd to his elder daughter, Bev: this is a PET. In 2030, Woody dies, leaving his remaining estate to his younger daughter, Kelly.*

*If Woody died within seven years of his gift to Bev, that gift will have become a chargeable transfer and his mortgage will have to be taken into account for BPR purposes. Kelly will then be denied any relief for the mortgage.*

*If, on the other hand, Woody was still alive on the seventh anniversary of his gift to Bev, that gift will have become fully exempt. Kelly will then be entitled to claim a deduction in respect of Woody's £1m mortgage, saving her £400,000 in IHT.*

I have assumed in this example that Woody's mortgage will meet the necessary conditions for a deduction, as explained in Section 2.10.

In summary, where liabilities have been incurred to purchase, enhance, or maintain qualifying business property, full relief for those liabilities can be restored by making a PET of the relevant business property and then surviving seven years.

## 7.16 THE MINIMUM HOLDING PERIOD

To qualify for BPR, the relevant property must generally have been owned by the transferor for a minimum of two years prior to the transfer.

There is an exception to this requirement where the property replaced other qualifying property (see Section 7.17) and both assets taken together had been owned by the transferor for at least two years out of the five-year period preceding the transfer. This effectively provides a form of rollover relief for business assets for IHT purposes.

The minimum ownership period requirement is also ignored on the second of two successive transfers of the same property within two years where:

i) the earlier transfer qualified for BPR,
ii) the second transfer would otherwise qualify for BPR, and
iii) at least one of the two transfers occurred on death

When a widow or widower inherits business property, their ownership period for the purpose of BPR includes the ownership period of their deceased spouse. However, a transferor spouse's previous ownership period is ***not*** included in the case of a lifetime transfer (although the general rule above will often apply where the transferee spouse dies soon after the transfer).

## 7.17 REPLACEMENT BUSINESS PROPERTY

The replacement of relevant business property by other relevant business property has been referred to a few times in the preceding sections. Broadly, this means on a disposal of the original business property, the same value was reinvested in new qualifying business property.

The replacement business property does not need to be in the same kind of business as the original business property, nor does it need to be the same type of property. For example, an individual could sell an unquoted manufacturing company and reinvest the proceeds in a partnership share in a hotel business.

Provided all the other necessary rules are met, BPR may still be available even when more than one replacement has taken place. Hence, in the preceding sections, where I refer to 'the two assets taken together', this could also apply to three or more assets, each of which replaced their predecessor.

Where a taxpayer relies on a replacement to qualify for BPR, the amount of relief available is generally restricted to the amount that would have been available had the replacement not taken place. For the specific purposes of this rule, however, the formation, alteration or dissolution of a partnership; or the acquisition of a business by a company controlled by the former owner of that business; are disregarded.

## 7.18 EXTRA RULES FOR LIFETIME TRANSFERS

Where BPR applied on a lifetime transfer and the transferor dies within seven years, some extra conditions must be satisfied for BPR to also apply at the time of the transferor's death. The conditions are:

i) The transferee must continue to own the original transferred assets throughout the period from the original transfer to the relevant date (see below)
ii) The original transferred assets must continue to be relevant business property for BPR purposes on the relevant date

Where the transferee retains only part of the original asset at the relevant date, BPR continues to apply to that part, as long as condition (ii) is satisfied.

**The Relevant Date and the Relevant Period**
For the purpose of the rules described in this section, the relevant date is the date of the transferor's death or, if earlier, the transferee's death. The relevant period is the period from the original transfer to the relevant date. Of course, the relevant date and relevant period are only relevant if the transferor dies within seven years of the original transfer.

The conditions set out above mean it is generally necessary for the assets to be qualifying business property in the transferee's hands at the time of the earlier of the transferor or transferee's death. This does not apply if the original assets were shares or securities that were either already quoted at the time of the original transfer, or remained unquoted throughout the relevant period.

Where a transferee has a minority holding of unquoted shares, these will cease to be relevant business property if the company obtains a quotation. This could result in an IHT bill if the transferor dies within seven years of the original transfer.

**Replacement Assets**
The transferee may retain their BPR entitlement if they dispose of the original assets and acquire replacement assets (as defined in Section 7.17). Qualifying agricultural property (see Section 7.28) also qualifies as a replacement asset for these purposes.

The following further conditions must be met:

a) The replacement assets must be acquired within three years of the transferee's disposal of the original assets
b) Both the transferee's sale of the original assets and their acquisition of replacement assets must take place on arm's length terms (see Section 2.1)
c) The whole consideration received on the sale of the original transferred assets must be expended acquiring the replacement assets
d) The transferee must own the replacement assets at the relevant date unless the transferor dies first and within the allowed period (see below)
e) Apart from the allowed period, either the original transferred assets or the replacement assets must be owned by the transferee throughout the relevant period
f) The replacement assets must be relevant business property in the transferee's hands at the relevant date (except as noted below)

**The Allowed Period**

The three-year period under condition (a) begins when the transferee enters a binding contract to sell the original assets. Fortunately, it is only necessary for them to enter a binding contract to acquire the replacement assets within the requisite period: completion can take place later if necessary. (There's more on binding contracts coming up in Section 7.19)

This three-year period, known as the allowed period, can extend after the transferor's death, so the replacement may sometimes take place after the transferor dies. For these purposes, condition (f) is amended so that the replacement assets need to be relevant business property in the transferee's hands when the transferee acquires them.

The legislation seems to suggest only one replacement is allowed under these circumstances, unlike other replacements, as considered in Section 7.17.

What all this means is, if you receive qualifying business property in a gift from someone else, you may find yourself with an IHT bill if you sell that property within seven years. However, if you can wait at least four years before selling the gifted property, you will have the opportunity to restore your BPR by acquiring replacement business property if your benefactor should pass away unexpectedly.

**Gifts with Reservation**

A lifetime transfer of qualifying business property could still be a gift with reservation (Section 4.8). This would mean the property effectively remained in the transferor's estate and IHT would be payable if the property did not qualify for BPR at the time of their death.

In particular, excessive salary payments to the transferor could make the transfer a gift with reservation: i.e. excessive salary paid to the transferor following the transfer of a business, partnership share, or shares or securities in a company. The same would apply to other benefits provided in excess of a normal commercial level, including excessive pension contributions.

**Lifetime Transfers Becoming Chargeable on Death**
If the transferee loses the BPR on a transferred asset, as explained above, then IHT will be payable if the transferor dies within seven years. Additional IHT may also be payable on a transferor's death when the transferred asset only qualifies for BPR at 50%. In both cases, any other available reliefs, such as the annual exemption, may be taken into account.

Where the original transfer was a chargeable lifetime transfer (e.g. to a trust), only that transferee will be affected by any loss of BPR. Where the original transfer was a PET, the loss of BPR means the whole of the transferor's estate must be recalculated on the basis set out in Section 4.5, but without the BPR.

## 7.19 HOW TO PRESERVE BUSINESS PROPERTY RELIEF

For anyone with a qualifying business, BPR is incredibly valuable. The trouble is you need to qualify for the relief at the moment a transfer takes place. That moment may be death in many cases and this carries some inherent problems.

Firstly, it is generally pretty unpredictable when this will be. Secondly, it may be some time after you cease to be interested in running a business. Most people will want to retire at some point and, unfortunately, this will often result in the loss of their BPR.

**Selling Up**
As soon as you have a binding contract for sale, you are, for IHT purposes, no longer regarded as owning the asset being sold. Instead, you are regarded as owning a right to the sale proceeds. That right is generally not a qualifying asset for BPR purposes. Hence, at one stroke of a pen, you can lose your BPR and substantially increase your family's IHT bill in the event of your death.

***Example:*** *Eddie owns an unquoted trading company, Cochran Ltd. The company is Eddie's only asset so, as things stand, Eddie has no need to worry about IHT.*

*Eddie gets an offer from a French company, Aznavour S.A., to buy Cochran Ltd for £10.325m. He decides to accept the offer, so he flies to Paris, takes the Metro to Aznavour S.A.'s offices and signs a binding contract to sell his company. Leaving the office, Eddie looks the wrong way crossing the street and steps in front of a bus. IHT bill: £4m!*

**This example is based on a true story** and readily demonstrates the ease with which BPR can be lost and the dire consequences that may result. An entrepreneur like Eddie might have been intending to reinvest his sale proceeds in a new business venture and hence might have regained the protection of BPR within a few weeks by virtue of the replacement property rules (Section 7.17). Perhaps Eddie should have considered taking out insurance to cover the IHT risk during this short interval!

When an individual who has sold a qualifying business within the last three years gets a little more warning of their demise, the replacement property rules might provide an answer. The protection of BPR can generally be maintained if the taxpayer reinvests all the sale proceeds from qualifying business property into new qualifying business property within three years.

**Exceptions to the Loss of Business Property Relief on Sale**
A binding contract for sale will not result in a loss of BPR if the contract is:

a) For the sale of an unincorporated business to a company that is to carry on that business where the purchase consideration is wholly or mainly shares or securities in that company, or
b) For the sale of shares or securities in a company for the purposes of reconstruction or amalgamation

**Liquidation and Winding Up**
BPR is lost on a company's shares if the company is in liquidation or being wound up. There is an exception to this, however, if the winding up is being carried out as part of a scheme of corporate reconstruction or amalgamation (e.g. a company reorganisation or merger of two companies).

**Retirement**
BPR is lost as soon as a partner retires from a qualifying partnership business. Any capital the retired partner leaves in the business is simply regarded as a loan and is ineligible for BPR.

One way to avoid this problem is for the partner to continue in partnership, but with a very small profit share. (Remaining in partnership does, of course, have commercial implications, which should also be considered.)

When a sole trader retires there is no business so there can be no BPR. The answer here may be to take on a partner and then, at a later date, to semi-retire: i.e. reduce to a very small profit share in the manner described above.

An individual owning qualifying shares or securities in a trading company can happily retire without any loss of BPR as their position depends on their shareholding and not on whether they actually participate in the company's business. Incorporating the business prior to retirement may therefore sometimes be a good way to preserve BPR.

**Buy-Out Clauses on Death: A BIG NO-NO!**
It is common practice for business partners to enter into an agreement whereby their executors will sell their partnership share to the surviving partners in the event of their death.

Similar agreements are also often used by shareholder/directors of unquoted companies whereby their executors sell their shares back to the company, or to their fellow directors, in the event of their death.

While these agreements make a good deal of commercial sense, from a BPR perspective they represent a disaster waiting to happen. This is because, at the moment of death, a binding sale contract will come into force and the estate will not hold relevant business property but, as we saw above, will instead hold a non-qualifying right to sale proceeds.

To avoid this problem, it is essential to avoid any sort of agreement that may form a binding contract on the death of a partner or director.

**Cross Options**

A better alternative is to use non-coterminous cross options. In other words, the business partners should enter into an agreement whereby, in the event of a partner's death, their executors will have an option to sell the deceased's partnership share and the surviving partners will have an option to buy it.

Similarly, private company directors would enter into an agreement whereby, in the event of a director's death, their executors will have an option to sell the deceased's shares or securities in the company and either the company itself or the surviving directors will have an option to buy them.

To be on the safe side, it is wise to ensure the options are non-coterminous. Broadly, this means the option to purchase and the option to sell may only be exercised at different times. (E.g. the deceased's executors must exercise the option to sell within six weeks of the deceased's death and the surviving business partners, or directors, must exercise the option to purchase more than six but less than twelve weeks after the deceased's death.)

HMRC has specifically confirmed this approach is acceptable in the case of a business partnership and there is no reason to suppose the same principles would not be equally valid in the case of unquoted company shares or securities.

Using cross options will therefore preserve any BPR entitlement while also satisfying the original commercial objective of allowing the deceased's share of a business to be bought out.

**Other Approaches for Partnerships**

HMRC has confirmed the following methods for dealing with a deceased partner's share of a business will preserve any BPR entitlement available:

- Partnership ceases on death, partnership assets to be realised and deceased partner's estate receives appropriate share of proceeds
- Partnership continues and deceased's estate represents the deceased
- Partnership share falls into deceased's estate with surviving partners having an option to purchase at either a valuation or an agreed formula-based price
- The deceased's partnership share accrues to the surviving partners but the deceased's estate is entitled to payment at either a valuation or an agreed formula-based price
- Cross options (as explained above), which must be exercised within a set period following the partner's death

## 7.20 MAXIMISING BUSINESS PROPERTY RELIEF

Where an individual owns and controls a qualifying trading company, the whole value of that company could effectively be exempt from IHT. As that individual nears the end of their life, it may make sense to maximise the value of the company.

Furthermore, any assets held personally by the individual and used in the company's business would only qualify for 50% BPR. Again, it might make sense to ensure these were held in the company.

***Example:*** *Madge is a very wealthy old woman. Among her many assets is her unquoted trading company, Ciccone Ltd, which is currently worth £4m. This value takes account of the fact the company owes £2m for the purchase of new equipment and has a bank overdraft of £1.5m. Madge also owns a factory worth £10m, which is used by the company.*

*If Madge were to die with things as they stand, her personal representatives would be able to claim BPR as follows:*

| | |
|---|---|
| *Ciccone Ltd: £4m @ 100%* | *£4,000,000* |
| *Factory: £10m @ 50%* | *£5,000,000* |
| *TOTAL* | *£9,000,000* |

*Realising she isn't immortal after all Madge decides to undertake some IHT planning. First, she transfers the factory into the company. She is able to avoid CGT on this transfer by using a holdover relief election. SDLT is, however, payable on the market value of the property. In this case, the SDLT amounts to £489,500.*

*Madge then uses £4m out of her substantial private wealth to subscribe for further new shares in Ciccone Ltd. This enables the company to pay off the bank overdraft, the debt for the new equipment and the SDLT on the property transfer.*

*Ciccone Ltd will now be worth £17.5m and, after just two years, the whole of this value will be covered by BPR.*

*The overall value of Madge's estate will be virtually unchanged except for the £489,500 paid in SDLT. However, this simple piece of planning will save her family £3.6m in IHT!*

The transfer of the factory will provide an immediate IHT saving, but it will take two years for Madge's new shares in Ciccone Ltd to qualify for BPR. This delay can, however, be easily avoided. New shares issued by way of a rights issue are treated as part of the original shareholding for the purposes of BPR.

Hence, a new investment into an existing qualifying trading company, which is structured as a rights issue, may be eligible for full BPR immediately.

Although the transfer of the factory in the above example can be carried out free of CGT, there may be other important tax consequences if the company subsequently sells the property. The potential advantages or disadvantages of holding property through a company are covered in depth in the Taxcafe guide *Using a Property Company to Save Tax.*

The IHT planning undertaken by Madge worked because her company was in debt and was using the factory in its business. If, on the other hand, she had injected so much capital into the company that it had a surplus in excess of its usual trading requirements, there would have been a restriction on her BPR under the excepted assets rules (see Section 7.9).

The restriction would have operated by reference to the amount of the non-trading surplus as a proportion of the company's total net assets. If the surplus were large enough, the company might even have failed the wholly or mainly test (see Section 7.6) and thus ceased to qualify for BPR altogether!

## 7.21 DIRECTOR'S LOAN ACCOUNTS

Most small company owners have a director's loan account with their company. This account represents money due to them from their company (a credit balance) or money they owe to their company (a debit balance).

Director's loan accounts can arise in several ways, including cash injected into the company by the director, cash withdrawn, or an accumulation of non-cash transactions such as unpaid salary, dividends, or rent.

The IHT impact of a director's loan account depends on whether we are looking at a credit balance or a debit balance.

**Credit Balances**

A debt due to you from your own company is a completely separate asset to your company shares. Furthermore, it is highly unlikely this asset will qualify for BPR. As explained in Section 7.7, it is only debts in the form of securities that actually contribute to your control of the company that qualify for BPR.

A credit balance on a director's loan account can, however, readily be converted into a qualifying asset for BPR purposes simply by issuing new shares to yourself in place of the balance on your loan account. If this is done by way of a rights issue then, as explained in Section 7.20, the new shares are treated as part of the original shareholding for the purposes of BPR and may therefore qualify for relief immediately.

There is also the problem that, as a separate asset, your director's loan account may pass to a different beneficiary on your death. This may cause a few practical difficulties in some cases, and may not be what you would ideally like to happen, so it will be sensible to make a specific provision to deal with your director's loan account in your Will.

Alternatively, a director's loan account may sometimes be a useful way to provide your spouse, or another beneficiary, with a source of tax-free income. For example, you could leave company shares qualifying for BPR to one of your children, but leave your director's loan account to your spouse.

Future company profits could then be used to repay the director's loan account, giving your spouse an effective source of tax-free income. This is a tax efficient structure but is probably only suitable where the surviving family members are happy to co-operate.

A director's loan account has other advantages during your lifetime, when it is probably preferable to investing in additional shares. As with many things, there are different factors to weigh up and it is perhaps only as you grow older that you might wish to convert your director's loan account into shares. For some of the lifetime benefits of a director's loan account, see the Taxcafe guides *Putting it Through the Company* or *Using a Property Company to Save Tax.*

**Debit Balances**

A debt due from you to your own company will enhance your company's value provided the debt is recoverable (i.e. you have sufficient private assets to repay the debt). Relatively small balances that have arisen through normal everyday transactions should not affect the company's status for BPR purposes. However, large balances may effectively become investment assets in the company's hands, and could either be excepted assets (see Section 7.8), or may even threaten the company's qualifying status under the wholly or mainly test (Section 7.6).

As with any other liability, the director's loan account will need to be repaid out of the assets of your estate in order to be deductible on your death.

Debit balances on director's loan accounts may also have Corporation Tax consequences for the company, as well as personal tax consequences for the director. See the Taxcafe guide *Salary versus Dividends* for further details.

## 7.22 SHELTERING INVESTMENTS WITH BUSINESS PROPERTY RELIEF

BPR on company shares may be reduced, or possibly lost altogether, if a non-trading asset, such as an investment property or quoted share portfolio, were transferred into the company. Such a transfer may also give rise to CGT liabilities, plus SDLT in the case of a property.

However, as we have already seen, there would nevertheless remain the possibility of arguing that a hybrid business, qualifying under the wholly or mainly principle (see Section 7.6) existed, so that the investment property or quoted share portfolio might be sheltered from IHT within the trading company. But how far can we push this?

If investments are simply being dumped into a trading company, HMRC is unlikely to accept the hybrid business argument and, as we saw in Section 7.6, may argue the company is simply being used as a repository for non-business assets.

The important distinction to remember is that investments can only be sheltered within a trading company qualifying for BPR if they form part of the company's business. A random cobbled together collection of non-trading investments will not be good enough.

The best way to make use of the trading company shelter would therefore be to build an investment arm to the company's business over several years.

It would be vital to ensure this part of the business remained comfortably less than 50% of the company's overall business, bearing in mind the various possible tests set out in Section 7.6.

To maintain full BPR on the company's shares, its investment business arm would need to be an integral part of the company's overall business and it is important to reflect this in the company's records, including management accounts, directors' board minutes, cashflow projections, etc.

***Example:*** *After making the transfer of the factory and subscribing for new shares, which we saw in Section 7.20, Madge begins to make some quoted investments within Ciccone Ltd. She runs the entire enterprise as a single business, ensuring that management accounts, directors' board minutes and other company documentation all record the fact the investment arm is an integral part of Ciccone Ltd's business.*

*A few years later, the total value of the company is £35m, including £10m worth of investments and trading assets worth £25m.*

*By building the investment portfolio within Ciccone Ltd instead of privately, Madge has reduced her IHT exposure by another £4m.*

A similar approach could also be taken to shelter investments from IHT within a trading partnership.

It would be difficult for a sole trader to achieve the same result, however, as HMRC would view them as having two businesses: one qualifying for BPR and one not. Nevertheless, this problem might perhaps be overcome if the investments were an integral part of the same business.

One good way to argue that investments are an integral part of any business is to make investments in companies operating in the same industry. These investments will provide the investor with valuable information on their competitors, including access to their competitors' shareholders' meetings, and there is therefore a strong argument this can be regarded as an integral part of the business.

Under the wholly or mainly test for BPR purposes, a company could still qualify with just under 50% of its activities being non-trading activities. However, for the purposes of a number of CGT reliefs, including business asset disposal relief and holdover relief on a gift of shares, the company may lose its trading status if just 20% of its activities are non-trading activities. This could have significant adverse consequences. Loss of business asset disposal relief could result in an extra £100,000 of CGT per shareholder. We will look at holdover relief in Chapter 12.

Historically, the criteria to be used for the 20% test had been expected to follow broadly the same principles as we saw in Section 7.6 for the wholly or mainly test. However, recent case law has given better guidance on this issue and we will look at this in Section 12.4.

If making investments via a trading company, it is important to ensure the company's Memorandum and Articles of Association permit this activity. Any activity not so permitted is strictly illegal and thus cannot be regarded as part of the company's business.

## 7.23 CHANGING THE BUSINESS TO SAVE INHERITANCE TAX

It is worth bearing in mind that a business only needs to qualify for BPR throughout the two-year period before the transfer. Hence, the business owner could build up a valuable non-qualifying business over many years and then change it into a qualifying business later. If the owner survives at least two years after the change, they can avoid IHT on the business.

***Example:*** *Steve has built up an unquoted property investment company, Tyler Properties Ltd, over many years. He is now 80 years old and wishes to retire. In early 2023, Steve retires and his daughter Liv takes over the running of the company. Steve continues to own the company and Liv is paid a salary.*

*Liv immediately begins to change the company's business to one of property development. This process is completed by March 2024. Sadly, in May 2026, Steve dies and leaves Tyler Properties Ltd to Liv. As the company had carried on a qualifying trading activity for the previous two years, the shares left to Liv are fully covered by BPR and no IHT is due.*

The change in the company's business activity may give rise to some additional Corporation Tax costs. However, where the change takes place gradually, over a number of years, these should not be too severe.

Remember also that the change in activity does not need to be absolute, as it is only necessary for the company to pass the wholly or mainly test (see Section 7.6) during the last two years prior to the transfer.

For IHT purposes, Steve would also have been able to claim BPR on a lifetime transfer of his Tyler Properties Ltd shares any time after the company had been carrying on a qualifying business for two years.

However, this would mean Liv would need to continue the qualifying business for up to another seven years in order to retain BPR (see Section 7.18). This could also lead to a CGT liability for Steve on the share transfer if the company still held any investment assets at that time.

## 7.24 BUSINESS SUCCESSION PLANNING

From a tax perspective, the last thing a dying person should do is sell a business that qualifies for BPR!

The day before the sale, the business would have been completely covered by BPR and available to pass on to their family free of IHT. The day after the sale, the proceeds would be completely exposed to IHT, resulting in the loss of up to 40%.

This is on top of any CGT that arose on the sale. As we shall see in Chapter 12, CGT could also generally be avoided if the family sold the business shortly after the original owner's death.

In practice, unfortunately, and much to HMRC's delight, it will often be necessary to sell the business before the owner's death. Very often, a large proportion of a business's value can be lost when its proprietor dies. After all, it is better to let HMRC take 40% of a great deal than to deny them their share of very little.

Ideally, business succession planning is something that should be looked at much earlier on, when the original proprietor is still hale and hearty and looking forward to a well-deserved retirement. If a deathbed sale situation does arise, however, one way to avoid the pitfalls described above would be to sell the business in exchange for unquoted shares in a trading company. Full BPR would then be preserved and CGT can also generally be avoided.

## 7.25 SMALLER SHAREHOLDINGS

***Any*** shareholding in an unquoted trading company qualifies for 100% BPR. This includes shares in AIM companies. The problem is when one considers the generally volatile nature of unquoted shares, combined with the minimum two-year holding period, putting your wealth into these types of assets just to save IHT is a pretty risky business. Nevertheless, under the right circumstances, it is certainly something to consider. Let's look at an example.

***Example:*** *Noel wins a substantial sum on the National Lottery. "Great," his brother Liam says, "how 'bout helpin' me out with me business then?" Noel agrees to give Liam £100,000 to help get his new business started. However, if Noel simply gives Liam the money, this will be a PET and if Noel dies within seven years, it will have to be brought back into his estate.*

*So, what Noel does instead is to subscribe for shares in Liam's company, Wonderwall Ltd. After just two years, the Wonderwall Ltd shares will qualify for BPR and Noel can then give them to Liam free from IHT (subject to the points set out in Section 7.18).*

## 7.26 THE AIM EXEMPTION

I've said it enough times but I know you think it's too good to be true, so here it is again: shares traded on the Alternative Investment Market (AIM) are eligible for 100% BPR. In other words, IHT really is voluntary and here's how to avoid volunteering in five easy steps:

i) Sell everything you've got unless it qualifies for 100% BPR or APR
ii) Put £325,000 on deposit (perhaps more: see below)
iii) Buy an annuity to give yourself sufficient guaranteed income to get by on (this step is optional but sensible)
iv) Put everything else into a portfolio of qualifying AIM shares
v) Survive two years

Widows and widowers with a full TNRB entitlement can increase the deposit under step (ii) to £650,000. Parents and grandparents may be able to exclude their home from step (i) if it will qualify for the RNRB (see Section 3.4), or add equivalent funds to the deposit under step (ii) if the downsizing provisions apply (see Section 13.11).

Too drastic for you? Perhaps, but the point to remember is, although AIM shares are classed as unquoted for most tax purposes, including BPR, they are still traded on the London Stock Exchange and are thus effectively liquid assets (albeit that, due to the relatively low level of trading, it can sometimes be difficult to sell AIM shares at a fair price).

Are they risky? Well, yes, all investments are risky, but AIM shares have sometimes outperformed the FTSE. At present, there are approximately 850 companies quoted on AIM with a combined market value of around £150 billion.

Furthermore, the risk is substantially reduced if you invest in a portfolio of shares and there are financial products available to enable you to do this with professional fund managers choosing your AIM investments for you.

The fund managers will monitor the performance of your investments and will make changes to the portfolio to protect your investment and your BPR. Such changes can usually be made without any loss of BPR due to the replacement property rules (see Section 7.17).

And you can afford a bit of risk anyway, can't you? Think about it: if you lose, say, 20% of your investment, but save 40% in IHT, your family are still better off. Better still, you can eliminate the risk altogether by investing in a protected IHT service with a built-in life insurance policy. If your investment has fallen in value when you die, the life policy will pay out the shortfall. The life policy itself can be made tax-efficient by being written into trust (see Section 11.8). All you need do is survive the requisite two years. You can then leave your family up to 67% better off, even if your AIM portfolio has performed badly!

Naturally, a scheme like this does not come cheap and the fund managers' charges can be quite expensive. Furthermore, the life insurance premiums will typically absorb any income from the investment: and you will still have to pay Income Tax on any dividends paid by the AIM companies in your portfolio that total in excess of your dividend allowance (see Appendix A).

However, under the right circumstances, it could be worth bearing these costs for the sake of the ultimate 40% tax saving. For an elderly person with surplus funds, the potential to avoid IHT after surviving just two years represents a huge incentive.

Furthermore, anyone investing the proceeds from the sale of other qualifying business property within the last three years could obtain BPR immediately, thus exempting their entire investment from IHT even if they die shortly afterwards.

And it's worth remembering an investment in AIM shares is not locked away permanently. If your circumstances change and you need to realise some of those funds, which are no longer surplus to requirements after all, you can simply sell some of your AIM portfolio. This makes an AIM portfolio very attractive to anyone who wishes to save IHT without actually giving any of their money away. The portfolio provides a means to protect some of your wealth from IHT when you are unsure whether you can genuinely afford to live without it.

On the other hand, in view of the costs inherent in a protected AIM portfolio investment, a wealthy person with funds that are quite definitely surplus to requirements and a life expectancy of well over seven years might do better to simply give that surplus away and take out term life insurance to cover the risk of a premature death.

Nevertheless, while the full five-step plan outlined above may not be for you, there could still be a place for some AIM shares in your IHT planning strategy.

While AIM shares are eligible for BPR in principle, it remains important that the companies in which you invest are themselves carrying on qualifying businesses. This will, however, include AIM companies with a hybrid business that passes the wholly or mainly test (see Section 7.6).

If your AIM shares get a full listing, your BPR will be lost (unless you control the company). Having said that, if this does happen, you will probably have made a nice profit, so it wouldn't be all bad would it? Alternatively, you could sell the AIM shares before they are listed and reinvest the proceeds in replacement business property any time within the next three years, thus retaining your BPR.

Capital gains and dividends received on AIM shares are subject to CGT and Income Tax respectively in the normal way. There are no special reliefs applying to AIM shares for these taxes. (You could hold AIM shares via an ISA to avoid these problems, although this may not always be the best use of your ISA allowance.)

## 7.27 AIMING TOO HIGH

As with any other form of qualifying business property, liabilities incurred after 5th April 2013 and used, directly or indirectly, to purchase qualifying AIM shares must be deducted from the value of those shares for BPR purposes.

This means it is no longer possible to obtain additional BPR by borrowing against other assets to purchase AIM shares. In this context, it is important to bear in mind HMRC takes a very broad view of what is meant by 'indirectly'.

***Example:*** *Ella owns a house worth £1.5m and has savings and investments totalling £1.2m. In 2023, she sells her investments and invests the proceeds, together with her savings, into qualifying AIM shares. (I have ignored CGT on the sale of her investments for the sake of illustration, but in practice this needs to be taken into account.)*

*A short time later, Ella mortgages her house for £1m. She gives £600,000 to her grandchildren and uses the remaining £400,000 to replace some of her savings: to assist in funding her mortgage and provide her with a bit of a 'cushion'.*

According to HMRC's guidance, Ella should be treated as having used £400,000 of her mortgage to indirectly finance the purchase of her AIM shares, restricting her BPR to £800,000 (£1.2m – £400,000). Their logic is that Ella could have achieved substantially the same result by investing just £800,000 of her savings in AIM shares and taking out a mortgage of £600,000 to provide funds to give to her grandchildren.

As always, HMRC's guidance is not actually the law, but it can often be persuasive and, until the matter is actually tested in court, it would be wise to operate on the basis their interpretation is correct. In other words, it would be sensible for someone in Ella's position to restrict their AIM investment to the amount they can actually afford without taking on any additional borrowing.

## 7.28 AGRICULTURAL PROPERTY RELIEF (APR)

APR applies in a broadly similar way to BPR. The following types of property may be covered:

i) Agricultural land or pasture
ii) Buildings used for the intensive rearing of livestock or fish
iii) Stud farms
iv) Farmhouses, cottages and other farm buildings
v) Woodlands

Property under (iv) or (v) must generally be occupied on a basis ancillary to property also occupied under (i), (ii) or (iii); although buildings used to grow indoor crops, such as mushrooms, may qualify in their own right without the need for any additional agricultural land.

For transfers of value (on death or otherwise) after 5th April 2024, the relief will only apply to agricultural land in the UK. Currently, it also applies to agricultural land anywhere in the European Economic Area (EEA), the Channel Islands, or the Isle of Man.

To qualify for APR, the land or buildings must either have been:

a) Occupied (i.e. used) by the transferor for agricultural purposes for a period of at least two years prior to the date of transfer, or
b) Owned by the transferor and used for agricultural purposes (by anyone) for at least seven years prior to the date of transfer

Occupation by a company controlled by the transferor is treated as occupation by the transferor for the purposes of (a) above. Occupation by a partnership is treated as occupation by the partners.

APR is given at rates of 50% or 100%, depending on the exact circumstances of the transfer and subject to the usual raft of provisions designed to prevent abuse. It is essential that agricultural activities are being carried out on the land at the time of the transfer. Furthermore, the relief is restricted to the agricultural value of the land or property. This is the value of the land or property if transferred subject to a condition it must remain in agricultural use permanently.

Any excess value may be eligible for BPR in some cases. Where the transferor is actively farming the land themselves, this will usually qualify as a trading activity for BPR purposes.

Farming syndicate arrangements are available to provide IHT shelters for investments of £200,000 or more.

A separate IHT deferral relief is available for woodlands in the UK or the EEA that do not qualify for APR. Again, this will be restricted to the UK only from 6th April 2024.

The Government is currently consulting on the possibility of expanding the scope of APR to cover certain types of environmental land management.

**Agricultural Liabilities**
The rules set out in Sections 7.10 to 7.15 apply equally to liabilities incurred to finance agricultural property, woodlands, or (where appropriate) shares and securities in companies carrying on these activities.

## 7.29 FARMHOUSES

If you ever discuss IHT in your local pub or golf club, some bright spark is bound to tell you they have avoided IHT by buying a farm.

For a start, the mere fact they are around to make this bar room boast means they have not actually avoided IHT yet. More specifically, the problem with a lot of so-called farmhouses is they are really just a country house with some farmland nearby. This alone is not enough to secure APR.

A normal size farmhouse occupied by a working farmer is indeed eligible for APR but it is essential the house is 'of an appropriate character' and occupied for the purposes of farming throughout the two years prior to the relevant transfer (or seven years where occupied by someone other than the owner).

To be occupied for the purposes of farming, the house must be occupied by the person with day-to-day responsibility for running the farm (e.g. a farm manager). A farm owner with only limited involvement in the day-to-day running of the farm does not occupy their home for the purposes of farming. So, simply buying an old farmhouse isn't necessarily enough to claim APR.

Of course, the fact the farmhouse doesn't qualify does not necessarily preclude the rest of the farm from qualifying, so our bar room braggart may not be entirely wrong, but this will generally only be a small comfort, as the majority of the value will usually be in the house.

Even when a farmhouse does qualify for APR, the relief is restricted to its agricultural value: the value it would have if sold subject to a covenant requiring it to remain in agricultural use. In some cases, there will be a substantial difference between this and the house's open market value and the excess will not be eligible for APR. Whether any of the excess value is eligible for BPR will depend on the circumstances of the case.

The major problem for genuine farmers is that the house must be occupied for the purposes of farming throughout the two years prior to the relevant transfer (or seven years where occupied by someone other than the owner). Elderly farmers who are seeking to retire should therefore consider passing the farmhouse to their children while it still qualifies for relief.

## 7.30 THE SAFETY NET

Given the numerous and highly complex conditions that must be satisfied to obtain BPR or APR, the matter will often be in doubt when the business owner dies.

If the owner simply leaves the business or agricultural property to their surviving spouse, the matter will still not be resolved as this transfer will usually be exempt anyway. However, if the deceased left the property to a discretionary trust in their Will, HMRC would need to examine the case and, hopefully, the matter will soon be resolved. But how does this help?

If BPR or APR is denied, there should be time to appoint the assets to the surviving spouse free from IHT (see Section 18.3). The tax is at least deferred and the executors will know where they stand. Furthermore, the surviving spouse may have time to correct whatever defects were in the property so there is a better chance of claiming relief on their subsequent death.

If it turns out that full BPR or APR ***is*** available on the first death, there is a chance to do some further planning, as outlined in Sections 7.31 and 15.2.

## 7.31 MAKE HAY WHILE THE SUN SHINES

If an individual dies leaving property that is fully exempt under BPR or APR, there is a strong argument to suggest it would be wise to pass this property directly to the deceased's children, or other younger beneficiaries, rather than risk any possibility the relief may be lost before the deceased's surviving spouse or partner dies.

BPR or APR could be lost during the surviving spouse or partner's lifetime due to either a change in legislation or a change in the nature of the business. In the case of AIM shares, there is also the possibility the shares might get a full listing so, again, it may make sense to pass these to the next generation while they still qualify for relief.

In the case of a family business, the fear of losing the relief may place unwelcome constraints on the business. By passing the business directly to the next generation, such constraints are effectively removed (although the problem will of course eventually return).

This approach will not suit every family, of course, and most people will want to be sure their spouse or partner is financially secure before they are happy to pass the family business straight to their children.

For those who literally are making hay, i.e. running the family farm, it is often a good idea to pass the farmhouse directly to the children on the first spouse's death since APR may subsequently be lost if the surviving spouse is unable to run the farm on their own.

Furthermore, for all types of business, passing the business directly to the children (or other ultimate beneficiaries) on the first death may help to ensure the widow or widower's estate does not exceed £2m on the second death, thus preventing the loss of their RNRB due to tapering (see Section 3.4).

# Chapter 8

# IHT Planning With Trusts

## 8.1 WHAT IS A TRUST?

In its simplest form, a 'trust' is an arrangement under which someone is given the legal title to an asset and 'trusted' to hold that asset on behalf of one or more beneficiaries.

Trusts have a long and honourable history as a well-established mechanism for protecting the vulnerable, such as widows, orphans or disabled people. They originated in the Twelfth Century when crusaders would entrust their assets to another person before setting off to fight in the Holy Land.

**Some definitions:**
**Trustee:** The person trusted to hold the asset
**Beneficiary:** The person on whose behalf the asset is held
**Settlor:** The person who transferred the asset into the trust
**Absolutely:** When assets finally leave the trust and become property of the ultimate beneficiary, we say the beneficiary holds those assets 'absolutely'
**Testator:** A deceased person who left a valid Will (which may have been used to set up a trust)

Very often, the settlor will also be a trustee. Legally, there is nothing to prevent the settlor from also being a beneficiary, although this usually renders the trust ineffective for IHT planning purposes and can also give rise to some unwanted CGT liabilities.

**Settlements and Settled Property**
In legal parlance (and within tax legislation), the act of putting assets or funds into a trust is referred to as a 'settlement'. When a trust is created, this is also referred to as a 'settlement'.

The assets held within the trust are known as settled property. Every time new assets or funds are put into the trust a new item of settled property is created. Each item of settled property has its own separate identity for IHT purposes and this is especially important when there are changes to the IHT treatment of trusts.

***Example:*** *On 20th March 2024, Marc set up the Jeepster Discretionary Trust and transferred £1m into it. On 25th March 2024, Marc transferred another £1m into the trust. Although there is only one formally constituted trust, it contains two distinct items of settled property, one settled on 20th March 2024 and one on 25th March 2024.*

It is important to remember IHT law applies not only to a trust in its entirety, but also to each individual item of settled property within that trust. In our example, the Jeepster Discretionary Trust is one settlement containing two items of settled property.

A single trust may hold settled property subject to an interest in possession while other property is held on discretionary trust. For IHT purposes, each item of settled property is treated according to the rules relating to that particular item of property.

A trust may therefore be regarded as an envelope, which may contain any number of different items of settled property of differing types.

In most cases, for the sake of simplicity, we will generally assume each trust has only one type of settled property. Always remember, however, that IHT law applies to each item of settled property in its own right.

Fundamental changes were made to the IHT treatment of trusts in 2006. These changes have far-reaching consequences and it will often make a critical difference whether property was settled before or after the change. Naturally, when planning for the future, we are only concerned with the current regime and any potential future changes. Nonetheless, as we shall see later in this chapter, many people will still be affected by the earlier rules.

Before we move on to look at some of the useful IHT planning techniques trusts provide, we need to understand more about trusts and how they are treated for tax purposes.

## 8.2 WHAT TYPES OF TRUST ARE THERE?

In essence, there are really only two types of trust: an interest in possession trust and a discretionary trust. The distinction between these two main types revolves entirely around whether any beneficiary is entitled to enjoy an interest in possession in settled property, and this is a crucial factor in determining how the trust will be treated. We will look at what constitutes an interest in possession in Section 8.3; and what constitutes a discretionary trust in Section 8.4.

For IHT purposes, it is necessary to further sub-divide the two main types into a number of other categories, each of which is subject to different rules. These categories are listed in Sections 8.5 and 8.7 and the factors that determine which category each item of settled property falls into are considered later.

As explained in Section 8.1, a single trust may hold items of settled property that fall into two or more different categories. Hence, we may sometimes get a sort of hybrid trust subject to different rules on its different parts.

## 8.3 WHAT IS AN INTEREST IN POSSESSION?

Whenever a specific individual is beneficially entitled, for a specified period, to the income from, or to otherwise enjoy, an asset within a trust, that person has an interest in possession.

Where more than one person is to share the income or enjoyment of the assets for a specified period, this is also an interest in possession. The income may be shared in any proportion specified in the Trust Deed.

If, however, the trustees have discretion over the income paid to the beneficiaries, this would make the trust a discretionary trust.

***Example:*** *Nicole transfers several rental properties into the All Saints Trust. Under the terms of the trust, the annual rental profits must be paid to the beneficiaries as follows:*

- *Half to Nicole's sister, Natalie*
- *The first £10,000 of the remainder to her friend, Melanie*
- *The remaining balance to her niece, Shaznay*

*Each beneficiary's interest is an interest in possession because each of them receives a specific defined amount under the terms of the Trust Deed that is not dependent on the discretion of the trustees.*

### Life Interests

Where a beneficiary is entitled to an interest in possession for the remainder of their life, we refer to this as a life interest (sometimes known as a liferent). A trust subject to a life interest is often referred to as a life interest trust.

Generally speaking, the IHT treatment of a life interest trust is exactly the same as any other interest in possession trust.

### The Remainder

The remainder is a term used to describe a right to assets that comes into force after an interest in possession ends.

The most common example is when a person leaves a life interest in property to their spouse with the remainder to their children. This means on the spouse's death the property passes absolutely to the children.

### Reversion to Settlor

It is possible to create an interest in possession trust where the remainder interest reverts to the original settlor. This, in itself, does not invoke the gift with reservation rules (Section 4.8) as long as the settlor is excluded from benefit during the period the interest in possession exists (in practice, as discussed in Section 9.2, the settlor's spouse would usually also need to be excluded).

**Income Tax Treatment**
All other things being equal, an interest in possession trust is generally to be preferred whenever possible as it enjoys a more beneficial Income Tax regime than a discretionary trust. See Section 8.20 for further details.

## 8.4 DISCRETIONARY TRUSTS

A discretionary trust is basically any trust, or part thereof, where no person is entitled to an interest in possession. The trustees have discretion to decide who to allow the enjoyment of the trust's assets, who to pay the income of the trust to, and how much.

There is usually a defined class of beneficiaries from whom the trustees can choose, such as 'all my grandchildren', for example.

It is possible for a discretionary trust to have just one beneficiary, as long as there is a theoretical possibility of there being at least one other additional beneficiary at some time and the trustees have discretion over whether, and when, to pay out income.

The assets of a discretionary trust will always be relevant property (see Section 8.17) unless the trust qualifies as:

- A bereaved minor's trust (Section 8.9),
- An 18 to 25 trust (Section 8.14),
- A disabled trust (Section 8.11), or
- A charitable trust (Section 3.5)

## 8.5 INHERITANCE TAX REGIMES FOR TRUSTS

In essence, there are three IHT regimes for settled property within trusts:

- The relevant property regime,
- Trust property included in the beneficiary's estate, and
- Exempt trusts

Where settled property falls into the relevant property regime, it is subject to IHT charges in its own right, as detailed in Sections 8.17 to 8.19. Such settled property is referred to as relevant property for IHT purposes.

Most other categories of settled property are treated as if they belong absolutely to the beneficiary and are included in the beneficiary's estate for IHT purposes, as explained in Section 2.5.

The scope of the third regime, exempt trusts, was severely curtailed by the changes made by Gordon Brown in 2006 but, as the name implies, it provides complete exemption from IHT for certain types of trust.

The various categories of trust fall into these three regimes, as follows:

**Relevant Property:**

Discretionary Trusts (Note 1)
Post-22/3/2006 Interest in Possession Trusts (Note 2)
18 to 25 Trusts (Note 3)

**In Beneficiary's Estate:**

Pre-22/3/2006 Interest in Possession Trusts
Disabled Trusts
Immediate Post-Death Interests
Transitional Serial Interests
Bare Trusts

**Exempt:**

Bereaved Minors' Trusts
18 to 25 Trusts (Note 3)
Charitable Trusts

This table is naturally a simplification of the position, but hopefully useful.

**Notes**

1. Unless qualifying under another category, as noted in Section 8.4.
2. An interest in possession created after 21st March 2006 that does not qualify under any other category will fall into the relevant property regime. This will occur in the case of most lifetime transfers into trust, or new interests in possession coming into force on termination of a previous interest.
3. 18 to 25 trusts are effectively exempt until the beneficiary attains the age of 18 and then fall into the relevant property regime thereafter.

## 8.6 TRANSFERS INTO TRUST

### On Death

Transfers into trust on the transferor's death are generally chargeable to IHT in the same way whatever type of trust is involved. The regimes described in the previous section determine how the settled property is treated later; they do not usually alter the amount of IHT arising on the transferor's death.

The only exceptions are charitable trusts and the fact the spouse exemption applies to an immediate post-death interest for a surviving spouse (see Section 8.12). In all other cases, transfers into trust arising on death form part of the estate in the normal way and will be subject to IHT as usual.

### Transfers on Death and the Residence Nil Rate Band

Transfers of qualifying property, on death, into a trust for the benefit of one or more of the deceased's direct descendents, will qualify for the RNRB, where available, provided one of the following types of trust is used:

- Bare Trust
- Bereaved Minors' Trust
- Disabled Trust

- Immediate Post-Death Interest
- 18 to 25 Trust

**Lifetime Transfers**
As we saw in Section 4.2, most lifetime transfers into trust are now chargeable lifetime transfers. Lifetime transfers to disabled trusts or bare trusts are, however, PETs and transfers to charity are exempt.

## 8.7 THE TRUST HIERARCHY

All trusts must take their place in what I call the Trust Hierarchy. Every trust will be categorised as the highest type within the hierarchy for which it qualifies. For example, a trust that qualifies as an Immediate Post Death Interest (ranked sixth in the hierarchy) cannot be an 18 to 25 Trust (ranked eighth) even if it would otherwise qualify. The trust hierarchy is as follows:

1. **Charitable Trusts**
2. **Bare Trusts**
3. **Bereaved Minors' Trusts**
4. **Pre-22/3/2006 Interest in Possession Trusts**
5. **Disabled Trusts**
6. **Immediate Post-Death Interests**
7. **Transitional Serial Interests**
8. **18 to 25 Trusts**
9. **Relevant Property Trusts**

Readers will note that two of our categories from Section 8.5 are absent here. Discretionary trusts and post-22/3/2006 interest in possession trusts (not falling into any other category) will both be relevant property trusts.

The first step in our trust hierarchy deals with Charitable Trusts, which have exempt status. We will now proceed to examine each of the remaining steps of our trust hierarchy in turn. Remember, throughout this process, any trust that qualifies at one point in the hierarchy cannot also qualify lower down the hierarchy.

As we shall see in the sections that follow, several categories of trust must be created immediately on the settlor's death. However, in Chapter 18, we will see both deeds of variation and distributions from most trusts made within two years of the settlor's death will be treated as if they had occurred immediately on death. Hence, in practice, most of the trusts that need to be set up immediately on death can often be set up sometime within the following two years.

## 8.8 BARE TRUSTS

Assets that are simply held in someone else's name are held on 'bare trust', sometimes also known as an 'absolute trust'. A bare trust only exists where the beneficiary has full beneficial ownership of the trust assets and has an immediate and absolute right to both capital and income.

Most commonly, a bare trust exists when an adult holds property on behalf of a minor who will become absolutely entitled to the asset on reaching the age of 18 (sometimes 16 in Scotland). Bare trusts for minors occur frequently because persons under the age of 18 cannot take legal title to property in England or Wales. The position in Scotland is slightly different and legal title is sometimes possible at 16. Bare trusts may sometimes continue beyond this point until the beneficiary calls for the trust assets to be transferred to them.

Assets held on bare trust are not regarded as settled property for IHT purposes and are simply treated as belonging to the beneficiary. We will see some useful consequences of this in the next chapter.

## 8.9 BEREAVED MINORS' TRUSTS

The 'trust for a bereaved minor', to give it its proper name, is a very restrictive class of trust. Where the appropriate rules are met, trust property will be exempt from IHT and there will be no charges if a beneficiary dies or assets are transferred out of the trust. The basic conditions are:

- i) The beneficiary must be under 18 years of age
- ii) At least one of the beneficiary's parents is dead
- iii) The trust was set up under:
    - a. Intestacy,
    - b. The criminal injuries compensation scheme, or
    - c. The Will of a deceased parent
- iv) The beneficiary must be absolutely entitled to the trust assets by the age of 18 at the latest
- v) Trust assets may only be applied for the benefit of the minor until he or she reaches the age of 18
- vi) Trust income may either be applied for the benefit of the minor or given directly to them. (The minor may have an interest in possession, if the settlor so desires.)

For the purposes of these rules, a parent includes a natural parent, a step-parent, an adopted parent and any other person with parental responsibility (e.g. a legal guardian).

While the above rules are clearly designed for a single beneficiary, a trust may still qualify with two or more beneficiaries, as long as each of them obtains absolute entitlement to their share of the trust assets at the age of 18.

The major problem with this type of trust is the beneficiary must gain absolute possession of the assets at the age of 18. Many people are horrified at the prospect of the entire family fortune suddenly being at the whim of someone so young. The risk of them frittering everything away before they have the wisdom to look out for their own future is all too obvious.

Thankfully, these concerns were at least partly recognised when the concept of the '18 to 25 Trust' was introduced. We will come on to these trusts in Section 8.14, but it is worth noting that a bereaved minor's trust can be converted to an 18 to 25 trust without charge.

**Small Payments for Non-Qualifying Purposes**
Small payments that do not qualify under points (v) or (vi) above are permitted. These are limited to the lower of £3,000, or 3% of the value of settled property in the trust, each year.

## 8.10 OLD INTEREST IN POSSESSION TRUSTS

Interests in possession already in existence on 21st March 2006 continue to be treated as if the beneficiary owns the asset outright for IHT purposes. Subject to certain exceptions, the termination of the beneficiary's interest, on death or otherwise, represents a transfer of the underlying asset for IHT purposes.

The old rules apply to settled property transferred into trust before 22nd March 2006. Any new transfers of assets into an existing trust will constitute new settled property and will be subject to the current rules.

**Changes to Terms**
Where the terms of a pre-22/3/2006 interest in possession trust are altered, including a change to the period of the interest, this will result in the settled property subject to that interest in possession becoming relevant property.

The trust would then be subject to the IHT charges explained in Sections 8.18 and 8.19. However, where there is no change to the actual beneficiary, there would not be a chargeable lifetime transfer and hence no entry charge.

See Section 8.13 for exceptions applying where the terms of an old interest in possession trust were altered before 6th October 2008.

**Spouses and Civil Partners**
Where a pre-22/3/2006 interest in possession comes to an end on the beneficiary's death and a new interest in possession in favour of the deceased's spouse comes into being, this new interest will be a transitional serial interest (Section 8.13). The spouse exemption will apply to the settled property that falls into the deceased's estate under these circumstances.

## 8.11 DISABLED TRUSTS

Assets within a trust for the benefit of a qualifying disabled person are exempt from the relevant property provisions and are instead treated as part of the beneficiary's estate.

Self-settlement by a person with a condition expected to lead to a qualifying disability is permitted. This extension only applies to self-settlements; other settlors must wait until the beneficiary's condition deteriorates enough for them to qualify under the general rules.

A disabled trust may be either a discretionary trust or an interest in possession trust. Further rules apply to the use of funds held by a discretionary trust.

The rules governing disabled trusts are mainly designed to cover beneficiaries with a mental disability but will often also cover a person with a terminal illness. This provides the opportunity for the settlor to put property into trust during their terminal illness. While this will not save any IHT, it will enable the trustees to manage all or part of the estate following the settlor's death without having to wait for the grant of probate or confirmation.

## 8.12 IMMEDIATE POST-DEATH INTERESTS

An interest in possession created immediately on death, either by Will or intestacy, is termed an immediate post-death interest and forms part of the beneficiary's estate for IHT purposes.

The settled property subject to the immediate post-death interest will therefore be included in the beneficiary's own IHT calculation if they should die while still entitled to the interest in possession or within seven years of the termination of that interest.

Most importantly, this means the spouse exemption is available on the creation of an immediate post-death interest. This provides tremendous additional potential for tax planning using the spouse exemption and we will explore this further in Section 9.6.

Furthermore, where an immediate post-death interest ends during the beneficiary's lifetime and property passes to a bereaved minor's trust under the terms of the original settlor's Will, this will be a PET. Combining this with the spouse exemption provides a potential opportunity to pass assets tax free to minor children. We will explore this in Section 9.7.

An immediate post-death interest may also be set up so that the settled property transfers to a bereaved minor's trust or 18 to 25 trust for the benefit of the original testator's children on the death of the original beneficiary (IHT is payable on the original beneficiary's death in the normal way in this case).

When a testator adds new settled property to an existing interest in possession trust this will also be treated as an immediate post-death interest.

A TNRB may be set against the value of an immediate post-death interest brought into the spouse's estate on their death.

## 8.13 TRANSITIONAL SERIAL INTERESTS

As explained in Section 8.10, a transitional serial interest comes into existence when an old interest in possession comes to an end on the beneficiary's death and is replaced by an interest in possession in favour of the deceased's spouse.

A transitional serial interest also arises where an interest in possession in a settlement made before 22nd March 2006 was replaced by a new interest in possession in the same settled property within the same trust before 6th October 2008. Where the terms of a pre-22/3/2006 interest in possession trust were altered before 6th October 2008, including a change to the period of the interest, this will also constitute a transitional serial interest.

In each case, the replacement interest forms part of the beneficiary's estate for IHT purposes.

When a transitional serial interest comes to an end and is replaced by a new interest in possession, the new interest will be relevant property and will be taxed as set out in Sections 8.17 to 8.19. The spouse exemption does not apply under these circumstances

Where changes are made to the terms of a transitional serial interest, including the period of the interest, this will again result in the property subject to the interest becoming relevant property.

## 8.14 18 TO 25 TRUSTS

To meet concerns raised by many bodies in the wake of the original Budget 2006 announcements, a further category of trust was created: the 18 to 25 Trust. The 18 to 25 trust is essentially the same as a bereaved minors' trust (Section 8.9) in all respects except the beneficiary must become absolutely entitled to the trust property by the age of 25 at the latest, rather than by 18.

Between the ages of 18 and 25, the beneficiary must either be entitled to an interest in possession or else the trust funds must be accumulated for their benefit (subject to the exception for small non-qualifying payments described in Section 8.9).

An 18 to 25 trust only retains its IHT exempt status until the beneficiary is 18. Thereafter, the trust assets effectively become relevant property.

There is no IHT charge when the trust assets become relevant property on the beneficiary's 18th birthday, but the exit charges explained in Section 8.19 will then apply as if the trust had been set up on this date.

This means there will be a maximum exit charge of 4.2% if the trust assets pass to the beneficiary at the age of 25 (in addition to the IHT already paid on the parent's death: making a total charge of up to 44.2%!).

More details of the exit charges applying to 18 to 25 Trusts are given in Section 8.19. Exit charges also apply in the same way if the beneficiary of an 18 to 25 trust dies after the age of 18.

An 18 to 25 trust cannot arise if an immediate post-death interest is created instead, as this takes precedence under the trust hierarchy. An immediate post-death interest will often be preferable, as this avoids the exit charge applying to an 18 to 25 trust.

## 8.15 RELEVANT PROPERTY TRUSTS

Any trust not falling under another category in the trust hierarchy is subject to the relevant property regime. This includes most lifetime settlements, even those conferring interests in possession on the settlor themselves (known as self-settlements), or on their spouse, and revert to settlor trusts (Section 8.3).

Discretionary trusts generally fall within the relevant property regime, unless they qualify under one of the other categories set out in Section 8.7.

When settled property falls within the relevant property regime, IHT charges may arise when the settlement is made, when assets come out of the trust, and every ten years in between (so it's 'in, out, and, every ten years, we shake it all about').

Remember, as explained previously, this may apply to any new settlement, not just a newly constituted trust. There is, however, a partial exception for life policies held in trust and we will return to this in Section 11.8.

### Transfers on Death

Most interests in possession created on death will qualify as immediate post-death interests, as explained in Section 8.12, and should therefore escape the relevant property regime. Dangers arise, however, where the interest in possession does not arise immediately on death. In particular, a new interest in possession that replaces an immediate post-death interest may fall within the relevant property regime (unless, as always, it qualifies under a higher category in the hierarchy).

## 8.16 END OF TRUST INTERESTS WITHIN BENEFICIARY'S ESTATE

As we saw in Section 8.5, there are five types of trust that are regarded as forming part of the beneficiary's estate. Property within these trusts is subject to IHT at 40% when the beneficiary's interest comes to an end by reason of their death (subject to the exemptions explained in Chapter 3, including the spouse exemption, and the revert to settlor exemption explained below).

Under certain circumstances, property within a pre-22/3/2006 interest in possession trust may be eligible to pass into an immediate post-death interest trust, a bereaved minor's trust or an 18 to 25 trust on the original beneficiary's death.

### Interests Ending During the Life of the Beneficiary

If the beneficiary becomes absolutely entitled to the trust property, this will be a non-event for IHT, as the property remains within the same estate.

If the original settlor or the beneficiary's spouse becomes absolutely entitled to the property, or it goes to charity, the transfer will be exempt. In other cases, when the beneficiary's interest ends during their lifetime, a PET will take place if:

- One or more individuals become absolutely entitled to the trust property
- Property transfers to a bare trust
- Property transfers to a disabled trust
- Property subject to an immediate post-death interest transfers to a bereaved minors' trust

All other transfers on termination of a beneficiary's interest during their lifetime will be chargeable lifetime transfers and the transferred property will fall into the relevant property regime.

If the original beneficiary retains an interest in former trust property, this may constitute a gift with reservation. See Section 4.8 for further details.

### Revert to Settlor Trusts

When property reverts to the original settlor on the termination of a pre-22/3/2006 interest in possession trust, the resultant transfer of value is exempt from IHT. This exemption only applies when the property passes back to the settlor absolutely.

## 8.17 THE RELEVANT PROPERTY REGIME

For the rest of this guide, I will refer to any trust that falls into the relevant property regime as a relevant property trust. A relevant property trust is treated as a separate person in its own right for IHT purposes. This has the following consequences:

- Lifetime transfers into a relevant property trust are chargeable transfers, ***not*** PETs
- Transfers into a relevant property trust are generally ineligible for the spouse exemption
- Assets within a relevant property trust are not generally included in a beneficiary's estate for IHT purposes
- No charges arise on the death of a beneficiary or termination of their interest in the trust's assets, but
- A charge may arise when assets leave the trust (see Section 8.19)
- There is no revert to settlor exemption (see Section 8.16)
- Ten-year anniversary charges apply (see Section 8.18)

In essence, IHT may arise when assets go into a relevant property trust, when they come out of it, and every ten years while they're in it. Nevertheless, a relevant property trust's 'separate life' gives rise to some useful tax-planning opportunities, which we will consider further in Chapters 9 and 13.

**Death of Settlor**

When a settlor dies, PETs made within the last seven years of their life become chargeable lifetime transfers. This will often lead to an increase in exit and anniversary charges where the relevant property trust was set up within the same seven-year period and we will see examples of the impact of this in Sections 8.18 and 8.19. In some cases, we may even see a retrospective increase in exit charges as a result of the settlor's death.

## 8.18 TEN-YEAR ANNIVERSARY CHARGES

Unfortunately, to counter the advantages of a relevant property trust's separate life, these trusts are subject to an IHT charge on every tenth anniversary of their creation. We will now examine how this charge is calculated. It gets rather complex, but we will work through a practical example at the end to illustrate the main points.

The anniversary charge is calculated as follows:

i) Take the value of relevant property in the trust on the anniversary date.
ii) Add other settlements (into other trusts) made by the same settlor on the same date as any settlements into this trust (see Note below).
iii) Calculate the amount of IHT payable on a hypothetical chargeable lifetime transfer of a sum equal to the total of (i) and (ii) on the anniversary date, taking account of:
    a. The NRB, but not any other exemptions, and
    b. Any chargeable transfers made by the settlor in the seven years prior to setting up this trust (including any PETs becoming chargeable on the settlor's death).
iv) Using the amount derived at step (iii), the effective rate of IHT on the hypothetical lifetime transfer is calculated.
v) The effective rate is multiplied by 3/10ths and then applied to any amounts in (i) derived from assets held by the trust throughout the ten-year period.
vi) For amounts in (i) derived from assets held for less than ten years, the charge is reduced by one fortieth for every complete calendar quarter those assets were not held as relevant assets of the trust.
vii) The rate applying to charges under (vi) may be increased to take account of further chargeable lifetime transfers made by the settlor (other than to the trust itself), including any PETs becoming chargeable on the settlor's death.

**Note:** Under step (ii), we exclude settlements:

- Into a charitable trust,
- Into an immediate post-death interest trust for the settlor's spouse,
- Made before 10th December 2014, and not on the day this trust was set up, or
- Made at any time other than the day this trust was set up, where this trust was set up on the death of a testator before 6th April 2017, under a Will executed before 10th December 2014

***Example*** *(Exemptions/reliefs other than the NRB are ignored for the sake of simplicity): On 1st April 2014, Mel set up the Spice Discretionary Trust for her granddaughters, Emma and Melanie. She immediately transferred assets worth £80,000 into the trust. No IHT was payable at that time as the transfer amount was below the NRB.*

*On the same day, Mel transferred £50,000 into an interest in possession trust for her niece, Victoria. Previously, on 26th November 2013, Mel had given her sister Geri £135,000. Sadly, Mel passed away in January 2020 but, fortunately, the NRB covered her lifetime transfers.*

*On 1st April 2024, the assets in the Spice Discretionary Trust are worth £330,000. The anniversary charge is calculated as follows:*

| | |
|---|---|
| *Value of relevant property on anniversary date:* | *£330,000* |
| *Other settlement made the same day:* | *£50,000* |
| *Previous chargeable transfers:* | *£135,000* |
| *(transfer to Geri becoming chargeable on Mel's death)* | |
| *Cumulative total for hypothetical transfer:* | ***£515,000*** |
| *Less NRB* | *£325,000* |
| *Gives:* | *£190,000* |
| *IHT at lifetime rate (20%)* | ***£38,000*** |
| | |
| *Effective rate on the hypothetical transfer:* | |
| *(£38,000 divided by £330,000 PLUS £50,000)* | *10%* |
| | |
| *Rate for anniversary charge: 3/10ths of 10%* | *3%* |
| | |
| *IHT Payable: 3% x £330,000* | ***£9,900*** |

*The result of this rather tortuous calculation is that IHT of only £9,900 is payable on the assets in the Spice Discretionary Trust. Remember, had these assets been in Mel's estate at the time of her death, up to £132,000 would have been payable.*

The calculation of the anniversary charge is sometimes so complex that some trustees simply elect to pay the hypothetical maximum charge of 6% in order to save time. You may therefore wish to check the trustees are calculating the charge correctly or, if not, at least reducing their fees accordingly.

**Impact of Same Day Settlements**
The position in our example would have been better if Mel had waited until the next day to make the gift into Victoria's trust. The ten-year anniversary charge applying to the Spice Discretionary Trust would then have been just £8,400.

As explained above, the effective rate applying to each trust is increased as a consequence of both chargeable transfers in the previous seven years and other settlements made on the same day.

Naturally, it is easy to avoid making a lifetime settlement on the same day as a settlement into another trust, but it is difficult to avoid this happening where settlements are made on death. This was the reason for the changes introduced in 2014 that have effectively blocked a well-known planning strategy known as pilot trusts. In short, pilot trusts no longer work!

**Undistributed Versus Accumulated Income**
Trust income that has simply not yet been distributed to beneficiaries at the anniversary date is not included in relevant property for the purposes of the ten-year anniversary charge. (Nor for any exit charges: Section 8.19.) However, once the trustees have accumulated that income, it becomes part of the relevant property of the trust. Broadly, it is then treated like a new settlement made on the date of the accumulation (although there is no chargeable lifetime transfer).

Where the trustees have a duty to accumulate the trust income, it is treated as being accumulated as soon as it is received. Where the trustees have no power to accumulate income (e.g. in the case of an interest in possession trust) it will not usually be treated as accumulated at any time (but see further below).

In other cases (e.g. most discretionary trusts), the general rule is income is accumulated when the trustees decide not to distribute it to beneficiaries. Any income that has not been distributed or formally accumulated after five years is deemed to have been accumulated for IHT purposes.

## 8.19 EXIT CHARGES

Transfers of assets out of a relevant property trust may also give rise to IHT charges. These exit charges are based on broadly similar principles to the ten-year anniversary charge. The effective rate arrived at in each case is multiplied by three-tenths, and then also multiplied by one-fortieth for every complete calendar quarter expiring since the most recent ten-year anniversary, or since the creation of the trust in the case of transfers taking place within the first ten years.

For an exit charge arising in the first ten-year period, the hypothetical lifetime transfer used to derive the effective rate is based on the value of the assets in the trust at its commencement, plus any further settlements made into the trust between then and the date of the transfer.

***Example:*** *Let's assume the same facts as the example in Section 8.18, except that in 2019, Mel transferred another £30,000 into the Spice Discretionary Trust and, on 29th June 2023, the trustees gave £20,000 to Emma out of capital. The exit charge on Emma's gift is calculated as follows:*

| | |
|---|---|
| *Value of property settled on 1st April 2014:* | *£80,000* |
| *Other settlement made the same day:* | *£50,000* |
| *Previous chargeable transfers:* | *£135,000* |
| *Value of property settled in 2019:* | *£30,000* |
| *Cumulative total for hypothetical transfer:* | ***£295,000*** |
| *Nil rate band* | *£325,000* |

*IHT Payable:* ***NIL***

As this example demonstrates, IHT can often be avoided when the trust's assets are distributed to beneficiaries before the first ten-year anniversary of the trust. We will look at the opportunities this provides in Chapter 9.

To continue our look at exit charges, let's slightly revise our example.

***Example Revised:*** *Let's now assume the gift to Geri becoming chargeable on Mel's death was actually £235,000. This increases the cumulative total for the hypothetical lifetime transfer to £395,000. What does this do to Emma's exit charge?*

| | |
|---|---|
| *Cumulative total for hypothetical transfer:* | *£395,000* |
| *Deducting the NRB of £325,000 leaves:* | *£70,000* |
| *IHT at lifetime rate (20%)* | *£14,000* |

*Effective rate on the hypothetical transfer:*
*£14,000 divided by £160,000 (£80,000 + £50,000 + £30,000)* *8.75%*
*Rate for exit charge:*
*8.75% x 3/10 x 36/40* *2.3625%*

*IHT Payable: 2.3625% x £20,000* ***£473***

**Points to Note**

i) If Emma bears the tax, the exit charge will be £473, as above. However, if the trust were to bear the tax, grossing up would apply. The grossing up rate in this case would be 2.3625/97.6375 (100 – 2.3625), giving rise to a grossed up charge of £484.
ii) Only 36 calendar quarters are counted here. The 37th quarter does not end until 30th June 2023. As the transfer to Emma took place before then, this quarter had not yet expired. If the transfer had been made two days later, we would have had to include the 37th quarter.
iii) Under this revised scenario, IHT liabilities would arise on Mel's chargeable lifetime transfers to both the Spice Discretionary Trust and Victoria's interest in possession trust, as a result of her death within seven years of the gift to Geri (see Section 8.18). For the sake of illustration, I have assumed these liabilities were settled directly by the trusts, thus avoiding any grossing up of those earlier transfers.

Later exit charges are based on the effective rate applying at the previous ten-year anniversary, as adjusted for any further settlements into the trust since then.

Distributions of trust income do not give rise to exit charges. Care must be taken, however, that the income is not allowed to accumulate first before distribution.

**Exit Charges on 18 to 25 Trusts**
The exit charge applying to an 18 to 25 trust (Section 8.14) is based on the number of complete calendar quarters that have expired since the later of the date of the settlor's death, and the beneficiary's 18th birthday.

If it transpires that the beneficiary's 18th birthday is the later date, exit charges can be kept slightly lower by allowing beneficiaries to become absolutely entitled to their inheritance two days before one of their birthdays (somewhere between their 19th and 25th birthday, as desired). By following this technique, the maximum charge of 4.2% should never arise!

**Penal Exit Charges**
Bereaved minors' trusts and 18 to 25 Trusts are subject to a penal exit charge regime which, broadly speaking, will apply if trust assets are not distributed to the beneficiary by the age of 18 or 25 respectively. The maximum potential charge under this regime is 21%. The charge does not apply to distributions of assets due to the death of the beneficiary before attaining the relevant age (i.e. 18 or 25), or to the conversion of a bereaved minors' trust to an 18 to 25 trust (or vice versa).

## 8.20 INCOME TAX FOR TRUSTS

As I said in Section 8.3, interest in possession trusts generally have a better Income Tax position than discretionary trusts. Discretionary trusts pay Income Tax at the trust rate (currently 45%) on all trust income in excess of a small basic rate band of just £1,000 (except for dividend income, which has its own dividend trust rate, currently 39.35%).

In other words, after the first £1,000 of trust income, a discretionary trust is taxed as if it were an individual who is an additional rate taxpayer.

Some of the Income Tax paid by the trust can be recovered by the beneficiaries when income is paid out. However, at best, there remains a significant cashflow disadvantage and, at worst, the trust's Income Tax burden effectively becomes permanent when income is retained in the trust.

An interest in possession trust, on the other hand, is generally taxed at basic rate only. The beneficiary entitled to the income then includes that income in their own tax calculation and pays any higher rate Income Tax due (or reclaims any tax overpaid, as the case may be).

Looked at another way, an interest in possession trust is given the benefit of the doubt and taxed at basic rate, with any extra tax due paid by the beneficiary. A discretionary trust is treated as a worst case scenario and, apart from the first £1,000, taxed as if it were a wealthy individual, with the resultant excess tax then being reclaimed by the beneficiary.

There is an exception for trusts for vulnerable individuals, under which a discretionary trust can be taxed as if its income belonged directly to the vulnerable beneficiary. This generally only applies to disabled trusts, trusts for bereaved minors, and a few other cases where the beneficiary is under 18.

See Section 11.10 regarding lifetime settlements made for the benefit of your own minor children.

Charitable trusts are generally exempt from Income Tax unless they undertake trading activities.

## 8.21 STAMP TAXES FOR TRUSTS

Trusts pay Stamp Duty on purchases of shares, and SDLT on purchases of non-residential property, in the same way, and at the same rates, as other purchasers.

For purchases of residential property by a trust, these are treated as if they were a purchase by the beneficiary for SDLT purposes if:

- Purchased by a bare trust,
- The beneficiary will have the right to live in the property for life, or
- The beneficiary will have an interest in possession in the income from the property (see Section 8.3)

Broadly speaking, this means the 3% SDLT surcharge will not apply if the beneficiary has no other interest in residential property, if the new property is replacing the beneficiary's previous main residence, or if the property is purchased from the beneficiary's spouse. The trust remains liable for SDLT at normal rates (although no SDLT will be due on a purchase for no more than £250,000 completed by 31st March 2025).

All other residential property purchases made by trusts will be subject to the 3% SDLT surcharge unless they fall within one of the general exemptions applicable to all purchasers.

As explained in Section 1.4, different taxes apply to purchases of property in Scotland or Wales. While many of the principles are much the same, there are some important differences to be aware of, so local professional advice is essential. For further details regarding Stamp Taxes on property anywhere in the UK, see the Taxcafe guides *How to Save Property Tax* or *Using a Property Company to Save Tax*.

# Chapter 9

# More Advanced Planning With Trusts

## 9.1 THE RELEVANT PROPERTY TRUST SHELTER

Because relevant property trusts are effectively treated as separate persons for IHT purposes, they provide an opportunity to shelter assets in a vehicle that exists outside any individual's estate. (Subject, of course, to the anniversary and exit charges explained in Chapter 8.)

In Section 8.15, we saw that relevant property trusts may be created through most lifetime transfers into trust (but see Section 9.2). To create a relevant property trust on death will usually require a discretionary trust.

In effect, and subject to any other transfers you may be making, there is the opportunity to transfer assets equal in value to the NRB into relevant property trusts every seven years free from IHT.

In fact, taking into account the annual exemption and the fact the NRB will hopefully increase again one day, it should be possible to accumulate a considerable amount of value within the relevant property trust. Let's look at an example with a wealthy couple starting their IHT planning next year. Throughout this example, we will follow the assumptions set out in Section 3.2 regarding the future projected level of the NRB, ***BUT*** it is important to note these are only forecast projections used for the sake of illustration.

***Example:*** *Salvatore and Cherilyn are a wealthy couple. Neither of them has made any transfer of value prior to 6th April 2024. On that date they set up the Caesar & Cleo Family Trust with their children as beneficiaries and each transfer £331,000 into it. The first £6,000 of each person's transfer is covered by their annual exemptions for 2024/25 and 2023/24 (see Section 5.2) and the remaining £325,000 by their NRB.*

*Hence, while there is a chargeable lifetime transfer, no IHT is payable at this stage. A total of £662,000 is now sheltered in the trust.*

*On 6th April each year from 2025 to 2027, Salvatore and Cherilyn are able to put a further £3,000 into the trust each, covered by their annual exemptions. By 6th April 2027 a total of £680,000 has been transferred to the trust free from IHT.*

*From 2028/29 onwards, the Government finally starts to increase the NRB again, starting with an increase to £334,000 for the 2028/29 tax year. On 6th April 2028, Salvatore and Cherilyn are therefore each able to put a further £12,000 into the trust. £3,000 of each transfer is covered by the annual exemption, leaving a chargeable lifetime transfer of £9,000. This brings each person's cumulative chargeable transfers up to £334,000 (£325,000 plus £9,000), which is covered by the NRB for 2028/29. A total of £704,000 has now been transferred to the trust free from IHT.*

*The couple follow the same principle for the next two years, bringing the total cumulative amount transferred into the trust free from IHT as at 6th April 2030 up to £752,000. After 6th April 2031, however, the first transfers made on 6th April 2024 will not need to be counted in calculating the couple's cumulative chargeable transfers.*

*On 7th April 2031, Salvatore and Cherilyn will therefore each be able to transfer £337,000 into the Caesar & Cleo Family Trust free from IHT. This is because, at this point, each person's cumulative chargeable lifetime transfers in the last seven years are just £27,000.*

*The projected NRB at this point is £361,000, meaning each of them can make a new chargeable transfer of £334,000 without giving rise to any IHT. Adding the annual exemption gives a total tax-free transfer of £337,000 each. These latest transfers bring the total value transferred into the trust to date up to £1.426m.*

*Following the same principles, each individual is able to transfer a further £26,000 into the trust over the next two years meaning that, by 7th April 2033, a total of £1.478m has been sheltered.*

*However, on 6th April 2034, our shelter springs a leak: the ten-year anniversary charge. To calculate this charge, let's assume all the trust's income has been distributed to the beneficiaries each year, but the assets in the trust have grown at the rate of 7.5% per annum (compound). This produces a total value for the trust assets at 6th April 2034 of £2.395m.*

*The transfers made by each of the settlors will be treated separately, so each has their own NRB (which is now £391,000 per our projections).*

*The effective rate is derived by taking 20% of the value of trust assets in excess of two NRBs as a percentage of the value of those assets. In this case, the effective rate is 13.47% (£2.395m – 2 x £391,000 = £1.613m x 20% = £322,600, which, divided by £2.395m, produces a rate of 13.47%).*

*This rate is multiplied by 3/10ths and then one-fortieth of this result is deducted for each calendar quarter the relevant assets were not in the trust. The assets in the trust from the outset are therefore subject to a charge of 4.041%. The assets that have been in the trust for nine years suffer a charge of 3.637%, those held for eight years suffer 3.233%, and so on.*

*In total, the anniversary charge amounts to £68,805. This represents just 2.87% of the value of the assets in the trust. If Salvatore and Cherilyn still held those assets personally, they would be exposed to potential IHT charges of 40%, or £958,000. The potential saving is therefore huge.*

You don't need to be in a couple to use this technique, nor the more sophisticated version we will look at below. Both work just as well for an individual: you just have to halve all the numbers.

Note that I have made a fairly conservative assumption regarding future increases to the NRB: namely that it will merely rise in line with the CPI after the nineteen year freeze to 5th April 2028. However, it is possible the NRB may be subject to more significant increases at some stage in the future. If so, the value of this planning technique will be substantially enhanced.

**Using Serial Trusts**

There is one major drawback to the method used by Salvatore and Cherilyn. By using just one trust, they had access to just one extra NRB each. It would be better to set up a new trust every seven years and thus continually increase the number of NRBs available.

What Salvatore and Cherilyn should have done is to set up the Caesar and Cleo No. 2 Family Trust on 7th April 2031 and make their next seven years' worth of transfers into that trust. Then, on 8th April 2038, they could set up the Caesar and Cleo No. 3 Family Trust, and so on, for as long as they are able. For a start, this more sophisticated approach would have reduced the charge arising on 6th April 2034 to £41,433.

The longer-term calculations for this planning technique get quite horrendous but, if Salvatore and Cherilyn survive until 8th April 2044 then, using our projection methodology set out above, they would have the following assets in trust:

| | |
|---|---|
| Caesar and Cleo Family Trust: | £2.887m |
| Caesar and Cleo No. 2 Family Trust: | £2.083m |
| Caesar and Cleo No. 3 Family Trust: | £1.500m |
| Total: | £6.470m |

These figures take account of anniversary charges of £41,433 in 2034, £46,760 in 2041 and £119,542 in 2044. The total IHT paid so far is thus £207,735. This compares with potential IHT of almost £2.6m had these assets still been held by Salvatore and Cherilyn personally.

You may wonder whether using relevant property trusts to shelter assets is really effective in view of the anniversary and exit charges. It is worth bearing in mind, however, that the tenth anniversary charges arising under the method set out above work out at less than 3%.

Twentieth anniversary charges (if the assets are still in trust) will tend to be higher, say around 4%, and, if you get to a thirtieth anniversary, we can expect charges approaching 5%. These are all based on our projected growth rate explained above. More growth would mean higher charges, but the overall saving compared with leaving the assets in the individuals' estates would also be greater. However high the growth, anniversary charges will always be less than 6%, as this is the theoretical maximum.

In general, the anniversary charges within the trusts are likely to work out at less than 0.5% per annum on average. Even if there were no growth in value within the trusts, this means you would need to survive more than eighty years after starting the plan before the anniversary charges exceeded the IHT saved on your death.

However, in fact, because of the dynamic nature of the plan and the anticipated growth in value of the assets within the trusts, the ultimate savings will continue to grow year on year for as long as you live. Following the method (and assumptions) set out above (and using serial trusts), I have calculated the projected IHT savings for a couple based on the number of years they survive after starting the plan:

| ***Years Survived*** | ***Total Net Assets in Trust*** | ***Total Net Assets in Estate*** | ***Saving*** |
|---|---|---|---|
| | ***£000s*** | ***£000s*** | ***£000s*** |
| *1* | *£717* | *£691* | *£26* |
| *2* | *£776* | *£726* | *£50* |
| *3* | *£838* | *£765* | *£73* |
| *5* | *£1,013* | *£888* | *£125* |
| *7* | *£1,862* | *£1,418* | *£444* |
| *10* | *£2,377* | *£1,766* | *£611* |
| *15* | *£4,317* | *£3,021* | *£1,296* |
| *20* | *£6,430* | *£4,446* | *£1,984* |
| *25* | *£10,358* | *£7,058* | *£3,300* |
| *30* | *£15,885* | *£10,809* | *£5,076* |

**Notes**

i) In compiling the above figures, it is assumed the trusts are wound up at the time of the couple's death. This does not necessarily need to happen, but I have done so here to make the comparison fair. The 'Total Net Assets in Trust' are the remaining funds distributed to beneficiaries less the IHT charges suffered at this time.

ii) 'Total Net Assets in Estate' is the total net sum left in the estate after IHT from the same assets if these had been retained personally. To create a fair like with like comparison, it is assumed the deceased's NRB is used against these assets.

iii) Saving is, broadly speaking, the overall net tax saving. To be more accurate though, it is actually the additional net amount left to the beneficiaries after IHT.

iv) It is assumed neither member of the couple makes any other transfers of value outside the relevant property trust plan.

v) The above table takes the simplistic view that both members of the couple die at the same time. In reality this is unlikely to be the case, but the table still serves as a fair illustration of the savings that might be achieved.

vi) A single individual following the same technique would produce savings equal to half of those shown above.

vii) As explained above, the savings could be far greater if there are more substantial increases in the NRB at some point in the future.

It is interesting to note the projected savings start almost immediately, with £26,000 saved even if the couple die after just one year. This arises because, once the assets are in the trust, any capital growth is immediately safeguarded from inclusion in your estate.

The savings steadily increase over time but there are significant additional increments in the total saving at each seventh anniversary, as a new NRB effectively becomes available.

This table is a perfect illustration of the benefit of starting IHT planning as early as possible. The table is not given in tax terms due to the cashflow impact of ten-year anniversary charges, which render a direct tax paid comparison slightly unfair after the first ten years. Nevertheless, it does ably demonstrate that an excessive concern over anniversary and exit charges is generally unwarranted!

## 9.2 HOW USEFUL IS THE RELEVANT PROPERTY TRUST SHELTER?

As we have seen, using relevant property trusts can save millions of pounds when the planning is started early enough. In the case of straightforward cash settlements into the trust, a relevant property trust can even be used to give money to your own minor children tax efficiently, allowing parents to start their IHT planning early. We will look at using trusts to benefit minor children in more detail in Section 11.10.

### Practical Advantages

As we know from Chapter 4, assets can be passed directly to other individuals as PETs and all that is required is to survive seven years to ensure no IHT is payable. In the right circumstances, this is naturally a much simpler way to save IHT.

However, using a relevant property trust will often have significant practical advantages over giving assets directly to your ultimate beneficiaries, including:

- Control: although you cannot benefit from the gifted assets (see below), you will be able to retain control over them.
- Assets in the relevant property trust are outside any person's estate. This will avoid the danger of unexpected IHT liabilities arising if your beneficiaries should pre-decease you.
- Relevant property trusts can be used as a vehicle to skip a generation (or even two) and pass family wealth directly to grandchildren or great-grandchildren, while still providing the settlor's children with income during their lifetime.
- The income from, or enjoyment of, assets can be given to your beneficiaries at an early age without exposing them to the risk of losing the underlying capital due to their own inexperience, a bad marriage, or some other misfortune.

On top of these practical issues there is also the fact that assets can often be transferred into a relevant property trust free from CGT, and we will look at this in Section 9.4.

However, relevant property trust shelters are subject to some limitations and it is important to be aware of these when undertaking this type of planning.

**Lifetime Charges**
Any transfer of value into the trust in excess of the transferor's available NRB and any other lifetime exemptions available will give rise to an immediate IHT charge at 20% on the excess (or 25% if the settlor settles the tax personally: see Section 4.2).

**Settlor Must Not Benefit**
Unless the settlor is completely excluded from benefit, in theory and in practice, the assets held within a trust will be subject to the gifts with reservation rules (Section 4.8), thus rendering the trust ineffective for IHT planning purposes. Worse still, while the trust assets would be subject to the gifts with reservation rules, the trust would still be subject to the anniversary and exit charges covered in Sections 8.18 and 8.19 and the initial transfer into the trust will remain a chargeable lifetime transfer.

Strictly speaking, a benefit derived by the settlor's spouse does not necessarily give rise to a gift with reservation, but there is often a danger the settlor may share such a benefit. Hence, in practice, it is usually wise to ensure the settlor's spouse is also excluded from benefit.

## 9.3 HOW TO AVOID ANNIVERSARY AND EXIT CHARGES

Anniversary and exit charges can easily be avoided by:

a) Distributing all trust assets to the beneficiaries before the tenth anniversary of the trust's creation, and
b) Ensuring the cumulative value of relevant transfers does not exceed the NRB when the assets are distributed

Remember, the value of relevant transfers for this purpose includes:

i) All transfers of relevant property into the trust
ii) Accumulated income within the trust (see Section 8.18)
iii) Chargeable transfers made in the seven years before setting up the trust (including PETs becoming chargeable on death)
iv) Other settlements made on the same day as any settlements into this trust (subject to the exclusions noted in Section 8.18)

We will see a simple example of how anniversary and exit charges may be avoided in Section 9.4. Even when following this strategy, up to ten years of capital growth in the value of trust assets can be accumulated free from IHT. However, in order to achieve the significant longer-term benefits we saw in Section 9.1, or to maintain some of the practical advantages discussed in Section 9.2, it may actually be preferable, in the long run, to suffer ten-year anniversary charges.

## 9.4 HOW TO AVOID INHERITANCE TAX AND CAPITAL GAINS TAX AT THE SAME TIME

As explained in Section 4.9, the transfer of assets other than cash will generally be treated as a sale at market value for CGT purposes.

However, because a transfer to a relevant property trust is a chargeable transfer for IHT purposes, the transferor is given the ability to hold over any capital gains arising on the assets transferred.

This means no CGT is payable on the transfer and the trust is treated, for CGT purposes, as having acquired the asset at the same price as that originally paid by the transferor.

Furthermore, when, at a later date, the trust then transfers the asset to the ultimate beneficiary, the trustees and the beneficiary may, once again, claim that the capital gain should be held over. Hence, by this method, appreciating assets may be passed on free of both IHT and CGT.

***Example:*** *Eric has an investment property worth £325,000, which he wishes to pass to his adult daughter, Patty. Eric is concerned he will have a substantial CGT bill if he gives the property directly to Patty.*

*Instead, therefore, Eric sets up the Slowhand Trust with Patty as the beneficiary. He then transfers the property to the trust and elects to hold over the capital gain arising. Eric has made no previous transfers of value, so his chargeable transfer of £325,000 is covered by his NRB.*

*A couple of years later, the trust transfers the property, now worth £375,000, to Patty. Patty and the trustees jointly elect to hold over the capital gain arising, so Patty is deemed to have acquired the property for the price Eric originally paid.*

*There is no exit charge on the transfer to Patty as the NRB covers the £325,000 that the property was worth when Eric put it into the trust. The fact the property is now worth £375,000 is irrelevant.*

As we can see from the example, where the original transfer was covered by the settlor's NRB, increases in the value of trust assets will not give rise to additional charges as long as those assets are distributed to beneficiaries within ten years of the trust's formation.

Only the transferor needs to elect to hold over the gain going into the trust, whereas the trustees and the beneficiary must jointly elect to hold over the gain when the asset is transferred out of the trust.

A simple interest in possession trust will usually suffice for the purpose of this technique, which is extremely useful for passing on investment property and other appreciating assets to adult children or other beneficiaries, and we will explore its benefits further in Section 9.5. However, it is subject to a few restrictions.

**Settlor-Interested Trusts**
In Section 9.2, we saw that a trust is ineffective for IHT planning purposes if the settlor themselves is able to benefit from that trust. However, the definition of a settlor-interested trust for CGT purposes goes much further.

Where the settlor, their spouse, or a dependent minor child of the settlor, can benefit in any way from a trust, that trust is a settlor-interested trust. Holdover relief is not available for transfers of assets into a settlor-interested trust. Gifts of land and buildings, or other appreciating assets, to such trusts may thus give rise to an immediate CGT charge. Additionally, if a trust becomes settlor-interested at any time within six years after the end of the tax year in which holdover relief was previously claimed, the relief is withdrawn and a CGT charge will arise.

**Private Residence Relief**
Where gains have been held over on the transfer of residential property, neither the trust nor the beneficiary will be entitled to any private residence relief on the property for CGT purposes.

**Charge Required**
Gains cannot be held over when assets leave the trust within three months of the initial settlement or within three months of an anniversary charge. This is because the hold over relief is only available where an IHT charge arises, so there must be a technical liability for an exit charge (Section 8.19); although there is no problem if this works out at nil.

## 9.5 INVESTMENT PROPERTY TRUSTS

The technique described in the previous section, which allows assets to be passed on free from both IHT and CGT, is well suited to an investment property business. The restriction on private residence relief will often be irrelevant in the case of investment properties. In addition to adult children, the technique works just as well when the trust is used to pass property to an unmarried partner, grandchild, nephew, niece, other relative, or friend. It is not generally possible to use it to pass existing investment property to your own minor children however, as CGT holdover relief would not be available.

Where two settlors jointly transfer property into the trust, two NRBs will be available. A couple could therefore use this technique to transfer up to £650,000 worth of rental property to their adult child free of both CGT and IHT. All they need to do is survive the requisite seven years.

After seven years, the couple will each have a new NRB available and could therefore do it all over again. A couple with a life expectancy of over 21 years could conservatively expect to be able to pass over £3m worth of rental property to their adult children free from tax!

**Selling Property to the Trust**

The technique can be refined to pass on more valuable property by selling the property to the trust for a low value. The sale price can then be left outstanding as a loan, or possibly a charge against the property.

For IHT purposes, this represents a sale at undervalue and, as we saw in Section 2.1, this means the transfer of value arising is the difference between the sale price and the property's market value. This provides a useful mechanism to tweak the transfer value to ensure it is covered by the settlor's NRB and other available exemptions.

For CGT purposes, it remains possible to hold over the part of the gain that exceeds the actual sale price. Hence, no CGT liability will arise if the sale price is set low enough. See Section 12.4 for more information on partial holdover claims.

However, the main fly in the ointment will be SDLT. Subject to the exceptions set out in Section 8.21, charges will generally arise on residential property transfers where the sale price is £40,000 or more. For non-residential property, charges will apply to any sale price in excess of £150,000.

***Example:*** *Paul and Linda jointly own a residential investment property worth £800,000 and wish to pass it to their adult daughter, Stella. They bought the property for just £200,000 some years ago.*

*A direct transfer of the property to Stella would give Paul and Linda a total CGT bill of up to £168,000 (£600,000 x 28%). Fortunately, neither Paul nor Linda has made any other transfers in the last seven years. The couple therefore decide to transfer the property into an interest in possession trust for Stella's benefit in June 2023 and to elect to hold over the gain arising for CGT purposes. However, a straightforward gift would give rise to an immediate IHT charge at 20% on the excess of the property's value over £662,000 (see Section 9.1), i.e. £27,600.*

*Hence, instead of a simple gift, Paul and Linda sell the property to the trust for £138,000, and take a charge over the property for this amount. This reduces the transfer of value to £662,000 (£800,000 – £138,000), meaning no IHT arises on the transfer.*

*For CGT purposes, the transfer is still deemed to take place at market value but, as the actual consideration received is less than the property's original cost, Paul and Linda can still hold over the gain arising, leaving them with no CGT to pay.*

*The sale price of £138,000 will give rise to an SDLT charge of £4,140 (see the Taxcafe guide* How to Save Property Tax *for details of SDLT rates).*

*Two years later (let's say in June 2025), the trust transfers the property to Stella, subject to the outstanding charge for £138,000 due to Paul and Linda. Stella and the trustees jointly elect to hold over the gain arising.*

*Most of the original transfer of value (£662,000) is covered by Paul and Linda's NRBs, leaving just £12,000 exposed to an exit charge at 1.2% (two years represents eight calendar quarters so the charge works out at 20% x 3/10 x 8/40 = 1.2%). Stella therefore pays an exit charge of £144.*

*Stella will have to pay a further £4,400 in SDLT, due to the outstanding charge, which is deemed to represent purchase consideration for SDLT purposes (the current temporary reduction in SDLT will have ended at this point, thus increasing the charge slightly). This brings the total tax cost of the exercise up to £8,684 (£4,140 + £4,400 + £144).*

I have assumed Stella already owns another residential property, so the additional 3% SDLT charge applies on both property transfers (see Section 8.21). If not, the exercise would be considerably cheaper, as no SDLT would be due on the transfer into the trust (during the period of the current, temporary reduction), and only £260 on the transfer out (after 31st March 2025).

The charge over the property can be dealt with in a number of ways. Perhaps, for example, Paul and Linda might waive it at some later stage. This would represent a PET and would escape IHT as long as the couple both survived a further seven years.

Despite the drawback of SDLT, the example demonstrates the huge tax-saving potential of using trusts to pass investment property to adult children or other beneficiaries. In this case, the couple faced an unpleasant choice between an immediate CGT charge of £168,000 and an eventual IHT bill of at least £320,000. By using a trust, they were able to pass a valuable investment property to their daughter almost tax free. In many cases, the same result can be achieved completely tax free.

**Existing Mortgages**

When undertaking this planning technique, it is important to take any outstanding loans or mortgages already secured against the property into account.

Where there is an existing mortgage over a property, it may be difficult to transfer it into the trust subject to that mortgage. It may be necessary for the trust to take out a new mortgage for the requisite amount and use those funds to buy the property. The beneficiary would then either take over that mortgage or, once again, take out a new mortgage to cover the same amount.

Where it is possible for either the trust or, at a later stage, the beneficiary, to take over an existing mortgage, the outstanding balance will represent deemed purchase consideration for tax purposes.

Whatever method is used, the balance on the existing mortgage will have the same effects for tax purposes as the low sale price we looked at in the example: namely, it will reduce the transfer of value for IHT purposes, and will represent deemed consideration for SDLT purposes. As far as CGT is concerned, the gain can still be held over as long as the mortgage balance does not exceed the original cost of the property. In other cases, a partial holdover remains possible, but some CGT liability may arise.

## 9.6 PASSING ASSETS TAX-FREE TO ADULT CHILDREN AND OTHER BENEFICIARIES

As we saw in Section 8.12, it is possible to leave assets to an immediate post-death interest trust in favour of your spouse free from IHT. This has the tremendous advantage that you can benefit from the spouse exemption and yet still be certain your assets will eventually pass to your children (or other intended beneficiaries). As explained in Section 8.3, this is achieved by bequeathing the remainder to your ultimate intended beneficiaries.

In many cases, you may want the immediate post-death interest to persist for the remainder of your spouse's life. This means IHT will arise on their death. Alternatively, if the immediate post-death interest is terminated during the spouse's lifetime, the assets can be passed to the ultimate beneficiaries as a PET that will become fully exempt seven years later, as long as the spouse survives to the end of this period.

This is a useful variation on the technique explained in Section 6.12, as it provides certainty the assets will pass to your intended beneficiaries. It is important to retain the assets in the trust for at least two years and a day after your death. In fact, it may be wise to keep them in the trust a little longer than this (say three years) as HMRC frequently challenges life interests of only just over two years under the associated operations rules (see Section 11.11).

Generally, it is preferable to avoid any fixed arrangements for the trust's early termination and leave it to your widow or widower to give up their interest voluntarily. This may not always be desirable, however, and we will look at some alternative options in Section 9.7 (plus one set out below).

Assets must pass to adult children or other beneficiaries absolutely in order to be a PET. Unlike the technique described in Section 9.7 (for minor children), it is not possible to use an 18 to 25 trust to pass assets to young adult children tax-free, as the transfer from the immediate post-death interest would be a chargeable lifetime transfer.

For example, the deceased might leave an interest in possession to their surviving spouse, which terminates on their child's 21st birthday, when the assets pass absolutely to the child. As long as the deceased's spouse survives until the child's 28th birthday (i.e. seven years later), the whole process should take place free from IHT.

As this is a more common-sense approach than passing assets to a minor, there is probably little risk of an attack under the associated operations rules.

## 9.7 PASSING ASSETS TAX-FREE TO MINOR CHILDREN

In many cases, where someone dies leaving both a spouse and minor children, they will be content for their assets to remain in their widow or widower's hands until the children reach adulthood. For guidance on how to get those assets into the children's hands tax-free after they reach the age of 18, see Sections 6.7, 6.12 and 9.6.

In some cases, however, the deceased may prefer their assets to pass to their children sooner, particularly if their spouse is unlikely to survive until the children are over 25 (i.e. more than seven years after the children reach adulthood), if they are separated from their spouse, or if their spouse is not their children's other parent.

As explained in Section 8.12, where an immediate post-death interest ends during the beneficiary's lifetime and property passes to a bereaved minor's trust under the terms of the settlor's Will, this will be a PET. This provides the opportunity to pass assets tax-free to minor children.

***Example:*** *James wishes to leave his estate to his five-year-old daughter Beatrice. If he left the estate directly to Beatrice or a trust for her benefit, the IHT arising would be colossal.*

*Instead, therefore, James leaves just £325,000 (his NRB) to a bereaved minor's trust for Beatrice and everything else to an immediate post-death interest trust in favour of his estranged wife, Heather. Heather's immediate post-death interest lasts for a fixed period of three years, after which the estate passes into Beatrice's bereaved minor's trust.*

*The bulk of James's estate initially passes into Heather's immediate post-death interest tax free under the spouse exemption and, three years later it passes into the trust for Beatrice as a PET.*

*As long as Heather outlives James by at least ten years, his entire estate can pass to Beatrice tax free.*

Technically, taking the strict letter of the legislation, Heather's interest would only need to last two years and a day, but I made it three years in the example since, as explained in Section 9.6, a shorter period could lead to a risk of challenge under the associated operations rules (see Section 11.11). The legacy to Heather could then be ignored and James's entire estate (except his NRB) could be subject to IHT.

Whether three years is even long enough is not clear, as any fixed period for Heather's interest may make the transfer to Beatrice's trust too much of a certainty for HMRC's liking. Clearly though, the longer Heather's interest lasts, the more robust the arrangement will be (but bear in mind the transfer to Beatrice's trust needs to take place before she is 18: after that, the assets would need to pass to her absolutely, as explained in Section 9.6).

Nonetheless, the associated operations rules are usually only used in blatant cases of tax avoidance, so a more subtle version of this approach is more likely to work, especially where the couple are still living together immediately before the transferor's death.

Immediate post-death interest trusts in favour of a surviving spouse that terminate on their remarriage are commonplace and would not generally be challenged. Other conditions that might terminate the spouse's interest, such as emigration or bankruptcy, for example, might also be acceptable.

The difficulty in a case like James's is he will want some certainty that the estate will pass to the child reasonably soon. A clause terminating the surviving spouse's interest when the child reaches a certain age might be subtle enough for the scheme to work (again, this needs to be before the child reaches 18 if you wish to use a bereaved minor's trust; otherwise the method described in Section 9.6 should be used instead).

Whatever method is used to trigger the termination of the spouse's interest, it must last at least two years and a day, and there will often need to be a risk that it could last a few years more for this strategy to be effective. This could mean the loss of several years' income for the ultimate beneficiary: although if it prevents them losing 40% of the capital, it could be worth it.

The surviving spouse may sometimes be prepared to give up their interest voluntarily. This would not create a bereaved minor's trust, but could result in a bare trust in favour of the child with similarly beneficial results. The implications of such a voluntary transfer were discussed in Section 6.12.

Note, as the transfer from the immediate post-death interest to the bereaved minor's trust or bare trust is a PET, holdover relief is not available for CGT purposes. Hence, the method may not be entirely tax free, as CGT would arise on the increase in value of any non-cash assets in the trust since the original owner's death.

## 9.8 DISCOUNTED GIFT TRUSTS

A useful type of trust used in IHT planning for many years is the Discounted Gift Trust or Reversionary Interest Trust. These trusts are usually provided by life insurance companies and different companies tend to give their trusts their own names but the basic principles employed are broadly similar.

A discounted gift trust is actually not a single trust, but a series of mini-trusts. The transferor gives a substantial sum to the discounted gift trust, which is then divided up among the mini-trusts with the following rights:

Mini-Trust 1: income accumulated for one year, after which the original funds in the Trust are returned to the transferor.
Mini-Trust 2: income accumulated for two years, after which the original funds in the Trust are returned to the transferor.
Mini-Trust 3: income accumulated for three years, after which the original funds in the Trust are returned to the transferor.
And so on ...

The accumulated income in the trusts is held for the benefit of the transferor's eventual beneficiaries. The effect of this is the transferor continues to receive an 'income' stream from their investment, despite the fact much of it is no longer in their estate for IHT purposes.

The statistical value of the reversionary interests in the mini-trusts does still have to be included in the transferor's estate, but this is less than the amount of the original investment and steadily reduces as time passes.

Actually, what the transferor is receiving is not, strictly speaking, income at all, but a return of capital. This has the added advantage of being free from Income Tax too!

The insurance companies providing these investments were quick to adapt to the changes made in 2006 and continue to provide discounted gift trust schemes using absolute trusts. This reduces the flexibility of the scheme but prevents a chargeable lifetime transfer arising on the initial investment.

Another form of discounted gift trust using relevant property trusts can also be set up but this will give rise to a chargeable lifetime transfer when the initial investment is made. Nevertheless, the structure may work satisfactorily for investments that do not exceed the NRB.

## 9.9 LOAN TRUSTS

Another popular scheme provided by many life insurance companies is the Loan Trust. In essence, the transferor does not make any transfer of value to the trust but simply lends funds to it. As there is no transfer of value, there can be no IHT charge.

Funds invested within the trust will (one hopes) experience capital growth, but the beauty of this scheme is that the capital growth is outside the original transferor's estate. All that the original transferor is due is a repayment of the original loan and hence this is the only value remaining in their estate.

The loan can be interest-free if desired (see Section 2.10) and the transferor may progressively withdraw their original loan capital. This capital can be spent on the transferor's living expenses, thus gradually removing its value from their estate. Alternatively, the transferor could gift the benefit of the loan to another individual as a PET (Section 4.3).

Meanwhile, the capital growth and accumulated income within the trust belongs to the beneficiaries and is thus also kept out of the transferor's estate.

A loan trust may be set up as an absolute trust in order to avoid any danger of becoming a relevant property trust. An absolute loan trust would be exempt from any anniversary or exit charges. Otherwise, as a relevant property trust, there would be some risk of anniversary and exit charges, but these could generally be avoided by ensuring the trust assets are distributed before the trust's net value exceeds the NRB (see Section 9.3 for further guidance on avoiding anniversary and exit charges).

## 9.10 EXCLUDED PROPERTY TRUSTS

Those who did not have a UK domicile of origin (see Section 16.2) but who have subsequently acquired UK domicile, or elected to opt-in for IHT purposes (see Section 6.15), may be able to exclude non-UK assets transferred into a trust for their benefit before they acquired UK domicile, or opted in.

Where such assets are still held in the trust at the relevant time, they may be excluded from the value of the beneficiary's estate for IHT purposes. This treatment even extends to property transferred into the trust by the beneficiary themselves: since the excluded property rules take precedence over the gifts with reservation provisions (see Section 4.8).

An individual who is shortly about to become UK domiciled (Section 16.3), or who is planning to opt-in (Section 6.15), may be able to transfer non-UK assets into a trust for their own benefit before this occurs and thus potentially prevent those assets from becoming subject to IHT.

An excluded property trust might also be used to shelter non-UK assets inherited from a non-UK domiciled individual and may be put in place via a deed of variation where appropriate.

Property held in trust ceases to be excluded property when a non-UK domiciled settlor acquires UK domicile as a consequence of resuming UK residence where they were born in the UK and have a UK domicile of origin (see Section 16.3).

As explained in Section 2.10, any liabilities incurred, directly or indirectly, to finance excluded property must be deducted from the value of that property and cannot be deducted from other chargeable assets. See also Section 3.7 regarding indirect holdings of UK residential property.

Further restrictions to excluded property trusts were put in place with effect from July 2020. Professional advice is essential.

Chapter 10

# Using Pensions in IHT Planning

## 10.1 A BENEFICIAL REGIME

In recent years, the UK pensions regime has become a steadily more attractive vehicle for IHT planning.

For a start, the value of an individual's pension savings generally fall outside their estate and hence completely escape IHT. There are some important exceptions to be aware of, however, and we will look at these in Section 10.2.

Having usually escaped IHT on the original scheme member's death, scheme funds can often still be held in an IHT-free environment throughout the member's beneficiaries' lifetimes, thus allowing the funds to be passed down through the generations free from IHT. We will look at the choices available to beneficiaries in Section 10.4, although it is important to stress that not all pension funds offer the full range of choices.

In many cases, the funds can even be paid out to beneficiaries free from Income Tax, although this depends on a number of factors, so we will look at this further in Section 10.5.

While pension savings held at the point of death may sometimes escape both IHT and Income Tax, it is important to understand the rules governing the two taxes operate independently of each other. Exemption from one tax does not imply exemption from the other and some payments may even be subject to both.

Payments, and other designations of pension scheme funds made before 6th April 2023 were, in some cases, subject to the Lifetime Allowance Charge at either 25% or 55%, depending on the circumstances. That charge has now been abolished, although the lifetime allowance itself still exists for 2023/24. (See Section 10.10 regarding the future position.)

In this chapter, we will look at the benefits of pensions in IHT planning. Pensions are, of course, predominantly meant to be used for retirement planning. While that is an important area of personal financial planning, and the main reason for most people to make pension contributions, it is not what we are looking at in this chapter. For a detailed examination of the lifetime benefits of pensions, as well as more information regarding pensions generally, see the Taxcafe guide *Pension Magic*.

**Some Terminology**
In this chapter, I will use the term 'death benefits' to refer to any pension savings or other benefits payable to, or for the benefit of, a pension scheme member's beneficiaries after their death. We will take a closer at what exactly may comprise these death benefits in Section 10.4.

Uncrystallised funds mean pension funds which remain completely untouched. A fund is typically crystallised when a member takes any benefit from it. As far as the taxation of death benefits is concerned, this is only relevant when a scheme member dies before the age of 75.

In some cases, pension scheme trustees effectively fill the same role as a pension scheme administrator but, for the rest of this chapter, I will just refer to scheme administrators.

## 10.2 PENSIONS AND INHERITANCE TAX

As stated in Section 10.1, pension savings are usually exempt from IHT. This is because, in the majority of cases, the scheme administrator has discretion over who to pay death benefits to. Provided the scheme administrator has this discretion, the death benefits do not fall into the member's estate and are thus not usually subject to IHT. There are some exceptions to be aware of, however, which I will look at below.

### Lack of Discretion

There are some pensions where the scheme administrator does not have discretion over who to pay death benefits to. These include:

- Buy-out plans (sometimes known as 'section 32' schemes)
- Retirement annuity contracts
- A few occupational schemes (including some statutory schemes)

Early entrants to Nest (the pension scheme set up by the Government to handle auto-enrolment) were also unable to give the scheme administrator discretion over payment of death benefits and could only nominate a named beneficiary, meaning their pension savings would fall into their estate for IHT purposes.

However, Nest members can now alternatively make an 'expression of wish' similar to most other pension schemes (see Section 10.3), thus providing the necessary discretion and ensuring their pension savings escape IHT.

### Is Lack of Discretion a Problem?

Where the scheme administrator does not have discretion over the payment of death benefits, it only means the value of the benefits falls into the member's estate, it does not necessarily mean any IHT will actually arise.

In particular, where the death benefits are payable to the member's widow or widower, they will be covered by the spouse exemption and hence remain exempt from IHT.

In other cases, the death benefits may be covered by the member's NRB (plus any available TNRB).

But where the death benefits are likely to give rise to an IHT charge, this can sometimes be avoided by nominating a discretionary trust as the member's named beneficiary. This restores the necessary discretion and will usually prevent an IHT charge from arising (but see further below). Trusts used to receive death benefits are sometimes known as 'bypass trusts'. We will take a closer look at the benefits and pitfalls of bypass trusts in Section 10.9.

**Taxable Transfers of Value**

Because most death benefits fall outside a pension scheme member's estate, any payments into a scheme, as well as certain other actions, are potentially transfers of value (see Section 2.1).

However, HMRC takes the view there is no transfer of value unless the member is in ill health at the time of the payment or other action. Furthermore, HMRC will assume the member was in normal health if they survive two years.

The result of all this is that the following actions can result in additional IHT costs if carried out within two years of death:

- Paying pension contributions
- Transferring funds to a pension scheme with better death benefits
- Putting buy-out plans or retirement annuity contracts into trust (as described above)

However, the member must have been in ill health so if, for example, they died in an accident, while HMRC may look at the position, there should not be any transfer of value. There must also have been a gratuitous intent. Hence, if the member was unaware that they had a life-threatening illness, there is again no transfer of value.

If there is a transfer of value, other exemptions may be available. For example, continuing to pay an established, regular pension contribution should be covered by the normal expenditure out of income exemption (Section 5.5). However, the spouse exemption is not available to cover these transfers of value, as they do not go directly to the spouse.

Where the transfer of value is taxable, it is treated as a lifetime transfer made within seven years of death in the same way as the gifts we looked at in Section 4.5. In some cases, it may be covered by the NRB but consequent additional IHT may then fall on the beneficiaries of the member's estate.

Calculating the amount of the transfer of value arising under these circumstances is a complex matter and would require specialist advice.

**Existing Annuities**

Where an annuity purchased during the member's lifetime was subject to a guarantee period, and the member dies before the end of that period, the present value of the future annuity payments, as calculated at the date of death, will fall into the member's estate ***if*** the annuity is either paid to the estate or at the direction of the deceased. This may lead to an IHT liability in the same way as any other asset in the deceased's estate.

Continuing annuity payments made at the discretion of the provider will, however, escape IHT.

See also Section 10.5 regarding the Income Tax treatment of annuity payments made to beneficiaries, which is unaffected by their IHT status.

**Paying the Deceased's Liabilities: A Risk Area**
Since, in most cases, pension fund death benefits fall outside the deceased's estate, they should not be used to settle the deceased's liabilities, as this would mean those liabilities cannot be deducted from the value of the estate for IHT purposes. See Section 2.10 for further guidance, including suitable methods to prevent this problem arising.

## 10.3 WHO INHERITS THE PENSION?

As we have seen, the pension scheme administrator usually has discretion over who to pay death benefits to. Nonetheless, in the vast majority of cases, the scheme administrator will follow the member's wishes, although these cannot be legally binding if the death benefits are to remain outside the member's estate for IHT purpose.

**Nominations**
Of course, the scheme administrator cannot follow the member's wishes unless they have a record of them. This is done through an expression of wish form, sometimes called a letter of wishes or a nomination form. Whatever it is called, it is crucial the scheme member nominates who they would like their death benefits paid to. Nominations can be changed at any time during the scheme member's lifetime and it is important to keep them up to date. For example, you might reach a point where you would like your death benefits to go to your grandchildren instead of your children: but you will need to tell the scheme administrator!

You can nominate anyone you like to receive your death benefits, but this is where the scheme administrator might occasionally choose not to follow your wishes. For example, if a member died leaving an impoverished widow and two minor children with no other means of support, but nominated their secretary to receive their death benefits, the scheme administrator might perhaps not follow their wishes.

On the other hand, in the absence of any dependants, the scheme administrator is likely to follow your wishes, no matter who you nominate.

It is possible to nominate a charity or a trust to receive your death benefits. In these cases, the death benefit can only be paid out as a lump sum. We will look at lump sum death benefits received by trusts in Section 10.9.

**What Happens if There is No Nomination?**
In the absence of a valid nomination, the scheme administrator may only be able to pay the full range of death benefits available under the scheme to your dependants.

A member's dependants are usually their spouse and any minor children, although this may also sometimes include young adult children still in full-time education or training, or disabled children of any age.

The key point is that your adult children are not usually your dependants and hence, if you wish your death benefits to go to them, it is advisable to nominate them.

If you have not made a valid nomination, the scheme administrator may only be able to pay death benefits to any non-dependant beneficiary as a lump sum and this could have dire Income Tax consequences (see Section 10.5), so it is generally best avoided.

## 10.4 WHAT DO THEY INHERIT?

The death benefits passing to your beneficiaries depend on what type of pension scheme you are in and on the terms of that particular scheme.

**Defined Benefit Schemes**
Some occupational pension schemes are defined benefit schemes, often known as final salary schemes. Any death benefits usually fall outside your estate and are thus exempt from IHT: but it's best to check.

Survivor's pensions may sometimes be paid to a dependant and are subject to Income Tax (see Section 10.5). This includes any lump sums of up to £30,000 paid as a 'trivial commutation'.

Where the pension includes life cover (generally in respect of death in service), a lump sum death benefit may be paid out. A pension protection lump sum may also be payable in some schemes. Lump sum death benefits are usually tax free but may be subject to Income Tax under some circumstances, as detailed in Section 10.5.

**Defined Contribution Schemes**
Most pension schemes are now defined contribution schemes, including most private pensions, self-invested personal pensions (SIPPs), and many modern occupational pension schemes, including those created under auto-enrolment.

What kind of death benefit may be payable depends on the terms of the scheme and on whether the member has purchased an annuity.

Purchasing an annuity during your lifetime will generally limit any death benefit to continuing annuity payments for the remainder of any guarantee period, or survivor's payments where a joint life annuity has been purchased. Continuing payments during a guarantee period may sometimes be subject to IHT (see Section 10.2).

The greatest death benefits are, of course, available where the pension fund has either not been touched at all, or has been put into drawdown.

In these circumstances, the entire fund remaining at the date of the member's death is available as a death benefit. This is where pensions provide tremendous scope in IHT planning and we'll look at this in more detail in Sections 10.6 and 10.7.

Subject to the terms of the scheme, the member's beneficiaries may take death benefits as:

- A lump sum
- Inherited drawdown
- An annuity
- A dependant's scheme pension

It is critical to be aware, however, that not all pension schemes allow drawdown and very few allow a dependant's scheme pension. In many cases, this leaves the beneficiary with the choice of a lump sum or an annuity. Annuities are not always suitable, especially if the beneficiary is in need of funds now. Hence, the only practical choice in some cases may be to take a lump sum. Furthermore, death benefits paid to a charity or a trust (see Section 10.9) must be paid as a lump sum.

Subject to the points made in Section 10.2, whatever form the death benefits take, they will usually fall outside the scheme member's estate and thus escape IHT. Whether the death benefits are subject to Income Tax depends on a number of factors and we will look at this in Section 10.5.

## 10.5 DEATH BENEFITS AND INCOME TAX

This guide is, of course, about saving IHT. But there's no point saving one tax if that saving comes at the expense of the same, or an even greater amount, of another tax. When it comes to saving IHT using pensions, the other tax we have to be concerned about is Income Tax (see Appendix A for details of current Income Tax rates and thresholds).

Before 6th April 2023, we also had to be concerned about the Lifetime Allowance Charge. That's gone for the time being but, as we will see in Section 10.10, it is quite possible it may return in the foreseeable future. Since IHT planning is all about the future, I have therefore annotated this section as follows:

Note 1: Such payments were previously subject to a Lifetime Allowance Charge at 55% instead of Income Tax.
Note 2: Such designations, etc, were previously subject to a Lifetime Allowance Charge at 25%.

At the end of this section, we will take a closer look at how much Income Tax arises where a payment made to an individual beneficiary during the current 2023/24 tax year is subject to Income Tax. The position after 5th April 2024 is discussed in Section 10.10.

Firstly though, we're going to look at which payments are subject to Income Tax. The good news is that many of them aren't and, in this section, we will refer to these as 'tax free'. However, while most of them will also escape IHT, that is not what we are discussing in this section and is subject to the points outlined in Section 10.2.

The position sometimes depends on the member's available lifetime allowance. Some of their lifetime allowance may have been used previously if they crystallised this, or any other pension fund by beginning to take benefits. Some individuals may also have an enhanced, protected lifetime allowance. In the absence of these factors, however, the lifetime allowance applying to death benefits taken in 2023/24 is £1,073,100.

The Income Tax status of a death benefit also often depends on a payment, designation, or other action, being made within 'two years'. In this context, and hence for the rest of this section (unless stated to the contrary) this means within two years of when the scheme administrator became aware, or might reasonably have been expected to be aware, of the member's death.

The relevant date for the purposes of both the two year time limit and when any critical action is deemed to have occurred is as follows:

- Lump sums: date of payment
- Inherited drawdown: designation of the drawdown fund
- Annuities: date beneficiary becomes entitled

**Lump Sum Death Benefits**

Where the scheme member died before age 75, a lump sum death benefit is generally tax free provided it is paid within two years and, in the case of uncrystallised funds, it is covered by the member's available lifetime allowance.

Lump sum death benefits are subject to Income Tax in the following situations:

- Where the scheme member died aged 75 or more
- Where the death benefit is paid out after more than two years
- In other cases, where uncrystallised funds in excess of the lifetime allowance are paid, but in these cases, only the excess is subject to Income Tax (Note 1)

Neither the two year time limit nor the lifetime allowance apply to pension protection lump sums under a defined benefit scheme, so these are always tax free when the scheme member dies before age 75.

Other lump sum death benefits payable under a defined benefit scheme on the death of a scheme member before the age of 75 will generally represent uncrystallised funds subject to the lifetime allowance. In these cases, any excess can sometimes be used to pay a survivor's pension to a dependant instead.

**Inherited Drawdown**

Where inherited drawdown is available, it may be available on both the original scheme member's death and again on the subsequent death of any later owner of the fund. We will look into the benefits of this in IHT planning in Section 10.6.

Drawdown payments are subject to Income Tax when:

- The previous owner of the fund died aged 75 or more,
- Uncrystallised funds are designated for drawdown after more than two years, or
- Payments commenced before 6th April 2015

Note 2 applies to uncrystallised funds in excess of the lifetime allowance designated for drawdown within two years of the death of a scheme member before the age of 75.

Subject to the above points, drawdown payments are generally tax free where the previous owner of the fund died before age 75.

An important point to note is that the Income Tax status of the same funds can change, as it usually depends on the age of the previous owner. For example, a scheme member might die aged 80, leaving their son with an inherited drawdown which will be subject to Income Tax. However, the son might later die aged 74 and leave the inherited drawdown to his daughter, who can then receive payments tax free.

**Annuities**

Annuities attached to a scheme pension are usually subject to Income Tax.

Otherwise, annuities paid to beneficiaries as death benefits are subject to the same rules for Income Tax purposes as payments from an inherited drawdown. Note 2 also applies again under the circumstances described above. (As noted above, the critical date for tax purposes is the date the beneficiary first becomes entitled to the annuity.)

**Dependent's Scheme Pensions**

These are rarely offered, but are subject to Income Tax.

**Payments Subject to Income Tax**

Payments subject to Income Tax are taxed at the recipient's normal Income Tax rates. In effect, the taxable death benefit is added to their other taxable income for the year and suffers Income Tax at the rates given in the table below.

**Marginal Income Tax Rates 2023/24**

| | | |
|---|---|---|
| First £12,570 | 0% | (Personal allowance) |
| £12,570 to £50,270 | 20% | (Basic rate taxpayer) |
| £50,270 to £100,000 | 40% | (Higher rate taxpayer) |
| £100,000 to £125,140 | 60% | (see below) |
| Over £125,140 | 45% | (Additional rate taxpayer) |

The 60% rate is the effective rate created by the withdrawal of the personal allowance from individuals with taxable income over £100,000.

***Example 1:*** *When Frank dies, his daughter Nancy receives a taxable lump sum death benefit of £50,000 from his pension scheme. She has an existing salary of £30,000 and no other taxable income. The first £20,570 of the death benefit is taxed at 20%, and the remaining £29,430 is taxed at 40%.*

The total cost to Nancy of £15,886 (31.8% of her inheritance) is perhaps not too bad when compared with IHT at 40%, but is that a fair comparison? What if Frank could have drawn down all his pension savings before he died and only suffered Income Tax at 20%? What if the remaining net sum of £40,000 was then covered by his NRB so he was able to pass it to Nancy free of IHT?

Alternatively, if Nancy had been able to place the funds in inherited drawdown, she would have been able to take her inheritance over a few years and only suffer Income Tax at 20%. Either way, taking a lump sum death benefit has cost her an extra £5,886 in Income Tax. And, in some cases, it could be much worse.

***Example 2:*** *Nina dies aged 85 with a pension fund worth £250,000. The scheme does not allow inherited drawdown and Nina's nominated beneficiary, her daughter Simone, does not wish to buy an annuity. Simone therefore takes the death benefit as a lump sum. She has other taxable income for the year of £80,000 and thus suffers Income Tax on the lump sum as follows:*

| | |
|---|---|
| *First £20,000 @ 40%* | *£8,000* |
| *Next £25,140 @ 60%* | *£15,084* |
| *Next £204,860 @ 45%* | *£92,187* |
| *Total* | *£115,271* |

In this case, Income Tax has eaten up 46.1% of Simone's inheritance, worse than IHT at 40%. This is only part of the story, however, and we will look at the IHT saving potential of pension savings in more detail in Sections 10.6 and 10.7.

Nonetheless, what these examples go to show is how important it is to nominate your beneficiaries (see Section 10.3) and make sure your savings are in a scheme that allows inherited drawdown, to give them the flexibility they need to make the most tax efficient use of your funds.

**Exceptions**
Different Income Tax rates apply to:

- Scottish taxpayers (higher rates apply to all taxable income over £25,688)
- The highest earner in a household where child benefit is being claimed and that individual has taxable income between £50,000 and £60,000
- Dividend income (which is subject to different rates and is also treated as the top part of an individual's taxable income for the year)

We'll look at the Income Tax rates on dividends in Section 10.8, and take a closer look at the impact of the other exceptions in Section 10.7. A taxable death benefit could also lead to an increase in the rate of CGT paid by a beneficiary disposing of an asset in the same tax year. More information on all these issues is contained in our other Taxcafe guides.

## 10.6 INHERITANCE TAX PLANNING WITH PENSIONS

Subject to the points in Section 10.2, most pension death benefits escape IHT. Many will also escape Income Tax. This makes pensions an incredibly valuable tool in IHT planning. But how great is the scope of this tool and what are its limitations?

We should also bear in mind that while pensions are currently a good way to pass wealth down the generations, that's not really their main purpose, and we at Taxcafe are concerned the tremendous benefits that exist now may be curtailed in future. We'll explore that issue in Section 10.10, which I urge you to read before relying on pensions as your IHT planning strategy.

Nevertheless, in this section, let's look at the benefits of the current regime:

- Pension savings will generally escape IHT provided the relevant contributions are made more than two years prior to death, or even later if you are in normal health at the time: this compares very favourably with the seven year period required to avoid IHT by making direct gifts or transfers into trust
- Your pension savings can grow in a tax-free environment, free of Income Tax, CGT, and IHT (all of which may be suffered by trusts: see Chapter 8), thus further enhancing the value of your beneficiaries' inheritance
- Where inherited drawdown is available, pensions can be passed down through multiple generations, escaping IHT every time (and continuing to grow in a tax-free environment)
- As pension savings do not generally sit in anyone's estate, there is no risk of IHT arising if your intended beneficiaries should predecease you
- If it turns out you need to access your pension savings during your lifetime, from age 55 (age 57 from 2028) you can drawdown up to 25% tax free and the rest as taxable income. In other words, if you are using a pension for IHT planning purposes, there is no need to lock the money away where you can't touch it (as is necessary when using trusts and most other forms of IHT planning, although AIM shares do also provide this flexibility)

- On top of all this, pension contributions generally attract Income Tax relief, making them one of the few IHT planning vehicles where you can also make tax savings when you implement your planning (unlike most others, which either have a tax cost to set up or are at best tax neutral at that point)

**The Fly in the Ointment**

While your pension savings will generally escape IHT under the current regime, there is a strong chance your beneficiaries will be subject to Income Tax on those savings. Subject to the further detailed points covered in Section 10.5, the basic rule applying in most cases is that your beneficiaries will ultimately suffer Income Tax on your pension savings if you survive to at least the age of 75.

According to the ONS, men currently aged between 40 and 74 can expect to live to between 84 and 87. Women in the same age bracket can expect to live to 87 or 88. In short, while there is a chance your beneficiaries could receive your pensions savings tax free, it is more likely they will suffer Income Tax.

This, in turn, means that a lump sum death benefit could attract a significant amount of Income Tax and we saw the consequences of this in Section 10.5. But this may not have told the full story as we did not factor in the Income Tax relief obtained by the scheme member during their lifetime.

For a basic rate taxpayer that relief is all given at source: for example, a cash pension contribution of £8,000 made by an individual is grossed up to £10,000 (the Government puts in the additional £2,000). Higher rate taxpayers receive additional tax relief through a reduction in their tax bill. The overall effect is that they receive total tax relief at their effective marginal rate of Income Tax: the same effective marginal tax rates as per the table in Section 10.5.

So, for example, if you're a higher rate taxpayer paying Income Tax at 40% and you make a cash pension contribution of £8,000, you get £2,000 of tax relief at source (the Government contribution to your pension fund) and a £2,000 reduction in your tax bill. This means it cost you just £6,000 to put £10,000 in your pension.

In Table A below we're going to look at what happens when an individual can afford a net cost of £10,000 to put money into a pension, after tax relief. For a basic rate taxpayer, that simply means a cash contribution of £10,000, which the Government will gross up to £12,500; for a higher rate taxpayer paying Income Tax at 40%, that means a cash contribution of £13,333, which the Government will gross up to £16,666 and also allow a reduction of £3,333 in the individual's tax bill: so it's the same net cost overall.

We'll ignore investment growth in this table, although we'll look at this issue a little further later.

The percentages given on the left of the table represent the individual's effective marginal Income Tax rate (see Section 10.5); the percentages across the top of the table represent the marginal Income Tax rate of the beneficiary receiving the lump sum death benefit; and the sums in the body of the table represent the net sum inherited by the beneficiary after Income Tax.

**Table A: Net Amount Received from £10,000 Investment**

| **Individual's** | **Beneficiary's Tax Rate** | | | | |
|---|---|---|---|---|---|
| **Tax Rate** | **0%** | **20%** | **40%** | **60%** | **45%** |
| **20%** | £12,500 | £10,000 | £7,500 | £5,000 | £6,875 |
| **40%** | £16,667 | £13,333 | £10,000 | £6,667 | £9,167 |
| **60%** | £25,000 | £20,000 | £15,000 | £10,000 | £13,750 |
| **45%** | £18,182 | £14,545 | £10,909 | £7,273 | £10,000 |

**Is it a Good Outcome?**

The first thing to bear in mind is, if that same £10,000 had still been in the individual's estate at the date of death (again ignoring investment growth) then, assuming it would not be covered by any exemptions, it would have suffered IHT at 40%. Hence, the beneficiary's net inheritance would be just £6,000. That means any amount in the table greater than £6,000 is better than could be achieved by, for example, investing the money in an ISA until the individual's death.

As we can see, where the individual and their beneficiary have the same tax rate, the same net sum as was originally invested is ultimately received back. That's logical enough and puts the pension on a par with simply giving away the money and surviving seven years (but you will generally only need to survive two using the pension).

Where the beneficiary's tax rate is lower than the individual's, more money than was invested is received back. Hence the pension savings not only escape IHT but also produce an additional overall net Income Tax benefit.

Sadly, however, the more likely outcome in the case of a large lump sum death benefit is that at least some of the amount paid to the beneficiary will be taxed at 45% or 60%, meaning, unless the individual obtained tax relief at the same rate, or more, the IHT saving comes at an overall Income Tax cost.

That could be a cost worth paying in some cases, as there is only one instance in the table where the pension does not beat simply holding the money as cash until the individual dies (even in an ISA). But there are a number of ways we can do better.

It's worth bearing in mind that, if you should die before the age of 75, your pension savings can generally pass to your beneficiaries tax free: unless they exceed your available lifetime allowance (see Section 10.5) and, even then, it is only the excess that suffers Income Tax. This means an early death will generally give rise to the beneficial outcome shown in the column headed '0%' in Table A above.

But, if you reach the age of 68 in good health, it's pretty likely you will reach the age of 75. This means two things: your beneficiaries will probably suffer Income Tax on your pension savings, but there's also probably time to make lifetime cash gifts that will become exempt from IHT when you have survived seven years (see Chapter 4).

While you live, you will be able to withdraw a tax-free lump sum of 25% from your pension (currently limited to a maximum of £268,275). However, this ability is not available to your beneficiaries after your death, and if you are then aged 75 or more, the whole of your death benefit will be subject to Income Tax.

So, if you reach 68 in good health without having yet taken your 25% tax-free lump sum, and you are confident you will not need the funds yourself, you could take the lump sum and give it to your beneficiaries. They will not pay any Income Tax on this sum either (as it's a gift) and IHT will be avoided when you have survived seven years.

You could, in fact, do this earlier (currently any time from the age of 55). We'll look at the pros and cons of waiting until you're 68 in Section 10.7 but, either way, when you subsequently die aged 75 or more, the overall total net sum received by your beneficiaries will be as per Table B below.

**Table B: Total Received from £10,000 Investment**

| **Individual's** | **Beneficiary's Tax Rate** | | | | |
|---|---|---|---|---|---|
| **Tax Rate** | **0%** | **20%** | **40%** | **60%** | **45%** |
| **20%** | £12,500 | £10,625 | £8,750 | £6,875 | £8,281 |
| **40%** | £16,667 | £14,167 | £11,667 | £9,167 | £11,042 |
| **60%** | £25,000 | £21,250 | £17,500 | £13,750 | £16,563 |
| **45%** | £18,182 | £15,455 | £12,727 | £10,000 | £12,045 |

All taxpaying beneficiaries benefit from this strategy if you reach age 75. The higher their marginal Income Tax rate, the more they benefit. The only beneficiaries who do not potentially benefit are non-taxpayers. It will be fairly rare for your beneficiaries to have no exposure to Income Tax on your death benefits if you die aged 75 or more, although it may be possible in the case of inherited drawdown and we will see an example later. If you were certain your beneficiaries would be non-taxpayers, this strategy would not be worthwhile, but that's going to be very rare.

In principle, there is nothing to stop you giving your tax-free lump sum to any beneficiary you choose. However, in the case of your own minor children, there are a number of other issues to be considered. These are examined in Section 11.10.

This strategy has the drawback that you have to survive seven years to get the full benefit. But if you should die sooner, the 75% of your savings still held in the pension will be free from Income Tax for your beneficiaries.

Hence, regardless of their Income Tax rate, they will ultimately benefit by at least the amounts given in Table C below (based on your tax rate).

**Table C: Total Received in Event of Early Death**

| Tax Rate | |
|---|---|
| **20%** | £11,250 |
| **40%** | £15,000 |
| **60%** | £22,500 |
| **45%** | £16,364 |

In this scenario, where you withdraw and give away your 25% tax-free lump sum but do not then survive seven years, your beneficiaries could be up to 10% worse off than if you had not made the withdrawal. However, you may feel the benefits if you do reach age 75 (as per Table B) are worth the risk: especially if your beneficiaries are higher rate taxpayers.

This 10% loss may not affect the same beneficiaries as those you give your 25% tax-free lump sum to. It may fall on the beneficiaries of your estate (as the lifetime gifts will use up some or all of your NRB) or, if you are married, it may fall on the beneficiaries of your spouse's estate (as their TNRB will be reduced: see Chapter 6).

It's also important to bear in mind the potential impact on (and of) other lifetime gifts you have made: see Section 4.5.

Conversely, where neither you nor your spouse (if you have one) have any exposure to IHT, there will be nothing to lose by taking and giving away the 25% tax-free lump sum. Even the tax-free investment growth can be reinstated if your beneficiaries put the money they receive into an ISA, or perhaps even better, into their own pension (subject to the limitations discussed in Section 10.7).

**Exceptions**
The same exceptions we looked at in Section 10.5 may affect both the individual's tax relief when making their pension contributions and the Income Tax burden on the beneficiaries receiving the death benefits. We'll look at some of these exceptions a little further in Section 10.7.

**The Added Benefits of Inherited Drawdown**
So far, we've seen that, even in the case of a lump sum death benefit subject to Income Tax, there are many instances where pension savings provide tax efficient IHT shelters.

Nonetheless, it must be recognised that, after you have reached the age of 75, the Income Tax burden on your beneficiaries can eat up a fair amount of the IHT savings and, in some instances, means other IHT planning strategies would have been more beneficial.

This is where inherited drawdown is a far better option than lump sum death benefits, as it will allow your beneficiaries to either draw down income when it will be taxed at a more palatable rate or, if they don't need the income themselves, pass on the funds to the next generation free from IHT. The next generation will face the same choices and, ultimately, someone is likely to be able to draw down the benefits either tax free or at a reasonable Income Tax rate.

It's also worth noting that inherited drawdown can be taken at any age (i.e. before age 55) and does not trigger the money purchase annual allowance (see Section 10.7). It may, however, lead to a tapered annual allowance if the recipient's total income exceeds the relevant thresholds as a result (again, see Section 10.7).

The funds held in inherited drawdown can also be used to purchase an annuity at any time if the beneficiary ever gets to the stage where they would prefer the certainty of a lifelong income. The Income Tax position on the annuity will be the same as the drawdown payments, but if the beneficiary is a basic rate taxpayer by this stage, the tax cost, where it applies, is only 20% (some may even be covered by their personal allowance).

Let's see how inherited drawdown may have helped the individuals in our examples in Section 10.5. We'll also take this opportunity to factor in the Income Tax relief obtained when the pension contributions were originally made. We will, however, continue to ignore investment growth for the time being (we'll look at that later).

I've also ignored the annual exemption: we'll assume the pension scheme members in the examples are already using it on other gifts. We'll also assume their estates will exceed the NRB and any other available exemptions.

***Example 1 Revisited:*** *Some years ago, Frank had £30,000 in cash available. He could have given it to his daughter Nancy and, provided he survived seven years, it would have been free of IHT. If he had died sooner, it would have meant his estate paid an extra £12,000 in IHT and, as Nancy is the beneficiary of his estate, she would have only benefitted by a net sum of £18,000.*

*But, instead, Frank, who was a higher rate taxpayer at the time, made net pension contributions totalling £40,000 (say over two years), to which the Government added £10,000 in basic rate tax relief to give him an extra £50,000 in his pension fund. His higher rate tax relief reduced his tax bills by a further £10,000, bringing the net cost down to the £30,000 he had available.*

*When Frank dies, Nancy is able to take the death benefit of £50,000. She has other taxable income of £30,000 so, as we saw in Section 10.5, taking it as a lump sum would cost her £15,886 in Income Tax, leaving her with a net amount of £34,114. That's already better than what she would have received if Frank had simply given her a cash gift but, instead, she takes the death benefit as inherited drawdown.*

*She draws down the funds over three years (no more than £20,570 in each year) and thus only pays a total of £10,000 in Income Tax, leaving her with a net sum of £40,000.*

*In the end, the pension scheme has enabled Frank to leave Nancy with £10,000 more than if he had simply made a cash gift and survived seven years, or up to £22,000 more than if he had died sooner or had held on to the cash himself.*

It's a remarkable thought: you could give your children £30,000 and they could end up with just £18,000, or you could use it to fund pension contributions and they could end up with £40,000, or even £50,000 if you should pass away before age 75.

Alternatively, if Frank had taken his 25% tax-free lump sum of £12,500 when he was aged somewhere between 55 and 68 (as discussed above), given it to Nancy at that time, then lived to at least 75, she could have ended up with a total net sum of £42,500.

***Example 2 Revisited:*** *Nina worked until she was 70, earning between £90,000 and £100,000 every year. She had more money than she needed, so she was able to make net pension contributions totalling £200,000, to which the Government added £50,000 in basic rate tax relief. The contributions all attracted higher rate tax relief too, saving Nina a further £50,000 in Income Tax, so they only cost her £150,000.*

*She could have given that same £150,000 to her daughter, Simone, but she was always worried she might need it herself one day or, if she died too soon, it would lead to an extra £60,000 in IHT. So, she felt happier having £250,000 in her pension fund than possibly leaving Simone with just £90,000.*

*When she was 74, Nina realised that Simone would soon be exposed to Income Tax on her pension fund death benefit so (unlike the first version of this example in Section 10.5) she transferred her pension savings to a fund that allowed inherited drawdown. This could have led to an IHT charge if Nina had been in poor health and had died within two years (see Section 10.2) but that was not the case here.*

*When Nina died many years later, Simone calculated that taking the death benefit as a lump sum would cost her £115,271 in Income Tax (Section 10.5). This would leave her with just £134,729, i.e. £15,271 less than if Nina had simply given her a cash gift of £150,000 and survived seven years; although it would still be £25,271 more than the effective net sum of £90,000 she might have ended up with if Nina had died sooner.*

*Instead of this, however, Simone placed the funds in inherited drawdown, giving her a number of choices:*

*Option 1: She could draw down £20,000 per year (to take her annual taxable income up to £100,000) and suffer Income Tax at 40%, but avoid the higher rates of 45% and 60%. If she used the whole fund in this way, she would end up with a total of £150,000: the same net sum that Nina's pension contributions originally cost, thus leaving her in the same position as if Nina had simply made cash gifts and survived seven years.*

*Option 2: She could wait until she retired. If her income then fell below the higher rate tax threshold (currently £50,270), there would be scope to draw down funds taxed at 20%. If she used the whole fund in this way, she would end up with a total of £200,000: £50,000 more than if Nina had simply made cash gifts.*

*Option 3: She could leave the funds in inherited drawdown and pass them on to her own intended beneficiaries. Those beneficiaries might be able to obtain the funds tax free (if Simone dies before age 75) or, more likely, might be able to draw them down and suffer Income Tax at only 20% if their income is below the higher rate tax threshold.*

Of course, it doesn't have to be one option only for Simone, she could apply a mixture of all three.

A further option for Simone might be to purchase an annuity. As discussed above, some people might prefer the certainty of a lifelong income and it will often only suffer Income Tax at 20% if they wait until they are a basic rate taxpayer. However, the drawback is the funds used to buy the annuity could effectively be lost to the family, as many annuities cease when the original purchaser dies.

In this example, it is arguable that Nina could have made regular cash gifts to Simone (instead of her pension contributions) and, if these had come out of surplus net income, they might have been immediately exempt from IHT as normal expenditure out of income (Section 5.5). However, that exemption may not have applied in this case, or there may have been some doubts over whether the gifts would be covered.

Making pension contributions provided Nina with the certainty these would escape IHT (she was in good health at the time) while also allowing the flexibility that she would be able to access the funds herself if she needed to. At the time, there was also the chance she might die before age 75 and thus be able to leave her pension savings to Simone free from Income Tax.

But when Nina moved her pension funds when she was 74, she could perhaps have also decided to take her tax-free lump sum of £62,500 (25% of her fund) and give it to Simone. This would have escaped IHT as, in this particular case, Nina survived more than seven years (although, as discussed in Section 10.7, the best time to do this in most cases is usually before you're 68). If Simone had then subsequently followed Option 2 above, the total net sum she would have received would be increased to £212,500.

**Multi-Generational Benefits**

So far, we've mostly focussed on passing funds down one generation, to the original scheme member's beneficiaries, typically their children.

But inherited drawdown provides the added benefit of being able to pass the funds on, free from IHT, down further generations.

Let's take Simone's case from Example 2 above. We've seen that, by either taking a lump sum or following Options 1 or 2, she would end up with somewhere between £134,729 and £200,000. But let's suppose she doesn't spend that money and it ends up in her estate so, when she dies it suffers IHT at 40%. That leaves somewhere between £80,837 and £120,000 to go to ***her*** beneficiaries.

Alternatively, by following Option 3, and passing the inherited drawdown to the next generation, Simone's beneficiaries might be able to take the whole £250,000 in the fund tax free (if Simone dies before age 75), or might be able to take it at an Income Tax cost of only 20%, so they receive a net amount of £200,000.

On the other hand, as Simone gets older, she might see that her children don't really need the money either. So she might change her nomination (see Section 10.3) in favour of her grandchildren, or even, eventually her great-grandchildren.

Inherited drawdown arrangements can be made for minor children (the funds are typically paid to the child's parent who is under an obligation to apply the funds for the child's benefit). Both minors and young adults in full time education generally tend to have little or no taxable income, so they can often receive up to £12,570 per year free from Income Tax.

For example, let's say Simone passes on her inherited drawdown to her five grandchildren and each of them is in full time education with no taxable income for four tax years. Each grandchild can therefore draw down £12,500 per year for four years with no tax payable and the entire £250,000 has been passed on completely free of both IHT and Income Tax.

(Nina could have done something similar a generation earlier by changing her nomination, but we've assumed that didn't happen.)

**Factoring in Investment Growth**

Pension funds are typically invested in a range of investments, including quoted shares, gilts, bonds, and commercial property. The aim is usually to produce good steady growth at an acceptable risk level. If you have your own SIPP, this opens up more possibilities, but residential property usually remains off the table.

The key point is the investments grow in a tax-free environment, with no Income Tax or CGT, and no anniversary or exit charges like those suffered by trusts.

So, broadly speaking, investment growth is usually going to make pension savings even more attractive. Hence, in all our tables and examples, where the net amount finally received by the beneficiary is equal to the net cost of the original pension contribution, the actual position in practice is generally going to be that the pension savings produce a better final outcome.

The only other way to get the same tax-free investment growth is to put money in an ISA. But, unless you give the money to your beneficiaries, they put it in an ISA, and you survive seven years, those funds will suffer IHT.

Let's go back to Example 2 again by way of illustration but let's now say that Nina only had £75,000 available (over the course of a few years). Her tax relief allowed her to use this money to fund net pension contributions totalling £100,000, grossed up to £125,000 by the Government. Over the years from then until her death, her pension savings doubled in value to the £250,000 we saw in the example which, in turn, left Simone with somewhere between

£134,729 and £200,000.

Now let's say instead that Nina simply gave £75,000 to Simone who then put it in an ISA (over the course of a few years). Nina survived more than seven years so there is no IHT to worry about and Simone's ISA experiences the same tax-free investment growth as the pension. Hence, by the time of Nina's death it is worth £150,000: the same sum as the cash gift we saw in the example above, where we ignored investment growth.

The first thing this proves is that investment growth does not alter the conclusions we have drawn so far. (For this reason, I will continue to ignore it in later examples in this chapter.)

It does show that a cash gift made more than seven years before the donor's death (or which is otherwise exempt from IHT) could be better than a pension contribution where the beneficiary's marginal tax rate is greater than the donor's.

But the pension contribution still carries many advantages, including the fact there is no need to survive seven years, the death benefits might turn out to be tax free, the contributor has access to their pension during their lifetime, and, of course, all the benefits of inherited drawdown.

Generally speaking, the only ways your money might see better investment growth than they would get in a pension are investing in residential property, your own business, or something risky that happens to pay off. Your own trading business or shares in an unquoted trading company will generally be exempt from IHT (see Chapter 7). As far as residential property is concerned, this is where many of the other IHT planning strategies in this guide come into play!

## 10.7 TACTICS AND LIMITATIONS

While it is sometimes possible to make pension contributions in excess of the limits discussed in this section, these will not generally attract Income Tax relief, so they are far less beneficial and we will ignore them for the purposes of this guide. Hence, when I say something is not possible, what I actually mean is it will not attract Income Tax relief: whether it is possible is another matter.

Unless stated to the contrary, the limits given in this section refer to gross pension contributions, including basic rate tax relief given at source. Hence, for example, a limit of £60,000 means the net cash contribution is limited to £48,000.

### Early Deaths

If you knew you were going to die before the age of 75, pension savings would be hard to beat as an IHT planning measure. Those savings would generally escape both IHT and Income Tax, as well as providing you with tax relief when you made the contributions.

As far as tax is concerned, it's a triple win! (Although I am sure your family would rather have you around for longer.)

As we saw in the '0%' column of Table A, Section 10.6, every £10,000 you invested in pension savings (net of tax relief) could leave your beneficiaries with between £12,500 and £25,000, depending on your marginal tax rate. Compare that with the £6,000 they could end up with if you died within seven years of making a cash gift.

In fact, even if you survive seven years, but not to age 75, the pension savings are still providing an Income Tax benefit which increases the value of your beneficiary's inheritance. The same is true where the savings could have been covered by other exemptions, like the annual exemption; or the relevant funds would have been exempt from IHT if they were still in your estate when you die (e.g. if covered by the NRB or the TNRB).

So, in the case of an early death, pension savings can do more than just saving IHT and can even benefit families where there is no IHT liability to worry about.

This makes pension savings extremely valuable for anyone who has a strong probability of dying before the age of 75, but more than two years from now. They will be most valuable for someone meeting these criteria but unlikely to survive seven years.

**Deathbed Planning**
As we saw in Section 10.2, pension contributions made within two years of death by someone in poor health could give rise to an IHT charge. But there are many reasons why it could still be worth making those contributions:

- Even if no IHT is saved, there will still be Income Tax savings if you die before age 75
- Inherited drawdown may be available to pass the funds down the generations free of IHT next time
- The resultant transfer of value might be covered by your NRB or other exemptions
- The transfer of value could work out at less than the amount you have managed to remove from your estate, thus still producing some IHT saving
- While there is a transfer of value, the contributions will generally lie outside your estate at death. If your estate is in the £2m to £2.7m bracket, this could increase the amount of RNRB available (see Section 3.4), thus providing an IHT saving at an effective rate of 20%
- You may survive two years after all, thus still getting the full IHT saving

**Changing Tack Between 55 and 68**
As we saw in Section 10.6, for the majority of people who live to at least the age of 75, the overall net benefit produced by your pension savings will generally be increased if you take your 25% tax-free lump sum and, if you can afford to, give it to your beneficiaries. Remember, the whole of your death

benefits will be subject to Income Tax if you survive to 75: there is no tax-free lump sum after death.

However, this does carry the risk that the gifted funds are exposed to IHT if you should die within seven years of making the gift. Married people whose spouse has a longer life expectancy may be able to reduce this risk by first gifting the money to their spouse, who may subsequently choose to give the funds to the ultimate beneficiaries (but see Section 6.7 for some potential issues to be aware of).

Currently, you can take your tax-free lump sum at any time from the age of 55 (increasing to 57 from 6th April 2028) and many people will do this for other reasons unconnected with IHT planning. From an IHT planning perspective, however, some people may prefer to wait until shortly before their 68th birthday: although there are pros and cons to this delay.

On the one hand, quite obviously, your chances of surviving seven years are generally better when you're 55 than when you're 68.

On the other hand, however, a lot can happen in the intervening thirteen years and you may have a better idea of whether you will need the tax-free lump sum for something else, including supporting you in your old age, or supporting your spouse in theirs. But if you gave it away when you were 55, you won't have those options and may have to take taxable income from your pension savings.

Sadly, some 55-year-olds won't even make it to 68. Some of those that do will have found out they are unlikely to live to 75. In these cases, the pension savings are best left where they are (from a tax point of view) as they are likely to escape both IHT and Income Tax.

But, if you're in normal health at the age of 68, you now have a stronger chance of reaching 75 than you did when you were 55. In other words, the position is a bit more certain.

Statistics can't tell us what is going to happen to each individual but, according to the ONS, a 55-year-old woman has about a 95% chance of surviving seven years, and around an 85% chance of living to at least 75. When she reaches 68, she has about a 90% chance of both surviving seven years and reaching 75.

A 55-year-old man has about a 92% chance of surviving seven years, and around an 80% chance of living to at least 75. When he reaches 68, he has about an 87% chance of both surviving seven years and reaching 75.

As well as the pension scheme member themselves, those intervening years will have made a big difference to their beneficiaries too. Their children, or other heirs will be more mature, meaning the scheme member may feel more comfortable about giving them a large cash gift. Some beneficiaries may have been the scheme member's minor children when the member was 55, but the member's children will usually be adults by the time the member is 68, meaning the issues covered in Section 11.10 will not arise.

Alternatively, the scheme member may wish to choose different beneficiaries at 68 than they would have at 55. Their children might now be financially secure enough that they wish to pass their wealth directly to their grandchildren, or to a trust for their benefit (see Chapters 8 and 9).

It will sometimes also be worth keeping the funds in the pension until the age of 68 in order to enjoy an extra thirteen years of tax-free investment growth, although this does depend on what your beneficiaries intend, and are able, to do with the gifted funds. In this context, it is worth pointing out you can stagger your tax-free drawdown over a number of years so your beneficiaries can invest the funds in an ISA, or their own pension, within the relevant limits (if they are not already fully utilising them). Arguably, if your beneficiaries are able to put the cash in their own pension, passing the funds to them as soon as possible may be most beneficial.

Another reason it may make sense to pass the funds to your beneficiaries sooner rather than later is the danger of changes in legislation, although what shape those will take is hard to predict.

There are many factors to consider when deciding whether to take your tax-free lump sum and pass it to your beneficiaries as soon as possible; to wait until just before your 68th birthday; or to leave the funds where they are.

Taking the lump sum after the age of 68 may pay off for some people, and we can see this in some of the examples in this chapter. But this does run the risk that your family could suffer ***both*** IHT on the 25% you have given away ***and*** Income Tax on the 75% left in your pension (if you die within seven years, but after reaching the age of 75).

Passing the tax-free lump sum to your beneficiaries by the age of 68 will generally leave them better off if you survive to the age of 75, and they will only lose out by a maximum of 10% if you die sooner (or someone could: see Section 10.6). It is still a bit of a gamble, but I'm afraid that's true of most IHT planning. I've done my best to give you the odds above; as far as the stakes are concerned, you need only look at the tables in Section 10.6.

While this strategy will usually leave your immediate beneficiaries better off (assuming you live to at least 75) it does mean the funds are now in their estates and the multigenerational benefits discussed in Section 10.6 have been lost (on the 25% of your pension savings withdrawn). But this either may not be an issue or can be resolved with some further planning.

Remember also there is a statutory maximum to the tax-free lump sum, which is £268,275 in most cases. I generally haven't factored this into my analysis in the rest of this section (or Section 10.8) but in practice you will need to bear it in mind if your pension savings exceed your available lifetime allowance (usually £1,073,100).

**After 75**

Everything changes once you reach the age of 75. Your pension savings will now be exposed to Income Tax in the hands of your beneficiaries. There are still many advantages though, especially with inherited drawdown (see Section 10.6).

It is not possible to make further pension contributions after the age of 75, although many people will have stopped before then anyway.

**Widows and Widowers**

Most people want to be sure their widow or widower will be comfortable after they've gone so, in practical terms, it often makes sense to nominate them to receive your pension death benefits.

However, from an IHT point of view this is a waste, as your death benefits will generally escape IHT anyway. Hence, where practical, it will make more sense to leave other assets to your spouse and nominate other beneficiaries (e.g. your children) to receive your pension death benefits.

**The Annual Allowance**

The annual allowance is the maximum amount of pension contributions you can make each year, although any unused allowance can effectively be carried forward for up to three tax years (provided you were a member of a qualifying pension scheme in the relevant year).

The annual allowance for 2023/24 is £60,000, but it was £40,000 in earlier years, so the maximum possible contribution in 2023/24 is £180,000.

Not everyone is entitled to the full annual allowance. If you have withdrawn more than your 25% tax-free lump sum, you can only make maximum contributions of £10,000 in 2023/24 (known as the money purchase annual allowance).

Those with total taxable income, after deducting pension contributions, of more than £200,000 ***and*** 'adjusted income' of more than £260,000, are subject to a tapered annual allowance, which reduces it to somewhere between £10,000 and £60,000, depending on the level of their income. Adjusted income for this purpose is total taxable income ***before*** deducting pension contributions ***plus*** any contributions made on the individual's behalf by their employer.

**Earnings**

As well as the limitations of the annual allowance, it is only possible to make pension contributions up to the greater of £3,600 or your earnings for the relevant tax year. Not all taxable income counts as earnings, as it is limited to employment income, self-employed trading income (sole traders or business partners), and profits from qualifying furnished holiday lets (see the Taxcafe guide *How to Save Property Tax* for details).

One group who are severely restricted when it comes to pension contributions are full-time landlords with no other income (other than those with furnished holiday lets). Without qualifying earnings, landlords are restricted to contributions of just £3,600 per year. The only way to improve the position is to use a company (see Section 10.8).

**The Rate of Tax Relief**

So, let's say you have your full annual allowance of £60,000 available and you have enough earnings to cover it. The next thing you need to think about is what rate of tax relief you're going to get for your pension contributions.

Remember, if you live to at least 75, your beneficiaries will be subject to Income Tax on your death benefits. That means there is only going to be an overall Income Tax saving on your death benefits if your beneficiaries pay Income Tax at a lower marginal rate than you, and there could be an overall Income Tax cost if they have a higher marginal rate.

However, in the majority of cases, there will be the opportunity to take the 25% tax-free lump sum from your pension and, if you give this to your beneficiaries and survive seven years (or it is exempt from IHT in some other way), this will enhance the overall saving available (see Table B, Section 10.6).

So, whether there will be an overall Income Tax saving on your pension savings as a whole, including the 25% tax-free lump sum, is slightly different.

In fact, if we operate on the most likely assumption that you will live to at least 75 and will have time to withdraw your tax-free lump sum, give it to your beneficiaries, and survive seven years, the ***overall*** rate of Income Tax they will suffer on your pension savings will be as follows:

| | | |
|---|---|---|
| Basic rate taxpayers | 15% | (20% less 25% tax free) |
| Higher rate taxpayers | 30% | (40% less 25% tax free) |
| Additional rate taxpayers | 33.75% | (45% less 25% tax free) |

A potential overall rate of 45% applies to any beneficiary foolish, or unlucky, enough to have taxable death benefits falling into the £100,000 to £125,140 income bracket.

In most cases, due to the statutory maximum of £268,275 for the tax-free lump sum explained above, these overall rates usually apply to the first £1,073,100 of your pension savings, with the beneficiary's full marginal tax rate effectively applying to any excess.

What all this means is there will usually be an overall Income Tax saving whenever you and your beneficiaries have the same marginal tax rate, and a greater saving where your marginal tax rate is higher than theirs.

Nonetheless, it still remains a fact that there could be an overall Income Tax cost if your beneficiaries' marginal tax rates are higher than yours. For example, if you are a basic rate taxpayer when you make your pension contributions, and your beneficiaries are higher rate taxpayers when they receive your death benefits, there remains an overall Income Tax cost equal to 10% of the gross contributions: even factoring in the 25% tax-free lump sum. That means a simple lifetime gift would have left your beneficiaries better off (provided you survived seven years).

So, while we saw some notable exceptions in Section 10.6, and they're worth thinking about, unless you can be certain your beneficiaries will be basic rate taxpayers or non-taxpayers, you will generally need to be a higher rate taxpayer to give them a fighting chance of coming out on top in the end.

In summary, for it to be both possible and worthwhile to make the maximum contributions of £60,000 per year, you will need earnings of at least £60,000; adjusted income of no more than £260,000 (see above); and usually also total taxable income of at least £110,270.

**Have You Got the Cash?**

In addition to earnings and taxable income, you will also need to have the cash available to make your pension contributions. However, you will only need to fund 80% of the gross contribution and the cash itself could come from anywhere. For example, an individual on a salary of £80,270 might not usually have any spare cash to fund pension contributions. But if one of their parents dies before the age of 75 and leaves them a lump sum death benefit of £24,000 they could use this to fund a gross pension contribution of £30,000 (they have enough earnings and they will get higher rate tax relief).

**How Much Time Have You Got?**

When I was in practice, most people who came to me for IHT advice were at least 60, generally older. So, the question is, how many years are left for them to make pension contributions and get tax relief at a minimum of 40%?

In other words, how much longer will they keep earning in excess of £50,270? Plus, even if they want to keep going until they drop, their contributions will have to stop at age 75 anyway.

For the reasons explained in Section 10.6, I have again ignored investment growth in the examples below.

***Example 1:*** *Darius is aged 60. He is already a member of a pension scheme and has sufficient savings for his own needs, but he is now starting to look at his pension savings as an IHT shelter and wants to put as much in there as he can while attracting higher rate tax relief.*

*He has an annual salary of £90,270 so, meeting his own criteria, he is able to make a gross contribution of £40,000 each year. He keeps working until he is 68, so he is able to build up additional pension savings of £320,000.*

***Example 2:*** *Chrissie is a partner in a large law firm. Her annual profit share is usually around £200,000, but she has a good year in 2023/24 and it increases to £250,000 this year. She is now aged 60 and has substantial private wealth. She has been a member of a pension scheme for several years, but has only contributed a small, nominal sum so far, as she has no need for retirement planning. Now realising the potential IHT benefits of her pension, she makes her maximum gross contribution of £180,000 in 2023/24 (see above) and then contributes a further £60,000 (gross) each year until the age of 74 (I would like to say she is still working at this point, but all that is actually required is that she is still receiving a partnership profit share, which is perhaps not quite the same thing).*

*When Chrissie retires at age 75, she has managed to build up an additional £1.02m in her pension fund that will escape IHT, while also obtaining tax relief worth a total of £461,271 (mostly at 45%), so the net cost is only £558,729. She has therefore saved £223,492 in IHT with this planning (£558,729 x 40%) but what matters is how much better off her beneficiaries are. In this context, the key comparatives are:*

*£558,729: the amount her beneficiaries could have received if Chrissie had made cash gifts and survived seven years, or*
*£335,237: the net amount her beneficiaries would have received after IHT at 40% if Chrissie had done no IHT planning*

*Having used the pension, the final net amount received by her beneficiaries depends on the rate of Income Tax they pay, as follows:*

*Non-taxpayers: £1.02m (£684,763 more than with no planning)*
*Basic rate taxpayers: £816,000 (£480,763 more than with no planning)*
*Higher rate taxpayers: £612,000 (£276,763 more than with no planning)*
*Additional rate taxpayers: £561,000 (£225,763 more than with no planning)*

*In practice, there will often be a mix of different tax rates for the beneficiaries but we can see that, with few exceptions (see below) whatever rate of tax they pay, the overall benefit to the family is more than just the IHT saving of £223,492, thus putting this planning ahead of simple cash gifts.*

*The maximum saving of £684,763 is entirely possible where inherited drawdown is used to pass wealth down the generations to grandchildren, great grandchildren, etc, as discussed in Section 10.6.*

*Furthermore, as we saw in Section 10.6, it is possible to increase the overall saving in other cases by taking the 25% tax-free lump sum (up to the statutory maximum of £268,275), giving it to the beneficiaries, and surviving seven years. If Chrissie were able to implement this strategy successfully, this would increase the final net amount received by her beneficiaries as follows:*

*Basic rate taxpayers: £867,000 (£531,763 more than with no planning)*
*Higher rate taxpayers: £714,000 (£378,763 more than with no planning)*
*Additional rate taxpayers: £675,750 (£340,513 more than with no planning)*

*In this particular example, Chrissie would need to live to at least 82 to achieve these savings, so she would need to weigh up the risks involved. A good compromise might be to take as much tax-free lump sum as she is able at age 68, give that to her beneficiaries, but leave the rest of her pension savings where they are: but that's her decision and there are pros and cons to both approaches.*

I have assumed in this example that, despite her substantial private wealth, Chrissie manages to arrange her affairs so she is never subject to a tapered annual allowance (see above).

There would be nothing to stop Chrissie also carrying out other IHT planning, such as setting up a trust, making lifetime gifts or using a family investment company for her property investments (see Chapter 14).

In theory, if she was only 40 when she started this planning, she could shelter over £2.2m in her pension this way. But there's a snowball's chance in Hell of the UK pensions regime remaining the same until she turned 75 in 2058!

In fact, it may not be anywhere near as long as that before we see restrictions that severely curtail the benefits of pension funds of this magnitude, and we'll look at some of the future potential changes in Section 10.10.

As an alternative strategy, a healthy, wealthy 40 year-old should have time to shelter around £2m in a trust, although the funds will not enjoy the same tax-free environment and will face anniversary and exit charges (see Chapters 8 and 9). Still, as I said, there is nothing to stop them doing both if they are wealthy enough (subject, again, to the points in Section 10.10).

**Who Benefits from Using Pensions to Pass on Wealth?**

As we saw at the beginning of this section, anyone might potentially benefit from using pensions to pass on wealth in the event of an early death. There are also the multigenerational benefits we looked at in Section 10.6 to consider and, of course, the flexibility the pension provides in that the funds don't have to be locked away where you can't touch them during your lifetime (although you will have to wait until you are 55, or 57 from 6th April 2028).

Leaving these points aside, for the majority who live to at least the age of 75, using pensions as an IHT shelter will generally only make sense when your beneficiaries will suffer Income Tax at a lower overall effective rate than the rate of tax relief you obtain for your pension contributions. As we saw above, however, when we factor in the 25% tax-free lump sum, if you plan things carefully, your beneficiaries' overall effective tax rate on your pension savings should generally only be a maximum of 75% of their marginal Income Tax rate.

Of course, while you probably have a pretty good idea what your tax rate is, it's hard to know what your beneficiaries' marginal Income Tax rates will be after your death. For this reason, it generally doesn't make sense to use pensions for IHT planning if you are a basic rate taxpayer.

If you're a higher or additional rate taxpayer, pensions will generally prove beneficial, usually providing overall Income Tax savings in addition to a substantial IHT saving. However, it remains important to bear in mind the exceptions below.

In addition to being at least a higher rate taxpayer, the greatest benefits are only available to those with significant earnings (as defined above). This makes pensions of most benefit to those who have taxable income well in excess of the higher rate tax threshold (£50,270) and are:

- Employed earners, particularly those with six figure salaries (or more)
- Owners of furnished holiday lets
- Partners in a trading business or professional firm

I include business partners because they are likely to retire at some point and also to have private assets outside the partnership. However, in the case of a family partnership, the position from an IHT planning perspective is more like a sole trader.

For sole traders, where their only asset is the business, this will often be free from IHT in any case (see Chapter 7). However, if they are likely to retire without either passing on the business to their children (or other heirs), or forming a company then, again, a pension could be a good way to pass on their accumulated wealth.

I haven't included company owners here because their position is usually rather different to everyone else's, so we will look at them in Section 10.8.

Individual landlords (other than those with furnished holiday lets) with no other source of income have little scope to use pensions. In fact, with a maximum annual contribution of £3,600, it would take 40 years to put just £144,000 into a pension. That might be worth doing in some cases, but it's hardly going to solve all their IHT problems.

**Exceptions**
So far in this section, we've considered both pension scheme members and beneficiaries with marginal Income Tax rates up to 45% (the additional rate). However, there are many people with a marginal Income Tax rate higher than this, including:

- Scottish additional rate taxpayers, who pay 47%
- Those with taxable income between £100,000 and £125,140, who suffer an effective marginal rate of 60%, or 63% if they are a Scottish taxpayer
- The highest earner in a household where child benefit is being claimed, who will suffer an effective Income Tax rate of at least 52.5% on income between £50,270 and £60,000 (more when there is more than one child eligible for child benefit)

If you fall into one of these categories, using a pension could lead to even greater savings. For example, if you have income of £125,140, you may be able to put £25,140 into a pension at a net cost of just £10,056 (£9,302 if you're a Scottish taxpayer). It's well worth making pension contributions if your income falls into the £100,000 to £125,140 bracket!

Conversely, if your beneficiaries fall into one of the above categories, the savings generated by using a pension may be reduced. Nonetheless, in most cases, an overall Income Tax cost could probably be avoided by using inherited drawdown so that your beneficiaries can either pass the wealth on another generation or wait until these extreme tax rates no longer apply. The last thing a beneficiary should do is draw down funds that will fall into the £100,000 to £125,140 income bracket!

Remember also that, when we take the 25% tax-free lump sum into account, the overall rate of tax suffered by your beneficiaries on your pension savings can usually be brought down to 75% of their marginal Income Tax rate.

Hence, for example, a Scottish additional rate taxpayer beneficiary might suffer an overall rate of 35.25% (47% x 75%), which is less than the tax relief a higher rate taxpayer would get on their pension contribution.

Another, though less extreme, exception to be aware of is that Scottish taxpayers are subject to higher rate tax at 42% on income over £43,662. This means, if you are a Scottish higher rate taxpayer with beneficiaries living elsewhere in the UK, a pension will be more beneficial ***but***, if you live in England, Wales or Northern Ireland and your beneficiaries live in Scotland, a pension will be slightly less beneficial (though generally still worthwhile if you're a higher rate taxpayer).

## 10.8 PENSIONS FOR COMPANY OWNERS

Most small company owner/directors have very little earnings to cover pension contributions because they usually only take a small salary and take the rest of their income as dividends.

However, the company can generally make pension contributions up to the annual allowance on their behalf and, provided the payment is justified as part of the director's remuneration package (i.e. by the work the director does for the company), it will attract Corporation Tax relief. There is no Income Tax relief because the director has not made the contribution personally.

Note that the company pension contribution needs to be included in the director's adjusted income for the purposes of the tapered annual allowance (see Section 10.7) so, if the director is taking total salary and dividends in excess of £200,000, the full annual allowance will not generally be available.

This all makes sense when the director is planning for their own retirement but, in this guide, we are only looking at IHT planning.

If the company is a trading company and the current owner intends to pass it on to their children (or other heirs), pension contributions will generally serve no purpose for IHT planning, as the value of the company should be covered by BPR (see Chapter 7). The only exception to this is where the company has significant amounts of surplus cash that may be treated as an excepted asset (see Section 7.9).

The value of a non-trading company, such as a property investment company, will be exposed to IHT, so making pension contributions could be an effective IHT shelter.

So, in summary, IHT can be saved by using pension contributions to either reduce the value of a non-trading company, or remove excepted assets from a trading company. Hence, these pension contributions will be beneficial in the event of an early death before age 75, or in other cases where death benefits can be passed tax free to beneficiaries (e.g. grandchildren or great-grandchildren with little or no taxable income).

However, once we start to look at the situation where beneficiaries suffer Income Tax on the death benefits, we have to dig a little deeper.

***Example:*** *Dean's only asset is his property company, Mamot Ltd. He is already taking enough dividends out of the company to meet his own needs and this has made him a higher rate taxpayer. He is now considering making a company pension contribution as a means of sheltering some of his wealth from IHT.*

*The company makes a contribution of £60,000. This provides Corporation Tax relief at an effective rate of 26.5% (see below), saving £15,900, so the value of the company is reduced by a net £44,100, thus ultimately saving £17,640 in IHT (£44,100 x 40%).*

*If, alternatively, the company had used the same sum of £44,100 (the net cost of the pension contribution) to pay an extra dividend to Dean, he would suffer at least £14,884 in Income Tax (at 33.75%: see below), leaving him with just £29,216. He could then give this to his beneficiaries and, if he survived seven years, it would be free of IHT. However, the IHT saved is effectively the same £17,640 as shown above.*

*The IHT savings are the same under both routes because there is the same reduction in the value of the company and thus also the same reduction in the value of Dean's estate.*

*However, as with everything, what really matters is how much better off Dean's beneficiaries are in the end and, assuming Dean lives to at least the age of 75, that will depend on those beneficiary's marginal Income Tax rates. The target to beat is the £29,216 cash gift Dean could have made. With a pension fund of £60,000, that means almost any beneficiary will be better off under the pension route, as it would take a marginal Income Tax rate of more than 51.3% before they were worse off.*

*In fact, if we factor in the ability for Dean to take his 25% tax-free lump sum, give it to his beneficiaries and survive seven years, his beneficiaries would need a marginal Income Tax rate of at least 68.5% before the cash gift was preferable.*

See Sections 10.6 and 10.7 for a detailed look at the pros and cons, and limitations, of the strategy referred to in the last paragraph, which is generally best done by the age of 68. See the exceptions given at the end of Section 10.7 for cases where marginal tax rates in excess of 51.3% may arise: plus how to prevent them from arising on death benefits by using inherited drawdown.

The pension contribution is clearly a good strategy for Dean in our example and he is probably fairly typical of a small private company owner. But there are, alas, a huge number of potential combinations of tax rates to consider in this scenario.

For accounting periods commencing after 31st March 2023, companies generally suffer Corporation Tax at the following rates:

| **Annual Profit** | **Marginal Tax Rate** | |
|---|---|---|
| Up to £50,000 | 19% | (Small Profits Rate) |
| £50,000 to £250,000 | 26.5% | (Marginal Rate) |
| Over £250,000 | 25% | (Main Rate) |

These rates can be affected by a number of factors, however, including the existence of associated companies, group companies, and investments held by the company (other than properties rented to unconnected third parties). For further details, plus the Corporation Tax rates applying in earlier accounting periods, see the Taxcafe guide *The Company Tax Changes.*

On top of this, we have to consider the Income Tax the owner/director would suffer on extra dividends paid to fund a cash gift. The Income Tax rates suffered on dividend income are currently:

| | |
|---|---|
| Basic rate | 8.75% |
| Higher rate | 33.75% |
| Additional rate | 39.35% |

Dividend income falling into the £100,000 to £125,140 income bracket will suffer an effective Income Tax rate between 50.625% and 56.25%, depending on how the recipient's other income is made up. It would be foolish to pay dividends falling into this income bracket in order to fund cash gifts, so we'll ignore these extreme rates in the rest of our analysis.

Dividends paid to the highest earner in a household where child benefit is being claimed, and falling into the £50,000 to £60,000 income bracket, will also lead to higher effective Income Tax rates and should, again, generally not be used to fund cash gifts.

So, combining our three Corporation Tax rates with our three main dividend tax rates, let's see how much of a cash gift a company owner can fund when they have a spare £10,000 of profit before tax available in the company.

**Table D: Cash Gift Funded from £10,000 Profit**

| **Dividend** | **Corporation Tax Rate** | | |
|---|---|---|---|
| **Tax Rate** | **19%** | **26.5%** | **25%** |
| **8.75%** | £7,391 | £6,707 | £6,844 |
| **33.75%** | £5,366 | £4,869 | £4,969 |
| **39.35%** | £4,913 | £4,458 | £4,549 |

We then need to compare this with the net sum the director's beneficiaries would end up with when the same £10,000 is used to fund a pension contribution. For this purpose, we'll assume the director takes their 25% tax-free lump sum by the age of 68, gives it to their beneficiaries and survives seven years (see Section 10.6). We'll also assume they are unaffected by the statutory maximum for the tax-free lump sum (see Section 10.7). On this basis, the beneficiaries end up with a total net sum as follows:

| | |
|---|---|
| Non-taxpayers: | £10,000 |
| Basic rate taxpayers: | £8,500 |
| Higher rate taxpayers: | £7,000 |
| Additional rate taxpayers: | £6,625 |

What this comparison tells us is that a company pension contribution will always be better than a cash gift if the director's beneficiaries are either non-taxpayers or basic rate taxpayers.

However, the pension is less beneficial than a cash gift if the director is a basic rate taxpayer and either their beneficiaries are additional rate taxpayers, or their beneficiaries are higher rate taxpayers and the company is paying Corporation Tax at the small profits rate of 19%.

For higher or additional rate taxpayer directors, the pension will generally be more beneficial. As usual, however, the exceptions listed at the end of Section 10.7 need to be borne in mind. The position may also be different if the director's pension savings exceed their available lifetime allowance (usually £1,073,100).

**Couples Can Double Up**

Many small companies are owned by couples. If a couple own and manage a company together as joint owner/directors, it may be possible to shelter up to £120,000 per year in total through company pension contributions. Each director will also have their own separate statutory limit for tax-free lump sums, so that up to £536,500 (in total) could often be taken and passed to the couple's children (or other beneficiaries).

**Other Options**

In this section, we have only compared the benefits of pension contributions against using the available cash to fund cash gifts. Small company owners with an exposure to IHT have other options to consider, such as passing on shares as lifetime gifts (see Sections 4.5 and 12.10), altering the company's business so the shares qualify for BPR (see Section 7.23), or passing on shares via a trust (the method described in Section 9.4 works equally well for shares). Married company owners can also use a family debt scheme to get the value of shares out of their estate (see Section 6.13).

## 10.9 BYPASS TRUSTS

In Section 10.2, we saw that the death benefits in certain types of pension scheme (generally older schemes started in the twentieth century) are not paid out at the discretion of the scheme administrator and are thus exposed to IHT. We also saw that the answer to this problem was to nominate a discretionary trust to receive your death benefits.

Scheme members sometimes also nominate a trust to receive death benefits for other reasons, such as the fact this will allow them to direct not only who receives the income derived from the trust funds after their death, but also who benefits from the trust funds later, after the original beneficiary's death.

Typically, a scheme member might do this if they are survived by a spouse or partner (the original beneficiary) and children from another, earlier relationship, who they perhaps want the bulk of the funds to go to eventually.

But bypass trusts of this nature carry some disadvantages. Firstly, the funds become relevant property, subject to anniversary and exit charges (see Chapter 8). While the lump sum paid to the trust only becomes relevant property at the date of the scheme member's death, the trust anniversary dates may be based on the date the trust arrangement was first set up or, in some cases, the date the pension was set up.

The bigger problem, however, is that the lump sum death benefit paid to the trust (and remember it has to be a lump sum) on the death of a scheme member at age 75 or more is subject to an immediate Income Tax charge at 45%. This charge also currently applies in any of the other scenarios where, and to the extent that, lump sum death benefits are subject to Income Tax, as explained in Section 10.5.

Some or all of that charge can be recovered as trust funds are paid out to beneficiaries, but this may take many years, especially if the scheme member wishes the bulk of the funds to be passed on after the original beneficiary's death.

***Example:*** *Paula dies aged 76 with a pension fund valued at £1m. She nominated the Yates Family Trust to receive her death benefit so the scheme administrator pays £550,000 to the trust and £450,000 to HMRC. In accordance with Paula's instructions, the trustees of the Yates Family Trust pay £22,000 to her partner, Michael each year. This payment is treated for Income Tax purposes as a gross payment of £40,000, with a tax credit of £18,000 (45% of the gross).*

*Michael has other taxable income of £22,270, so £28,000 of his grossed-up trust income is taxed at 20%, and £12,000 at 40%. That totals £10,400, so Michael will receive a tax repayment of £7,600 (£18,000 – £10,400).*

It may work out the same as inherited drawdown in the long run but, from a cashflow point of view, it's a disaster. And, this time, investment growth will make a big difference!

## 10.10 WILL IT LAST?

My friend Nick and I often joke about the Government's misuse of the word 'permanent'. We both agree the current pensions regime is certainly not permanent. It may not last long at all, and there is a fair chance that 2023/24 and 2024/25 will come to be seen as the 'high water mark' for pensions.

The current Government published its plans for pension death benefits as part of the November 2023 Autumn Statement. They don't intend to change very much in the short term. In fact, while they are scrapping the lifetime allowance, they are actually just renaming it as the 'lump sum and death benefit allowance' and it will remain £1,073,100 in 2024/25.

Hence, the Income Tax treatment of death benefits outlined in this chapter will remain largely the same in 2024/25: there will mostly just be some changes in terminology.

Some potential changes under the current Government proposals are that the treatment of death benefits in excess of the available 'lump sum and death benefit allowance' on the death of a scheme member under the age of 75 will be the same regardless of whether the relevant funds have been crystallised or not: with such excess sums being taxed as additional income in the hands of the beneficiary, or at basic rate (20%) if paid to a trust.

Looking further ahead, however, we have to consider the possibility there may be a change of Government soon and, while the lifetime allowance is scheduled for termination on 6th April 2024, Keir Starmer tells us that, if he gets his way, it will, like Arnold Schwarzenegger, be back.

If a future Labour Government restores the Lifetime Allowance Charge, it will curtail the usefulness of some of the planning techniques that currently exist. Pension savings in excess of £1.073m may no longer be efficient IHT shelters although, as always, there will be exceptions. In this context, it must be remembered the Lifetime Allowance Charge did not just apply to death benefits in excess of the lifetime allowance, it also applied, where relevant, to funds in excess of the lifetime allowance when these were crystallised, or when a scheme member reached age 75. In other words, building up a fund in excess of the lifetime allowance always had a tax cost, and may do so again in future.

The next general election has to take place by January 2025. It may come a little sooner but it is likely to fall during the 2024/25 tax year. To me, that suggests, if we get a change of Government, the Lifetime Allowance Charge is likely to be restored from 6th April 2025 (although new Governments have been known to make changes quicker than this: i.e. from the date of some Emergency Budget.)

Taking a broader look at the pensions regime, it's worth mentioning that, in 2022, the Institute for Fiscal Studies (a respected think tank) called for an end to the favourable tax treatment of pensions, and recommended including pension savings in the value of estates for IHT purposes.

So, while pension savings currently have enormous potential in IHT planning, it's important to bear in mind that things may change. That is, of course, true of any form of IHT planning. But perhaps the key difference is the odds of a detrimental change for pensions could be greater than many other IHT planning techniques. Proceed with caution, dear reader.

Chapter 11

# Practical Aspects of IHT Planning

## 11.1 THE BIGGER PICTURE

No-one should do IHT planning; they should do estate preservation planning. What is important is not just saving IHT, but preserving family wealth for the benefit of the next generation. Saving IHT is just one part of preserving wealth and it is important never to lose sight of this bigger picture.

When we come to the bigger issue of estate preservation, there are many other factors to be taken into account. In this chapter we will look at some of these other factors, as well as some practical aspects of IHT planning itself.

From early in my career, I was taught 'never let the tax tail wag the commercial dog'. In other words, it is almost always more important to get the commercial aspects right before letting tax planning dictate your actions.

For example, putting all your savings into a share of *'Dave's Dodgy Autos'* might be a great way to avoid IHT, but what's the use of that if Dave runs off to South America with all your money? When all is said and done, Rishi Sunak and Jeremy Hunt will only take 40%, so they are (just slightly) better than Dodgy Dave.

On the other hand, as we saw in Section 7.26, saving 40% may still be beneficial overall, even in some slightly uncommercial situations. It's a question of getting the right balance and is best expressed as follows:

***Bayley's Law:*** *"The truly wise taxpayer does not seek merely to minimise the amount of tax paid but rather to maximise the amount of wealth remaining after all taxes have been accounted for."*

After commercial issues, the next important issue to watch out for is other taxes. When undertaking tax planning, it is essential to consider all taxes, not just the one you're trying to save. We saw this in action in Chapter 10 with pension savings, where the Income Tax benefits and costs are generally more critical than IHT itself.

In other cases, IHT planning often involves transferring assets and this can have important implications for Income Tax, Corporation Tax, Stamp Duty (on shares and securities), or SDLT (on land and buildings). But the tax that interacts most frequently with IHT is CGT, and we will look at that particular 'clash of the titans' in Chapter 12.

While lifetime transfers of assets can often trigger other taxes, transfers on death usually escape them, with such transfers being exempt from Stamp Duty, SDLT, and CGT. These exemptions generally only apply to a direct transfer from the deceased's estate to the beneficiary, however, so more complex transactions may lead to tax liabilities.

In particular, where real property (land and buildings) is to be passed to a beneficiary subject to a mortgage, it will generally be better for the beneficiary to take on the existing debt, as this will be exempt from SDLT, rather than buy the property from the estate, or take out a new mortgage. As long as there is an arm's length commercial mortgage provider involved, the original debt should still be deductible from the deceased's estate (see Section 2.10).

As far as Income Tax is concerned, the deceased's personal representatives will generally need to submit a tax return for the period from the beginning of the tax year in which the deceased died up to the date of death. The deceased is entitled to a full year's worth of personal allowance, basic rate band, etc, for this period, so there is often a tax repayment due if they were paying tax under PAYE on a salary or private pension. Sadly, while such a repayment is welcome, it then falls into the deceased's estate and is subject to IHT.

The personal representatives will also have to submit further tax returns on behalf of the estate for the remainder of the tax year in which the deceased died and subsequent tax years until the estate has finally been wound up. The estate is taxed on any income or capital gains it receives during this period: although the uplift on death (see Section 12.2) usually ensures there is very little CGT to pay.

## 11.2 VALUATIONS

Valuation is a key part of IHT. We are frequently concerned with the value of land, buildings, unquoted shares, or unincorporated businesses.

Very often, the value of an asset owned by an individual is dependent on what proportion of a larger asset they own. We saw an example of this with Bjorn's chairs in Section 2.1. In practice, the most significant examples are in the case of unquoted shares. A controlling (over 50%) shareholding in a private company might be worth £5,000 per share, for example, while a small minority holding in the same company might be worth just £600 per share.

These changes in proportionate value can have major implications for any transfers of value that result in the transferor's shareholding falling into a lower value category.

***Example:*** *Mick owns a thousand ordinary shares in Fleetwood Ltd out of the company's total issued share capital of 10,000 shares. There is only one class of shares. It has been established that shareholdings of 10% or more (but less than 25%) can be valued at £2,000 per share but holdings of less than 10% are worth only £600 per share. Hence, at present, Mick's shareholding is valued at £2m (1,000 x £2,000).*

*Mick decides to give one share to his daughter, Stevie. This reduces the value of his remaining holding of 999 shares to £599,400 (999 x £600). The gift to Stevie is therefore treated as a transfer of value of £1.4006m (£2m - £599,400) despite the fact her share is worth just £600.*

*This preposterous result could be absolutely disastrous for Stevie. If Mick should die within three years of making this gift, Stevie could face an IHT bill of up to £560,240. All for a share worth just £600! Let's hope BPR is available on these shares and Stevie does nothing to mess it up. She certainly needs to hope Fleetwood Ltd isn't floated on the stock exchange within the next seven years (Section 7.18).*

There are clearly times when a gift should not be accepted!

Valuing unquoted company shares is a highly complex matter, but it is perhaps worth pointing out the requirements of company law relating to shareholders' resolutions effectively create some key thresholds where increases in share values can be expected to apply. These thresholds are: 10%; 25%; 50%; over 50%; over 75%; over 90%; and 100%.

## 11.3 RELATED PROPERTY

When valuing assets for IHT purposes, an individual's assets are treated as if they are part of a larger holding made up of all the assets held by the individual and their spouse; plus any assets held by a charity or similar exempt body at any time within the last five years that were originally transferred to that body by the individual or their spouse.

***Example:*** *Christine and John are an unmarried couple. Christine owns 3,000 of the 10,000 issued shares in Fleetwood Ltd; John owns 2,200. It has been established that shareholdings of 10% or more (but less than 25%) can be valued at £2,000 per share; holdings of 25% or more (but less than 50%) can be valued at £5,000 per share; and holdings of over 50% are worth £10,000 per share. Hence, at present, Christine and John's shareholdings are valued as follows:*

| | |
|---|---|
| *Christine:* | *3,000 x £5,000 = £15m* |
| *John:* | *2,200 x £2,000 = £4.4m* |

*Christine and John have a son, Lindsay, and eventually intend to leave their shares to him. As things stand, this would give rise to transfers of value totalling £19.4m.*

*Christine and John decide to get married. The related property provisions mean their shares must now be valued as a combined shareholding of 5,200 shares worth £52m (5,200 x £10,000). Leaving their shares to Lindsay will now give rise to transfers of value totalling £52m, or £32.6m more than before they married, thus potentially costing up to £13.04m in extra IHT (£32.6m x 40%).*

Christine and John will, of course, have gained the benefit of the spouse exemption and that may be worth more to them. Furthermore, if the shares qualify for BPR, the increase in value may not cause any problems. Nonetheless, while marriage is nearly always beneficial for IHT purposes, the example shows there could be some exceptions.

### Practical Problems and Solutions

These related property provisions can cause unexpected problems, with small gifts sometimes being given large hypothetical values for IHT purposes. However, the impact of the related property rules can be reduced if transfers are timed carefully. This is particularly relevant to unquoted shareholdings held by married couples where BPR may not be available.

***Example:*** *Jack and Diane are a married couple and both own shares in Mellencamp Ltd, an unquoted investment company. Jack owns 2% of the company and his shares are worth just £2,000. Diane owns 49% of the company and her shares are worth £245,000.*

*Under the related property rules, however, their shares must be valued as part of a combined shareholding of 51%. This shareholding, being enough to provide control of the company, is worth £510,000.*

*The couple now wish to give their son, John a 25% share in the company. Jack transfers his 2% stake to John first. This represents a transfer of value of £20,000 (2/51 x £510,000). Diane then transfers a further 23% to John. This represents a transfer of value of £115,000 (23/49 x £245,000), bringing the total to £135,000.*

*If Diane had made her transfer first, this would have been a transfer of value of £230,000 (23/51 x £510,000). Jack's subsequent transfer would then have been a transfer of value equal to 2/28ths of the value of a 28% shareholding, let's say £10,000 for the sake of argument.*

*By making the smaller transfer first, the couple have reduced the effective transfer of value by £105,000, providing a potential IHT saving of up to £42,000 (at 40%).*

**Post-Death Relief**

Where an inherited asset that was valued under the related property rules is sold within three years of the previous owner's death, it can be re-valued at the date of death (for IHT purposes), without taking account of the related property. The sale must be made on arm's length terms, must not be to a connected person (see Appendix B), and must not be made in conjunction with other related property sales.

## 11.4 JOINTLY HELD PROPERTY

Any form of property can be held jointly, including bank accounts, shares and securities, or land and buildings. The key point to note about jointly held property is that, on a joint owner's death, their share may sometimes pass by survivorship and not by intestacy or under the deceased's Will. This has major implications for IHT planning, as you may not be free to transfer your share of jointly held property in the most tax-efficient manner.

After the joint bank account, the next most common form of jointly held property in the UK is land and buildings, sometimes referred to as real property. In fact, most couples in the UK now own their home jointly.

In England and Wales, there are two different legal forms for jointly held property: Joint Tenants or Tenants in Common.

**Joint Tenants**
In a joint tenancy the ownership of each joint owner's share passes automatically on death to the other joint owner (or joint owners). This is what is meant by survivorship. Furthermore, neither joint owner is normally able to sell their share of the property without the consent of the other.

This may restrict the scope for IHT planning with the property and joint tenancies are therefore generally less desirable than tenancies in common purely from a tax planning perspective. Having said that, the security provided by the right of survivorship is often considered of more value by many couples.

**Tenants in Common**
Under a tenancy in common, the joint owners are generally free to do as they wish with their share of the property and there is no right of survivorship. The joint owners' shares in the property need not be equal. A tenancy in common therefore opens up a wide range of IHT planning opportunities that may not always be available under a joint tenancy.

**Practical Implications**
As explained above, each person's share in a joint tenancy will usually pass to the other joint owner by survivorship. In the case of the family home, the surviving joint owner will usually be the widow or widower of the deceased. Following the introduction of the TNRB (see Chapter 6), this will usually be the best result anyway.

Nevertheless, for the reasons explained in Section 6.8, this may sometimes still be bad IHT planning. It is, however, possible to break a joint tenancy via a deed of variation (Section 18.1) executed within two years after a joint owner dies.

Alternatively, it may be preferable to sever the joint tenancy during both owners' lifetimes, as this provides more certainty to the intended IHT planning. It is not always wise to rely on a deed of variation to rectify the situation!

Once a joint tenancy has been severed or broken, whether during the owner's lifetime or via a deed of variation, it becomes a tenancy in common.

A share in property held under a tenancy in common may be passed to anyone, under the terms of the deceased's Will, or possibly via a deed of variation, as explained in Section 18.1. Hence, whenever undertaking any IHT planning on the family home in England or Wales that involves passing a share of the property to anyone other than the surviving spouse, it may be wise to first ensure the property is held under a tenancy in common and not a joint tenancy.

Breaking a joint tenancy to create a tenancy in common can be achieved at a reasonably modest cost and should, in itself, be tax free, as it is not treated as a disposal for CGT purposes, nor an acquisition for SDLT purposes.

If you change your property to a tenancy in common and then draw up your Wills to put the appropriate IHT planning measures in place, remember to make sure you also buy any new property as tenants in common if you move!

### Scotland

In Scotland, joint ownership of real property mainly comes in a form known as Pro Indivisio, which operates in a broadly similar manner to a tenancy in common.

A form of beneficial joint tenancy is also available in Scotland using a survivorship destination. This cannot be severed unilaterally, which can sometimes lead to practical difficulties if one joint owner decides they wish to pass their share to someone other than their fellow joint owner. A survivorship destination can, however, be broken by a deed of variation where the surviving joint owner is prepared to co-operate.

Nonetheless, relying on using a deed of variation when the time comes may not always be wise so it may make sense to break the survivorship destination during both owners' lifetimes to better facilitate any IHT planning that involves passing a share of the property to someone other than the surviving joint owner. And be careful when you move house too!

### Valuing Jointly Held Property

A useful benefit of jointly held property is the fact a discount often applies to the value of a joint owner's share of the property.

***Example:*** *Two sisters, Mel and Kim, live together in Appleby Manor, which they own jointly. Sadly, Kim dies in September 2023, when Appleby Manor is worth £1.5m. Kim's half share is not valued at £750,000, as one might expect, but at a discount of 15%, i.e. £637,500. This discount produces an effective IHT saving of £45,000.*

The discount applies to reflect the practical difficulty in selling a joint owner's part share of a property. The discount also reflects the fact that the other joint owner has a right to occupy the property and is therefore akin to a sitting tenant, thus further reducing the value of a joint share in the property.

The 15% discount used above was established by an IHT case back in 1982. In a more recent case, it was suggested a discount of just 10% might now be more appropriate, especially where the surviving joint owner is not likely to remain in occupation of the property. Nevertheless, conventional wisdom seems to be that a 15% discount is still appropriate in the case of residential property occupied by the surviving joint owner. A lower rate of discount may be appropriate in other cases but it is certainly still worth claiming.

HMRC takes the view that the related property rules (see Section 11.3) prevent any discount applying where a property is held jointly by spouses. Furthermore, due to the different nature of joint property titles in Scotland, the usual discount does not generally apply to property in Scotland.

**Other Jointly Held Assets**
A jointly held bank or building society account in England or Wales passes in its entirety to the surviving joint account holder on the other account holder's death. In Scotland, a joint account holder's share of a joint account usually falls into their general estate to be dealt with according to the terms of their Will or under the laws of intestacy (see Section 11.7).

In either case, the deceased's share of the joint account is included in their estate for IHT purposes (although it will usually be exempt if it passes to their spouse). The deceased's share will generally be taken to be half the account balance and no discount can apply.

Other jointly held property, such as paintings, antiques and personal effects may be subject to a substantial discount due to the fact that a joint owner is generally unable to sell such property.

Unmarried couples can therefore save substantial IHT by jointly holding tangible moveable property (e.g. antiques) and separately passing each joint share to their intended beneficiaries (but not each other).

## 11.5 MORTGAGES

It is important to be aware that any transfer of property subject to a mortgage will require the lender's consent. If the transferee takes over the mortgage, the outstanding borrowings will be deemed to constitute purchase consideration and may give rise to a SDLT charge if they are £40,000 or more; or more than £150,000 in the case of commercial property.

Transfers to spouses are not subject to the extra 3% SDLT surcharge. Hence a spouse can currently take over a mortgage (or share of a mortgage) over a residential property with a balance of up to £250,000 without incurring SDLT.

Mortgages are deducted from the value of the property they are secured against for the purposes of the RNRB (see Section 3.4), unless they must be deducted from the value of another asset under the rules in Section 2.10.

## 11.6 RESIDENTIAL CARE FEES

While IHT is a major worry, many people are more concerned about losing their property to the local authority in order to pay nursing home or residential care fees in their old age. In some cases, the local authority may even be able to force a sale of a property that has previously been given away if they can show this was done to avoid payment of the fees.

In some instances it has been accepted that, where a property has been given away for IHT planning purposes, the local authority were unable to claim the taxpayer's motive was to avoid care fees. Nevertheless, this approach is not entirely reliable, as many families have found to their cost (see Section 12.8).

A better approach is often to take out long term care insurance or even emergency care assurance. The latter approach generally requires the payment of a single lump sum premium in exchange for an annuity covering the residential care fees. The amount of the premium is generally equal to around two to three years' worth of care fees.

Emergency care assurance is a useful strategy employed by many families who wish to have certainty about the cost of looking after their elderly relative. If necessary, the premium can be funded by way of a loan secured against the relative's former home, thus enabling the family to keep the property and perhaps even benefit from the CGT uplift on death (see Section 12.2).

## 11.7 WILLS, INTESTACY, AND STATUTORY RIGHTS

Most people are pretty relaxed about dying intestate (without a valid Will) until they realise what would actually happen. Most of us know we should make a Will, but a great many of us put it off until it's too late.

Quite apart from IHT planning, a Will is sensible as, without a valid Will, your assets will be divided up according to the ancient laws of intestacy and this may be very different to what you would have liked. More importantly, a Will is essential for nominating the future guardians of your children if, as Oscar Wilde would have put it, they are careless enough to lose both parents.

In the tables that follow, 'issue' generally means your children but, if your children pre-decease you, their children will take their place. For example, if you have three children and one of them pre-deceases you, leaving two children of their own, the share going to your children will be divided so that one third of that share goes to each of your surviving children and one sixth goes to each of your grandchildren by your deceased child.

In this section, domicile refers to domicile under general principles only (see Chapter 16) and does not include deemed domicile for tax purposes.

### Dying Without a Will: England and Wales

If you are domiciled in England and Wales, and die without a valid Will, your estate will be divided as follows:

**1. If you leave a spouse and issue:** The first £270,000 and all personal possessions go to your spouse. 50% of the balance is divided equally between your children. The remaining 50% is held on trust, with your spouse having a life interest and the remainder going to your children.

**2. If you leave a spouse but no issue:** If you have no surviving parents, siblings, nephews or nieces, your entire estate goes to your spouse. Otherwise, your spouse's share is restricted to £450,000 plus all personal possessions and 50% of the remaining balance. The other 50% of the balance goes to your parents if they survive you, to your siblings if both of your parents pre-decease you, or to your nephews and nieces if your siblings also pre-decease you.

**3. If you leave issue but no spouse:** Your estate is divided equally between your children.

**4. If you leave no spouse or issue:** Your estate goes to the nearest relatives to survive you, using the following order of precedence: your parents; siblings, or their issue (i.e. your nieces and nephews; grandparents; aunts and uncles.

**5. If no near-relatives survive you:** Your entire estate goes to the Crown!

**Dying Without a Will: Scotland**
If you are domiciled in Scotland and die without a valid Will, your estate will be divided as follows:

**1. If you leave a spouse and issue:** Your spouse gets: your interest in any dwelling (the family home) up to a value of £300,000 or, if the family home's value exceeds this amount, the right to receive the sum of £300,000; personal possessions up to the value of £24,000; the first £42,000 of the remaining estate; and one third of any other moveable property (i.e. anything other than land and buildings). Your children then get the remainder of your estate.

**2. If you leave a spouse but no issue:** Your spouse gets your interest in any dwelling and personal possessions, as above, plus the first £75,000 of the remaining estate and one half of any other moveable property. The rest of your estate falls into your free estate and is dealt with as set out below. If you have no surviving parents, siblings, nephews or nieces, your spouse will receive your entire estate.

**3. If you leave issue but no spouse:** Your estate is divided equally between your children.

**4. If you leave no spouse or issue:** Your entire estate will be dealt with under the rules for a free estate.

**Free Estate:** In dealing with your free estate, any claimant's children or remoter issue may take the place of a claimant who pre-deceased you, except where the deceased claimant was your spouse or parent. If you are survived by at least one parent and at least one sibling (or their issue), 50% of your free estate goes to your parents and 50% to your siblings or their issue. In any other case, the free estate goes to the nearest relatives to survive you, based on the following order of precedence: siblings; parents; your surviving spouse (for cases under (2) above); aunts and uncles; grandparents; grandparents' siblings; great-grandparents, etc. If your entire clan has been wiped out and you have no surviving relatives; yes, you've guessed it, everything goes to the Crown (who, in centuries past, often did the wiping out!)

So, as you can see, whether you live in Swansea, Penzance or Aberdeen (and probably Belfast too, although I don't have those rules available), you really shouldn't be relaxed about dying without a Will.

It is not unknown for widows to be forced to sell the family home due to the operation of the above rules and, without proper provision children could end up being taken into care.

The statutory rules set out above take no account of common-law partners, step-children or many other important personal relationships. A remote cousin could get everything in priority to a fondly loved step-child!

The Crown could even get your house in priority to a common-law partner you've lived with for decades. And you thought IHT was bad enough!

**Will Limitations**

A Will is rendered void by marriage, unless written in contemplation of that marriage. Furthermore, your Will can only determine what happens to assets falling into your estate and which you are free to dispose of as you wish. Jointly held property may be subject to survivorship (see Section 11.4), and most pension fund death benefits and life insurance proceeds will not fall into your estate (see Sections 10.2 and 11.8).

Apart from these points, in England, Wales, or Northern Ireland, you may generally distribute your estate as you wish under the terms of your Will. Surviving spouses may, however, apply to the courts for an increased share of the estate where the amount provided to them in the Will does not represent adequate financial provision for their care and maintenance. In essence, this is something akin to posthumous divorce proceedings. Similar applications may be made on behalf of dependent minor children of the deceased.

A different system operates in Scotland where legal rights take priority over the terms of the deceased's Will unless waived by the beneficiaries concerned. Legal rights for beneficiaries of a deceased domiciled in Scotland are:

**Surviving spouse:** Where there are no issue of the deceased, one half of the deceased's moveable property, otherwise one third.
**Surviving issue:** Where there is no surviving spouse of the deceased, one half of the deceased's moveable property, otherwise one third.

The question of whether you are domiciled in Scotland under general principles is the same as any other domicile issue (see Chapter 16). Deemed domicile applies only for tax purposes. Hence, you may have lived in London for many decades, but, if you or your parents were born in Scotland, you could still be domiciled in Scotland and your spouse and children will have legal rights as set out above.

Current proposals for the reform of the laws of succession in Scotland include a proposal to abolish legal rights for adult children. However, it is uncertain whether this proposal will be adopted.

## 11.8 LIFE INSURANCE

One simple way to prevent your estate from being excessively inflated on your death is to ensure all forms of life insurance cover you have are written in favour of other family members. Such policies are effectively held on bare trust (see Section 8.8). In that way, the proceeds will never fall into your estate but will go, instead, to your intended beneficiaries free of IHT.

This should also extend to any death benefit under an occupational pension scheme you are a member of. See Chapter 10 for further details.

Ideally, if they can afford to do without it, your spouse should not be the beneficiary under any of your life policies. In practice, this suggestion may sometimes be somewhat impractical, especially when you have a young family, but it is worth reviewing the position as you get older.

Payments of regular insurance premiums will usually be covered by the annual exemption or the exemption for normal expenditure out of income (see Section 5.5), so these do not usually present a problem.

Depending on the exact circumstances, and for the reasons outlined in Section 4.4, a large lump-sum premium paid on a policy written in favour of another individual may represent a PET, a chargeable lifetime transfer, or a mixture of both.

**Life Policies Written in Trust**

By writing a life policy into trust, you will be using a form of interest in possession trust rather than a bare trust. This retains the advantage of keeping the proceeds of the policy out of your estate but also means you can vary the intended beneficiaries over the course of your lifetime. Furthermore, this also ensures no IHT arises if any of those beneficiaries should pre-decease you. For these reasons, it generally made sense to write life policies into trust before March 2006.

For many policies written into trust before March 2006, it is business as usual and their beneficial treatment continues. HMRC has even confirmed that paying a regular premium on a policy already held by a pre-22/3/2006 interest in possession trust will generally continue to be classed as a PET if not already exempted under another provision.

One change of beneficiary before 6th October 2008 will have turned the trust into a transitional serial interest (Section 8.13) and it will effectively retain its beneficial treatment. Any other changes of beneficiary, however, will bring it into the relevant property trust regime (Sections 8.17 to 8.19).

Life policies written into trust after March 2006 will generally fall into the relevant property trust regime. This also applies where changes are made to existing policies and those changes were not already permitted under the terms of the policy on 22nd March 2006.

Where a life policy falls into the relevant property trust regime, it may potentially be subject to entry, exit and anniversary charges.

Payments of regular premiums will usually be covered by the annual exemption or the exemption for normal expenditure out of income (see Section 5.5), so these do not usually present a problem in themselves.

Any large lump-sum premium payments, however, will be chargeable lifetime transfers and will give rise to immediate IHT liabilities where the policyholder's NRB has been exhausted.

Ten-yearly anniversary charges will be applied to the policy (Section 8.18). Generally, the policy's value for this purpose will be taken to be the cumulative amount of premiums paid to date, although in cases where the policyholder is in poor health at the anniversary date, it is feared HMRC may argue a greater value should be used to reflect the likelihood of the policy's imminent maturity. (An image of a vulture has jumped into my mind!)

Worst of all, of course, an exit charge of up to 6% (see Section 8.19) will apply when the policyholder dies. That's still a lot better than 40% though!

**Insuring for Inheritance Tax Liabilities**
Much of the IHT planning discussed elsewhere in this guide depends on the transferor surviving a certain period after a transfer, or some other transaction, has been made. Often the period concerned will be seven years, but survival to other anniversaries can also be critical. When death occurs before the expiry of the critical period, unexpected tax bills can arrive as a nasty surprise. It is often a good idea, therefore, to take out some term life insurance on the transferor to guard against this possibility. It is important to make sure the transferor is not the beneficiary of the term insurance as this will inflate the value of their estate and lead to an effective grossing up of IHT liabilities.

## 11.9 LOTTERY SYNDICATES

Lottery, pools, and other gambling syndicates are breeding grounds for potential IHT problems. Just imagine this:

***Example:*** *Donny wins £15m on the National Lottery. It's in all the newspapers, so you can bet HMRC knows about it. He gives £3m to each of his brothers, Wayne, Merrill, Jay and Jimmy. Tragically, just a few weeks later, Donny is killed water skiing in Utah.*

*HMRC demands almost £6m in IHT from Donny's family as the transfers to his brothers were made only weeks before his death. "But we were in a syndicate," protest the brothers. "Prove it!" replies HMRC.*

The simple answer to this problem is to make sure you have documentary evidence of any syndicate arrangements.

## 11.10 MINOR PROBLEMS

You may have noticed I tend to base a lot of my examples around gifts to adult children. This is because transfers of value to minor children carry a few extra complications.

**Gifts to Minors by Parents**

Any gift from a parent to, or for the benefit of, their own minor child is subject to the Income Tax settlements legislation. This means the parent is subject to tax on any income derived from the gifted assets (subject to a general exemption for income not exceeding £100 per annum and the further exemptions for Child Trust Funds and Junior ISAs explained below). The Income Tax burden can often be reduced by making sure the parent with the lower level of income makes the gift.

The child has their own annual exemption and basic rate band for CGT purposes, so some savings can be generated on capital gains, such as where funds are invested in a stock market portfolio on behalf of the child.

Assets gifted to a child, or purchased with gifted funds, are usually held on bare trust, with one parent acting as trustee. Bare trusts are treated as if the child owned the assets directly for IHT purposes (Section 8.8); although it is important not to fall foul of the gifts with reservation rules (Section 4.8).

The best way for a parent to make large IHT effective gifts to minor children is generally to use relevant property trusts (Section 9.1). Such trusts will be settlor-interested trusts for CGT purposes (Section 9.4). Hence, given the inability to hold over capital gains, it will generally make sense to make cash settlements into the trust; although other assets might sometimes be suitable where there would be little or no CGT liability arising on the transfer.

When using a settlor-interested trust, it is essential to ensure the parent making the settlement cannot benefit. If both parents are making a settlement into the trust then neither can benefit. Even when there is only one settlor, it is generally wise to ensure their spouse cannot benefit. If a settlor can or, in practice, does benefit from a trust, the assets and funds within the trust will be treated as gifts with reservation (see Section 4.8) and the trust will be rendered ineffective for IHT planning purposes.

This makes it vital that any income, or other funds, derived from the relevant property trust is effectively ring-fenced and cannot be used in any way to benefit the settlor. This requires some careful management, as using trust income, or other funds, to settle any expenses or obligations that would normally fall on the settlor, as the beneficiary's parent, could render the trust ineffective for IHT purposes.

For smaller gifts, either a Child Trust Fund or Junior ISA may be the best vehicle to use (see further below).

**Grandparents, Aunts, Uncles, Etc**

Other family members may generally make gifts to minor children without the problems set out above. Hence, you could make gifts to your grandchildren or your nephews and nieces, and these will usually be PETs; or you could transfer assets into trust for these children and holdover any capital gains arising. Similarly, your parents or your siblings could make gifts to your children or into a trust for their benefit, with the same results. Be careful to avoid any kind of reciprocal arrangements as these might trigger the associated operations rules (Section 11.11).

Also, don't forget the gifts with reservation rules (Section 4.8) can apply to a gift to any person or any trust where you are not excluded from benefitting.

**Will Trusts for Minors**

HMRC appears to take the view that a minor cannot have an immediate post-death interest (Section 8.12), as trust law would make such a trust discretionary in nature. Anyone intending to leave assets in trust for the benefit of a minor should therefore consider using a bereaved minor's trust, an 18 to 25 trust, or even just a bare trust.

A bare trust carries some advantages for Income Tax and CGT purposes, as the minor's own allowances could be set against income and capital gains. A similar result may be obtained via the trusts for vulnerable individuals exception (see Section 8.20), but this carries a few limitations that will not always be desirable.

**Child Trust Funds and Junior ISAs**

Minor children born in the UK before 3rd January 2011 should have a Child Trust Fund. Junior ISAs are available to UK resident minors who were not eligible for a Child Trust Fund.

Parents, family, and friends of minor children may put up to £9,000 in total into the child's Junior ISA or Child Trust Fund each tax year. Monies are invested in a long-term investment account to grow free from Income Tax or CGT, like a normal ISA.

On maturity, funds within a Child Trust Fund may be transferred to an ISA in the child's name. Junior ISAs automatically convert to a normal ISA when the child reaches 18. No withdrawals are permitted before this time.

Payments into Child Trust Funds or Junior ISAs are PETs unless covered by an exemption, such as the annual exemption or the exemption for normal expenditure out of income.

Funds within a Child Trust Fund or Junior ISA form part of the child's estate and, crucially, ***not*** their parent's. They remain subject to IHT, however, in the tragic event that the child should die before the age of 18. (Yes, if a child's estate exceeds the NRB, they are subject to IHT like anyone else. Vultures!)

## 11.11 ANTI-AVOIDANCE MEASURES

There is a great deal of targeted anti-avoidance legislation aimed at blocking specific areas, or types, of IHT planning (e.g. the rules on deduction of liabilities: Section 2.10). In this section, it is worth looking at some of the more general anti-avoidance measures at HMRC's disposal.

Where there are two or more transfers of the same property, or two or more transactions that affect the same property, HMRC may invoke the associated operations rules. Broadly speaking, where these rules are applied, the transfers or transactions are treated as if just one transfer from the original transferor to the ultimate recipient had taken place, thus undoing any tax planning the intermediate steps aimed to achieve.

HMRC's powers under the associated operations rules are extremely wide-ranging and, as we have seen several times throughout this guide, there are many IHT planning techniques that might potentially be caught. Nevertheless, where there are sufficiently good non-tax reasons for carrying out the transactions, the application of the associated operations rules may still be avoided.

Time is a good defence against the associated operations rules: the longer the gap between one transaction and the next, the less likely the planning measures are to be attacked. Uncertainty is also important. Where subsequent transfers are uncertain of being carried out at the time of an earlier transfer, they are far less likely to be deemed associated operations.

It is also worth noting, as a general principle, death itself is not regarded as an associated operation or a step in a tax avoidance scheme (perhaps because, while the event itself is certain, the timing is not). This saves many planning techniques from being caught by the associated operations rules.

The general anti-abuse rule (GAAR) is targeted at 'artificial' and 'abusive' or 'aggressive' tax avoidance schemes that go beyond the scope of normal tax planning and use loopholes in tax legislation in a way not intended by Parliament. Where the GAAR applies, any tax advantage gained through the use of the 'abusive' scheme will be reversed.

We are told normal tax planning should not be affected and, to date, HMRC have not applied the GAAR to any of the IHT planning strategies in this guide. It also seems unlikely that the GAAR could affect any techniques not already at risk of attack under the associated operations rules. Nonetheless, there is a risk some more advanced IHT planning techniques might one day be challenged under the GAAR.

There is a legal obligation to disclose certain types of IHT planning techniques under the 'DOTAS' (disclosure of tax avoidance schemes) regime. In other words, the taxpayer using the technique must advise HMRC they have done so. Disclosure does not necessarily mean the scheme doesn't work, but it may lead to greater scrutiny from HMRC. Only more advanced techniques are affected, specifically those which:

- Reduce or eliminate the entry, anniversary or exit charges where assets or funds are placed in a relevant property trust (see Chapter 8)
- Reduce or eliminate charges on company participators (not referred to in this guide, but potentially an issue for family investment companies: see Chapter 14)
- Avoid the gifts with reservation rules (Section 4.8), without leading to a pre-owned assets charge (see Section 11.12)
- Reduce the value of a person's estate without creating a chargeable lifetime transfer or PET

The arrangements must also involve one or more 'contrived or abnormal' steps to require disclosure. Writing a Will is never regarded as abnormal, so anything put in place purely through a Will need not be disclosed.

By and large it is only commercial products, such as those covered in Sections 7.26, 9.8, and 9.9, or complex arrangements, such as those in Chapter 14, or Sections 15.1 and 15.2, that may need to be disclosed. These generally require professional advice, so ***my*** advice is: whenever an IHT planning technique is complex enough to require professional advice, seek advice regarding whether the scheme needs to be reported under DOTAS at the same time.

## 11.12 THE PRE-OWNED ASSETS CHARGE

An Income Tax charge may be levied on the former owner of an asset who continues to benefit from that asset, or on a donor who benefits from the use of assets purchased with funds they had previously gifted.

While this is an Income Tax charge, its purpose is to deter IHT planning. Hence there is a general exemption for assets already caught under the gifts with reservation rules (see Section 4.8) or that are otherwise still included in the donor's estate.

Assets subject to the charge are known as 'pre-owned assets' and, broadly, the charge taxes the annual value of these assets as a benefit-in-kind. For land and buildings, the annual value is the property's open-market rental value. For most other assets it is based on a fixed sum of 5% of their capital value. The initial values to be used are those prevailing on the date the asset first falls within the provisions. These values can be used for five years before the asset must be revalued.

Any amounts the former owner is paying for the use of the asset may be deducted from the annual value in arriving at the taxable benefit. These payments must be made under a legal obligation so, in the case of property, a formal lease is required.

The charge is designed to hit back at a number of IHT planning schemes but, technically, could also catch many unintended, innocent victims, as there is no motive test. Furthermore, there is no exemption for an unexpected change of circumstances in the same way as there is for gifts with reservation (Section 4.8).

HMRC have been accused of 'institutional disinterest' in the pre-owned assets charge as it is really designed to deter IHT planning and they seem to have very little interest in actually collecting it. Nonetheless, where the charge is technically due, it remains the taxpayer's duty to report it.

One of the greatest risk areas is gifts between unmarried partners. For example, if an individual gives their partner some money to help with the purchase of a property that they then live in together, that property is caught by the charge. Furthermore, the charge still applies even if the couple subsequently get married.

Such problems can usually be avoided by either purchasing the property in joint names or by marrying before the gift is made: although these simple strategies will not be available in every case.

**Exemptions**

Thankfully, there are a few exemptions from the charge, including:

i) Gifts to your spouse; or to a former spouse under the terms of a court order (including gifts to a trust for their benefit: although the exemption ceases to apply if their interest comes to an end before their death)

ii) Gifts for 'maintenance of family' (Section 5.4)

iii) Gifts wholly covered by the annual or small gifts exemption

iv) Sales of your entire interest in an asset made on commercial, arm's length terms (even if made to a connected party)

v) Sales of a part interest in an asset made on normal, commercial, arm's length terms to an unconnected party, or for consideration not in the form of money, or assets readily convertible into money (see Appendix B for a list of 'connected persons')

vi) The donor's total annual taxable benefits ***before*** deducting contributions paid by the donor do not exceed £5,000. This is an 'all or nothing' exemption so, if total taxable benefits exceed this amount, the ***whole*** sum (less donor contributions) is taxed

vii) The asset was acquired with funds derived from an outright gift of money seven years or more before the donor first enjoyed any benefit

viii) The donor has retained a suitable interest in the gifted asset, such as a parent who has given a joint share in a property to an adult child who lives there with them

Furthermore, the charge does not apply to non-UK residents, or to assets that would not be chargeable to IHT, such as foreign assets formerly held by, or purchased with funds donated by, a non-UK domiciled individual.

The charge does not apply where the donor's enjoyment of an asset is minor and incidental, such as social visits to the current occupier of a property. The charge can only apply to property if the donor is in occupation and HMRC's guidance suggests this requires an element of 'control and exclusion': for example, the ability to access the property freely, or store items at the property. However, use of a property that fulfils these criteria will amount to occupation, even if only occasional.

Finally, there is a 'Get Out Of Jail: But Not Free' card, in the shape of an option to elect out of the pre-owned assets charge by allowing the relevant asset to be included in the donor's estate for IHT purposes. The asset is then treated as a gift with reservation (see Section 4.8) and effectively remains in the donor's estate for as long as they continue to enjoy a benefit. The election should be made by 31st January following the tax year in which the charge would have first arisen, although HMRC generally accept late elections. Once made, the election is irrevocable.

The most likely application of the pre-owned assets charge is in the case of the family home. It should not generally arise under any of the planning methods described in Chapter 13, but the following points are worth noting:

- If the former home is sold after being given away, a charge could arise if the transferor benefits from an asset purchased with the proceeds.
- Methods that involve realising cash and giving it away could give rise to a charge if the donor benefits from the use of an asset purchased with the proceeds within a period of seven years after making their gifts.
- Methods that involve passing the deceased's share of the property to a trust or to someone other than their surviving spouse could pose a risk if the surviving spouse had originally given a share in the property to the deceased, or had given them the funds with which to purchase their share, and had done so before they were married.

## 11.13 FOREIGN ISSUES

As explained in Section 2.2, IHT continues to apply to overseas assets held by a UK domiciled individual.

However, it is important to understand some form of succession or inheritance tax may also apply to overseas assets in the country in which they are located. Furthermore, foreign succession law may also apply to those assets. You may also be subject to some form of succession or inheritance tax in any country where you are a national, a citizen, or a resident; or have been at some time in the past.

Lastly, it is worth noting some countries tax the beneficiary of a gift or inheritance. Hence, if you are leaving assets, or funds, to a beneficiary resident, or domiciled, overseas, this could create a foreign tax liability, and this may even end up falling on your estate.

As with all foreign tax issues, it is wise to take local advice if there is a chance you may be affected.

Chapter 12

# Interaction with CGT

## 12.1 A QUICK CAPITAL GAINS TAX UPDATE

Before we look at that 'clash of the titans' created by the interaction between CGT and IHT, I will provide a quick update on the current CGT regime.

Individuals currently pay CGT at five rates:
- 10% where business asset disposal relief (BADR) or investor's relief (IVR) is available (see Section 12.5)
- 18% on gains on residential property made by basic rate taxpayers
- 28% on gains on residential property made by higher rate taxpayers
- 10% on other gains made by basic rate taxpayers
- 20% on other gains made by higher rate taxpayers

Company shares are not classed as residential property, even when the company is investing in residential property. This point has some useful applications, as we will see in Chapter 14.

Basic rate taxpayers pay the reduced rates to the extent of any basic rate tax band remaining available. Generally speaking, therefore, once your combined taxable income and gains for the tax year exceed the higher-rate tax threshold (£50,270 for each tax year until 2027/28), you must pay CGT at either 20% or 28%, as appropriate, on any further amount of capital gains arising in the same tax year.

***Example:*** *Beyoncé has taxable income of £38,270 for 2023/24. After deducting her personal allowance of £12,570, she is liable for Income Tax on £25,700. This means £12,000 of her £37,700 basic rate band for 2023/24 remains available.*

*In February 2024, Beyoncé makes a capital gain of £31,000 on a residential investment property. After deducting her annual CGT exemption of £6,000 she is left with a taxable gain of £25,000. The first £12,000 of her taxable gain is taxed at 18% and the remaining £13,000 is taxed at 28%.*

Anyone with taxable income in excess of the higher-rate tax threshold simply pays CGT at 20% or 28% on all their capital gains after deducting the annual CGT exemption (except where BADR or IVR is available: see Section 12.5).

Disposals of UK residential property that give rise to any taxable gain must be reported to HMRC within 60 days of completion. Any CGT arising must also be paid by the same deadline. This includes gifts to another individual (other than your spouse), transfers into trusts, or companies, and any other disposal of UK residential property, even when the gain arising is held over.

The annual CGT exemption (£6,000 for 2023/24) is to be reduced to just £3,000 from 2024/25 onwards. As it will be so small in future, I am simply going to ignore it throughout the rest of this guide. In practice, however, it will often produce small additional savings.

For further details of the current CGT regime, including the application of any of the reliefs mentioned in this chapter to property, see the Taxcafe guide *How to Save Property Tax*.

## 12.2 THE UPLIFT ON DEATH

Do you remember my opening comments in Section 4.5? I'll refresh your memory: "For CGT purposes, death is often a good tax-planning strategy."

The reason for this rather dark-humoured remark is one simple fact. On death, the CGT base cost of all the deceased's assets is uplifted to market value at that date.

***Example:*** *In 1985, Jerry set up Killer Ltd with an investment of just £10,000. By July 2023, his controlling interest in Killer Promotions PLC (the same company) is worth £100m. Jerry's CGT bill on a sale of these shares would be almost £20m.*

*Sadly, Jerry dies in August 2023, and leaves his entire Killer Promotions PLC shareholding to his son, Lee. Lee sells the shares for £102m in March 2024. His CGT bill will be just £400,000 at most.*

Lee is treated as if he acquired the shares in August 2023 for a price of £100m. We call this the CGT 'uplift on death'. His taxable gain on the sale in March 2024 is therefore just £2m.

## 12.3 THE CAPITAL GAINS TAX vs INHERITANCE TAX DILEMMA

While death is very good CGT planning, lifetime transfers generally pose a problem. As explained in Section 4.9, a lifetime transfer of anything other than cash will give rise to a CGT disposal, which is deemed to take place at market value.

Hence, in the example in Section 12.2, if Jerry had given the Killer Promotions PLC shares to Lee before he died, he may have given himself a £20m CGT bill!

This creates a bit of a dilemma: the best way to save IHT is often to make lifetime transfers, whereas the best way to save CGT is to hold on to assets until death.

What we really want to do is minimise the overall tax burden or, to be more precise, follow ***Bayley's Law*** (Section 11.1). To do this, we need to start by considering what reliefs the assets will qualify for, both under the IHT regime and under the CGT regime. The three major areas to consider are:

- Business assets
- Transfers to spouses
- The family home

We will look at each of these areas in turn. Other assets that do not fall under any of these headings are dealt with in Sections 12.9 and 12.10.

## 12.4 GIFTS OF BUSINESS ASSETS

Where a qualifying business asset is transferred by way of gift, the capital gain arising may be held over. This provides an effective CGT deferral, but means the uplift on death will be lost.

***Example:*** *Kurt set up Nevermind Ltd in 2011 with a share capital of just 100 £1 ordinary shares. The shares currently qualify for both holdover relief and BADR (see Section 12.5).*

*In December 2023, Kurt gives 25 shares to his unmarried partner, Courtney, and they elect to hold over the capital gain arising. In effect, this means Courtney is treated as if she acquired the shares for £1 each: the price Kurt paid.*

*Kurt dies in March 2024 and, fearing a drop in value, Courtney decides to sell her Nevermind Ltd shares at their current value of £5,000 per share, £125,000 in total.*

*Courtney's base cost for her shares is just £25, so she ends up with a capital gain of £124,975. Her CGT bill, at 20%, is therefore £24,995 (assuming she is a higher-rate taxpayer).*

Sadly, despite its name, holdover relief on gifts of business assets does not actually apply to assets used in a 'business', but generally only to assets used in a trade. What will qualify as a 'trade' can be difficult to define, but it certainly does not include a property investment or property letting business (but see below regarding furnished holiday lets).

Broadly, the assets that qualify for holdover relief are:

- Assets used in a qualifying trade (including goodwill)
- Unquoted shares in a trading company (this time, unquoted does not include shares traded on AIM)
- A holding of at least 5% of a quoted trading company

To be a trading company for the purposes of both holdover relief and BADR, the underlying business must not include any substantial element of non-trading activities. HMRC generally accepts that non-trading activities are not substantial where neither non-trading income nor non-trading assets exceed 20% of the totals for the company as a whole. However, this test is only a yardstick and is not conclusive. In a recent tax case, it was held that non-trading activities would only be regarded as substantial where they were of material or real importance in the context of the company's activities as a whole.

Nonetheless, to avoid any argument over the issue, it is wise to keep both non-trading income and non-trading assets below 20% in order to safely preserve the company's trading status wherever possible.

Although not technically regarded as a trade, furnished holiday letting counts as a qualifying activity for both holdover relief and BADR purposes, provided it meets certain strict criteria. Additionally, anything that qualifies for APR (Section 7.28) also qualifies for CGT holdover relief.

However, many modern farms include elements of what HMRC would regard as investment activities, such as letting cottages, letting land out for solar energy or wind farms, or wayleave (right of access) payments for electricity pylons and mobile phone masts. Where these elements are significant (based on the criteria discussed above), holdover relief may not be available.

Holdover relief on gifts of business assets is not available for a transfer of shares or securities to a company, or on any transfer to a settlor-interested trust (Section 9.4). A claim for holdover relief requires a joint election by the transferor and the transferee (or by the transferor alone where the transferee is a trust).

## 12.5 BUSINESS PROPERTY RELIEF (BPR) AND BUSINESS ASSET DISPOSAL RELIEF (BADR)

As we have already seen, the uplift on death provides enormous potential to save CGT. Whether that saving is achieved at an IHT cost, however, is highly dependent on whether BPR or APR is available. Another important factor for business assets is the question of whether BADR is available.

**Business Asset Disposal Relief (BADR)**
Where a disposal of business assets qualifies for BADR the rate of CGT applying is reduced to 10%. Each individual may only claim BADR on a maximum cumulative lifetime total of £1m of capital gains (£10m for disposals before 11th March 2020). Thereafter, the CGT rate will revert to the normal rates set out in Section 12.1.

The qualifying rules for BADR are different to the rules for BPR or holdover relief, so it is essential to consider each relief separately in every case. Broadly speaking, BADR is available on the disposal of:

i) The whole or part of a qualifying business
ii) Assets formerly used in a qualifying business that has ceased or been disposed of
iii) Shares or securities in a 'personal company'

A qualifying business for this purpose is generally a trade, although, once again, qualifying furnished holiday letting businesses also qualify.

A part of a business can only be counted for these purposes if it is capable of operating as a going concern in its own right and HMRC interprets this point very strictly. However, an interest in a business, such as a partnership share, may qualify.

A disposal of assets formerly used in a qualifying business must take place within three years after the cessation or disposal of the business.

In all cases, the individual making the disposal must have owned the qualifying business for at least two years prior to its disposal, or cessation, as the case may be.

**Personal Company**

The definition of a personal company for the purposes of BADR is broadly as follows:

i) The individual holds at least 5% of the ordinary share capital
ii) The holding under (i) provides at least 5% of the voting rights
iii) The company is a trading company (based on the same criteria we looked at in Section 12.4)
iv) The individual is an officer or employee of the company (an officer includes a non-executive director or company secretary)
v) The individual's shareholding gives them at least a 5% interest in both the distributable profits and net assets of the company, OR
On a disposal of all the company's ordinary shares, the individual would be entitled to at least 5% of the proceeds

Each of these rules must be satisfied for at least two years prior to the disposal in question or, if earlier, the cessation of the business. In the latter case, the disposal must again take place within three years after cessation. Furnished holiday letting is again accepted as trading where it meets the relevant qualifying criteria.

**Associated Disposals**

BADR may sometimes extend to assets owned personally but used in the trade of a personal company, or a partnership in which the owner is a partner. A number of restrictions apply to these associated disposals, however. Broadly, the relief is only available where the owner is also disposing of at least a 5% stake in the company or partnership, or is disposing of their entire remaining stake, having held at least a 5% stake at some time in the past.

The assets must have been used in the company or partnership's business for at least the two year period immediately prior to the sale of the business stake or, if earlier, cessation of the business. In the latter case, the disposal must again take place within three years after cessation. The asset needs to have been owned for at least three years at the date of disposal.

The relief is restricted where the asset has not been used in the business throughout the seller's ownership or where any payment has been received for the use of the asset after 5th April 2008.

**Investor's Relief (IVR)**

IVR is available to investors subscribing for new issues of ordinary shares in unlisted trading companies after 16th March 2016. Shares must be held for at least three years and the investor must **not** be an officer or employee of the company. Shares qualifying for IVR are subject to a CGT rate of 10%. The relief is subject to a lifetime limit of £10m of capital gains: this is a separate allowance to the limit applying to BADR.

Where an individual holds shares qualifying for IVR, the implications for IHT planning discussed in this guide will be the same as in the case of shares qualifying for BADR.

**Critical Interactions**
The interaction between BPR and either BADR or IVR has enormous consequences for estate preservation planning. There are three possible combinations we need to consider, so let's examine each in turn.

**BPR & Either BADR or IVR Available**
These assets can be passed on free from IHT and it will therefore often make sense for the transferor to hang on to these assets and transfer them on death to obtain the CGT uplift with no IHT cost.

If it is not possible to hang on to the original assets until death, the same result can sometimes be achieved by exchanging these assets for replacement assets, as explained in Section 7.17. To avoid any CGT liabilities on the exchange, the replacement assets generally need to be one of the following:

i) Shares issued in exchange for shares in the transferor's own company (e.g. a 'takeover')
ii) Shares issued in exchange for the transfer of an unincorporated business into a company
iii) Business property acquired within the three year period following the disposal of the original assets. (E.g. buying business premises to replace previous premises used in the same business or the acquisition of property for use in a new qualifying business.)

Any new business under (iii) will need to qualify as a trading business. A qualifying furnished holiday letting business would also suffice for this purpose from a CGT perspective, but is unlikely to qualify for BPR (see Section 7.4).

Assets qualifying for holdover relief on gifts of business assets (see Section 12.4) can generally be transferred during the transferor's lifetime without any CGT liability. However, while this avoids CGT on the transfer, it also denies the transferee the benefit of the uplift on death.

On the other hand, a transfer of assets qualifying for BADR or IVR will be subject to CGT at a rate of just 10%. In many cases, it will make sense **NOT** to claim holdover relief on the transfer, so the transferee may benefit from an increased CGT base cost on the assets. This is particularly relevant where the transferee is considering a sale of the asset in the near future (although the potential impact of such a sale when the transferor dies within seven years needs to be considered: see Section 7.18).

**BPR but Not BADR or IVR**
These assets can be passed on free from IHT but would often attract an immediate CGT charge of up to 20% or 28% in the case of a lifetime transfer.

If the Killer Promotions PLC shares in our example in Section 12.2 qualified for BPR, Jerry would have been able to leave them to Lee free of IHT. As we saw in Section 12.2, Lee was treated as if he had bought the shares at market value at the date of Jerry's death, thus drastically reducing his CGT bill.

In this situation, it will therefore generally make sense to hang on to the assets and only transfer them on death. CGT uplift will be obtained and both IHT and CGT can be avoided if the transferee sells the assets shortly afterwards. At the very least, there should be a substantial reduction in CGT, as we saw in Section 12.2.

Again, it may be possible to achieve the same results when the assets are exchanged for replacement assets before death. The opportunity to avoid CGT on such an exchange is more limited, however, and item (iii) outlined above may no longer apply in some cases.

Lifetime transfers of these assets will often give rise to immediate CGT liabilities, as holdover relief on gifts of business assets (Section 12.4) may not be available. Even where it is available, the uplift on death will be lost and the transferee will most likely suffer CGT at up to 20% or 28% on the held over gain when they ultimately sell the asset (although there will be a few instances where the transferee is eligible for BADR and thus pays CGT at just 10%).

**BADR or IVR but Not BPR** (Although it's difficult to foresee an individual qualifying for IVR but not BPR on the same shareholding)

This scenario could apply where:

i) A qualifying business has ceased within the last three years
ii) A furnished holiday letting business qualifies for BADR but not BPR
iii) An individual has shares or securities in a quoted company that qualifies as their personal company for the purposes of BADR

In these cases we face a major dilemma. A lifetime transfer (before the expiry of the three year period in the first case) will give rise to a maximum CGT charge of just 10%, but the opportunity to achieve the CGT uplift on death will be lost and the transferee may face a charge of up to 20% or 28% on the future growth in the asset's value. On the other hand, if the assets are still held at the time of death, IHT will be fully chargeable.

Furthermore, in the first case, it is unlikely the assets will be eligible for holdover relief on gifts of business assets (see Section 12.4). Even where this relief is available, it only provides a CGT deferral and the uplift on death will be lost.

In practice, it may be difficult to establish the best course of action, but an early transfer will often produce an overall saving.

***Example:*** *Sanjeev has a large estate well in excess of the NRB, including a 5% shareholding in a quoted trading company that qualifies for BADR. Sanjeev's base cost in these shares for CGT purposes is £2m.*

*In February 2024, Sanjeev transfers his shares to his daughter Meera when they are worth £3m. He decides not to claim holdover relief in order to secure the benefit of BADR. His resultant CGT bill is therefore £100,000. In March 2031, Sanjeev dies when the shares are worth £5m. As the transfer to Meera took place more than seven years previously, no IHT is due. If Sanjeev had still held the shares at this time, the IHT arising would have been £2m.*

*Meera now sells the shares, giving rise to a capital gain of £2m and a CGT bill, at 20%, of £400,000 (she is a higher-rate taxpayer and is not eligible for BADR). Hence, while father and daughter between them have paid £500,000 in CGT, the overall net tax saving for the family is £1.5m.*

*In fact, if we take account of the additional IHT saved due to the £100,000 reduction in the value of Sanjeev's estate when he paid his CGT bill, the overall net saving is actually £1.54m.*

Clearly, in this example, it was worth incurring a relatively low CGT cost, as the asset was successfully removed from Sanjeev's estate by way of a PET more than seven years before his death. On the other hand, if Sanjeev had died immediately after his transfer to Meera, there would have been no IHT saving (other than the £40,000 saved due to Sanjeev's CGT bill). The CGT liability would have been incurred needlessly when Meera could have had a CGT uplift on her father's death. Furthermore, if Sanjeev had left a surviving spouse, the transfer to Meera would have used up his NRB, leaving no TNRB to be used against the spouse's estate.

Between these two extremes lie an almost infinite variety of outcomes. As a general guide, I have produced the table below (Version 1). It follows broadly the same lines as the example, but with a few minor modifications based on the following assumptions:

- i) There is an existing gain of £1m giving rise to a CGT liability of £100,000
- ii) The asset is currently worth £3m and its future value will increase at a rate of 7.5% per annum (compound)
- iii) The transferee will sell the asset immediately after the transferor's death and will not be entitled to BADR
- iv) The transferee is a higher-rate taxpayer
- v) The transferor will not hold over the gain arising on the transfer
- vi) The asset is not residential property
- vii) The NRB and any TNRB to which they are entitled would have been fully utilised against other property within the transferor's estate if the transfer had not taken place
- viii) The transferor survives just beyond the relevant anniversary
- ix) The NRB in future years is as per our forecast in Section 3.2

| Transferor Dies After | Value on Death | IHT on Transfer* | CGT on Final Sale | IHT if Still in Estate | Net Saving or (Cost)** |
|---|---|---|---|---|---|
| < 1 year | £3,000,000 | £1,200,000 | £0 | £1,200,000 | (£60,000) |
| 1 year | £3,225,000 | £1,200,000 | £45,000 | £1,290,000 | (£15,000) |
| 2 years | £3,466,875 | £1,200,000 | £93,375 | £1,386,750 | £33,375 |
| 3 years | £3,726,891 | £986,000 | £145,378 | £1,490,756 | £299,378 |
| 4 years | £4,006,407 | £772,000 | £201,281 | £1,602,563 | £569,281 |
| 5 years | £4,306,888 | £560,160 | £261,378 | £1,722,755 | £841,218 |
| 6 years | £4,629,905 | £349,760 | £325,981 | £1,851,962 | £1,116,221 |
| 7 years | £4,977,147 | £0 | £395,429 | £1,990,859 | £1,535,429 |
| 10 years | £6,183,095 | £0 | £636,619 | £2,473,238 | £1,776,619 |

* Includes additional tax on estate arising as a result of the transfer (due to the transfer using up the deceased's NRB in the event of their death within seven years). For this purpose, it is assumed no TNRB is available to the deceased.
** Net saving/(cost) takes account of the CGT paid on the original transfer less the IHT saving arising as a result of this cost.

As we can see, under this scenario, the transferor only needs to survive two years to make the transfer worthwhile.

The above savings are based on the assumption that the transferor's NRB (and any TNRB available) would be used up on other assets within their estate. This will not be the case if they would have otherwise left everything to their UK domiciled spouse and the points to be considered in this situation are covered in Chapter 6.

**Transferees Eligible for Business Asset Disposal Relief**

A lifetime transfer becomes even more attractive where the transferee will also be eligible for BADR on the transferred asset. In our example above, this might apply if the company Sanjeev held his shares in became Meera's personal company after the transfer.

In practice, this could generally be achieved by ensuring at least 5% of the ordinary shares are transferred and the transferee is, or becomes, an officer or employee of the company. The following table (Version 2) sets out the position arising under the same scenario as before except the transferee now qualifies for BADR on the transferred asset.

| Transferor Dies After | Value on Death | IHT on Transfer | CGT on Final Sale | IHT if Still in Estate | Net Saving or (Cost) |
|---|---|---|---|---|---|
| < 1 year | £3,000,000 | £1,200,000 | £0 | £1,200,000 | (£60,000) |
| 1 year | £3,225,000 | £1,200,000 | *£46,688 | £1,290,000 | (£16,688) |
| 2 years | £3,466,875 | £1,200,000 | £46,688 | £1,386,750 | £80,063 |
| 3 years | £3,726,891 | £986,000 | £72,689 | £1,490,756 | £372,067 |
| 4 years | £4,006,407 | £772,000 | £101,281 | £1,602,563 | £669,281 |
| 5 years | £4,306,888 | £560,160 | £161,378 | £1,722,755 | £941,218 |
| 6 years | £4,629,905 | £349,760 | £225,981 | £1,851,962 | £1,216,221 |
| 7 years | £4,977,147 | £0 | £295,429 | £1,990,859 | £1,635,429 |
| 10 years | £6,183,095 | £0 | £536,619 | £2,473,238 | £1,876,619 |

* It is assumed in the case of the transferor's death after one year that the transferee keeps the shares for another year to qualify for BADR.

Remember the £1m cumulative lifetime limit for BADR applies to each individual. Hence, a transferor and transferee may be able to obtain combined relief on up to £2m between them. In this scenario, the transferee is paying CGT at 10% on the first £1m of the shares' growth in value after the transfer and at 20% on any excess.

### Residential Property

Let's now look at the same scenario where the transferred asset is residential property that qualifies for BADR but not BPR. This might be the case for a portfolio of furnished holiday lets, for example (see Section 7.4 regarding the status of furnished holiday lets for BPR purposes).

To begin with, we will assume the transferee will not qualify for BADR: perhaps, for example, they might convert the properties to normal residential lettings after the transfer. This gives us Version 3 of the table:

| Transferor Dies After | Value on Death | IHT on Transfer | CGT on Final Sale | IHT if Still in Estate | Net Saving or (Cost) |
|---|---|---|---|---|---|
| < 1 year | £3,000,000 | £1,200,000 | £0 | £1,200,000 | (£60,000) |
| 1 year | £3,225,000 | £1,200,000 | £63,000 | £1,290,000 | (£33,000) |
| 2 years | £3,466,875 | £1,200,000 | £130,725 | £1,386,750 | (£3,975) |
| 3 years | £3,726,891 | £986,000 | £203,529 | £1,490,756 | £241,227 |
| 4 years | £4,006,407 | £772,000 | £281,794 | £1,602,563 | £488,769 |
| 5 years | £4,306,888 | £560,160 | £365,929 | £1,722,755 | £736,667 |
| 6 years | £4,629,905 | £349,760 | £456,373 | £1,851,962 | £985,829 |
| 7 years | £4,977,147 | £0 | £553,601 | £1,990,859 | £1,377,258 |
| 10 years | £6,183,095 | £0 | £891,267 | £2,473,238 | £1,521,971 |

If the transferee ***did*** qualify for BADR, the outcome would be the same as Version 2 of the table above until the transferee's gain exceeded £1m. Thereafter, the position would be as follows (Version 4):

| Transferor Dies After | Value on Death | IHT on Transfer | CGT on Final Sale | IHT if Still in Estate | Net Saving |
|---|---|---|---|---|---|
| 4 years | £4,006,407 | £772,000 | £101,794 | £1,602,563 | £668,769 |
| 5 years | £4,306,888 | £560,160 | £185,929 | £1,722,755 | £916,667 |
| 6 years | £4,629,905 | £349,760 | £276,373 | £1,851,962 | £1,165,829 |
| 7 years | £4,977,147 | £0 | £373,601 | £1,990,859 | £1,557,258 |
| 10 years | £6,183,095 | £0 | £711,267 | £2,473,238 | £1,701,971 |

## 12.6 TRANSFERS TO SPOUSES OR CIVIL PARTNERS

As we know, transfers to your spouse are usually exempt from IHT. Furthermore, subject to the further points below, transfers to your spouse are also usually exempt from CGT. However, only transfers on death will benefit from the CGT uplift explained in Section 12.2. It therefore makes sense to hold on to assets that are subject to CGT, and which you ultimately intend to leave to your spouse, so they can benefit from the uplift on death.

Alternatively, a lifetime transfer of assets to your spouse could be used to get a CGT uplift on their death. You need to be pretty sure the assets are going to come back to you though!

**Separation and Divorce**

Unlike the IHT exemption, the CGT exemption for transfers between spouses does not always apply to transfers between separated spouses. Under draft legislation currently making its way through Parliament, for transfers after 5th April 2023, the general CGT exemption extends to transfers made before the earlier of:

a) The last day of the third tax year after the tax year in which the couple separate; or
b) The date on which their divorce is finalised, their marriage or civil partnership is annulled or dissolved, or they are formally, legally separated under a separation order or judicial separation

Hence, for example where a couple separate in June 2023, and none of the events under (b) above have yet occurred, the general exemption ends on 4th April 2027 (I'm sure the Government intended to make it 5th April but the way the legislation is currently drafted it's the 4th!)

In addition to the general exemption, it is also proposed that transfers between spouses made under a formal legal divorce or separation agreement at any time after 5th April 2023 will also be exempt.

A further useful proposal is that transfers of the former marital home to ***any*** person after 5th April 2023 as part of a divorce or separation agreement may be exempt from CGT. The exemption applies to a transfer of the whole or a part share in an individual's former main residence where their separated spouse still resides in the property (as their main residence) and the transferor has not elected for any other property to be treated as their main residence in the interim.

As we saw in Section 6.6, transfers made as part of a formal, legal divorce or separation agreement are generally exempt for IHT purposes. Hence, if enacted, this proposal means it may be possible for an estranged spouse to transfer the whole or a part share in the former marital home to their children, or a trust for their benefit, free from both CGT and IHT.

## 12.7 CAPITAL GAINS TAX AND THE FAMILY HOME

I could write an entire chapter on this subject alone. In fact, I have, but that chapter already appears in the Taxcafe guide *How to Save Property Tax*.

To put it simply, your home is exempt from CGT for as long as you live in it as your only or main residence, and for at least nine months thereafter. Full exemption will generally apply as long as you moved into the property within two years of acquisition and did not use it for anything else in the interim. Other periods of absence may result in a partial loss of your exemption, although additional reliefs are sometimes available.

Each married couple or single individual may have just one main residence for CGT purposes at any given time.

Hence, as far as CGT is concerned, a lifetime transfer of your qualifying main residence while you are still living there, or within the next nine months thereafter, will usually be exempt.

So, what's the problem? Well, apart from the IHT problems we will look at in the next chapter, there are two major CGT problems with giving away your main residence: the transferees lose the ability to benefit from the CGT uplift on death and; unless they move into the property, the transferees also lose any main residence exemption.

In essence, the transferees will be treated for CGT purposes as having acquired the property at its market value on the date of transfer and will be exposed to CGT on any growth in value thereafter.

**Practical Implications**
A sale of the parent's home at any time within nine months of them ceasing to occupy it as their main residence would generally be fully exempt from CGT if they were still the owner at that time. This additional nine month period is extended to three years if the owner is disabled or resident in a care home.

Furthermore, if the parent retained the property until death, it would be subject to the uplift on death, giving the children complete exemption from any gain arising during the parent's lifetime, even if the parent had been absent from the property for a longer period.

Conversely, if a child owns their parent's current or former home, but does not occupy it as their main residence, it is effectively treated like an investment property and is fully exposed to CGT on a subsequent sale.

The capital gain in such cases will be based on the property's increase in value since the time the child acquired it, not since the time of the parent's death. The relevant transfer may have been several years earlier, when the property's value was considerably less, thus leading to a much larger taxable gain.

The interplay between CGT and IHT can produce one of three results:

i) The IHT saving may outweigh the CGT exposure that has been created. This is fine and means the planning is still worthwhile
ii) The IHT saving comes at the price of a similar level of potential CGT liability. Such instances may still be worthwhile, as they may still produce a significant cashflow saving by deferring the tax arising. (This will often be the case where the beneficiaries have no intention of selling the property, or at least not for some considerable time)
iii) The IHT saving results in a significantly greater amount of potential CGT. This, clearly, would be foolhardy if the beneficiaries are contemplating any sale of the property in the foreseeable future

The introduction of the RNRB (Section 3.4) has significantly altered the potential outcomes of this interplay in many cases. Far more cases will now fall into the third category, meaning that retaining the property in the parent's ownership until death will often be the most sensible thing to do.

In fact, in most cases where a married couple, widow, or widower, intends to leave the family home to their children, there will be little point in trying to avoid IHT on it, as properties worth up to £1m will often be fully covered by the available exemptions. My suggestion for most such people is therefore to focus their IHT planning on other assets and keep the family home where it is. But there remain many exceptions to this, and we will look at these in the next chapter.

Where the parent still resides in the property, a simple transfer will usually be a gift with reservation. As we shall see in the next section, it would generally be wise to refrain from making any transfer that would be a gift with reservation, as there would be no IHT advantage but all the CGT disadvantages would remain. We will look at ways to resolve this problem in the next chapter.

## 12.8 CAPITAL GAINS TAX AND GIFTS WITH RESERVATION

As explained in Section 4.8, when a transfer falls foul of the gifts with reservation rules, it will be ineffective for IHT purposes until such time as the relevant reservation comes to an end.

This has absolutely no impact on the CGT treatment of the asset. The transfer that was subject to a gift with reservation may still give rise to CGT liabilities based on the market value of the asset transferred, and the new legal owner of the transferred asset will lose the benefit of any reliefs to which the transferor may have been entitled, including main residence relief on the transferor's home.

Generally, with few exceptions, this situation should be avoided as it usually creates CGT problems without saving any IHT.

***Example:*** *Tina is an elderly divorcee. In 2003 she gave her house to her son, Robert, but continued to live there until April 2021, when she moved into a nursing home. The house was worth £275,000 in 2003 but £725,000 by 2021.*

*Tragically, Tina dies in March 2024, leaving only a few small possessions with no material value and just enough cash to pay her last month's nursing home fees and funeral expenses. However, as she only moved out of her house in 2021, its value at that date must be brought back into her estate, resulting in an IHT bill of £160,000.*

*To help pay the IHT, Robert sells the house in August 2024. Let's assume the house is still worth £725,000 at this point. For CGT purposes, he is treated as having acquired the house for just £275,000, thus giving rise to a CGT bill of £126,000 on top of the IHT bill (he is a higher-rate taxpayer so his capital gain of £450,000 is taxed at 28%).*

I have seen this type of situation many times and it's an absolute tragedy. Had Tina simply held on to the house, Robert would have paid ***LESS*** IHT, since the RNRB would have been available, and his IHT bill would have been reduced to £90,000. He would also have paid little or no CGT on a sale of the property shortly after Tina's death. The transfer in 2003 has cost Robert almost £200,000 in unnecessary extra tax.

Many families have attempted this type of planning to their cost. To make it even worse, many of these transfers were done to avoid paying residential care fees (see Section 11.6) but, as a result of a number of rule changes and successful cases taken by the local authorities this part of the plan has often failed as well.

We will return to gifts with reservation of the family home in Section 13.12, although the above example has already ably demonstrated that, in the vast majority of cases, gifts with reservation should be avoided like the plague!

## 12.9 EXEMPT TRANSFERS

There are a few classes of assets other than cash that are exempt from CGT. For IHT planning purposes, these assets can often be regarded much like cash, since a lifetime transfer will not give rise to any CGT liability, but could save IHT if the transferor survives seven years (or even just three in some cases). The following assets may be exempt from CGT:

- Enterprise Investment Scheme shares (only the shares themselves, not any gain held over and only if certain qualifying conditions are met, including a minimum holding period of at least three years)

- Tangible movable assets worth less than £6,000 (also known as chattels). This includes items like paintings, antiques, and silverware
- Government securities (also known as gilts)
- Foreign currency held by an individual
- Motor vehicles
- Tangible wasting assets with an expected life of less than 50 years (machinery, computers, household equipment, etc.)
- Medals and certain other awards (although, as stated in Section 3.8, these are usually exempt from IHT when still held by the original recipient or their heirs)

Note that exemption from CGT does not necessarily provide exemption from other taxes. Anyone trading in any of these items would be classed as a dealer and subject to Income Tax and National Insurance on their profits.

As far as chattels are concerned, a lifetime transfer means foregoing the CGT uplift on death, so it might lead to increased CGT liabilities at a later date for the transferee where the assets are later worth over £6,000. The transfer is likely to remain advantageous overall though if an IHT saving is achieved.

Married persons must bear in mind these transfers could lead to a reduction in their spouse's TNRB if the transferor does not survive seven years. The pros and cons of this were discussed in Chapter 6. Items like motor vehicles and other wasting assets will also generally reduce in value, meaning the loss of TNRB will be greater than the ultimate reduction in the transferor's estate, leaving the family worse off on a death within seven years.

Other ways to make lifetime transfers free from CGT include:

- Transferring assets while you are non-UK resident: you must be non-resident for at least five years, this doesn't work for land and buildings in the UK, and foreign tax implications must be considered.
- Cashing in an ISA and passing over the proceeds

As always, it remains important to remember the loss of the CGT uplift on death and, for married persons, the potential impact on your spouse's TNRB.

## 12.10 OTHER ASSETS

So, what about those other assets, which do not qualify as business assets or main residences, which aren't exempt, and which you're not planning to give to your spouse? Here we are considering assets that do not qualify for BPR, BADR, IVR, or holdover relief on a gift. This will make a lifetime transfer less attractive from a CGT perspective. Nevertheless, the opportunity to save IHT by way of an early transfer remains.

### Assets Other Than Residential Property

We'll return to the scenario in Version 1 of our table in Section 12.5, except for one change: BADR is ***not*** available to the transferor. On this basis, the position arising is as follows (Version 5):

| Transferor Dies After | Value on Death | IHT on Transfer | CGT on Final Sale | IHT if Still in Estate | Net Saving or (Cost)* |
|---|---|---|---|---|---|
| < 1 year | £3,000,000 | £1,200,000 | £0 | £1,200,000 | (£120,000) |
| 1 year | £3,225,000 | £1,200,000 | £45,000 | £1,290,000 | (£75,000) |
| 2 years | £3,466,875 | £1,200,000 | £93,375 | £1,386,750 | (£26,625) |
| 3 years | £3,726,891 | £986,000 | £145,378 | £1,490,756 | £239,378 |
| 4 years | £4,006,407 | £772,000 | £201,281 | £1,602,563 | £509,281 |
| 5 years | £4,306,888 | £560,160 | £261,378 | £1,722,755 | £781,218 |
| 6 years | £4,629,905 | £349,760 | £325,981 | £1,851,962 | £1,056,221 |
| 7 years | £4,977,147 | £0 | £395,429 | £1,990,859 | £1,475,429 |
| 10 years | £6,183,095 | £0 | £636,619 | £2,473,238 | £1,716,619 |

* Net saving/(cost) takes account of £200,000 CGT paid on the original transfer less the resultant IHT saving arising due to the reduction in the value of the transferor's estate.

Apart from BADR being unavailable, all notes and assumptions made for Version 1 of this table in Section 12.5 apply. I also assume the transferor is a higher-rate taxpayer. In this scenario, such a transfer remains beneficial if the transferor survives at least three years.

**Residential Property**

The position is altered if the assets are residential property which is subject to higher CGT rates. Based on the above assumptions, but assuming the assets transferred are residential property, the position is as follows (Version 6):

| Transferor Dies After | Value on Death | IHT on Transfer | CGT on Final Sale | IHT if Still in Estate | Net Saving or (Cost)* |
|---|---|---|---|---|---|
| < 1 year | £3,000,000 | £1,200,000 | £0 | £1,200,000 | (£168,000) |
| 1 year | £3,225,000 | £1,200,000 | £63,000 | £1,290,000 | (£141,000) |
| 2 years | £3,466,875 | £1,200,000 | £130,725 | £1,386,750 | (£111,975) |
| 3 years | £3,726,891 | £986,000 | £203,529 | £1,490,756 | £133,227 |
| 4 years | £4,006,407 | £772,000 | £281,794 | £1,602,563 | £380,769 |
| 5 years | £4,306,888 | £560,160 | £365,929 | £1,722,755 | £628,667 |
| 6 years | £4,629,905 | £349,760 | £456,373 | £1,851,962 | £877,829 |
| 7 years | £4,977,147 | £0 | £553,601 | £1,990,859 | £1,269,258 |
| 10 years | £6,183,095 | £0 | £891,267 | £2,473,238 | £1,413,971 |

* Net saving/(cost) takes account of £280,000 CGT on the original transfer less the resultant IHT saving arising due to the reduction in the value of the transferor's estate.

As we can see, under this scenario, it will take three years before a lifetime transfer of residential property provides any advantage.

The position would be different if the property qualified for main residence relief in the hands of either the transferor or the transferee. The situation for a main residence was examined in Sections 12.7 and 12.8, and will also be the focus of Chapter 13.

In conclusion, the tables in this section, and Section 12.5, tell us that early transfers of assets that are appreciating in value will often lead to significant overall tax savings in the end. However, married persons must remember the tables take no account of the impact of these transfers on the deceased's spouse's TNRB: see Chapter 6 for a thorough examination of this issue.

## 12.11 CAPITAL GAINS TAX AND TRUSTS

A trust for a vulnerable individual may elect to be taxed as if any capital gains arising belong directly to the beneficiary (except that any capital losses made by the individual cannot be set against the trust's gains). However, as explained in Section 8.20, this will generally only apply to disabled trusts, trusts for bereaved minors, and other trusts where the beneficiary is under 18.

Most other trusts (apart from bare trusts and charitable trusts) are subject to CGT at the higher rates of 20% or 28% and generally have an annual CGT exemption equal to half that applying to individuals (see Section 12.1). This is further reduced where the settlor has set up more than one trust.

In Chapter 8, we considered the various different types of trust and saw some of them had their own separate life for IHT purposes and some did not. With the exception of bare trusts, however, trusts are treated as a separate legal entity for CGT purposes. This effectively means, subject to any exemptions or reliefs that may be available: transfers into a trust are treated as disposals made at market value; and transfers to beneficiaries from a trust are again treated as disposals at market value.

In the case of a bare trust, it is only the transfer to the trust that represents a disposal for CGT purposes. Thereafter, the assets of the trust are generally treated as belonging to the beneficiary for the purposes of both IHT and CGT.

### The Capital Gains Tax Uplift on Death

Assets subject to an interest in possession that fall into a beneficiary's estate for IHT purposes (see Chapter 8) will generally qualify for the same CGT uplift on the death of the beneficiary as assets held absolutely (see Section 12.2). However, the uplift does not apply where property reverts to the original settlor absolutely on the beneficiary's death (but does if the settlor only obtains an interest in possession).

The CGT uplift on death also generally applies to assets in a bereaved minor's trust, or an 18 to 25 trust, on the death of a beneficiary under the age of 18.

### Held Over Gains

When an interest in possession that is not within the relevant property trust regime (Chapter 8) ends on the death of the beneficiary and a capital gain was held over when the same assets entered the trust (see Sections 9.4 and 12.4), that held over gain becomes chargeable. The held over gain can usually be held over again provided IHT is chargeable on the beneficiary's death, or the assets qualify as business assets for hold over relief purposes (Section 12.4).

**Hold Over Relief on Absolute Entitlement**

CGT hold over relief is generally available when the beneficiary of a relevant property trust, a bereaved minor's trust or an 18 to 25 trust becomes absolutely entitled to trust assets. There is no restriction on holdover relief when assets are ***leaving*** a settlor-interested relevant property trust.

In some cases, it may be worth changing the terms of a pre-22/3/2006 interest in possession trust so that it becomes a relevant property trust (see Chapter 8). Although this will expose the trust to anniversary and exit charges, the ability to hold over any capital gain arising when assets leave the trust may produce greater CGT savings than any resultant IHT cost.

Chapter 13

# The Family Home

## 13.1 WHEN OUR MAIN ASSET BECOMES OUR MAIN LIABILITY

For most of us, the family home is our major asset. In the past, it has often also been the main cause of IHT liabilities. However, with both the TNRB (see Section 6.2) and RNRB (Section 3.4) now available in many cases, for many people the family home is no longer a problem from an IHT standpoint.

Many people now have exemptions totalling £1m available to cover their family home, made up as follows:

| | |
|---|---|
| Nil rate band | £325,000 |
| Transferable NRB | £325,000 |
| Residence NRB | £175,000 |
| Transferable RNRB | £175,000 |
| Total exemption available: | £1,000,000 |

As discussed in Section 12.7, many married couples, widows, or widowers, intending to leave their home to their children no longer need to worry about IHT on the family home and would do better to focus on other assets.

It is also important to remember giving your home away may mean you are unable to benefit from the RNRB. We will look at this issue further in Section 13.12. Selling your home will have a different effect, however, and we will return to this subject in Section 13.11.

But not everyone fits neatly into the Government's 1950s-style vision of a world where everyone gets married, raises a family, and lives happily ever after: until the time comes to hand 40% of everything over to them!

There are many people who will still not enjoy the £1m of exemption George Osborne promised back in 2007. These people are among many others who still face potential IHT liabilities on the family home, including:

- Those with a home worth in excess of £1m
- Single, divorced, or unmarried people. You have to become a widow/widower in order to benefit from the TNRB or transferable RNRB. This does not apply to everyone! Those who never become a widow or widower will only be able to enjoy maximum total exemptions of £500,000 (at current rates)
- Widows and widowers with a property worth in excess of £325,000 and who do not have the benefit of a full TNRB. Those whose former spouse used some or all of their NRB will not be able to enjoy the full £1m of exemption detailed above unless they remarry. In some cases, they may also be unable to claim any of their former spouse's RNRB. See Chapter 6 and Section 3.4 for more details

- Those with estates worth in excess of £2m and a home worth in excess of £650,000; or £325,000 if they never become a widow or widower. These people will lose some or all of their RNRB due to the tapering provisions (Section 3.4)
- Those who do not intend to leave their family home to direct descendants. Not everyone has children, and not everyone who does intends to leave their home to those children. If you do not leave your home to your direct descendants (see Section 3.4 for details), or to the right kind of trust for their benefit (see Section 8.6), then you will not be entitled to the RNRB. This will leave your home exposed to IHT on any value in excess of £650,000; or £325,000 if you never become a widow or widower.

As we can see, there are many people who still need to take action to protect the family home from IHT.

As already mentioned in Section 4.8, the major stumbling block to effective IHT planning with the family home is the gifts with reservation provisions. Another issue to consider is the pre-owned assets charge, although this will rarely apply in practice: the potential risks posed to the planning techniques in this chapter were summarised in Section 11.12.

Despite these drawbacks, there are still a number of methods for saving IHT on the family home. Many of the methods described in this chapter will also have CGT implications for the transferee. These are discussed in more detail in Section 12.7. For more information on CGT, SDLT, or any related reliefs, on residential property, see the Taxcafe guide *How to Save Property Tax*.

The methods described in Sections 13.5 to 13.7 are only beneficial for married couples where one or both spouses already have a TNRB available (see Section 6.8). Any methods that involve mortgages, loans, or other borrowings will only work if those liabilities are repaid out of the assets of the deceased's estate, or if there is a valid commercial reason for non-repayment (see Section 2.10 for further details).

See also Sections 6.6 and 12.6 regarding a potential opportunity for married couples who are separating or divorcing to pass on the whole or a part share in the family home free of both IHT and CGT.

## 13.2 MOVE OUT THEN GIVE IT AWAY

If you can afford to, and are willing to do it, you can simply move out of the property then give it away. The gift is a PET that will escape IHT as long as you survive seven years. Furthermore, as long as you make the gift within nine months of the date you move out of the property, it will also be exempt from CGT under private residence relief.

If you are prepared to do this, you could then move into rented accommodation, or buy a more modest property.

No gift with reservation should arise as long as you never move back into the property, or only do so under unforeseen circumstances that meet the requirements detailed in Section 4.8.

## 13.3 SELL UP OR RE-MORTGAGE

If you can't quite afford to follow the strategy in Section 13.2, you could, instead, sell your current home, buy a smaller one, and give away the surplus left-over cash. All you need to do then is survive another seven years. If you're feeling really brave, you could even give away all the sale proceeds and move into rented property. While this is good IHT planning, it doesn't leave you with much security in your old age and it might cause some problems with the local authority if you ever need to go into a residential care home.

Alternatively, if you would prefer to stay in your current home, another way to get most of its value out of your estate is to re-mortgage the property then give away or spend the borrowed funds.

The outstanding mortgage balance will be deducted from your estate (subject to the rules explained in Section 2.10) and this will reduce your IHT bill as long as you have either given away the borrowed funds and survived seven years, or spent the borrowed funds before you die.

The major drawback to this method is the need to service the mortgage from your retirement income. Hence, a sensible refinement may be to buy an annuity with some or all of the mortgage proceeds. This will enable you to service the debt and give away or spend any surplus. The problem then, of course, is that in the event of a premature death shortly after purchasing the annuity, a lot of your home's value will have been lost: not to His Majesty's Treasury, but to the annuity provider.

A better approach might be to release equity in your property, either by selling or re-mortgaging it, and invest the proceeds in a discounted gift trust (Section 9.8) or loan trust (Section 9.9). These investments provide an effective income stream, but also carry the advantage that your wealth is not lost in the event of a premature death.

Alternatively, you could sell your property and invest the proceeds in AIM shares (Section 7.26). You would need to limit your investment to the amount you can genuinely afford, as any subsequent borrowings, including any mortgage on a new property, would be deemed to have indirectly funded the purchase (Section 7.27). Hence, while AIM shares provide a complete shelter from IHT (after two years), they are probably only suitable where you sell the family home, buy something smaller, and just invest the surplus.

A final alternative may be to invest some of your proceeds in a pension, although this is subject to the limitations discussed in Section 10.7, including the fact you need to be under 75 and still have sufficient earned income.

## 13.4 SALE AT MARKET VALUE

If you sell your property to your children, or other beneficiaries, at full market value, no transfer of value will take place and hence the property will immediately be excluded from your estate for IHT purposes.

However, whether the sale proceeds are paid in cash or left outstanding as a loan, they will remain in your estate. Your beneficiaries will also have to pay SDLT. The rates can be quite prohibitive for a more valuable property and they will have to pay the 3% surcharge on top if they have any other residential property.

Any prior arrangement to give any part of the sale proceeds back to the purchaser, or waive any loan balance, will render this planning void, since the sale would not have taken place on arm's length terms, as required, and a transfer of value will have taken place.

Furthermore, there must not be any obligation on the purchaser to allow you to continue to occupy the property. This means you will subsequently only be able to live in the property under an informal licence to occupy, which is totally at the purchaser's whim. This will not suit everyone!

If the purchaser pays you in cash, perhaps in instalments, you will be free to spend the proceeds, perhaps to support yourself in your retirement. Any future growth in the property's value is also safely excluded from your estate.

As you spend the proceeds and the property grows in value, the reduction in your taxable estate starts to accumulate. These savings also start immediately after the sale and it is not necessary to survive for any period to benefit. Alternatively, you could invest the proceeds in one of the IHT shelters suggested in Section 13.3.

On the other hand, as time passes there is a danger that the adverse CGT considerations discussed in Section 12.7 could outweigh any IHT savings. Combining these with the SDLT cost of putting the plan into place may sometimes render this technique too costly to be worthwhile.

## 13.5 THE WIDOW'S LOAN SCHEME & THE FAMILY HOME

The method described in Section 6.11 generally works just as well for the family home as for any other assets. Probably better, in fact, as there is an asset on which to secure the loan and thus give it the necessary commercial substance. As explained in Chapter 6, however, this method is now only worth exploring where one or both spouses already has a TNRB available.

***Example:*** *Oscar and Freddie are registered civil partners and equal joint tenants in common of a house worth £1.3m. Each of them already has a full TNRB available from the death of a previous spouse. Freddie dies in December 2023 and leaves an amount equivalent to twice the NRB, £650,000, to a discretionary trust. He leaves everything else to Oscar.*

*No IHT is payable on Freddie's death, since the legacy to the discretionary trust is covered by his NRB and TNRB and the rest of his estate is covered by the spouse exemption.*

*The trust takes a charge for £650,000 over the couple's house and then passes the title to Freddie's share over to Oscar. Oscar survives Freddie by just over two years and passes away in January 2026. At this time, the house is worth £1.4m.*

*The value of the house in Oscar's estate is reduced to £750,000 by the £650,000 charge taken by Freddie's discretionary trust (provided the charge meets the necessary conditions explained in Sections 2.10 and 6.11). After deducting the NRB of £325,000 and Oscar's TNRB from his previous marriage, just £100,000 of the house's value is subject to IHT at 40%, giving a charge of £40,000.*

*Without the widow's loan scheme, the whole value of the house would have been subject to IHT on Oscar's death. After deducting the NRB and his TNRB, a value of £750,000 would have been subject to IHT at 40%, giving a charge of £300,000. The widow's loan scheme has thus produced a saving of £260,000.*

Further details of how to implement the widow's loan scheme and some of the pitfalls to be avoided are given in Section 6.11.

## 13.6 LEAVE A SHARE TO THE CHILDREN

Another method that may be worth considering where one or both of a married couple are already entitled to a TNRB is to simply leave a share in the property to your children, who will then, after your death, own it jointly with your surviving spouse. See Section 6.8 for guidance on the value this share should ideally have in order to optimise the overall IHT position. Any RNRB to which you are entitled should also be taken into account. Remember, as explained in Section 11.4, a joint share in a property held as tenants in common may be any proportion and need not be an equal share.

If your surviving spouse and children sell the property immediately after your death, there should be no CGT liability: the children will benefit from the CGT uplift on death (see Section 12.2) and the surviving spouse should be covered by the main residence exemption.

Opinions differ, however, on the more common situation that arises when the property is retained and the surviving spouse continues to occupy it.

The surviving spouse's joint share gives them a continuing right of occupation. Some experts think this means the survivor can remain in the property without paying any rent and the children's share of the property does not need to be included in their estate. Hence, as planned, when the surviving spouse dies, their estate would only include their share of the property.

Other experts, however, believe the surviving spouse's continuing occupation amounts to an interest in possession and the children's share of the property would therefore fall into their estate unless they pay rent for their occupation of that share. Still others consider a relevant property trust would come into being in respect of the children's share of the property. The consequences of this are explored below.

Unfortunately, at present, it is not yet clear which set of experts is correct and HMRC has refused to comment. Personally, I've always favoured the view of the first set of experts, which means the IHT planning will work as intended, although it must be admitted the position is now far from certain.

If the method does work as intended, it still has the drawback that the children are exposed to CGT on the growth in value of their share of the property after the first parent's death. However, the resultant CGT liability arising will often be considerably less than the IHT saving. Furthermore, if the family intend to retain the property in the long term, CGT is less of a concern anyway.

Another issue to consider is the fact this simple route relies on your children, and, more particularly, ***their*** spouses or partners, getting along OK with your spouse after you're gone. In practice, this is not always the case, and families in this situation have been known to come to blows (both metaphorically and physically). The joint owners have even been known to force the surviving spouse into selling the former family home against their wishes.

The best way around these practical problems is for the children to set up a trust with the surviving spouse as both trustee and beneficiary. After inheriting a share in the property, the children transfer this into the trust. The provisions of the trust are that the property reverts to the children, as settlors, on the death of the surviving spouse.

The drawback is that the trust set up by the children will be a relevant property trust (see Chapter 8). The transfer into the trust will be a chargeable lifetime transfer, and the trust will be subject to anniversary and exit charges. Nevertheless, these charges may well be substantially less than the amount saved by keeping part of the property out of the surviving spouse's estate. In many cases, where each individual child's share of the property is worth less than the NRB, the structure may, in practice, still avoid IHT altogether.

The children will be unable to benefit from any CGT uplift (in respect of the trust's share of the property) on the surviving spouse's death. However, if the trust were then to sell its share of the property, the main residence exemption should be available as the property had been the main residence of the trust beneficiary (the surviving spouse). The trust could then pass the sale proceeds to the children.

Hence, while this technique may be slightly flawed in theory, it will often work reasonably well in practice.

The children may be subject to a gift with reservation if they have any use or enjoyment of the property during the life interest of the surviving spouse. As the property is ultimately intended to pass to the children, this will not generally pose much of a problem, although there is the risk one of the children might pre-decease the surviving spouse. Minor, incidental use of the property, such as limited social visits, should not cause any difficulty, however.

## 13.7 LEAVE A SHARE TO A DISCRETIONARY TRUST

In Section 6.10, we looked at the drawbacks to using a discretionary Will Trust and the possible problem of it being treated as an immediate post-death interest and thus falling into the surviving spouse's estate. As explained in Chapter 6, this is now only a problem for certain 'second time around' married couples.

A possible solution to this problem, where it still exists, is to leave an appropriate share in the family home (see Section 6.8 for what is appropriate) to a discretionary trust in which the surviving spouse is ***not*** a beneficiary.

As explained in Section 13.6, as a joint owner, the surviving spouse already has a right to occupy the property, so the fact they are not a beneficiary of the discretionary trust does not make any practical difference to them.

After an interval of at least two years and a day, the discretionary trust can be changed into an interest in possession trust in favour of the surviving spouse. This will be a relevant property trust and hence will not fall into the surviving spouse's estate. Anniversary and exit charges may apply but these may be avoided if the trust's share of the property is not worth more than the NRB.

This technique is a fairly new idea and, as such, it is currently untested. Even the experts are still debating whether it actually works in practice!

## 13.8 THE FULL CONSIDERATION METHOD

The gifts with reservation rules can be bypassed if, after giving the property to your children, you pay them a full commercial rent for continuing to live in it. Payment of the rent would also further reduce your estate for IHT purposes.

It is ***essential*** rental payments are made under an enforceable legal obligation, rather than a mere casual arrangement. Hence, a formal lease will generally be required and the rent should be subject to a regular review, in line with normal commercial practice. The pre-owned assets rules (Section 11.12) require a review every five years, but a more frequent review may be required to prevent a gift with reservation.

The major drawbacks to this method are the fact your children have to account for Income Tax on the rent they receive and are also fully exposed to CGT on the future growth in value of the property.

## 13.9 CO-OWNERSHIP

This method is popular with widows, widowers and other single parents who have single, adult children. Quite simply, you put the property into joint ownership with one or more of your adult children then live together with them there.

The transfer of one or more shares in the property is a PET as long as the child or children are living there. It is the children's occupation of the property that prevents the transfer being a gift with reservation.

However, if one or more of the donee children should subsequently move out of the property while the parent is still in occupation, the gift with reservation rules will come into play: unless the parent pays a full market rent for their use of the child's share; or the child rents their share to another occupier.

It is important each party bears their share of the household running costs. If any child were to pay the full household running costs, or even just part of the parent's share, a gift with reservation would have taken place and the IHT planning will be undone.

While in practice this method works best when the children remain single, there is nothing in principle to prevent it from continuing to work when they marry, or even have children of their own. It just gets crowded!

## 13.10 THE THREE-WAY SPLIT

Following the introduction of the TNRB, most married couples should now be protected from IHT on a property worth up to twice the NRB. This method may exempt a property worth up to three times the NRB (£975,000 at current rates).

To follow this method, we need to make an assumption about which spouse will die first. If we get this wrong, the survivor will have to think again (but should not get an immediate IHT bill). For the sake of illustration, let's assume it is a heterosexual marriage and the husband will probably die first (statistics would support us on this).

First, if the property is in England or Wales, we put it into a tenancy in common. Next, we divide the ownership so that two thirds goes to the husband and one third to the wife. On the husband's death, he leaves half his share (one third of the total) to a life interest trust in favour of his wife, with the remainder to the children (or other beneficiaries). This will qualify as an immediate post-death interest (Section 8.12) and hence fall within the wife's estate. Most importantly, it will be an exempt transfer. Later, the wife allows an early termination of her life interest and passes that one third share of the property to the children. This will be a PET, and will be exempt from IHT as long as she survives another seven years.

The husband leaves the other half of his share to a discretionary trust, thus utilising his NRB. At some convenient date more than two years later, this trust can be wound up and the property share will be passed to the children. Alternatively, to protect the widow, it may be better to keep the trust going and perhaps pay some modest anniversary charges.

When the widow dies, her NRB can be utilised against her remaining one third share of the property.

As discussed in Section 13.6, some experts would argue the widow has an interest in possession in the discretionary trust's share of the property and the scheme would therefore fail. Again, the position on this is not clear.

Before the introduction of the TNRB, many people took the view this scheme was worth a try as there was nothing to lose. Now, however, the scheme generally represents something of a gamble since it means sacrificing the TNRB. It will certainly only be worth considering where the property is worth considerably in excess of twice the NRB, plus any available RNRB.

## 13.11 DOWNSIZING

The RNRB may be claimed against other assets or cash left to direct descendants, or certain types of trust for their benefit (see Section 8.6), to the extent these assets are covered by the sale proceeds of a former qualifying private residence sold after 8th July 2015 (see Section 3.4 for details of direct descendants and qualifying private residences).

Such a claim under the 'downsizing' provisions may be made when an individual dies with no qualifying private residence, or an individual had a more valuable qualifying residence at some time after 8th July 2015.

To be more precise, the downsizing provisions actually apply when you previously had a more valuable residence ***as a proportion*** of the RNRB applying, or deemed to apply, at that time. As the RNRB has increased significantly since it was first introduced, this is not the same thing as a more valuable residence in absolute terms. In fact, a ***less*** valuable residence sold before 6th April 2020 may sometimes allow you to increase your RNRB claim using the downsizing provisions.

The RNRB applying, or deemed to apply, at the time of the property's sale for the purpose of these provisions is:

| **Sales completed** | **Residence Nil Rate Band** |
|---|---|
| 9th July 2015 to 5th April 2018 | £100,000 |
| 6th April 2018 to 5th April 2019 | £125,000 |
| 6th April 2019 to 5th April 2020 | £150,000 |
| After 5th April 2020 | £175,000 |

There is no need to actually trace the sale proceeds of the former qualifying private residence; it is simply a case of using the amount of those proceeds to derive the available exemption. Nonetheless, the relief may only be claimed against amounts, or the value of assets, which actually do go to qualifying beneficiaries or trusts. Furthermore, only actual sale proceeds (not deemed proceeds) may be used in the calculation of the relief available.

A widow or widower may include any RNRB transferred from their deceased spouse within their downsizing claim. The maximum claim is derived as follows:

i) Calculate the proportion of the individual's maximum available RNRB actually used against qualifying property on their death
ii) Calculate the proportion of the individual's maximum available RNRB that could have been used if the individual had died immediately before selling the former qualifying residence, based on the assumption the actual sale proceeds received for the property represented its open market value
iii) Deduct the proportion derived under step (i) from the proportion derived under step (ii)
iv) The maximum relief available under the downsizing provisions is derived by multiplying the individual's maximum available RNRB by the proportion derived under step (iii)

The amount of RNRB used for the purposes of the calculation at step (ii) is dependent on the date of sale of the former residence, as detailed above. To this we add any RNRB transferred from the individual's deceased spouse: BUT the transferred RNRB is not the amount available at the time of the property's sale, it is the amount available at the time of the widow or widower's death.

***Example 1:*** *Billie has been divorced for many years. In March 2017, she sold her house for £80,000 and moved into a care home. When she dies in March 2024, she does not own any qualifying property and leaves her entire estate to her son, Duke. The sale proceeds for Billie's house amount to 80% of the RNRB deemed to have been available to her at that time (£100,000). The maximum amount of RNRB to which she would be entitled on her death is £175,000. Hence, she may claim an exemption of £140,000 (£175,000 x 80%) under the downsizing provisions.*

***Example 2:*** *Marty is a widower whose wife died many years ago with a very modest estate. In August 2018, he sold his home for £225,000 and moved into a small bungalow. When Marty dies in January 2024, he leaves his entire estate to his daughter, Kim, including the bungalow, which is then worth £105,000.*

*If Marty had died in August 2018, he would have been entitled to a RNRB of £125,000. To this we must add a full RNRB entitlement transferred from his late wife, but we count this as £175,000, the amount applying at the time of Marty's death. This produces a total of £300,000, so the sale proceeds of £225,000 for Marty's former home are deemed to represent 75% of his maximum entitlement (£225,000/£300,000 = 75%).*

*When Marty dies, his maximum RNRB entitlement is £350,000 (2 x £175,000). He therefore uses only 30% of his entitlement (£105,000/£350,000 = 30%).*

*Marty is able to claim 45% (75% less 30%) of his maximum RNRB entitlement under the downsizing provisions. Hence, £157,500 (£350,000 x 45%) of other assets left to Kim can be exempted under the RNRB, in addition to Marty's bungalow.*

Where an individual dies owning a qualifying private residence, but does not leave that property to a direct descendent, or a qualifying trust for their benefit, any RNRB available is effectively reduced by the value of that qualifying private residence.

For example, if Marty had left his bungalow to his brother, Ricky, the RNRB available to exempt the assets left to Kim would have remained £157,500, but there would be no exemption on the bungalow itself.

**Making the Most of the Residence Nil Rate Band**

Thanks to the downsizing provisions, many married couples, widows, and widowers will be able to get the maximum benefit from the RNRB by ensuring they own a private residence worth at least £350,000 at some stage. To get the maximum possible relief, they will also need to ensure they:

- Have equity of at least this amount in the property (after deducting any mortgage against it),
- Sell the property for actual proceeds (rather than give it away, etc), or keep it until they die
- Leave at least one of any qualifying properties they own at the time of their death to their direct descendants, or a suitable trust for their benefit (see Section 8.6), and
- Leave sufficient further sums to qualifying beneficiaries or trusts in order to fully utilise the relief available under the downsizing provisions

The third and fourth steps can take place on the second death. The third step becomes unnecessary where no qualifying properties are held at the time of death.

**Earlier Property Sales**

The maximum potential RNRB may also be available as a result of an earlier sale of a qualifying property for at least the following amounts (net of any mortgage over the property):

| | |
|---|---|
| Sales between 9th July 2015 and 5th April 2018: | £275,000 |
| Sales during 2018/19: | £300,000 |
| Sales during 2019/20: | £325,000 |

**Single People & Unmarried Couples**

Similar principles apply to single or divorced people, and unmarried couples, but each individual will need to own a share in a property, net of any mortgage, worth at least £175,000 at some stage after 8th July 2015, or to have sold a share in a property for at least the following amounts (again, net of their share of any mortgage):

| | |
|---|---|
| Sales between 9th July 2015 and 5th April 2018: | £100,000 |
| Sales during 2018/19: | £125,000 |
| Sales during 2019/20: | £150,000 |

For an unmarried couple, the third and fourth steps described above will need to take place on ***each*** death.

## 13.12 THE RESIDENCE NIL RATE BAND AND GIFTS WITH RESERVATION

Many of the planning techniques described in this chapter involve a lifetime transfer of the family home and are designed to avoid a gift with reservation. Sadly, if the planning is not carried out correctly, a gift with reservation may still arise (e.g. failing to pay full market rent under the full consideration method in Section 13.8). A gift with reservation will also arise on a simple gift of the property while the original owner is still in occupation. We looked at the CGT implications of a gift with reservation of the family home in Section 12.8, but what happens to the RNRB in these situations?

***Example Part 1:*** *Marilyn has been a widow since her husband, Jack died in 2018. Jack left his entire estate, worth £1m, to Marilyn, including their family home, at 63 Fitzgerald Gardens. In May 2023, Marilyn gives Fitzgerald Gardens to her son, Curtis, when the house is worth £425,000, but continues to live there on her own.*

The gift of Fitzgerald Gardens represents a gift with reservation. Hence, if Marilyn should die while still residing in the property, its value will be included in her estate. As she gave the property to a direct descendant, she will be able to claim the RNRB against it. Including the RNRB transferred from Jack, she can claim up to £350,000 at current rates (see Section 3.4).

However, as we saw in Section 4.8, if Marilyn dies within seven years of making the transfer, we must also prepare a second calculation, on the basis that the transfer ***did*** take place. While this second calculation will be based on the property's value at the date of transfer, the RNRB will not be available as the transfer has not taken place on death.

***Example Part 2:*** *In June 2026, Marilyn is taken seriously ill. Things are touch and go for a while, it is not clear if she will recover. Her advisers, Miller & Co., prepare some deathbed planning options for her. At the same time, they carry out a preliminary assessment of her IHT position if she should die. Under the first calculation, Fitzgerald Gardens, now worth £535,000 is included in her estate but she is able to set off her RNRB entitlement of £350,000, leaving £185,000 exposed to IHT and resulting in a charge of £74,000 on the house (at 40%).*

*In the second calculation, the gift of Fitzgerald Gardens in 2023 becomes a chargeable lifetime transfer. While the gift is covered by Marilyn's NRB and part of her TNRB, it still results in an extra £425,000 of her remaining estate being exposed to IHT, increasing her IHT bill by £170,000. As this calculation produces the greater tax, this is the one used if Marilyn were to die. The gift of Fitzgerald Gardens would thus cost Marilyn's family an extra £96,000.*

Once more than seven years have elapsed since the gift with reservation, the second calculation is no longer required. The property remains in the transferor's estate for IHT purposes and, where it has been gifted to a direct descendant, the RNRB continues to be available. As far as IHT is concerned, it is really as if the transfer had never taken place.

However, while the gift with reservation is ineffective for IHT purposes, it can be disastrous for CGT (see Section 12.8). On the other hand, where tax is not a concern, there is the practical advantage that title to the property has already passed without the need to wait for probate. It might also avoid a few family squabbles in some cases.

The IHT position changes again when the reservation comes to an end. Surprisingly, in many cases, this may actually make matters worse!

***Example Part 3:*** *Thankfully, Marilyn makes a full recovery and continues to live in Fitzgerald Gardens for several more years until, in June 2031, she decides she is tired of living alone and moves in with her sister, Jane. This means the reservation over Fitzgerald Gardens comes to an end, and Marilyn is treated as making a PET. By this time, Fitzgerald Gardens is worth £760,000.*

If Marilyn dies any time in the next seven years, the deemed PET in 2031 will become a chargeable lifetime transfer of £760,000 and the RNRB will ***not*** be available. This means her NRB (and TNRB) will be used first against Fitzgerald Gardens, thus costing her family an additional £304,000 in IHT on her death (see Note 2).

***Example Part 4:*** *Sadly, Marilyn passes away in June 2033 when Fitzgerald Gardens is worth £875,000. If the reservation had still applied, the property would be treated as part of her estate, but the RNRB, which is £205,000 by this time, would have been available. With Jack's transferred RNRB, this would have given Marilyn a total exemption of £410,000, leaving only £465,000 of Fitzgerald Gardens' value exposed to IHT, giving rise to a charge of £186,000. Ending the reservation has therefore cost Marilyn's family an additional £118,000 (£304,000 – £186,000) in IHT.*

Where a property eligible for the RNRB is subject to a gift with reservation, ***ending*** the reservation within seven years prior to the original owner's death could lead to additional IHT of up to £140,000 at current rates, possibly more in future.

In many cases, it may be unlikely the original owner will survive for seven years after ending the reservation. It may therefore be better to keep the reservation going. But this could be difficult if the original owner's health begins to fail and they need to be taken into care. Nonetheless, with up to £140,000 at stake, it may be worth the additional cost of having them cared for at home.

A potential alternative strategy in this scenario might be to rent the property out and ensure the rental income goes to the original owner, or is applied for their benefit: perhaps to pay nursing home fees. Better still: avoid the gift with reservation in the first place!

**Notes to the Example**

1. I assumed throughout the example that Marilyn's estate will not exceed the threshold for tapering of the RNRB (currently £2m: see Section 3.4).
2. Future values for the NRB and RNRB are based on our projections in Section 3.2. Based on those projections, on a death after 5th April 2033, Fitzgerald Gardens would use up £760,000 of Marilyn's NRB and TNRB, leading to the cost of £304,000 in the example. On an earlier death, Fitzgerald Gardens would completely use up Marilyn's NRB and TNRB with the excess exposed to IHT. As this would be less than three years after the deemed PET, there would be no taper relief. Hence the overall cost would again be £304,000.
3. See Section 12.8 regarding the CGT implications of a gift with reservation of the family home, which again apply in this example.

**Summary**

The position on a gift with reservation, where the RNRB is available on the gifted property, can be summarised in most cases as follows (assuming the property is increasing in value):

**Death within seven years of gift; reservation still in effect:** IHT is charged on the greater of the property's value at the date of death ***less*** the amount of RNRB available; **or** the property's value at the date of the gift. This leaves the family worse off than if the gift had never taken place: unless the property increases in value between the date of gift and the date of death by more than the amount of RNRB available; in which case it leaves the family no better or worse off for IHT purposes.

**Death more than seven years after gift; reservation still in effect:** IHT is charged on the property's value at the date of death ***less*** the available RNRB. This leaves the family no better or worse off for IHT purposes.

**Death within seven years after the reservation has ceased:** IHT is charged on the property's value at the date the reservation ceased. This leaves the family worse off than if the gift had never taken place: unless the property increases in value between the date the reservation ceases and the date of death by more than the amount of RNRB available.

**Death more than seven years after the reservation has ceased:** the property escapes IHT. This obviously leaves the family better off for IHT purposes, but, like all the other scenarios, the CGT position also needs to be taken into account (see Section 12.8).

To summarise the summary, there are two seven-year periods (the first and third scenarios) when the gift with reservation is likely to leave the family worse off. Although these periods may overlap, this still means up to fourteen years of increased exposure to IHT.

Where there is a gap between these periods (the second scenario) the family is no better off during the interval. Only the fourth scenario produces an IHT saving: and even then there is likely to be a CGT cost.

**Valuable Properties or Estates**

The position may sometimes differ where the value of the property at either the time of the gift, or the time the reservation ceases, was more than the amount of the NRB, plus any available TNRB, at the time of the transferor's death. In the case of the transferor's death more than three, but less than seven, years after the original gift, this will reduce the IHT arising under the second calculation. However, where the reservation still applies, this can, at best, still only leave the family no better or worse off than if the gift had never taken place.

Once the reservation ceases, the position will remain the same as described above for the first three years thereafter. It is only when the transferor dies more than three years after the reservation ceases that transfers of these more valuable properties may begin to produce additional IHT savings, although detailed calculations are required to fully assess the position where the transferor does not survive the full seven years.

I have also assumed throughout this section that the RNRB is available, and will not be eliminated by the tapering provisions (Section 3.4). If the RNRB was not available, there would generally be IHT savings on a death any time after the reservation ceases, although the CGT costs would remain.

## Chapter 14

# Family Investment Companies

### 14.1 INTRODUCTION TO FAMILY INVESTMENT COMPANIES

A 'family investment company' is a broad term used to describe companies set up to hold investments, including investment property, rental property, etc; and also used to pass wealth to, or share it with, adult children or other family members.

In addition to the IHT planning benefits we will explore in this chapter, holding investment or rental property through a company can also produce substantial tax savings on income and capital gains during your lifetime. These are explored in detail in the Taxcafe guide *Using a Property Company to Save Tax*, as well as tax issues around transferring property to a company, including CGT, SDLT, and the rates, charges and reliefs applying under both taxes, as referred to in this chapter.

Family investment companies come in a number of forms, with a variety of share structures, loan accounts, etc. In this chapter, we will explore some of the most popular structures.

### 14.2 SHELL COMPANIES AND LOAN ACCOUNTS

A simple method to create a family investment company is to start by setting up a new, 'shell' company with a small nominal value, say £100. New companies can easily be set up via an online service at a very modest cost (less than £50 in many cases, but more if you require a complex share structure).

The next step is to transfer the shares to your adult children or other intended beneficiaries. It is important to do this while the company is still an empty shell as this means the transfer of value is very small, just the value of the nominal share capital and in most cases, covered by your annual exemption.

You now transfer your investments, rental property, etc, to the company in exchange for an interest-free loan account, repayable on demand. The loan account means you have received full consideration for the transfer: hence no transfer of value has taken place and no IHT charges can arise.

***Example:*** *Joe and Katherine are a married couple with ten adult children and wish them all to benefit equally from their substantial residential rental property portfolio, worth £4m, and comprising twenty properties. They also have cash and other investments of £1m and a home of their own worth £800,000. At present, they have no other income apart from their rental property and a small amount of savings and investment income. In future, they will each receive a modest state pension, but they have made no other pension provision.*

*They set up a family investment company (FIC), Gary Investments Ltd, with a nominal share capital of £100 and then give 10% of the shares to each of their children. These transfers are covered by their annual exemptions and are thus immediately exempt from IHT and cannot be subject to the pre-owned assets charge.*

*They now transfer their entire property portfolio to the company in exchange for an interest-free loan account of £4m. Unfortunately, while this is free from IHT (as no transfer of value has taken place) it must be treated as a sale at market value for the purposes of both CGT and SDLT.*

*Let us suppose the portfolio was originally purchased for a total cost of £1.5m. This means the couple have capital gains of £2.5m, giving rise to CGT of £700,000 (at 28%: I have assumed they are both higher rate taxpayers).*

*Additionally, the company has a SDLT bill of £120,000. Joe and Katherine lend this sum to the company to enable it to pay the SDLT. They also lend the company a further £80,000 to give it some working capital, thus taking their loan account balance to a total of £4.2m.*

*The property portfolio yields an annual profit before tax of £275,000. After paying Corporation Tax at 25% and setting aside a small reserve, the company is able to repay £200,000 to Joe and Katherine each year, giving them sufficient money to live on. While this is effectively an income stream, it is tax free, as it is a loan repayment and therefore not subject to Income Tax.*

*Ten years later, the loan account balance has reduced to £2.2m; the rental property portfolio is worth £7.5m; Joe and Katherine's home is worth £1.5m; and the NRB and RNRB have increased to £381,000 and £205,000 respectively. Let's take a look at the couple's IHT exposure at this stage:*

| | | ***With FIC*** | ***Without FIC*** |
|---|---|---|---|
| *Property portfolio* | | - | *£7.5m* |
| *Home* | | *£1.5m* | *£1.5m* |
| *Loan account* | | *£2.2m* | - |
| *Cash and investments** | | *£0.1m*** | *£1m* |
| *Total assets* | | *£3.8m* | *£10m* |
| *Less:* | *NRBs* | *£0.762m* | *£0.762m* |
| | *RNRBs**** | *£0.41m* | - |
| *Chargeable estate* | | *£2.628m* | *£9.238m* |
| *IHT exposure at 40%* | | *£1.051m* | *£3.7m* |

** Assumed no growth as after tax income and capital gains used to pay living costs*
*** Reduced by payment of CGT, SDLT and loan of further £80,000 to the company*
**** Using the company, the couple's estates now amount to less than £2m each, so they should be able to benefit from their RNRBs if they plan carefully. Without the company the tapering provisions (Section 3.4) will mean no RNRBs are available*

After ten years, the family investment company has reduced Joe and Katherine's IHT exposure by £2.65m. However, this has come at a significant cost, with a total of £820,000 in tax paid at the outset. Nonetheless, there is still an overall net saving, after ten years, of over £1.8m.

You might wonder if Joe and Katherine could have achieved greater savings by simply giving properties directly to the children. Let's say they gave two properties to each child, so their total CGT bills would be the same. This would avoid the SDLT charges but, as the gifts to the children would be PETs, the value of the properties would remain in Joe and Katherine's estates, still exposed to IHT, for the next seven years. Furthermore, it is unlikely that all the properties would have an equal value, making it impossible to treat the children fairly, as Joe and Katherine wish.

But the biggest problem with these direct gifts is they would leave Joe and Katherine with almost nothing to live on in their retirement!

To summarise, a family investment company has the following advantages:

- There is no transfer of value, hence IHT savings start to accumulate immediately
- There are no immediate IHT charges on transfers in excess of the NRB
- The loan account provides a tax-free income stream
- Profits and capital gains arising within the company are subject to Corporation Tax at 25% at most, instead of Income Tax at up to 45% (even more in some cases) and CGT at up to 28%
- Children or other beneficiaries can benefit equally, or in whatever proportions you wish (this can be difficult to achieve with direct transfers or bequests)

To further illustrate the benefits of a family investment company, the table below shows the overall saving achieved under the scenario set out in the example above, with the following additional assumptions:

i) Property values grow at a compound rate of 7.5% per year
ii) The first parent to die leaves their entire estate to the surviving spouse
iii) Joe and Katherine spend all the cash they receive from the company, from pensions, and from their investments
iv) Rental profits from the property portfolio remain at the same level
v) Income Tax rates and thresholds remain at 2023/24 levels: see Appendix A (they are currently expected to remain at these levels until at least 2027/28 in any case)
vi) The Corporation Tax rate for companies with annual profits in excess of £250,000 remains 25%

| Second Death After (Years) | Estate without FIC | Estate using FIC | IHT Saved | Overall Net Saving/(Cost)* |
|---|---|---|---|---|
| 1 | £6,160,000 | £4,960,000 | £480,000 | (£312,594) |
| 2 | £6,547,000 | £4,824,500 | £689,000 | (£76,188) |
| 3 | £6,963,025 | £4,693,838 | £907,675 | £169,893 |
| 5 | £7,891,021 | £4,448,503 | £1,377,007 | £694,037 |
| 7 | £8,963,436 | £4,227,239 | £1,894,479 | £1,266,321 |
| 10 | £10,892,951 | £3,948,825 | £2,777,650 | £2,231,710 |
| 15 | £15,202,611 | £3,667,102 | £4,614,204 | £4,205,294 |
| 20 | £21,389,685 | £3,698,281 | £7,076,562 | £6,804,682 |

* After accounting for up-front tax charges of £820,000; but also including annual tax savings on rental profits from the residential property portfolio of £27,406 each year. This saving increases to £41,203 per year after the first death, although this potential increase is not accounted for in the table.

Taking the additional Income Tax savings into account, we can see it takes just three years before the family investment company starts to produce an overall saving. As this is based on the date of the second death, this means most couples would have a good chance of benefitting from this method.

Unlike the example above, the table ignores any further savings that might be yielded if the RNRB becomes available. This will require some additional planning after the first death, but could lead to a further saving of up to £140,000 (at current rates).

**Problems and Limitations**

The major problem with this strategy is the up-front tax cost. The couple need to have sufficient liquid resources (cash and short-term investments) to cover this cost. As a very broad rule of thumb, if we say the value of your rental properties has roughly doubled since purchase, the up-front tax cost is likely to be around 17% to 20% of the value of your portfolio (it was slightly over 20% for Joe and Katherine as their portfolio had more than doubled in value).

If you do not have enough liquid resources, you will need to sell some properties, which, in turn, will lead to more CGT. Selling a former home can be helpful, however, as some or all of the gain will usually be exempt from CGT, and an arm's length sale will usually preserve your RNRB entitlement (see Section 13.11).

Alternatively, a former home may be a suitable property to transfer to the company at a lower CGT cost, although this might jeopardise your RNRB. See the Taxcafe guide *How to Save Property Tax* for further details on the CGT exemption for a former home.

In our example, I have also assumed the properties were debt-free. It may be difficult to transfer properties subject to a mortgage.

The loan account in the example will run out after twenty-one years, hopefully long enough for Joe and Katherine. Getting the duration of the loan account right is a matter of luck, or perhaps good timing, but the closer the second death is to the date the loan account is exhausted, the better.

If one or both parents survive for longer, they will need to use other resources to fund their living expenses. It is important that the children/company owners do not support them, as this could lead to problems under the gifts with reservation rules (Section 4.8), effectively bringing the value of the company shares back into their estate. In a case like Joe and Katherine, this might be the time to sell the family home and downsize (see Section 13.11), perhaps putting some surplus funds into a suitable IHT shelter, as explained in Section 13.3.

Another potential problem, in some families, is the practical issue of running the company. Sibling rivalry may render this impossible and there may also be the worry of outside influences, such as the children's partners. Some of the children may also be less mature than others, which may be a cause for concern. In the next section, we will look at some possible solutions to some of these issues.

**Not Limited**
An unmarried couple could use a family investment company in a similar way, except that IHT charges would arise on the first death. The loan accounts would need to be kept separate and it would be important to ensure both of the couple's NRBs and RNRBs were fully utilised on their deaths. Similarly, a single or divorced parent could use a family investment company, but would only benefit from a single NRB and RNRB.

A family investment company could be used to pass investment assets to other beneficiaries, such as nieces, nephews, siblings, or friends. The only difference to the figures given in the example above is that no RNRB would be available on the deceased's home where this is not left to direct descendants.

## 14.3 OPTIONAL EXTRAS

There are a number of potential refinements and improvements to the strategy discussed in the previous section.

**Golden Shares**
The parents may have a concern that their children will not be able to manage the company effectively together. To combat this, the parents can hold a 'golden share' that carries no rights to dividends, is non-transferable, and will be redeemed and cancelled on the second death. As such, the golden share will have little or no value in its own right. However, the share will carry the power to appoint or remove directors and to block any resolution to remove a director appointed by the golden shareholders. Hence, the golden

share allows the parents to intervene, if necessary, and thus ensure the smooth running of the company (often the mere threat of intervention will be enough!)

**Shares in Trust**
The family investment company's shares can be gifted to a trust rather than directly to the children. This could be used as a means to retain control over the shares allocated to a less mature (but adult) child until such time the parents feel they are responsible enough to participate directly in the company's management.

Alternatively, shares can be placed in a discretionary trust to benefit grandchildren or other family members (but not the donor's own minor children). Furthermore, if each parent sets up a separate discretionary trust to hold shares, the widow or widower could, if desired, be included as a beneficiary of the other parent's trust after the first death.

Provided the shares are held in the trust for less than ten years, no IHT charges should arise. Alternatively, it may be worth paying some anniversary or exit charges (see Chapter 8) to secure longer-term benefits (both practical and financial).

**Reducing the CGT Cost**
CGT savings may be achieved by delaying some of the transfers until a tax year when the parents' taxable income is below the higher rate tax threshold, thus enabling some of the capital gains to be taxed at 18% instead of 28% (or 10% instead of 20% for assets other than residential property). The impact on the SDLT charges arising should be taken into account, however, as this will affect the multiple dwellings relief on the transfer of residential properties.

Another way to reduce the CGT arising on the transfer may be to select properties giving rise to lower CGT bills, such as more recent acquisitions, or a former home (but bear in mind the potential impact on your RNRB).

**Avoiding the SDLT Cost**
It might be possible to avoid, or reduce, the SDLT on the transfer by initially going into partnership with your children for a few years before forming the family investment company. This will mean delaying the formation of the company. It will also mean you need to retain some shares (although, with careful planning, your shareholding may be kept small). For more details on the tax-saving potential of using partnerships as a preliminary step to forming a company, see the Taxcafe guide *Using a Property Company to Save Tax.*

**Accelerating the IHT Savings**
If the parents reach the point where they feel they have sufficient personal resources outside the company to sustain them for the rest of their lives, they can gift the benefit of some or all of the remaining loan account to the children. This will be a PET and the gifted amount will escape IHT if the donor parent survives seven years. Note, however, there may be CGT consequences for the donee on a subsequent repayment of the debt.

## 14.4 GROWTH SHARES

By creating a different share structure, incorporating growth shares, a family investment company can be used to pass on some or all of the future growth in value of your investments or rental property free from IHT. In many cases, the company can be set up with no up-front tax costs, or at least much less than using the technique in Section 14.2.

***Example:*** *James and Mary, a married couple, run a residential rental property business in partnership together. They each spend an average of more than twenty hours per week working in the business. The portfolio comprises ten houses purchased over several decades at a total cost of £1.5m and currently worth a total of £6m. Their only other significant asset is their home, worth £1.2m. They now wish to start passing on some of their wealth to their sons, Paul and Michael, but the cost of using the method in Section 14.2 would be over £1.6m (£1.26m in CGT and £355,000 in SDLT), which they simply cannot afford.*

*Instead, they transfer their property business to a new company, Walton Investments Ltd, in exchange for Class A Ordinary Shares. This transfer qualifies for incorporation relief for CGT purposes, meaning their capital gains of £4.5m can be held over against the value of their shares and no CGT liability arises at this point. The transfer of partnership property to a company controlled by the same individuals is also exempt from SDLT. Hence, there is no up-front cost of forming the company.*

*The company issues Class B Ordinary Shares to Paul and Michael. These carry the right to any growth in value in the company in future, but the first £6m of the company's assets belongs to the Class A shareholders. Hence, in effect, the Class B shares are currently worthless, there is no transfer of value, and no IHT can arise.*

*While the current value of the Class A shares, £6m, remains in James and Mary's estates, the future growth in the property portfolio's value will now effectively belong to Paul and Michael. Furthermore, if James and Mary are able to limit the dividends they withdraw from the company, any surplus after tax profits can either be paid to their sons, or accumulated within the company for their benefit.*

**Notes to the Example**

i) The transfer was only exempt from SDLT because James and Mary were operating as a partnership. In other cases, including joint ownership, SDLT will arise, and it would be necessary to operate as a partnership for a few years in order to obtain exemption.

ii) CGT incorporation relief is usually available where the business owners spend an average of at least twenty hours per week working in the business. In other cases it will depend on circumstances.

iii) Whether the Class B growth shares have any voting rights is entirely up to you. If you wish to retain control over the company, the Class B shares can be non-voting.

iv) Similarly, it is up to you whether the growth shares carry rights to dividends. My recommendation would be that they do, but this is at the discretion of the Class A shareholders (this is important to ensure the B shares have no value at the date of issue).

**Next Steps**
At this stage, James and Mary still hold £6m worth of shares. However, to date, they have not made any transfers of value. They could therefore transfer £650,000 worth of Class A shares into a trust for Paul and Michael's benefit and hold over the capital gains arising, using the method described in Section 9.4 (which works just as well for shares).

To transfer any significant further amount of shares to their sons within the next seven years, the couple face a choice of either paying CGT on a direct transfer, or IHT at the lifetime rate if they pass on shares via the trust. Since CGT only applies to the gain (not the full value), this will be the cheaper option.

If we suppose there are 10,000 Class A shares, the capital gain arising on the transfer of each individual share will be £450 (£4.5m/10,000), giving rise to a CGT bill, at 20%, of £90 (see Section 12.1: I am assuming James and Mary are higher rate taxpayers).

Funding that cost would entail taking additional dividends out of the company, on top of what James and Mary already need to fund living expenses. Hence, there would also be an Income Tax cost. For a higher rate taxpayer to take an extra £90 out of their company, they need to take a dividend of £135.85 (so that, after paying Income Tax at 33.75% on the dividend they are left with the net £90 they need: see Section 10.8 for dividend tax rates).

This means the total tax cost of passing each share worth £600 (£6m/10,000) to one of their sons is £135.85, or 22.64%; and it will be more if the couple's total taxable income goes over £100,000 (each). For an IHT saving of £240 (£600 x 40%), which will take seven years to achieve, many might not consider this to be worthwhile.

Alternatively, it might be possible to pass small parcels of shares into a series of trusts over many years, with significant extra additions every seven years, using the methodology described in Section 9.1. As the Class A shares will not increase in value, anniversary and exit charges will be negligible. Based on our assumptions regarding the NRB, if James and Mary start this strategy in 2024/25, they could have sheltered a further £3.418m worth of shares from IHT by 2045/46 (including the initial £650,000 described above). If the couple are both, say, 60 now, it is not unreasonable to suppose they will survive long enough to achieve this. (Arguably, one might say they have only sheltered £2.378m, as their projected NRBs of £520,000 each by this time, will have been fully utilised.)

A third alternative is to pursue a mix of direct transfers, with their consequent CGT and Income Tax costs, and transfers via trust, utilising the available exemptions, over many years.

Whichever method is used, there are some limiting factors to be aware of. As the parents' shareholding reduces, the amount of income they are able to take from the company will also reduce. Hence, they cannot take this past the point where they have insufficient income to live on. Furthermore, if they wish to retain control of the company, they will need to keep more than 50% of the Class A shares in either their personal ownership or within the trusts (and not allow the B shares any voting rights).

## 14.5 PICK AND MIX

The method described in Section 14.2 produces the greater IHT savings, but comes at a significant up-front tax cost. The method in Section 14.4 can be implemented with no up-front tax cost in many cases, but only achieves IHT savings on future growth in value of rental property or other investments (unless further steps are taken). It is, however, possible to have a compromise solution that combines some of the benefits of both methods.

***Example Revisited:*** *Let's go back to the same opening position we had for James and Mary at the start of the example in Section 14.4. However, let's now assume they have cash and short-term investments of at least £420,000 available to fund any up-front tax costs.*

*As before, they transfer their rental property business to Walton Investments Ltd in exchange for Class A shares but, this time, there is also cash consideration of £2m in the form of an interest-free loan account repayable on demand. This means the value of their Class A shares is now £4m (£6m – £2m).*

*Their incorporation relief is restricted to the part of the gain attributable to their shares, £3m (£4.5m x £4m/£6m), and £1.5m of their gain is exposed to CGT at 28%, giving them a CGT bill of £420,000, which they are able to fund from their savings.*

*The Class B shares can then be issued to Paul and Michael in the same way as before (except it is now the first £4m of the company's net assets that belongs to the Class A shareholders, rather than £6m).*

*Instead of taking taxable dividends, James and Mary can now take tax-free loan repayments that will reduce their loan account, thus producing significant additional IHT savings, similar to those we saw in Section 14.2, as well as significant annual Income Tax savings.*

Class A shares can subsequently be passed to Paul and Michael using the methods described in Section 14.4. The costs of direct transfers will be considerably less as James and Mary may only be basic rate taxpayers if they are funding their living costs wholly or mainly through tax free loan repayments, thus reducing some of the CGT to just 10% (see Section 12.1). This reduced CGT bill can also be funded through further loan repayments rather than taxable dividends.

## 14.6 MORE OPTIONAL EXTRAS

Once again, there are some potential refinements or improvements to the strategies discussed in Sections 14.4 and 14.5.

**Parent/Directors' Ongoing Income**

The method described in Section 14.4 will leave the parents with no income from their rental portfolio, so they will probably need to take dividends out of the company to fund living expenses.

However, provided the parents continue to play an active role in the business, they will first be able to take small annual salaries, which will provide Corporation Tax relief at up to 26.5% (see Section 10.8). Where the parents have no taxable income from outside the company, salaries of £12,570 each will be covered by their personal allowances and thus be free from Income Tax. In the case of a family investment company like Walton Investments Ltd, the salaries will usually also be free from National Insurance thanks to the employment allowance.

Hence, in many cases, paying these salaries will provide an annual Corporation Tax saving of up to £6,662 at no tax cost to the parents themselves.

Under the hybrid method explained in Section 14.5, the parents have a loan account and can thus take tax free loan repayments. However, taking the same level of salary described above will both provide the same annual Corporation Tax saving and prolong the life of the loan account.

For example, taking the same facts as the revised version of the example in Section 14.5, if James and Mary need total net income of £150,000 per year, they could increase the life of their loan account from thirteen years to sixteen, while producing Corporation Tax savings totalling up to £106,592 over the same period, by taking annual salaries of £12,570 each.

Going further, if the couple have no other sources of income from outside the company and are concerned the loan account may be exhausted too soon, it may be worth them also taking dividends of £37,700 each every year (assuming the company is making sufficient profits to fund these). The total combined Income Tax cost would be just £6,510, giving the couple total annual after tax income of £94,030 before they even need to consider loan repayments. Based on the same assumptions as before, this would extend the life of James and Mary's loan account to over thirty-five years.

But, let's not forget, the purpose of the family investment company was to save IHT, so extending the life of the loan account too far may be counter-productive!

A better solution may be to take the tax efficient salaries, the low tax dividends, and as much further money by way of loan repayments as the company can afford each year. The amount that is surplus to the parents' requirements can be invested in an IHT shelter, such as a loan trust, gift trust, AIM shares, or perhaps even gilts if the parents intend to emigrate some day (see Section 3.7).

If the parents begin to receive any taxable income from outside the company, including the state pension, they will need to revise their plans from then onwards, as the same level of salary and dividends will no longer be tax efficient. In fact, for directors over state pension age, a larger salary can often be more beneficial overall, but the dividends would need to be reduced to make sure they didn't become higher rate taxpayers. For a detailed examination of tax efficient company profit extraction for company owners of all ages, see the Taxcafe guide *Salary versus Dividends*.

Lastly, it is important to point out that if and when the parents fully retire from the business, they should no longer be paid a salary, as this will not attract Corporation Tax relief and will represent a gift with reservation, thus undermining the IHT savings that have been achieved. However, if they remain active as directors, attending board meetings, reviewing company accounts, etc, those duties alone should continue to justify a small salary, certainly at least £12,570 each.

**Pension Contributions**

Where the parents continue to run the business after the transfer, it may be possible for the company to make pension contributions of up to £60,000 per parent per year (see Sections 10.7 and 10.8). These will attract Corporation Tax relief and will also provide an effective IHT shelter, as discussed in Chapter 10.

As with salary payments, it is vital the parents do sufficient work in the business to justify the pension contributions made on their behalf, otherwise Corporation Tax relief may be denied and a gift with reservation may arise.

**Golden Shares**

If the parents may eventually wish to give 50% or more of the Class A shares to their children, they may also wish to hold a golden share (see Section 14.3) so they are able to retain control over the company. The golden share should ideally be issued at the outset before there are any concerns over values, voting rights, etc.

**Shares in Trust**

The Class B shares could be put in a trust rather than issued directly to the children, if desired. This could provide the same potential benefits as discussed in Section 14.3. If this is done at the outset, the shares would be virtually worthless, hence no transfer of value will have taken place, and no IHT charges can arise in the first ten years.

**Accelerating the IHT Savings**

If the parents have followed the method set out in Section 14.5, it may later be possible to create additional IHT savings by gifting some or all of their loan account to the children (subject, again, to the comments in Section 14.3).

Chapter 15

# Other Advanced IHT Planning Ideas

## 15.1 BUSINESS BUY BACK

Assets qualifying for 100% BPR or APR (see Chapter 7) can be transferred to a trust free from IHT. At some later stage, the transferor may decide to purchase the business back from the trust at market value. The end result would be that funds equal to the value of the business (at the time of the buy back) have been passed into the relevant property trust regime (and are thus outside any individual's estate) without incurring any entry charge on the transfer.

***Example:*** *Sheridan and Smithy own an unlisted trading company, Two Pints Ltd, which they founded some years ago for an initial investment of £1 each; the company is now worth £2m. They transfer their shares to the Barry Family Discretionary Trust to benefit their adult children, Gavin and Stacey. The transfer qualifies for BPR so no IHT arises.*

*The transfer qualifies for business asset disposal relief (see Section 12.5), so Sheridan and Smithy decide not to claim holdover relief for CGT purposes. Each of them has a capital gain of £1m, on which they each pay CGT of £100,000 (at 10%).*

*A few years later (more than two), Sheridan and Smithy buy the company back from the trust for its then market value of £3m. As the trust has held the company for the benefit of Gavin and Stacey for more than two years, it may also claim business asset disposal relief on its gain of £1m, so it pays CGT at 10%, i.e. £100,000.*

*Sheridan and Smithy pay Stamp Duty of £15,000 on the purchase (£3m x 0.5%), bringing the total tax costs incurred to date to £315,000.*

*However, a net sum of £2.9m (£3m – £100,000) has now been placed in trust with no entry charge, leading to an eventual IHT saving of £1.16m. Taking account of the tax costs incurred by Sheridan, Smithy, and the trust, (and the consequent reduction in their estates), the overall net saving achieved is £971,000 (£1.16m – £315,000 + £315,000 x 40%).*

*Furthermore, this saving will be achieved after two years not seven (i.e. once Sheridan and Smithy are eligible for BPR on the shares again) and no exit charges will apply to funds paid out to the trust beneficiaries within ten years of when the trust was set up.*

By way of comparison, a couple putting a net sum of £2.9m into a relevant property trust by way of a lifetime transfer would incur immediate IHT charges of at least £450,000 (£2.9m – 2 x £325,000 = £2.25m x 20% = £450,000). Furthermore, exit charges of at least 0.1164% would arise for each calendar quarter the funds were held in the trust, and it would take seven years before the funds were exempt from IHT on the couple's deaths.

**Some Provisos**

There must be no fixed arrangement to buy the business back from the trust at the time of the original transfer. Even an intention to purchase the business back may be enough to require disclosure under the DOTAS regime (see Section 11.11).

The transferor must actually pay the funds required to purchase the business back from the trust. Any amount left outstanding as a loan would not be deductible from the purchaser's estate, as it would be deemed an artificially created debt (see Section 2.10).

The purchaser will need to hold the business for another two years before they are eligible for BPR again. If they were to borrow to fund the purchase, those borrowings will be deducted from the value of the business for BPR purposes (see Section 2.10).

While the entry charge may be avoided under this technique, the trust will still be subject to anniversary and exit charges (see Chapter 8) if the funds (or assets purchased with them) remain in the trust for ten years or more after it was formed. Income accumulated within the trust (see Section 8.18) might also give rise to some exit charges, even within the first ten years, if this exceeds the NRB (or twice the NRB where there are two settlors). Such charges are likely to be modest, however.

## 15.2 THE DOUBLE DIP

Where full BPR or APR is available on a business owner's death (see Chapter 7), the relevant assets can safely be left to a discretionary trust free from IHT. The deceased's spouse (or unmarried partner) can then buy the relevant property from the discretionary trust for full market value.

Due to the rules on deduction of liabilities used to acquire relievable property (see Sections 2.10 and 7.10), the purchase will need to be funded from other existing assets and not by way of borrowing.

On the survivor's death, the chargeable value of their estate will effectively be reduced twice: through BPR or APR on the qualifying property; and then again by using other chargeable assets or funds for the purchase. This provides the effective 'double dip', illustrated by the following example.

***Example:*** *On his death, Damon leaves the family business to the Parklife Discretionary Trust and the remainder of his estate to his widow, Justine. Justine buys the business from the trust for £1m, its current market value, using funds inherited from Damon.*

*On Justine's death, her estate comprises the family business, worth £1.2m, and other assets worth £650,000. Her IHT calculation is therefore as follows:*

| | |
|---|---|
| *Total estate value* | *£1,850,000* |
| *Less: Business property relief* | *£1,200,000* |
| *Chargeable estate* | *£650,000* |

*Justine's chargeable estate is covered by her NRB of £325,000 plus her TNRB received from Damon, leaving her executors with no IHT to pay. If Damon had left the business to Justine rather than the trust, she would not have used £1m of other funds to purchase it. Those funds would then have been in her estate on her death, giving rise to an IHT bill of £400,000.*

Hence, as we can see from the example, this technique effectively enables a surviving spouse or partner to benefit from a double deduction in respect of qualifying business or agricultural property.

The purchase of the business shortly after the original owner's death should give rise to little or no CGT due to the uplift on death (Section 12.2). The same would apply to any inherited assets sold to fund the business purchase.

However, the major drawback is the purchase of the business must be funded from other existing assets: either assets already held by the surviving spouse or partner, or other assets inherited from the deceased spouse or partner. Funding the purchase through borrowing will not be effective. This restriction severely limits the usefulness of this technique, although it will still be possible to use it in some cases.

There are a few other little 'flies in the ointment' here:

- Stamp Duty or SDLT will be payable on the surviving partner's purchase of the business
- Although inherited assets will benefit from the uplift on death, the surviving spouse or partner may suffer CGT if they have to sell any of their own existing assets to fund the purchase of the business
- The discretionary trust will be subject to higher rates of Income Tax on income from the funds it holds; although the effects of this can be mitigated by paying income out to beneficiaries (see Section 8.20)
- The discretionary trust will be subject to anniversary and exit charges (see Chapter 8) if it holds assets with a value in excess of the NRB for ten years or more

Having said all that, it is worth bearing in mind the technique allows funds equal to the market value of the deceased's business to be put into a discretionary trust with no entry charge (and no exit charges during the first ten years: subject to my comments in Section 15.1), so it is a very efficient way to set up a trust.

Note that, in the example, I assumed Damon and Justine were married. This technique works almost as well for unmarried partners but, in such a case, Damon's estate would have suffered IHT on his other, non-business assets, and Justine would not have been entitled to a TNRB (unless she already had one from a previous deceased spouse).

## 15.3 MONEY BOX COMPANIES

In one IHT case a company with a business consisting of lending money to other associated companies was held to be carrying on a qualifying business for BPR purposes. Thus it seems money lending can be a qualifying business.

However, an important factor in this particular case was the fact the loans were unsecured and repayable on demand. This meant the company's business comprised a business of making loans rather than one of investing in loans and this was enough to enable the company's owner to obtain BPR. The fact the loans were made to associated companies did not seem to affect the position. This is good news since it is doubtful whether many people will wish to make unsecured loans to non-associated companies.

This decision opens up some interesting planning possibilities. A person with a non-qualifying company, such as a property investment company, for example, could set up a money-lending company to make loans to the non-qualifying company.

The loans would need to be unsecured and repayable on demand and the volume of activity carried on by the money-lending company would need to be enough to make it a business (Section 7.3). The money-lending company would need to charge interest to provide the necessary profit motive.

Under these circumstances, it would be possible to reduce the value of the non-qualifying company while the value of the money-lending company may be eligible for BPR, thus saving IHT when the owner of both companies dies.

The non-qualifying business probably needs to be in a company in order to get the necessary reduction in value that saves the IHT. (See Section 15.4 for further benefits of putting non-qualifying businesses into a company)

Strategies involving setting up multiple companies may lead to additional Corporation Tax costs in some cases. See the Taxcafe guide *The Company Tax Changes* for details.

## 15.4 CORPORATE DEBT

As we saw in Section 7.12, liabilities owed by a company reduce the value of that company and hence also the value of its shares. When a person dies owning shares in a company, it is the value of those shares that is brought into their estate and there is no need to claim a separate deduction for the company's liabilities. Hence, there is also no need to meet the rules described in Section 2.10 regarding the payment of liabilities out of the assets of the deceased's estate.

It may therefore make sense if borrowings to finance investments not qualifying for any form of relief are made through a company.

***Example:*** *Phil has offered to lend his brother Don £500,000 to help him start a property investment business. The loan will be unsecured and interest-free. If Don borrowed the money personally and later died still owing this money to Phil, his executors would need to repay Phil out of the assets of Don's estate in order to claim a deduction for IHT purposes (see Section 2.10).*

*Instead, Don sets up a company, Ever Lee Investments Ltd. He then gets Phil to lend the money to the company. The debt to Phil will now automatically reduce the value of Don's shares in Ever Lee Investments Ltd without having to worry about meeting the rules in Section 2.10.*

This technique solves the problem of having to repay a loan on the borrower's death but if such a loan was used to indirectly finance relievable property or excluded property, the other rules described in Section 2.10 would then apply.

# Chapter 16

# Domicile and Emigration

## 16.1 DOMICILE PRINCIPLES

For IHT purposes, an individual is treated as UK domiciled if ***any*** of the following apply:

i) They are UK domiciled under general legal principles,
ii) They are deemed to be UK domiciled, or
iii) They have made an 'opt in' election

Looking at it another way, as far as IHT is concerned an individual can only enjoy the potential advantages of being non-UK domiciled if they are ***neither*** UK domiciled under general principles ***nor*** deemed to be UK domiciled; ***and*** they have ***not*** made an 'opt in' election.

We looked at 'opt in' elections in Section 6.15. As far as everyone else is concerned, you first have to establish whether you are UK domiciled under the general principles we will examine in Section 16.2 and then work out whether you are deemed to be UK domiciled under the rules in Section 16.3. Only if you manage to pass both tests can you be treated as non-UK domiciled for IHT purposes and thus exempt all your foreign assets (plus certain other items as discussed in Section 3.7) from the tax.

**Double Tax Treaties**
The following countries have Double Tax Treaties with the UK covering IHT: France, India, Irish Republic, Italy, Netherlands, Pakistan, South Africa, Sweden, Switzerland, and the USA. These may affect your position if you are domiciled in one of these countries under general legal principles.

## 16.2 LEGAL DOMICILE

In essence, your legal domicile is the country you consider to be your permanent home. This does not necessarily equate to your country of birth, nor to the country in which you happen to be living at present. Domicile should not be confused with residence, which is a far more transitory concept.

At this point, it is worth noting that, technically speaking, you cannot actually have UK domicile but will, instead, have your domicile in England and Wales, Scotland, or Northern Ireland. As we saw in Section 11.7, this can be important when it comes to intestacy or legal rights.

It is usually safe to simply refer to UK domicile for IHT purposes, although we will see some instances where the distinction between the different nations of the UK can be important later. It is also worth noting that the Channel

Islands and the Isle of Man are not part of the UK for tax purposes, including IHT and domicile.

**Domicile of Origin**

At birth, each person acquires the domicile of the person on whom they are legally dependent at that time. That person will usually be their father, but it is their mother if their father is dead or their parents are living apart and they have a home with their mother, but not with their father. The domicile you acquire at this point is known as your 'domicile of origin'.

Throughout your minority, you continue to have the same domicile as the person on whom you are legally dependent. If that person changes their domicile during this period then your domicile also changes and you acquire a 'domicile of dependency'. You only become capable of having your own independent domicile when you reach the age of 16 (or, in Scotland, 14 for a boy, 12 for a girl).

***Example:*** *Farrokh was born in Zanzibar in 1946 and lived with both of his parents at that time. His father was domiciled in India, so Farrokh acquired an Indian domicile of origin. In 1960, Farrokh's parents moved to England, taking Farrokh with them. They intended to remain in England permanently. At this point, Farrokh acquired a UK domicile of dependency.*

**Re-acquiring a Domicile of Origin**

If it ever becomes uncertain which country you regard as your permanent home, your domicile will revert to your domicile of origin (and not any domicile of dependency you may have had).

**Domicile and Marriage**

Subject to the 'opt-in' election described below, marriage no longer affects domicile. However, women other than US Nationals, who married before 1st January 1974, adopted their husband's domicile as a domicile of dependency.

Non-UK domiciled individuals with a UK domiciled spouse may elect to be treated as UK domiciled for IHT purposes. See Section 6.15 for further details.

**Domicile of Choice**

In most cases, a person's domicile of origin remains their domicile for the rest of their life. A different domicile can only be acquired, as a 'domicile of choice', where a person emigrates and can prove their intention to reside permanently or indefinitely in their new home country.

Acquiring a new domicile for tax purposes, as a domicile of choice, can be very difficult. This is both good news and bad news since it cuts both ways and HMRC has had just as much difficulty proving a taxpayer has acquired the UK as their domicile of choice as taxpayers have had in proving they have acquired a domicile somewhere else.

To acquire a new domicile, as a domicile of choice, it is necessary to not only demonstrate an intention to adopt the new country as your permanent home, but also to follow this up by action and subsequent conduct.

If the taxpayer abandons their domicile of choice, without demonstrating a clear intention to adopt a new domicile of choice somewhere else, then their domicile automatically reverts to their domicile of origin.

***Example:*** *Brian has a UK domicile of origin. Twenty years ago, he emigrated to Spain and became Spanish domiciled. He declared this intention on form P85, which he lodged with the Inland Revenue (now HMRC) shortly before he departed for the Costa del Sol. In 2024, Brian gets a terrific offer to work in Los Angeles, so he leaves Spain and moves to California. Brian is uncertain, however, whether he wishes to remain in California permanently. As Brian's permanent home is now unclear, his domicile reverts to the UK!*

If you intend to emigrate to avoid UK IHT, make sure you pick the right country first time! Although Brian might eventually be able to establish Californian domicile, this will now be more difficult because he has a track record of abandoning his so-called permanent home. Hence it will be harder to prove he has no intention of returning to the UK.

Note that I referred to Californian domicile and not US domicile. Strictly speaking, domicile relates to a territory rather than a country (e.g. a State in the USA). In countries with a federal system, like the USA, you will need to decide which territory you are adopting as your new permanent home, not just which country. This may severely restrict your freedom of movement. California may be big enough, but what about Rhode Island?

**Shedding a UK Domicile of Dependency**

If you have a UK domicile of dependency, but a non-UK domicile of origin, it will be far easier for you to re-acquire your domicile of origin than to acquire a domicile of choice. In this situation, you only need to leave your domicile of dependency for long enough to be in a position where the country that is your permanent home is uncertain in order to re-acquire your non-UK domicile of origin.

Remember that England and Wales, Scotland, and Northern Ireland are different territories for this purpose. Hence, for example, a person with an English domicile of dependency might be able to shed that domicile by moving to Scotland or Northern Ireland, even if they do not intend to remain there permanently.

Shedding a UK domicile of dependency will not, however, prevent you becoming deemed UK domiciled after 15 years of UK residence (Section 16.3).

**Retaining a Domicile of Origin**

If you are lucky enough to have a non-UK domicile of origin it is far, far, easier to retain this as your domicile than to acquire a domicile of choice. As stated above, it is very difficult for HMRC to prove an individual has acquired a new domicile of choice. This is especially true if the individual states it is their intention to return to their country of origin one day.

***Example:*** *Grace was born in Jamaica, of Jamaican parents. She has, however, lived in the UK for over 30 years, having moved here in her early twenties. Despite this, she has always stated she intends to return 'home' when she retires. She therefore remains domiciled in Jamaica.*

In this case, an intention does not have to be backed up by action, but should be more than a vague notion that you would like to 'die in the land of your fathers'. Intentions such as 'to retire to your home country' or 'return home after your spouse's death' are the sort of thing that will usually suffice.

To strengthen your non-UK domiciled status, it may also be worth buying a grave plot in your domicile of origin. This is accepted as a strong indication of your intention to return to that country.

It's worth remembering you will keep your domicile of origin if there is some doubt about where you intend to make your permanent home. It might be enough to state you intend 'retiring abroad' if there is reasonable substance to your intentions. You might even retain a non-UK domicile of origin by expressing doubt about whether you intend to live in England or Scotland!

**Punitive Charges**

Non-UK domiciled individuals resident in the UK for seven or more of the previous nine UK tax years may be subject to punitive Income Tax charges unless they elect to pay UK tax on foreign income and capital gains. These charges cease if the individual attains deemed UK domicile, as explained in the next section.

## 16.3 DEEMED DOMICILE

Non-UK domiciled individuals are generally deemed to be UK domiciled for all UK tax purposes for the current tax year (even if they are no longer UK resident) if they:

- Were UK resident for at least 15 of the previous 20 UK tax years, and
- Are UK resident in at least one of the four tax years made up of the current year and three previous years,

One practical upshot of this is that Individuals with deemed UK domicile prior to leaving the UK may retain it for up to a further three years thereafter.

In most cases, it is usually possible to avoid becoming deemed UK domiciled by spending at least six UK tax years out of every twenty abroad (not necessarily in your domicile of origin).

However, individuals born in the UK, with a UK domicile of origin, but who have acquired a non-UK domicile of choice, and who were UK resident in either of the previous two UK tax years, are treated as UK domiciled if they remain UK resident in the current tax year.

Since 2013/14, an individual's tax residence has been determined under the statutory residence test. In some cases, this may effectively hasten, or prolong, their deemed UK domicile. See the Taxcafe guide *How to Save Property Tax* for further details of the statutory residence test.

## 16.4 A GUIDE TO EMIGRATION

Emigrating to avoid IHT must be done early and carefully. Furthermore, while emigration can be an excellent strategy for avoiding or reducing IHT, it will not lead to any saving in respect of most UK assets, and generally only leads to a saving in respect of foreign assets. There are some important exceptions, however, as we saw in Section 3.7.

An individual who ceases to be UK domiciled under general principles will continue to have deemed UK domicile for IHT purposes for a further three years thereafter.

In other words, if you have UK domicile under general principles, you will first need to acquire another domicile and then wait a further three years before you are no longer treated as UK domiciled for IHT purposes. As we saw in Section 16.2, this process is easier for those who do not have a UK domicile of origin, although they still need to be wary of the deemed domicile rules.

For those with a UK domicile of origin, it is far harder to acquire another domicile and become non-UK domiciled than it is to simply become non-UK resident. The difference can be summed up as follows:

- To become non-UK resident, you generally need to leave the UK for at least one complete UK tax year
- To become non-UK domiciled you need to adopt another country (or territory) as your new, permanent home, and then wait at least three years

Generally, you will only enjoy any IHT savings if you become non-UK domiciled, although a key exception is gilts (UK government securities), where you will often only need to achieve non-resident status (Section 3.7).

Non-UK residence can generally be achieved by remaining outside the UK with only limited return visits. Usually you can spend up to 90 nights in the UK per tax year, although the position is now governed by the statutory residence test, which has a few quirks and pitfalls you need to be wary of and may mean you need to restrict your visits further (see the Taxcafe guide *How to Save Property Tax* for details).

For anyone with a UK domicile of origin, the process of becoming non-UK domiciled is much more difficult. You will need to establish a new domicile of choice elsewhere. There is no set procedure for doing this; like many things in tax, each case is examined on its merits, but here are a few practical tips:

- Declare your intentions to HMRC on form P85 before leaving the UK
- Buy a home in your new country
- Take your family with you (including the pets)
- Take whatever steps you can to establish citizenship, nationality, etc, in your new country
- Take up employment in your new country (or, alternatively, establish your own business there)
- Register on the electoral roll in your new country
- Buy a grave plot in your new country (this is given a great deal of importance by the tax authorities when looking at domicile)
- Try to visit the UK as little as possible
- Make sure your former home in the UK is not available for your use: preferably, it should be sold
- Ensure residential accommodation is not available to you elsewhere in the UK: if you must visit the UK, try to stay in hotels
- Sell as many UK assets as you can and close your UK bank accounts
- Resign membership of clubs, associations, etc, in the UK. Ideally, you should try to make a clean break with your previous life in the UK
- Write letters or emails (e.g. to your solicitor) expressing your intention of never returning to reside in the UK
- Write a Will in your new country
- Try not to move on again to another territory

You don't necessarily need to do all these things but, the more you do, the better. Following these guidelines should generally ensure you become non-UK resident as well as non-UK domiciled. However, the statutory residence test could potentially lead to a few instances where an individual manages to achieve non-UK domicile, but remains UK resident for tax purposes.

As we saw in Section 16.3, an individual born in the UK with a UK domicile of origin, who was UK resident in either of the previous two UK tax years, is deemed to be UK domiciled if they remain UK resident in the current tax year. Hence, for most people born in the UK, it remains essential to achieve non-UK residence, as well as non UK domicile.

For the reasons explained in Section 16.2, you may need to think in terms of your new home territory, rather than country, when applying the above guidelines (e.g. Queensland rather than Australia).

If you really must retain any connections with the UK (and I don't recommend it), try to make it a different nation. For example, if you have an English domicile of origin and you wish to keep a UK bank account, make it an account with a Scottish or Northern Irish branch.

**Interaction with Capital Gains Tax**

If you need to sell UK assets in order to save IHT, you need to be wary of incurring CGT liabilities in the process. Land and buildings in the UK remain subject to UK CGT and the related reporting requirements (see Section 12.1), even when you are non-UK resident. Your own home will usually be exempt though, provided you have occupied it throughout your ownership. Furthermore, you may still make some CGT savings by waiting until you are non-UK resident before selling UK property. See the Taxcafe guide *How to Save Property Tax* for further details of all aspects of CGT on UK property.

Most other assets cease to be subject to UK CGT once you become non-UK resident, provided you remain non-UK resident for at least five years. Hence, you can usually avoid CGT on assets other than UK land and buildings simply by waiting until you are non-UK resident before you sell those assets.

While you can sometimes be non-UK resident for part of a UK tax year, this only applies under certain circumstances. Hence, it is generally safer to work on the basis that you only become non-UK resident at the beginning of the next UK tax year after you leave the UK and you then need to remain non-UK resident for five complete UK tax years.

As we saw in Section 6.14, a sale of assets transferred to you from your spouse while you were UK resident could lead to a CGT liability for them if you sell those assets when you are non-UK resident but they are still UK resident.

**Look Before You Leap!**
If you become resident or domiciled in another country, you will be subject to that country's tax regime. Believe it or not, some of them are worse than us! Hence, it is essential to take local advice in your destination country (or territory) before you go.

Chapter 17

# The Inheritance Tax Planning Timetable

## 17.1 IT'S NEVER TOO EARLY TO START

Most tax advisers will tell you it's never too early to start IHT planning, but when you're struggling to pay a mortgage and make some headway at the beginning of your career, IHT will probably be the last thing on your mind.

Nevertheless, as we saw in Section 9.1, the earlier you start, the more effective your planning will be, and if you are lucky enough to have the wealth to follow the kind of planning in that section, long term planning will help to pass on more family wealth to the next generation, or even the one after that.

Even if you have little wealth, your first step should be to ensure any life policies are written in favour of other family members.

## 17.2 MARRIAGE

First of all, marriage is a good time to remind the family to do ***their*** IHT planning by making the exempt gifts set out in Section 5.3. This is also a good time to put money into trust for your children, even before they're born!

Next, remember to make a new Will. An existing Will is rendered void on marriage unless it was made in contemplation of your union.

Once you are married, it may be worth taking steps to ensure your NRB is fully available to transfer to your spouse on your death. As we saw in Chapter 6, this may not always be the best course of action but is certainly something you should at least consider.

## 17.3 BECOMING A PARENT

This is the one that focuses the mind and gets most people thinking about IHT planning. It's time to step up the ante and begin thinking about tax efficient trust structures for your children (see Section 11.10). Get your parents to give money directly to your children instead of you (if you can afford to do without it).

It's time to re-write your Will again as well; you will need to think about how to provide for your children if you die prematurely. Consider what kind of structure you would like to put in place from the choices available (see Chapter 8). Don't forget to appoint a guardian too!

Now you're a parent, the RNRB comes into play and you should start to factor it into your planning (see Sections 3.4, 13.11, and 13.12).

## 17.4 ADULT CHILDREN

You can now start giving assets directly to the children without the need for any trust structures. Making use of the annual exemption may make sense, although most of us seem to have little choice anyway!

Normal expenditure out of income can be established to pass on substantial sums to the children and, when they marry, you can use the exemptions in Section 5.3.

You may want to consider putting a family debt scheme in place (Section 6.13), or using a family investment company (Chapter 14).

## 17.5 YOUR FIRST GRANDCHILD

Time to start looking at trust structures again; as we saw in Section 11.10, gifts to grandchildren are much more tax effective. Bare trusts for grandchildren are useful and avoid the problems you get with your own minor children.

You may want to re-write your Will again. Think about skipping a generation. What's the point of leaving money to the children if they're already well established? It might be better left to the grandchildren, so IHT doesn't come up again for another two generations.

## 17.6 GRANDCHILD'S EIGHTH BIRTHDAY

Your grandchild's eighth birthday is a key date. From the next day onwards, you will be able to put money into a relevant property trust for their benefit and pass it to them absolutely within less than ten years, i.e. before any anniversary charges can arise (see Section 8.18). This opens up a number of additional planning opportunities, as we have seen in previous chapters.

## 17.7 MIDDLE AGE

I'm not sure exactly when middle age is. A client of mine once said it was always ten years older than him and, the older I get, the more I like that definition. For the purposes of this guide, though, it is perhaps better defined as still working, but financially comfortable. This is when it may be worth considering maximising pension contributions, not so much for your own retirement planning, but as an IHT shelter: see Chapter 10 for details.

If your pension savings are more than you are likely to need for your own retirement, it is worth considering taking your tax-free lump sum and giving it to your beneficiaries somewhere between the age of 55 and 68. As explained in Chapter 10, this will generally enhance the overall tax-saving potential of your pension savings.

## 17.8 RETIREMENT

As pensions or other savings income starts to come in, you may now be able to afford to pass on income-producing assets, perhaps by using a trust (see Section 9.4). Alternatively, a family investment company may be a good vehicle to allow you to retire and still enjoy a tax-free income stream.

If you decide to downsize your home, you may be able to benefit from some of the planning strategies considered in Section 13.3, while still preserving your RNRB entitlement (Section 13.11).

If you have assets qualifying for BPR or APR (see Chapter 7), consider how to preserve the relief after your retire (see Sections 7.19 and 7.29). Consider also whether it is better to pass these on now or hold on to them so your children (or other beneficiaries) can obtain a tax-free uplift on death for CGT purposes when you pass away.

If you take the tax-free lump sum from your pension at this point, consider whether to gift the funds to your children, as discussed in Chapter 10.

## 17.9 LOSING A PARENT

If one of your parents dies intestate or with a Will that isn't tax efficient, a deed of variation (Section 18.1) can be used to put IHT planning into place retrospectively.

When your first parent dies, you should consider whether it is better for them to use their NRB on assets that might be appreciating in value (see Section 6.7) or for it to transfer to your surviving parent (assuming they are married).

If you don't need the money, get your legacies transferred to your children (or even grandchildren) instead. Gifts to charity may also reduce the IHT bill (see Sections 3.5, 3.6 and 18.1).

## 17.10 STILL TOGETHER AFTER ALL THESE YEARS

Elderly married couples face a bit of a dilemma. If you're both getting older, it may make sense to start giving away surplus wealth as PETs that will hopefully become exempt if you survive seven years.

However, if you die within seven years of making any PET or chargeable lifetime transfer, this will restrict the proportion of your NRB that transfers to your spouse. As we saw in Chapter 6, this may have adverse consequences, although there are also times when such transfers will be advantageous, especially when assets appreciating in value are gifted.

You need to weigh up these conflicting factors before making any lifetime transfers that are not immediately exempt. While such transfers may sometimes be beneficial for elderly married people, any potential impact on your surviving spouse's TNRB should also be considered.

If you do decide to make lifetime transfers that are not immediately exempt, it will generally make sense for these to be made by the spouse with the longer life expectancy.

## 17.11 LOSING A SPOUSE

You have two years to put a deed of variation into place to make sure your late spouse's estate is dealt with tax efficiently. Obviously, the key point is to maximise the benefit of their NRB, either by having it transfer to you, or by using it to pass on appreciating assets free from IHT (see Section 6.7).

If your spouse leaves property qualifying for BPR or APR, it may make sense to pass this directly to the children (or other beneficiaries), in case the relief is later lost. This is often particularly important in the case of a family farm where the surviving spouse may no longer be able to run it. Alternatively, you may want to put a 'double dip' in place (Section 15.2).

Generally, your spouse's RNRB will transfer to you and should form part of your own subsequent planning. However, there will be some instances where it will be better to utilise your spouse's RNRB at this stage, if you can (e.g. if their estate was less than £2m, but you now expect yours to significantly exceed this level).

This is also a good time to assess your own financial needs and start making plans to give away any surplus. Consider your own life expectancy and review the appropriate action set out in Sections 17.13 to 17.15.

### 17.12 REMARRIAGE

Remarriage provides another opportunity to make some of the exempt gifts outlined in Section 5.3. On this occasion, the ability to make tax-exempt transfers into trust for the benefit of your children may be particularly useful.

If either or both of you are a widow or widower, you may have an existing TNRB entitlement (see Section 6.8). If so, you should now consider taking steps to maximise the benefit of your existing TNRB. The methods discussed in Sections 6.9 to 6.11 and 13.5 to 13.7 are available to save your family up to £260,000.

This is also a good time to consider your new combined estate and decide whether there are surplus assets that can be given away. If your spouse already has an existing full TNRB entitlement, you will be able to make lifetime transfers without risking any loss of relief. If they have an existing partial TNRB entitlement, some lifetime transfers may still be made without risk.

Once again, you should re-write your Will, as any previous Will not made in contemplation of your new marriage will be rendered void.

### 17.13 LIFE EXPECTANCY OVER SEVEN YEARS (Per the ONS: men under 84, women under 86)

There's still time to make PETs that should hopefully have time to become fully exempt. Ending the reservation on a gift with reservation will give it time to become exempt also (but beware of the potential risks arising in the case of the family home: see Section 13.12).

Remember, if you are single and survive at least three years, some savings may still be made. If you are still married, however, some caution may be required (see Section 17.10, but also Section 17.12 if this is not your or your spouse's first marriage).

Longer-term planning strategies, such as family investment companies (Chapter 14) may still be viable but, after this, it's probably too late. Having said that, they would still have worked for Captain Sir Tom Moore; Vera Lynn; Joan Graham; the Queen Mother; Kirk Douglas (if he was British); and many others!

I was looking forward to adding Prince Phillip to this list of centenarians, but sadly he didn't quite make it. Nonetheless, he deserves a mention, if only for the fact he once said, "All money nowadays seems to be produced with a natural homing instinct for the Treasury."

## 17.14 LIFE EXPECTANCY THREE TO SEVEN YEARS (Men aged 84 to 94 and women aged 86 to 95)

Transfers made now should still benefit from tapering (see Section 4.5), so some tax may be saved if you are single. Transfers by married people at this stage carry a strong risk of having an adverse impact on your spouse's TNRB unless they are immediately exempt (see Section 17.10 but also Section 17.12 if this is not your or your spouse's first marriage).

Whether you're married or not, it's time to really start making the most of the annual exemption, the small gifts exemption, and normal expenditure out of income (these are all immediately exempt).

A loan trust or discounted gift trust may make sense at this point, and possibly also gifts of appreciating assets not qualifying for BPR (but see Chapter 12 regarding the CGT implications).

You may be able to save IHT by emigrating. If you survive at least three years after establishing non-UK domicile, you can avoid IHT on non-UK assets and certain other items of excluded property (see Section 3.7).

## 17.15 LIFE EXPECTANCY TWO TO THREE YEARS (Men aged 94 to 99 and women aged 96 to 100)

Now's the time to think seriously about those AIM shares, but never forgetting 'Dodgy Dave' (see Section 11.1). Anything that gets your money into qualifying business property (see Chapter 7) may still save IHT if you can survive two years. Rights issues and transfers of assets into a company under your control may provide immediate savings.

Loan trusts and discounted gift trusts may still save you money even now, as well as other transfers of appreciating property (but watch the CGT position).

While it may be too late to achieve non-UK domicile, you may still have time to become non-UK resident. Investing in gilts and emigrating abroad could still save substantial amounts of IHT (see Sections 3.7 and 16.4 for details).

## 17.16 LOSS OF CAPACITY

If you expect to lose the ability to take care of your own affairs in the near future, it will make sense to appoint a power of attorney. A power of attorney, or next of kin, can apply to the Court of Protection to make a Statutory Will on your behalf.

The Court of Protection can also authorise your attorney to make lifetime gifts on your behalf, but this is generally limited to modest birthday and Christmas presents. The attorney is not usually entitled to make the more substantial gifts needed for IHT planning purposes. Where you have already set up a standing order to use your annual exemption, or make your normal expenditure out of income (Section 5.5), it is possible the attorney may be able to allow this to continue, but this point is not clear and may be challenged by HMRC.

In view of these problems, it is sensible to put as much IHT planning as possible in place before you lose capacity: everything becomes considerably more difficult once an attorney has been appointed. Write a new Will, make appropriate gifts, and consider the actions set out in the next section. A disabled trust may also be a good idea at this stage (Section 8.11). Do as much as you can before it's too late!

## 17.17 DEATHBED PLANNING

So, if you've really left it far too late, what can still be done? Some of this may seem a little flippant and, as I said in Section 1.1, I have no wish to cause any offence to anyone. Tax planning may be the farthest thing from your mind at this stage, and who could blame you. Nevertheless, here are some of the things you could think about if time is running out:

**Deathbed Marriage:** The biggest deathbed planning point, if you're still single at this stage, is to marry your partner. No point trying to hang on to your freedom now, just get on with it. That's exactly what one of HMRC's most famous adversaries, Sir Ken Dodd, did two days before his death.

It will almost always be worth marrying at this stage, even if you have very few assets, as any unused proportion of your NRB or RNRB will transfer to your spouse.

**Last Gasp Gifts:** If you haven't used your annual exemption (Section 5.2) for this, or the previous, tax year, get gifting. If you've made no previous gifts, one simple £6,000 payment to one of your nearest and dearest will save your family £2,400. For the rest of your family and friends, there's the small gifts exemption (Section 5.2). Every person you can find to give £250 will save your estate £100 in IHT.

Remember, however, as explained in Section 4.7, if made by cheque, these gifts will not be effective unless the cheque clears before you pass away. Online banking may therefore be better if you feel up to it.

**What about the House?** Although your family may be able to sort things out with a deed of variation (Section 18.1), it could make things easier for them if you change the title to a tenancy in common now.

**Make Pension Contributions:** If you're aged under 75 and still have earnings for this tax year, you may be able to make pension contributions. These probably won't escape IHT at this stage but, as explained in Section 10.7, they could still yield significant savings.

**Maximising the Residence Nil Rate Band:** As explained in Section 3.4, some or all of the RNRB is withdrawn if your estate is worth more than £2m at the time of your death. Hence, while PETs and chargeable lifetime transfers made shortly before your death will not usually save IHT, it may be possible to use them to reduce the value of your estate and thus prevent your RNRB being withdrawn.

***Example:*** *It is March 2024 and Nelson, a widower, is dying. His late wife Sheena died some years earlier, leaving her modest estate to him. Nelson's estate is worth £2.7m, including his home, worth £1m, which he plans to leave to his children, and various cash and savings totalling £700,000. As things stand, Nelson's RNRB will be completely withdrawn by tapering and the IHT on his estate will total £820,000 (£2.7m – £650,000 = £2.05m x 40% = £820,000).*

*Instead, Nelson gives all his cash and savings to his children shortly before he dies. These transfers become chargeable on his death and IHT of £20,000 (£700,000 – £650,000 = £50,000 x 40% = £20,000) will be payable on them. However, the gifts reduce the value of Nelson's estate to £2m, meaning he will be entitled to a RNRB of £350,000. IHT of £660,000 (£2m – £350,000 = £1.65m x 40% = £660,000) will now be payable on his estate.*

*The total IHT arising on Nelson's death is thus £680,000 (£20,000 + £660,000), meaning the lifetime gifts have led to a saving of £140,000 (£820,000 – £680,000).*

A married person could easily reduce the value of their estate to £2m by giving the excess to their spouse shortly before they died. This would generally be an exempt transfer (unless the couple had mixed domicile: see Section 6.14) and would have no impact on the TNRB; but it would mean the deceased's RNRB was available to transfer to their widow or widower.

Where assets other than cash are transferred, the CGT consequences will need to be considered. We looked at these in detail in Chapter 12. However, in some cases, it may be worth taking a CGT hit to save more in IHT.

***Example Revisited:*** *The facts are exactly as before, except Nelson transfers various assets worth £700,000 to his children, rather than cash. The transferred assets stand at an overall capital gain of £500,000 and do not include any residential property. Nelson is a higher rate taxpayer so CGT of £100,000 arises on the transfer. Nelson's CGT liability is deducted from his estate, so this increases the total IHT saving to £180,000 (£140,000 + £100,000 x 40%). Overall, the family remains £80,000 better off (£180,000 – £100,000).*

For transfers to a spouse, there would generally be no immediate CGT cost but the uplift on death (Section 12.2) would be lost and this may eventually lead to a higher CGT cost that should be taken into account.

Transfers of assets qualifying for BPR or APR may also help to reduce your estate, as these are still counted for the purposes of the RNRB tapering rules (see Section 3.4). Where CGT holdover relief also applies (Section 12.4), the transfer can be made free of CGT. However, once again, the uplift on death will be lost and you need to consider whether this may be more valuable to your heirs in the end.

If you are married, it is important to remember, apart from transfers that qualify for 100% BPR or APR, other transfers at this stage that are not immediately exempt, will affect your spouse's TNRB, so you need to bear this in mind too.

**Remember Your Normal Gifts:** The exemption for normal expenditure out of income (Section 5.5) applies to lifetime gifts only. To get that final year's exemption, you need to make sure you've made that expenditure before you go.

**Consider Setting up a Disabled Trust:** As explained in Section 8.11, it may make sense to set up a disabled trust during your terminal illness. This may make things easier for your beneficiaries.

**Spend!** 'There are no pockets in shrouds,' they say, so why not spend it before HM Treasury gets hold of it. Any money you spend that qualifies as maintenance of family (Section 5.4) will escape IHT. For example, you could spend £3,000 buying clothes for your teenage daughter instead of leaving her a legacy of £3,000 that produces an IHT charge of up to £2,000.

You could also think about buying depreciating assets. "How will that help my family?" you may ask, but think about this:

***Example:*** *Ian knows he has only a few months to live and wants to give his friend Chas a last gift. What Chas would really like is a new car and the model he has his eye on, a Rhythm Stick Blockhead, costs £75,000 new.*

*Ian buys a Rhythm Stick Blockhead but doesn't give it to Chas straight away. Instead, he leaves the car to Chas in his Will. When Ian dies a few months later, the car, now second-hand, is worth only £45,000 and this is the value to be used for IHT purposes. If Ian had simply given the car to Chas brand new, a sum of £75,000 would have been included in his estate. Hence, by leaving the car in his Will instead, Ian has saved up to £12,000 in IHT.*

**Contractual Obligations:** The liabilities under any contractual obligations existing at the date of your death will be deductible from your estate provided they meet the rules set out in Section 2.10. Hence, if your beneficiaries would like something done to an asset that is about to pass to them under the terms of your Will, why not contract for the work to be done at your expense?

**Review (or Make) Your Will:** While you're still of sound mind, there is still time to change (or make) your Will. Maximising the value of your NRB should be top of the list if you are married (see Chapter 6) and you should consider the RNRB if you have children or grandchildren.

As we shall see in Section 18.1, your beneficiaries can enter a deed of variation within the next two years as long as all affected parties agree. What you might need to consider at this stage, however, is whether any beneficiaries in your current Will are likely to stand in the way of IHT saving measures by refusing to agree to a deed of variation. Furthermore, as we shall see in Section 18.1, deeds of variation have some significant drawbacks that can be avoided by making the relevant provisions in your Will instead.

The easiest way to save IHT at this stage is to change your Will to leave some or all of your estate to charity (see Section 3.5). Your existing beneficiaries may not be happy but it's your decision (mostly: see Section 11.7).

If you wish to benefit from the additional relief for charitable legacies we examined in Section 3.6, you may wish to include the relevant provision in your Will as, again, one of your beneficiaries might not agree to the necessary deed of variation. Furthermore, as explained in Section 3.6, there have been some doubts over whether deeds of variation can be used for this purpose. There are also a few technical hurdles to be overcome.

All in all, while deeds of variation are an extremely useful IHT planning tool, it will generally make sense to put as much of your IHT planning in place via your Will as you can.

**Go Home or Stay Away:** In Chapter 16, we looked at the issues of retaining a foreign domicile of origin, shedding a UK domicile of dependency, or obtaining a foreign domicile of choice. In borderline cases, the outcome will be heavily influenced by your final actions. To keep or re-acquire a foreign domicile of origin, it may be wise to go home to die.

To maintain a foreign domicile of choice it will be best if you remain in your adopted country. Buying a grave plot and arranging your funeral in your new adopted country will also be helpful to your cause.

**Maximise Your Business Property:** While, as explained in Section 7.16, the business property itself generally needs to have been held for at least two years to qualify for BPR, you can enhance the value of existing business property at any time. This might, for example, include:

- Paying business debts from private resources
- Paying off liabilities incurred to finance the acquisition, enhancement, or maintenance of business property (again from private resources)
- Buying additional assets for use in your business (as long as these are funded from existing private resources, not from borrowing): for example, could you buy the business premises you currently rent?
- Rights issues of shares by a qualifying private company
- Transferring assets into a qualifying private company (Section 7.20): such transfers may have CGT or SDLT consequences, which should be considered

Remember, if you have disposed of qualifying business property within the last three years, you can restore full BPR by buying replacement property (see Section 7.17), including qualifying AIM shares.

**Deathbed CGT Planning:** What you should ***not*** generally do at this stage is make disposals that give rise to CGT liabilities. (Although there are exceptions, as we have seen.) If you sell assets before you die, your estate will be liable for the CGT arising based on your original base costs for those assets. Subject to this liability, the net proceeds of the sale will remain in your estate and will be subject to IHT.

If you hang on to those assets, the IHT may be a little greater (as there is no CGT liability to deduct) but, as we saw in Chapter 12, your personal representatives or beneficiaries will be able to sell them later with little or no CGT liability. Conversely, therefore, the best deathbed planning for CGT purposes might be to accumulate more assets: especially, as we saw in Section 12.6, from your spouse!

Chapter 18

# Planning after Death

## 18.1 DEEDS OF VARIATION

Perhaps the last resort in IHT planning is the deed of variation. This is an essential planning tool where a family finds the terms of the deceased's Will (or intestacy) have an undesired effect. Where all affected beneficiaries are in agreement, it is possible to vary the Will in order to create a better result.

As the deed of variation is a legally binding document, it is wise to consult a lawyer when completing it. Strictly speaking, the IHT rules only require the document to be a written instrument, although a formal deed is generally recommended.

**Conditions**

i) The required variations must be recorded in writing within two years of the death (this is the deed)
ii) All existing beneficiaries affected by the variations to the Will or intestacy should sign the deed. (New beneficiaries benefitting from the variations do not need to sign, although this does no harm)
iii) The deed should include a statement that the signatories intend the deed to have effect for IHT purposes
iv) Where the deed results in additional IHT being payable on the deceased's death, a copy must be sent to HMRC within six months of the date of the deed. At the same time, HMRC must also be notified of the amount of additional tax due
v) The variation must not be made for any consideration in money or money's worth, except in the case of other compensatory variations to the deceased's Will or intestacy

It is also common practice for the deceased's personal representatives to sign the deed, although this is not required by law.

Variations made by such a deed are treated for IHT purposes as if they had been made by the deceased. This treatment extends to the pre-owned assets regime (Section 11.12). This means a beneficiary who becomes a party to a deed of variation and, as a result, gives up a right to all or part of their inheritance, is not themselves regarded as having made any transfer of value (neither chargeable nor otherwise).

Deeds of variation may be used to create any type of trust or implement many of the other planning techniques described throughout this guide.

**Deed of Variation Drawbacks**
Variations made under a deed of variation effectively rewrite history and are treated as if they had been made by the deceased: ***but not for Income Tax purposes!***

For Income Tax purposes, the original beneficiary (under the deceased's Will or laws of intestacy) is regarded as having made a transfer to the new beneficiary, or to any trust that receives property under the deed of variation. This could result in the settlements legislation applying where the new beneficiary is a minor child of the original beneficiary (see Section 11.10).

Where a deed of variation is used to make, or increase, charitable legacies, there are a few additional formalities that need to be observed. It is essential the charity (or trustees of a charitable trust) is notified of the existence of the deed. HMRC will look for evidence that the charity or trustees are aware assets or funds are being redirected to them under the deed. Copies of an exchange of letters between the parties involved should be sufficient for this purpose.

As explained in Section 3.6, there have been doubts over whether it is possible to use a deed of variation to increase charitable legacies in order to benefit from the reduced IHT rate. This may no longer be the case, so it will certainly be worth a try, but it is better to make the appropriate provisions in a Will.

Where property is passed to a new beneficiary under either a deed of variation or by way of a transfer out of a relevant property trust within two years of the settlor's death (see Section 18.3), and the new beneficiary makes a PET of that same property shortly afterwards, there is a strong chance HMRC will apply the associated operations rules (Section 11.11). This would mean the deceased is treated as having left the property directly to the ultimate recipient which, in most cases, is likely to make it fully chargeable to IHT.

## 18.2 DISCLAIMERS

Under a simpler procedure a beneficiary can disclaim their inheritance. Only conditions (i) and (v), as listed in Section 18.1, need to be satisfied, and the deed should only be signed by the person making the disclaimer. The disclaimed inheritance will generally fall into the residue of the estate and be dealt with accordingly.

This procedure may be particularly useful where NRB legacies have been included in older Wills and the family decide it would be more sensible for the surviving spouse, as the residuary beneficiary, to receive the entire estate.

In addition to its simplicity, a disclaimer has the added advantage that the disclaimed legacy is treated as passing directly from the deceased to the new beneficiary for Income Tax purposes. This is therefore a much better way to pass a legacy directly to the original beneficiary's minor child.

A disclaimer is not possible where the original beneficiary has received any benefit from their legacy since the deceased's death (e.g. by living in an inherited property). However, it will often remain possible to use a deed of variation to achieve the same result: for IHT purposes at least!

## 18.3 TRANSFERS OUT OF TRUSTS WITHIN TWO YEARS

Transfers of property placed into a relevant property trust on the death of the settlor that take place within two years of the settlor's death, are treated as if they were legacies made by the deceased directly. Such transfers are exempt from exit charges (see Section 8.19).

Where the transferee is another trust, it will be treated as if it had been established under the deceased's Will. This provides scope to set up an immediate post-death interest, a bereaved minors' trust, or an 18 to 25 trust. In effect, this enables testators to create a discretionary trust under the terms of their Will that can be converted, as appropriate, within the two years following their death.

Once again, these provisions do not apply for Income Tax purposes. Hence, the relevant property trust will be liable for Income Tax on income received prior to the transfer. See also Section 18.1 regarding the risks of making a PET of the same property shortly after the transfer out of the trust.

## 18.4 SECOND CHANCES

One might say the procedures outlined under Sections 18.1 to 18.3 already provide a second chance to get the IHT planning right. However, only one variation under the procedure in Section 18.1 is allowed in respect of any item of property. Similarly, only one transfer of any item of property can fall under the rules explained in Section 18.3.

Nonetheless, it is possible for the same item of property to be subject to a deed of variation and later transferred out of a relevant property trust within the rules set out in Section 18.3 (or vice versa). The variation and the transfer must both take place within two years of death to be effective for IHT purposes.

## 18.5 POST-MORTEM RELIEF

Where a beneficiary, or the deceased's personal representatives, sells certain types of inherited assets for less than their probate value, they may claim post-mortem relief for their effective loss. The relief decreases the value of the deceased's estate for IHT purposes and a refund of the IHT already paid may be claimed where appropriate.

The assets must not be sold to a connected person (Appendix B), and must be sold for a freely negotiated price, on arms' length terms, within a specified period after the deceased's death. Actual sale price must be used for the purposes of this relief; there is no discount in respect of jointly held property (see Section 11.4). The specified period is twelve months for quoted shares; or three years for land and buildings.

The beneficiary must take account of all sales within the relevant period. Hence, when some inherited assets have also been sold at a profit, it is only the beneficiary's overall net loss on assets of that type that may be claimed. Furthermore, in the case of land and buildings, profits made on sales during the fourth year after the deceased's death must also be taken into account.

In effect, the values of all the inherited assets sold by the beneficiary within the specified period are adjusted to their sale price. This is to prevent 'cherry picking', i.e. only claiming for losses without taking account of profits.

However, a form of cherry picking can still be achieved by leaving the relevant assets to a discretionary trust in the first instance and then appointing all loss-making assets to one beneficiary prior to sale, and within two years of the deceased's death. As explained in Section 18.3, the beneficiary is treated as if they had inherited these assets absolutely, thus enabling them to make the post-mortem relief claim.

A similar form of post-death relief is available to assets subject to the related property rules: see Section 11.3.

# Appendix A

## UK Tax Rates and Allowances: 2022/23 to 2024/25

| | Rates | 2022/23 | 2023/24 | 2024/25 |
|---|---|---|---|---|
| | | £ | £ | £ |
| **Income Tax (1)** | | | | |
| Personal allowance | | 12,570 | 12,570 | 12,570 |
| Basic rate band | 20% | 37,700 | 37,700 | 37,700 |
| Higher rate/Threshold | 40% | 50,270 | 50,270 | 50,270 |
| Personal allowance withdrawal | | | | |
| Effective rate/From | 60% | 100,000 | 100,000 | 100,000 |
| To | | 125,140 | 125,140 | 125,140 |
| Additional rate | 45% | 150,000 | 125,140 | 125,140 |
| | | | | |
| Starting rate band (2) | 0% | 5,000 | 5,000 | 5,000 |
| Personal savings allowance (3) | | 1,000 | 1,000 | 1,000 |
| Dividend allowance | | 2,000 | 1,000 | 500 |
| Marriage allowance (4) | | 1,260 | 1,260 | 1,260 |
| | | | | |
| **Capital Gains Tax** | | | | |
| Annual exemption | | 12,300 | 6,000 | 3,000 |
| | | | | |
| **Inheritance Tax** | | | | |
| Nil rate band | | 325,000 | 325,000 | 325,000 |
| Main residence nil rate band | | 175,000 | 175,000 | 175,000 |
| RNRB taper threshold | | 2m | 2m | 2m |
| Annual exemption | | 3,000 | 3,000 | 3,000 |
| Small gifts exemption | | 250 | 250 | 250 |

**Notes**

1. Different rates and thresholds apply to Scottish taxpayers (except on savings income and dividends)
2. Applies to interest and savings income only
3. Halved for higher rate taxpayers; not available to additional rate taxpayers
4. Available where neither spouse/civil partner pays higher rate tax

Appendix B

# Connected Persons

The definition of connected persons differs slightly from one area of UK tax law to another. Generally, however, an individual's connected persons include the following:

i) Their husband, wife or civil partner
ii) The following relatives:
    - Mother, father or remoter ancestor
    - Son, daughter or remoter descendant
    - Brother or sister
iii) Relatives under (ii) above of the individual's spouse or civil partner
iv) Spouses or civil partners of the individual's relatives under (ii) above
v) Spouses or civil partners of an individual under (iii) above
vi) The individual's business partners
vii) Trusts where the individual is:
    - The settlor (the person who set up the trust or transferred property, other assets, or funds into it), or
    - A person connected (as defined in this appendix) with the settlor
viii) Companies under the control of the individual, either alone, or together with persons under (i) to (vii) above

Additionally, for the purposes of the pre-owned assets charge (Section 11.12), connected persons also include:

- Aunts and uncles
- Nephews and nieces
- Companies under the control of any of these relatives
- Trusts where any of these relatives are a beneficiary

Appendix C

# Sample Documentation

1. Memorandum recording a gift

MEMORANDUM OF GIFT FROM

Roger Meadows of 3 Taylor Street, Penzance

TO

Ian Deacon of 4 Queen Street, Belfast

MEMORANDUM that on 15th August 2023 Roger Meadows transferred by way of gift to Ian Deacon the sum of one million pounds (£1,000,000)

Dated: 20th August 2023

Signed by Roger Meadows:

Signed by Ian Deacon:

**Note:** Any IHT arising at the time of the transfer will be the transferor's liability. In practice, however, most transfers to other individuals will be PETs, meaning no IHT actually arises at that stage. Any further IHT arising in the event of the transferor's death within the next seven years will usually be the transferee's liability. If this is not desired, a memorandum along the lines of Item 3 below will be appropriate.

2. Memorandum recording transferee's liability for IHT on a lifetime transfer

MEMORANDUM OF GIFT FROM

James Stewart of 15 Castle Street, Stirling

TO

Mary Stewart of 42 Palace Road, Linlithgow

MEMORANDUM that on 16th November 2023 James Stewart transferred by way of gift to Mary Stewart (subject to the payment of any Inheritance Tax) the assets listed in the schedule below to the intent that they have become and are the absolute property of Mary Stewart and IN CONSIDERATION of such transfer Mary Stewart undertook to pay any Inheritance Tax in respect of such gift assessed upon James Stewart or his personal representatives and indemnifies James Stewart and his personal representatives accordingly.

SCHEDULE

- Property at 87 Flodden Avenue, Berwick upon Tweed
- Ten thousand Ordinary £1 Shares in Darnley plc
- The sum of five thousand pounds (£5,000) in cash

Dated: 21st November 2023

Signed by James Stewart:

Signed by Mary Stewart:

3. Memorandum recording a gift (all IHT to be borne by the transferor)

MEMORANDUM OF GIFT FROM

Noddy Hill of 6 Slade Street, Wolverhampton

TO

David Holder of 9 Flame Avenue, Birmingham

MEMORANDUM that on 29th February 2024 Noddy Hill transferred by way of gift to David Holder the sum of two million pounds (£2,000,000). The said Noddy Hill hereby further undertakes that he or his personal representatives shall pay any Inheritance Tax assessed in respect of such gift out of the assets of his general estate and indemnifies David Holder accordingly.

Dated: 29th February 2024

Signed by Noddy Hill:

Signed by David Holder:

# Appendix D

## Abbreviations Used in this Guide

| | |
|---|---|
| AIM | Alternative Investment Market |
| APR | Agricultural Property Relief |
| BADR | Business Asset Disposal Relief |
| BPR | Business Property Relief |
| CGT | Capital Gains Tax |
| CPI | Consumer Prices Index |
| DOTAS | Disclosure of Tax Avoidance Schemes |
| EEA | European Economic Area |
| FIC | Family Investment Company |
| FOTRA | Free of Tax to Residents Abroad |
| GAAR | General Anti-Abuse Rule |
| HMRC | HM Revenue and Customs |
| IHT | Inheritance Tax |
| ISA | Individual Savings Account |
| IVR | Investor's Relief |
| LLP | Limited Liability Partnership |
| Ltd | Limited (i.e. a limited company) |
| NRB | Nil Rate Band |
| ONS | Office for National Statistics |
| PET | Potentially Exempt Transfer |
| RNRB | Residence Nil Rate Band |
| RPI | Retail Prices Index |
| SDLT | Stamp Duty Land Tax |
| SIPP | Self-Invested Personal Pension |
| TNRB | Transferable Nil Rate Band |
| UK | The United Kingdom of Great Britain and Northern Ireland |

Milton Keynes UK
Ingram Content Group UK Ltd.
UKHW021006290724
446271UK00007B/409

9 781911 020868